Honoring the Civil War Dead

John R. Neff

Honoring the Civil War Dead

Commemoration and the Problem of Reconciliation

University Press of Kansas

Published by the University Press of Kansas (Lawrence, Kansas 66049), which was organized by the Kansas Board of Regents and is operated and funded by Emporia State University, Fort Hays State University, Kansas State University, Pittsburg State University, the University of Kansas, and Wichita State University

Library of Congress Cataloging-in-Publication Data

Neff, John R.
     Honoring the Civil War dead : commemoration and the problem of reconciliation / John R. Neff.
          p. cm. — (Modern war studies)
     Includes bibliographical references and index.
     ISBN 0-7006-1366-8 (cloth : alk. paper)
     1. United States—History—Civil War, 1861–1865—Monuments.
     2. United States—History—Civil War, 1861–1865—Influence.
     3. Soldiers' monuments—United States—History   4. Soldiers' monuments—Southern States—History.   5. Nationalism—United States—History.   6. Nationalism—Southern States—History.
     7. Reconciliation—History—19th century.   8. Reconciliation—History—20th century.   9. United States—Politics and government—1865–1933.   10. Southern States—Politics and government—1865–1950.   I. Title.   II. Series.
     E641.N44 2005
     973.7′6—dc22   2004025530

British Library Cataloguing-in-Publication Data is available.

Printed in the United States of America

10 9 8 7 6 5 4 3 2 1

For John and Patricia, my parents:
A better start I could not have had.

T he final use of the greatest men of a Nation is, after all, not with reference to their deeds in themselves, or their direct bearing on their times or lands. The final use of a heroic-eminent life—especially of a heroic-eminent death—is its indirect filtering into the nation and the race, and to give, often at many removes, but unerringly, age after age, color and fibre to the personalism of the youth and maturity of that age, and of mankind. Then there is a cement to the whole people, subtler, more underlying, than any thing in a written constitution, or courts or armies—namely, the cement of a death identified thoroughly with that people, at its head, and for its sake. Strange, (is it not?) that battles, martyrs, agonies, blood, even assassination, should so condense—perhaps only really, lastingly condense—a Nationality.

—Walt Whitman, *Death of Abraham Lincoln*

Contents

Tables, Figures, and Illustrations

Tables

Figures

Illustrations

Acknowledgments

A LTHOUGH RESEARCH AND WRITING ARE SOLITARY TASKS, the completion of a work of history cannot be accomplished by an individual alone. Like many before me, I have accrued over the years innumerable debts, largely beyond my ability to repay, except in this paltry recognition of the invaluable gifts given me.

I would like to thank, for their generous, always cheerful, and exemplary assistance, the staff of Interlibrary Loan and Rick Beaumont, Government Publications Depository, both of Rivera Library, University of California, Riverside. For the sharing of their expertise as well as access to their collections, I would like to express my deep appreciation to Jennifer Ford and Leigh McWhite, Special Collections, J. D. Williams Library, University of Mississippi; the kind folks at the A. K. Smiley Library Heritage Room, Redlands, California; Special Collections, University of California, Santa Barbara; the Huntington Library, San Marino, California; Bill Irwin and staff at the Perkins Library, Duke University, Durham, North Carolina; John Coski, Eleanor S. Brockenbrough Library, Museum of the Confederacy, Richmond, Virginia; the staff of the Virginia Historical Society, Richmond; Leslie Rowland, director of the Freedmen and Southern Society Project, University of Maryland, College Park; and the unfailing, patient, and largely unheralded staff research assistants of the Library of Congress Manuscript Division, Microfilm and Reading Rooms, and the National Archives and Records Administration. This work would not have been possible without your assistance, and I am grateful.

Special notice must be made of several who contributed personally to my research efforts: Karen R. Tupek and Therese Sammartino of the Veteran's Administration; Scott Hartwig and the staff at Gettysburg National Military Park, for their kind hospitality; Bill Martin and the staff of the Fort Sumter National Military Park; Walter A. Gray Jr., Beaufort National Cemetery; Lincoln T. Berry, with whom I spent a pleasant afternoon at the Soldier's Home National Cemetery, Washington, D.C.; and Fred Espinak, NASA/Goddard Space Flight Center, Planetary Systems Division, for answering patiently my arcane questions about century-old eclipses.

Acknowledgments

To those who have invested so much of themselves in me, I cannot pay any adequate dividend other than to reinvest that commitment in my own students: William Patey, John Reagan, Sara Mason, Ronald W. Yoshino, David C. Sloane, Richard Johnson, David Levering, John Moore, Charles Wetherell, Piotr Górecki, thank you all. I will always hold a special gratitude to John A. Phillips, whose warmth, professionalism, wit, sage advice, and ties I will try to carry with me always. John, I can truly never thank you enough.

Numerous scholars have worked diligently to make this work better than they found it and along the way improved the historian who wrote it. Roger L. Ransom, Richard Godbeer, and P. Sterling Stuckey deserve special mention since they suffered with it first and with me longer than anyone else. Sterling, you in particular have been so generous, and I will always treasure your elegant grace, warmth, and wisdom. My friends and colleagues at the Department of History, University of Mississippi, have provided unflagging and enthusiastic support, especially Robert Haws, Charles Eagles, Joe Ward, Sue Grayzel, Josh Howard, Ted Ownby, Douglass Sullivan-González, Jeff Watt, and Harry P. Owens. David Sansing, thank you for my own Gettysburg Address. I would like to make a special note of my indebtedness to Winthrop Jordan, with whom I have been lucky to be associated these last few years. He is the very definition of a gentleman and a scholar, and his encouragement and advice have been a special blessing. I would also like to acknowledge the efforts of my various readers, anonymous and otherwise, whose thoughtful and insightful critiques strengthened this work throughout, particularly Donald Shaffer, University of Northern Colorado. Of course, I am particularly grateful to Michael Briggs, Larisa Martin, Susan McRory, Jan Butin, Susan Schott, and the rest of the staff of the University Press of Kansas.

Among the rest to whom I owe far too much and will happily spend the rest of my life making good on the debt, I would like to thank Peter McCord, Jennifer Hildebrand, and William C. Johnson, partner in crime; adoptive siblings John P. Lloyd, another brother, and Sharon Chism, my sister, who despite distance is never very far away. Thank you Robert, my brother, and Mark ("bil"), for your love and support; I am immensely proud of you both. I am grateful to all my family for their understanding and encouragement, but especially Ben, Molly, and Kathy, who not only made this and everything else possible, but also make it all worthwhile.

Introduction
"All Care for the Dead Is for the Sake of the Living":
The Loyal and the Rebel Dead

> In what census of living creatures, the dead of mankind are
> included. . . . Methinks we have hugely mistaken this matter
> of Life and Death.
> —*Herman Melville, Moby-Dick (1851)*

THE COMMEMORATION OF THE AMERICAN CIVIL WAR is so important that
our understanding of the social, intellectual, and cultural repercussions
of that conflict will remain incomplete until it is more fully understood. As
Northern and Southern Americans of the late nineteenth century thought
about their recent past, they sought to preserve their understanding of that
war in immortal oratory and in equally imperishable marble and bronze. Individually and collectively, Civil War monuments—the thousands erected in
town squares, battlefields, and cemeteries, North and South—are more than
lodestones of memory or prods to the national consciousness. The effort involved suggests a greater significance, one which transcends the figures or carv-
ings that ornament them. The frequency with which individuals and groups of
ordinary citizens erected such monuments—a rate that far outstrips any other
period of our history—speaks to the importance of such activities in their lives.
Through commemorative activities, Americans who had survived the war preserved their perceptions of the most traumatic event of their lives and of their
nation's life. This impulse to interpret and express meaning was nowhere more
significant, nor more eloquent, than in the commemoration of the war's soldier dead. For the national government and all American citizens following the
war, the commemoration of the war's dead provided the quintessential forum
for engaging—and, most important, expressing—the war's meaning. Quartermaster General Montgomery C. Meigs noted the abiding connections that
Americans felt in the act of honoring and commemorating the fallen. "All care
for the dead," he wrote, "is for the sake of the living."[1]

Honoring the Civil War Dead

The commemoration of the dead, in all its myriad forms, provides a particularly rich source that documents how Americans derived meaning from that nearly incomprehensible tragedy of war. These commemorations ranged from the intensely private to the extravagantly public, including individual mourning, pageants of collective grief, the rude battlefield disposition of bodies, the creation of national cemeteries, the erection of monuments, and annual Memorial Day observances. All these commemorative acts intentionally delineated at least three sets of relationships. First, they explicitly described the relationship between the dead and the cause for which they had died. The process of relating the fallen to their cause was perhaps the first, most immediate response on the part of their fellow participants and other observers of the war. Confronted with death on a previously unimaginable scale, those who had survived the conflict sought to understand loss by attributing to it a greater purpose. The death of soldiers required axiomatically that their cause must have been worthy of such a high cost. Soldiers lost their lives as "martyrs," as a "sacrifice," especially on the "altar of the nation," language that each side used to ennoble both the dead and their separate causes.

Second, these commemorative acts also described the relationship between the men and women who undertook them and the lost soldiers they honored. No monument is erected by those unconnected or unconcerned with the soldier dead: commemoration is an explicit statement of connection. More precisely, that relationship between the living and the dead was often stated as an indebtedness. The impulse to commemorate often arose out of this sense of obligation to those who had died for a shared cause or for one's sake.

Third, and, for the purposes of this study, most important, the act of commemoration articulates the relationship between those involved in the memorial activity and the social, political, or cultural context in which they find themselves. Monuments and other forms of commemoration seek explicitly to preserve ideals and values in order to communicate them undiminished to the future. In many cases, the need to commemorate indicates a belief that such ideals, unless preserved in this enduring manner, are at risk among future generations who will neither understand nor appreciate the significance of the sacrifice. In this instance, commemorative activities ask future generations to remember the soldier dead of the Civil War, but also ask that the historical interpretations of those who erected the monuments and provided the oratory be preserved as the appropriate way to understand the past.

All three of these dimensions were apparent when, thirty years after the war, Chicago's ex-Confederate Association obtained permission from the secretary of war to erect a memorial within the soldiers' section of that city's Oakwoods Cemetery. During the war, Chicago had been home to Camp Douglas, one of a string of military prisons arranged throughout the Northern states from Illinois to Massachusetts. The rigors of prison and an outbreak of smallpox took the lives of at least 4,500 Confederate inmates, who after the war were taken from their original burial grounds and reburied in long rows in Oakwoods. In the generation since the war's end, the graves had remained largely unmarked, although a few privately erected stones dotted the greensward. The ex-Confederate Association expended nearly $25,000 for a monument and dedication ceremonies. The monument erected by the association is a towering soldier-topped shaft of Georgia granite, rising from a broad plinth.[2]

In their commemoration and memorialization, the association's members desired, first, to point out the contribution and sacrifice made by their soldiers, even as prisoners of war, to the Southern cause. Second, by their acts and their dedication to this task of memory, the members also wished to express their own connection to the men they honored. Their diligence in erecting such a grand statement of memory reflected on their own continued commitment to that cause for which these prisoners had given all. Finally, they sought to make at least two specific commentaries on the present and communicate those ideas to the future. Primarily, the act of honoring these Confederate dead allowed the veterans in Chicago to remind everyone of the anguish of Civil War prisons. But, more pointedly, placing such a prominent edifice, cut from Southern stone, in the midst of such an important Northern city allowed the assembled veterans to assert their sense of their separate heritage, and to implicitly celebrate their defiance of the war's results. By understanding these activities within their context, it becomes clear that such commemorations are, in effect, responses to their context. This is not to suggest that such commemorations are anything other than sincere and even devout acts. It does argue that any statement of ideal or principle—even though made in reference to the past—takes place within, and therefore reflects, a particular "present-mindedness" on the part of those involved. In sum, monuments tell us at least as much, and perhaps far more, about the people who build them than about the individuals they are intended to honor.

Such commemorative activities have recently become of great interest to historians. With a sensitivity to public performance, ritual, and social memory, historians have begun to explore acts of commemoration as moments of public discourse expressing important connections between the individuals and groups participating in such activities and the objects of their commemoration. To date, much of this work has been European in orientation, especially—but not exclusively—devoted to the aftermath of World War I. As England, France, and Germany sought to make sense of the horrific costs of the Great War, they erected monuments and imposed order on battlefields and cemeteries. Throughout, these nations wrestled with the very real political and social quest to understand and honor the relationship of the individual soldier to the nation for which he died.[3]

Similar commemorations occurred in the United States after the American Civil War, but they have not yet received the same level of scholarly attention. The American example shares many of the aspects that have so fascinated European scholars—the social responses to death, the interpretation of war and loss through commemorations and monuments, and the political negotiations between government and citizens in the process of creating and assigning meaning to war. But characteristics of late nineteenth-century American commemoration have no parallel in the European experience. The fundamental nature of Civil War commemoration contained tensions between divergent Northern and Southern interpretations of the war not apparent in the early-twentieth-century European commemorations. Following World War I, no European nation confronted large portions of its own populace intent on commemorating the activities of the enemy. But, since reunification was an express goal of the victorious Union, the commemoration of the Confederate experience formed a crucial, contentious aspect of postwar national memorialization. In the years following the American Civil War, Northerners and Southerners struggled to understand their separate commemorations within a larger, reunified national context.

Several recent works have contributed significantly to our understanding of the reunion movement that characterized the United States in the late nineteenth century. This scholarship attempts to delineate the process of reunification across the divides—sectional, political, and racial—wrought by decades of antagonism and the turmoil of war. The central narrative of most concerns the reconciliation of the veterans, particularly at the numerous blue-gray reunions that became increasingly frequent in the last decades of the century and the first decades of the next. These reunions captured the popular imagination at the time and have dominated our thinking about reunification since. In particular, the familiar photographs of veterans from both armies shaking hands across the stone wall on which the Pickett-Pettigrew Charge was shattered came to symbolize, for them and for us, the metaphoric reconciliation of the sections. So powerful was this image that the National Park Service adopted it as the symbol of Gettysburg's one hundredth anniversary as a park, an image commemorating not the acts that inspired the preservation of the grounds in the first place, but the subsequent reconciliation of Northerners and Southerners to those acts. Additionally, historians have carefully delineated the great desire that Americans expressed for reunion. North and South, Americans created emotional counterparts to political and economic sectional concerns, a "romance" through which the sections could court unity. So powerful was the need to find reconciliation to such a disruptive war, even the logical consequences of the Union victory—predicated at least in part on emancipation—could be rather easily relinquished in the name of the reunited nation. While black freedom was a bitterly fought and hard-won struggle during the war, in this literature postwar black citizenship and political participation were sacrificed for the sake of white reconciliation.[4]

While the focus on reunion has certainly been important to our better understanding of the decades following the Civil War, and while it has been easily justified given the obvious preoccupation with reconciliation apparent in the literature of the period, by itself it fails to portray the complexities that confronted American society. At the very least, such a focus neglects the pain-ridden emotions inspired by the war among at least a portion of the nation's populace that expressed little desire to pursue reconciliation. Often minimized—at the time and by historians since—as the province of either "unreconstructed" Southerners or "bloody-shirt" Northerners, the persistence of animosity long after war's end remains an important and largely ignored social strand in postwar society. The clearest evidence of a persistent divergence in American society—of a lack of reconciliation—is found in the commemoration of the war's soldier dead. In the processes associated with mourning and memorializing, it was incumbent upon the living to interpret and render sensible the sacrifice of those no longer among them. These expressions, monumental and oratorical, necessarily involved justifications of the separate nationalist visions of the soldiers who had died, who had given their lives for such contrasting and irreconcilable goals.

Importantly, historians have lately become interested in death and its universality following the war, but have, I believe, drawn the wrong conclusions. Drew Gilpin Faust has suggested that, as Southerners and Northerners became preoccupied with the memorialization of the dead, many of the political clashes attendant on Reconstruction "became gradually muted as much of the nation redirected its interest in the war to the work of memorialization, into a focus on the heritage of loss and mourning common to both sections." Similarly, David Blight argues that, increasingly over time and especially after the mid-1870s, veterans and civilians from both sections found that their mutual commemoration of the dead provided a foundation for future reconciliation. This focus on the reconciliatory effect of memorialization and memory was first posited by Paul Buck, who wrote in 1937: "Wearied of the partisan excesses into which they had been led by the difficulties of Reconstruction, not yet knowing the solution, yet conscious that the implied hostility and hatred were not of their seeking, the people of the mid-1870s found in Memorial Day an escape through which they could express their yearning for sectional peace."[5] Buck's passive language freed him from having to assign culpability for the origins of those Reconstruction difficulties while at the same time emphasizing the desire "of the people" to seek reconciliation. However, such interpretations subsume the commemoration of the dead under larger political, economic, and social motivations encouraging reunion rather than appreciating them as a significant social movement in their own right; although contemporaneous and related, remembering the dead proved to be an impediment to national healing.

The reunion movement was real and genuine, but it was not the sole response to the war. While surviving veterans could, perhaps, become reconciled to their former enemies, could participate in some public display that worked to allay sectional tensions, the dead could not be so easily reconciled. From the days of the war through the decades afterward, to remember and honor the dead was to recall their cause and the reasons for their deaths. Reconciliation would always run counter to the undeniable fact that many young men lay in graves because of the actions of the enemy, and no reunion, encampment, or political oration could deny that essential reality. To commemorate the dead was to recall and honor the men themselves, the cause they championed, and especially the relationships between the dead, their cause, and the living. Whether the death was recent or distant in time, commemoration invoked specific statements of these relationships, and, because those deaths were frozen in time, in a specific and unchangeable context, no amount of subsequent reconciliation could alter the nature of those relationships. The loyal and the rebel dead would always remain so, locked within a specific historical moment. Therefore, as Americans sought to understand their war against the shifting social fabric seeking reunion and—as Blight has suggested[6]—forgetfulness, the commemoration of the dead remained the polestar of sometimes bitter memory.

The significance of the dead to postwar America will always elude us until we more fully understand the divergent national visions and myths that are reflected in their commemorations. The Southern postwar memorial efforts remembered their cause: from the beginning, Confederates worked toward a goal of separation. Only within an independent nation, they believed, could they assure themselves of control over their economic prosperity, their political viability, and their social safety, all of which revolved around the necessity of sustaining the institution of slavery. The anguish of defeat would always be augmented by the disillusionment of reincorporation with a people—Northerners—thought to be absolutely antithetical to Southern ideals. In response, Southerners collectively imagined a vision of the war and the world that had preceded it in order to establish comforting pathways of memory that held nobility in defeat in higher esteem than victory. The South lost 260,000 soldiers in its unsuccessful bid toward independent nation building, and the Lost Cause was the social and cultural manifestation that explained that loss. That mythology bore the burden of explaining how a people so blessed and prosperous became humbled by divine Providence through war, how a society groping for independence from what it perceived to be tyranny could remain—after so much loss and destruction—still subordinate to that national power. Defeat, itself, was denied by the myth—the Confederacy was not defeated militarily in combat but, instead, overwhelmed by numbers.[7] With this mythos, Southerners warmed themselves at the banked embers of a waning nationalist fire.

What has so far remained unclear to scholars is that, following the war, the North was as active as the South in mythmaking.[8] The Union armies lost more than 360,000 soldiers, losses that also required explanation, but because the North had a different relationship to the war its myths were necessarily different than their Southern counterparts. Northern war goals were twofold:

of first priority was the reestablishment of national integrity, Union; second, after 1862, the destruction of the institution of slavery. The second goal was mostly accomplished before the war ended, through the efforts of the enslaved, the enforcement of the president's Emancipation Proclamation by Union soldiers, and the passage and ratification of the Thirteenth Amendment in 1865. This second goal would prove to be the most socially significant product of the Civil War, and its immediate accomplishment was obvious to all; the liberation of four million men and women residing in fourteen states was astounding proof of Northern military victory.

However, the first goal, perhaps counterintuitively, was far more elusive. The triumph of Union was never as easily defined or as evident as the destruction of slavery. Although it was the most obvious of Northern goals, there existed no clear threshold beyond which all could know that victory had been accomplished. Was Union won when the Confederate armies surrendered, making the mere lack of open, violent opposition the standard of unity? The tumultuous events of Presidential and Congressional Reconstruction scarcely provide any moment where an observer might safely state that the people— North and South, black and white—were united. White Southerners acquiesced, under military occupation, to the transformation of their state governments under Congressional Reconstruction, but it required the presence of the military to enforce the acquiescence. Was Union assured with the Redemption of the former Confederate states after the resurgence of white-supremacist Democratic political dominance, or was it not until some point yet further along? Was the Civil War finally won when the sons of Northern soldiers fought alongside the sons of Southern soldiers against Spain? With the sectional division so fresh, every political, economic, and social dispute could all too easily be attributed to a resurgence of wartime passions. When could Northerners be confident that Southerners had again become loyal citizens of the nation? At what point was the Union victory exemplified in the unity of the nation? These questions plagued the triumphant North and invoked the necessity for all on the winning side to interpret, and mythologize, their victory. Clearly, the nation had not been successfully sundered, but Reconstruction proved that neither was it entirely whole.

Northern myths had to explain what that victory ultimately meant for the nation, and in some way demonstrate the truth of that national victory. In the central tenets of the Northern mythology—the Cause Victorious, perhaps—the nation had been reunited virtually at the time of Confederate surrender. Further, the federal government had since that point in time exercised wise and even benevolent dominion as the logical consequence of victory, which resulted in a ubiquitous and sincere national allegiance among all Americans. Under this rubric, the death inflicted by the war, the dislocation and destruction, as well as the implied and explicit critiques of the American nation resulting from such a widespread insurrection, all were made to serve the development of a stronger nation in the Northern image, a nation tempered in the fires of treasonous rebellion. As the Confederacy toppled, but before the fall of Richmond, the New York Herald confidently asserted, "This war will abolish all sectional lines. Hereafter we shall be but one people, instead of two different people under one government. When the war is over we shall all be Americans, instead of being divided into Northerners and Southerners."[9] This statement avoids characterization as naive optimism only when it is understood as a simple and reasonable assertion of the expectations that accompanied Northern victory.

The greatest irony of the Cause Victorious, and the reason it has so far escaped scholarly attention, is that the myth—untrue in 1865—eventually became much more than myth. The literature of reunion has skillfully outlined the sometimes tortured pathways toward reconciliation, but that goal was imagined and asserted by Northerners almost from the moment the war ended. As the destruction of slavery was clearly an accomplishment of the war, the nation whole and uncontested—while mythical at war's end—became a nationalist blueprint that guided Americans to produce that triumphant sense of unity, to make myth become a reality. Therefore, the initial assertions of the Cause Victorious were usually more strident than accurate, for the essential character of the mythology was to describe in carefully coded language a nationality reunited in imagination long before reconciliation had been actually accomplished. The myth of the Lost Cause is conspicuous in our national consciousness because it sought to reassert a world that could not be remade—if it had ever existed at all. Alternately, the national myth of Northern Americans actually became our collective consciousness and, hence, was rendered nearly invisible. The myth reshaped American society after the war and, in so doing, succeeded like few myths before it. The commemorative response to the soldier dead is a particularly useful guide to these multiple and conflicting mythologies created by the war.

Because these concepts and their expression are susceptible to ambiguity, it is important to be as concise as possible. In my understanding of myth, following the work of Joseph Campbell, myths are metaphors, that is, explanations created by a people in order to understand how their present emerged out of their past and why their present looks as it does.[10] In understanding the myths, we come closer to understanding the people for whom they were a necessity. As myth often carries connotations of falsity or untruthfulness, it should be stated that Northern perceptions were false only in the sense of their timing. While the unity optimistically expressed after the war was, indeed, inaccurate at that time, this is not to suggest that such nationalistic unity was never achieved or that such a metaphoric understanding of the war's lasting effect of a divided nation was naive or unrealistic. The significance of that myth's falsity, of its "untruth," is less important than its significance as a demonstration of the distance, in a specific time and place, between perception and reality. Finally, the Cause Victorious was a logical and reasonable consequence of the war, and any critical assessment of it here is not intended to suggest that the mythology was unjustified or anything other than a legitimate response to the extraordinary circumstances resulting from that devastating national crisis.

As Northerners derived their myth from the desire to provide contextual meaning for their present, in the shadow of the war death was necessarily integral to it. Walt Whitman provides the most cogent contemporary observation of that myth, in which death and nationalism are intertwined inextricably. Toward the end of a life that had been so profoundly affected by the Civil War, Whitman returned often in his prose to the human costs of war. Most significantly, nearly fifteen years after the death of Abraham Lincoln, Whitman tried to sum up the meaning of the president's life and assassination. In trying to estimate Lincoln's worth to the nation, Whitman ultimately discounted his life and actions, the very things that most Americans still regard as significant. "The final use," he wrote, "of the greatest men of a Nation is, after all, not with reference to their deeds in themselves, or their direct bearing on their times or lands." While these are certainly important, Lincoln's greatest service to his nation was more indirect, more subtle. Whitman believed that Lincoln provided an influence—a "color and fibre"—in a way that united the nation. But it was not the life of Lincoln that had been most important to this process; it was his death. While a "heroic-eminent life" could inspire this unity, the poet asserted that it was the product "especially [of] a heroic-eminent death." It was "the cement of a death identified thoroughly with that people, at its head, and for its sake." Of course, as many Americans did, Whitman understood that the death of Lincoln and the deaths of soldiers were of a piece, melded in their common sacrifice for the nation. Each soldier's death also qualified as "heroic-eminent," having been identified with a people, in their defense and on their behalf, as more than a century of commemoration after that war would attest. "Strange, (is it not?)," Whitman concluded, "that battles, martyrs, agonies, blood, even assassination, should so condense—perhaps only really, lastingly condense—a Nationality."[11]

This book, proceeding from the touchstones of memory and nationalism, explores the role of death in condensing, and occasionally defying, American nationality. Chapter 1 establishes the nature of the overwhelming death associated with the war. In the beginning, the war presented civilians and soldiers with death, both in quantity and in kind, far outside anyone's experience in both its devastating volume and its violence wrought on individuals and social traditions. Contrary to much current scholarship, the American Civil War challenged fundamentally the social rituals and mores associated with death in America. In addition, the historical literature of Civil War combat gives short shrift to the experience of battlefield death. Death was a soldier's constant companion, and from the heights of command to the lowest foot soldiers the military forces of both sides grappled with the demands of the dying, including the desire for the decent interment of comrades and the speedy disposal of the enemy dead. Throughout the conflict, soldiers and civilians tried to restore folkways associated with traditional death rituals and customs, and almost always failed. Moreover, again for both civilians and soldiers, the actions taken in response to the dead clearly expanded the animosity of the combatants to encompass the dead as well.

In Chapter 2, as a final act of war searing itself into the public consciousness, one particular death came to reach every Northern citizen, became, in fact, a surrogate death for all. Abraham Lincoln's murder, perhaps inevitably, invited interpretation as symbolic of the individual deaths of hundreds of thousands of soldiers. Significantly, it is within the public response to Lincoln's assassination—the response to Whitman's "heroic-eminent death"—that the Northern myth of American nationalism finds its first voice. Even though, during the conflict, many observers looked beyond the war and pondered the future of the nation, their arguments were largely political. It is only within the rhetoric surrounding the death of Lincoln that the nation's future becomes fully intertwined once more with a providential hand, which, having seemingly chastised the nation through war, was again construed as hovering favorably over the nation's destiny. In the eulogies of ministers and other orators, a wondrous confusion of sentiments finds expression—anger and despair, blame and penitential anguish, cries for vengeance and exhortations for forgiveness—yet significant in virtually every oration is the certainty that Lincoln's death was necessary for the consecration of the new, reconciled nation. From religious motifs to realpolitik, Lincoln's death becomes something required—mythically—for the "new birth of freedom" that he foretold among mounded graves in the unfinished cemetery at Gettysburg.

Chapters 3 and 4 discuss the separate commemorative traditions of Northern and Southern Americans. In the months and years following the war, both sides mourned their soldiers lost but acted on their similar impulses in starkly different fashions. Northerners faced the grim responsibility of more than 300,000 graves scattered across at least seventeen states. The first phase of federal activity focused on the decent and honorable interment of Union soldiers into the newly established National Cemetery System, an effort that required the intertwining of private, local, state, and national efforts. The difficulties involved in fully incorporating black men into the nation were mirrored in the inconsistent burial policies applied to soldiers of the U.S. Colored Troops. Of course, Southerners responded to the best of their means, but when commemoration of the rebel dead could be—as it often was—interpreted as a treasonous act, Southern activities organized and accomplished largely by women, were of necessity more somber, less expansive, but no less sincere or impassioned. For both North and South, the regional development and practice of Memorial Day gave a unique annual opportunity to interpret the dead, their separate causes, and their separate nationalisms. From its very beginnings, and in opposition to our current understanding, Memorial Day observances preserved sectional animosity with a potency not possible in any other national venue of discourse. As long as commemorative activities included the soldier dead, they would remain divisive. Finally, the death and funeral of Jefferson Davis became the South's contrapuntal accompaniment to the North's earlier mourning of Lincoln. As had Northerners earlier, white Southerners expressed a newfound assertiveness through the reinvigoration of a nationalist funeral.

Chapter 5 explores the special internal challenges to the Northern mythology posed by the extension of citizenship to black men and former Confederates. The broadening of citizenship implicit in Reconstruction charged national memorial activities with a racial consciousness that had before been absent from national gestures. Although the national cemeteries are, from their inception, among the first publicly funded racially integrated cemeteries in American history, the inclusion of black soldiers within the commemoration of the Union soldier dead was fraught with difficulty. Similarly, part of that nationalist ideal embodied in the Cause Victorious demanded the incorporation of even former enemies within the definition of fellow citizens. The necessity of incorporating African Americans and former enemies into the imagined national community at once fostered reconciliation but also invited greater expressions of hostility and disdain for the unwanted.

Chapter 6 follows the lingering effects of commemorative separatism into the twentieth century. In the shadow of Davis's death, former Confederates mounted an assault on the great symbolic center of national honor and sacrifice, Arlington National Cemetery. The efforts to gain inclusion into those hallowed grounds, and the subsequent efforts on the part of the federal government to secure care and protection for Confederate graves nationally, might be seen as a remarkably cooperative conclusion to the last animosities stemming from war. But the motivations of both sides are complex and defy such easy explication. Indeed, it is clear that sectional concerns about commemoration have persisted throughout the 140 years since the end of the Civil War.

Although the brief outline presented above employs broadly inclusive terms, at no point were Northern or Southern perspectives ever monolithic. Some source materials utilized in this work—diaries and letters—speak only of an individual point of view. Some were intended for groups of various sizes—sermons for congregations, orations for a particular audience, editorials for a newspaper's readership. Yet, in all these, the sentiments expressed were recorded or otherwise preserved because someone thought it important to do so. Except in the case of diaries, and sometimes even then, these records were intended to convey ideas and thoughts to others in a persuasive manner, to speak to others of the same mind. The majority of sermons and orations from the nineteenth century have survived because they were thought important enough to be published—by listeners who wanted to retain what they had heard in more tangible form, by publishers who thought that a market existed for such material, by authors who wanted to convince others. This very process presumes a wider audience that to some degree responded to the thoughts and memories so recorded.

Honoring the Civil War Dead

The study of memory as a means to understanding historical experience is still relatively new, at least on this side of the Atlantic.[12] However, the period of national reconciliation provides an especially good laboratory for such explorations. In the first place, memories of the war—no matter how private—became public, shared, tangible actions. Each act of commemoration, every monument and speech, even the adornment of graves with flowers on Memorial Day, all expressed eloquently those aspects of the recent conflict that were thought significant. Additionally, the generation that experienced the war self-consciously adopted the didactic mission of relating that significance to the next. Memories thus became articles of faith, at times resulting in the perpetuation of the war in subsequent generations with a vehemence that outstripped that of the war generation. Although at times elusive, memories of the war and the soldiers it consumed are, in this way, accessible and palpable.

A last word of caution. This study does not presume that Americans were inordinately obsessed with death following the Civil War or even—Whitman aside—that death was the most important catalyst of memories about the war. Nor does it suggest that the commemoration of the war dead is the only source of evidence documenting the shifting nationalist identities of the period. It does argue, however, that so far death is a neglected avenue through which we can approach evidence of what citizens of various stripes and stations were thinking and doing in the late nineteenth century.

It is certain that memory, and the future's perception of their war, was on the minds of many. As he was writing his first inaugural address, Lincoln sought the advice of his political colleagues, among them William H. Seward. Seward suggested that Lincoln add a final paragraph that would read, in part, "The mystic chords which proceeding from so many battle fields and so many patriot graves pass through all the hearts and hearths in this broad continent of ours will yet again harmonize in their ancient music when breathed upon by the guardian angel of the nation." Lincoln thought the idea a good one but with his own sense of meaning and poetry altered the wording to read:

> The mystic chords of *memory,* stretching from every battle-field, and patriot grave, to every living heart and hearthstone, all over this broad land, will yet swell the chorus of the Union, when again touched, as surely they will be, by the better angels of *our nature.*

With these subtle alterations, Lincoln elevated Seward's political message into one of national identity. The "chorus of the Union" would be renewed and reestablished not by external forces—Seward's "guardian angel"—but by each individual recalling through personal memory his or her own associations with the nation.[13] Poignantly, before the Civil War had even begun, Lincoln had understood and expressed what the reconciliation of the nation would require.

"This Mysterious Providence": Americans' Initial Responses to Civil War Death

In glades they meet skull after skull
Where pine-cones lay—the rusted gun,
Green shoes full of bones, the mouldering coat
And cuddled-up skeleton;
And scores of such. Some start as in dreams,
And comrades lost bemoan

. . .

Few burial rites shall be;
No priest with book and band
Shall come to the secret place
Of the corpse in the foeman's land

. . .

A riddle of death, of which the slain
Sole solvers are.
　—*Herman Melville, "The Armies of the Wilderness" (1866)*

L ITTLE IS KNOWN OF DANIEL HOUGH, except that he was the first to die. The surviving documents left to us provide only a sketch of his life. He was an Irish immigrant, a farmer, born in Tipperary in 1826, standing about five feet, eight inches tall, with a fair complexion, hair so light as to appear gray, and blue eyes. He enlisted in 1849, as a private in the First U.S. Artillery, and the army seems to have been his only career in America. He reenlisted twice, at the end of each five-year tour of duty, and twelve years later he was still with the First U.S. Artillery and still a private. He had apparently suffered from some mental instability around 1857—his commanding officer described him then as "so crazy as to be unmanageable"—but after a brief stay in a Washington, D.C., asylum he had returned to his regiment. On the spring afternoon of 14 April 1861, the thirty-five-year-old Hough was a part of Company E, Abner Doubleday commanding, standing ready to service their cannon on the battered parapet of Fort Sumter.[1]

For a day and a half, Hough and the rest of the Union garrison at Sumter had endured the punishing artillery fire of the Confederate batteries encircling Charleston Harbor. On the evening before, Major Robert Anderson concluded arrangements with Confederate General Pierre G. T. Beauregard that would effect the withdrawal of Federal troops from their hopeless position. But, before departure, Anderson had negotiated the right to salute his flag as he lowered it for the last time.[2] And so, with the breeze off the sea fresh in their faces, the gun crews stood amid shattered masonry and debris, awaiting the order to begin firing.

Anderson planned for a salute of one hundred rounds, although powder was in short supply. The doors to the magazine had been damaged during the bombardment, preventing his men from retrieving more powder. Even had the magazine been readily accessible, the Confederates had heated their cannon shot during the bombardment, which had, in turn, ignited the wooden structures within the fort. Late into the morning, the barracks still smoldered, and sparks continued to swirl in the compound. So Anderson's men improvised; all through the morning, they scrounged discarded blankets and other fabric that could be sewn hastily into cartridge bags and filled with the small amount of black powder that had been cached at the various gun emplacements. By two o'clock in the afternoon, the makeshift cartridges had been stacked near the remaining undamaged guns on the seaward parapet—massive ship-killing eight- and ten-inch-diameter Columbiads—and the gun crews began their salute.[3]

All along the shoreline of Charleston's harbor, newly minted Confederates, soldiers and civilians alike, lined the water's edge to witness the final act in the first Southern victory. Anxiously they counted off the rounds, for few knew in advance the number that Anderson intended to fire. Many thought that the traditional twenty-one guns would be fired. But, as the guns continued beyond that number, some thought that Anderson might order thirty-four rounds, to insult the secession movement by insinuating that South Carolina and the other seceded states were still numbered among the thirty-four states of the Union. But the guns continued to thunder, the deep-throated roars rolling across the expanse of water. As the Charlestonians counted, a newspaper reporter later wrote, all could hear a "sound as of two reports, and the impression was that two guns had been fired together." After a pause, the guns continued to a total of fifty, then stopped. Anderson curtailed his salute because the war had inflicted its first death.[4]

Company E had manned the great black gun on the far right of the parapet. Daniel Hough worked as the rammer, responsible for sponging out the gun's tube to extinguish any smoldering powder residue and then ramming home the new powder cartridge and shot. At some point during the salute, as Hough stood before the cannon and forced a powder cartridge down the tube, it exploded prematurely, firing the ramrod out like a projectile and tearing Hough's right arm from his body. Flaming fabric, either the cartridge wrapping or perhaps Hough's own clothing, was blown back by the wind onto the remaining cartridges stacked near the gun. The resulting second explosion injured the rest of the gun crew; Edward Gallway and James Fielding were grievously wounded, three others less seriously so. Although Fielding eventually recovered in a Charleston hospital, Gallway died of his wounds some hours later.[5] Daniel Hough had been killed almost instantly, the first death of the American Civil War.

Once the remaining guns had finished the abbreviated salute, Hough's body and the wounded were carried down to the fort's parade. A local minister, the Reverend W. B. Yates, was summoned from Charleston to perform the funeral services for Hough. The death of Private Daniel Hough and the injuries to the others in his command affected Major Anderson deeply. He reportedly told Yates that he had prayed daily to protect his men from harm during the bombardment and that just the night before he had returned thanks to God for so singularly answering his prayers. During the attack, only four men had been slightly injured from flying shards of mortar and brick despite the terrific pounding inflicted by Confederate guns. But Anderson, gesturing toward Hough and the dying Gallway, said, "This mysterious providence, you must admit, Rev. Yates, is beyond our finite comprehension."[6]

The next four years would prove that there was much beyond the finite comprehension of all Americans. In April 1861, no one could have anticipated the scope of human destruction that the war would bring or have foretold its effect on the American nation. In the months preceding the attack on Fort Sumter, speculations of a bloodless separation had been numerous. Confident that Northerners would not fight to retain the disaffected states, Southerners boasted that secession would be accomplished without bloodshed. Alabamian Leroy Pope Walker, who later became the Confederacy's first secretary of war, blustered that he would be able to sop up every drop of blood shed in the conflict with his handkerchief, certain that his scrap of fabric would be more than equal to the task. More ghoulishly, Senator James Chesnut of South Carolina offered to drink all the blood that would be spilled.[7] Both men would have been hard-pressed to carry out their boasts following the tragic events of Sumter, and the loss of Hough and Gallway foreshadowed but dimly the four long years of death that would follow. Even those who sought or expected bloodshed—and there were many—could not have been adequately prepared.

The unimaginable scope of soldier death, and its effects on American society and culture, remains one of the most powerful legacies of the Civil War. Although its significance has rarely been explored, death forms a crucial chapter in the history of the war and its aftermath. Union and Confederate armies had to include death within their calculus of war, including the reactions of surviving comrades, the continuing objectives of combat, the loss of military strength and its replacement, even the logistics of burial. Beyond the battlefield, no social history of the war can afford to ignore the relationship between the soldier dead and their civilian survivors. The death inflicted during the war disrupted dramatically the folkways associated with death ritual and defied every previous custom with which Americans sought to tame death. Furthermore, the animosities of war, both reflected in and growing out of the treatment of the dead, continued to shape public thought and discourse for decades through the postwar commemoration of more than half a million men and remained an anguished divide in national reconciliation.

Numbers quickly overwhelm us, or perhaps comfort us in their anonymity, but they are an efficient means of providing a comparative context for the death incurred by the Civil War. Our best current estimates are that 620,000 soldiers died in the Civil War, about one-third as a result of military action, and about two-thirds from disease. As Maris Vinovskis has suggested, the social impact of such numbers exceeds by far anything in American experience.[8] Led by a relatively small career officer class, the U.S. military had met with inordinate success, given its size and largely ad hoc status, and at relatively little human cost. The Revolutionary War, the military conflict that compelled international recognition of the new nation's identity, required slightly more than 25,000 lives, in a contest with professional soldiers serving one of the great military powers of the world, Great Britain. In 1812, a second defense of national sovereignty and access to the seas cost another 6,780 lives. After nearly a generation of peace, America's first imperial war—with Mexico—was won at the cost of another 13,000 American lives. As significant as these earlier military actions were, they pale in comparison with the Civil War. The number of casualties inflicted in three days at Gettysburg exceeded the number of fatalities in all previous American wars[9] (see table 1). More Americans were lost at Cold Harbor in an hour than in the four years of the War of 1812; 7,000 men—husbands, fathers, and sons who would never return to their lives and loved ones—killed or mortally wounded at the rate of more than 116 a minute, nearly two every second.[10]

During the Civil War, nearly 14 percent of all combatants were killed, and the total number was equal to nearly 2 percent of the national population. One hundred years later, American involvement in Vietnam—a conflict similarly marked by great social strife—presents a startling contrast. In the Vietnam War, fewer than 1 percent of American soldiers engaged were killed, still almost 60,000. But, as a percentage of the population, nearly 3.72 *million* soldiers would have had to die—nearly sixty-five times the actual number killed—for Vietnam deaths to be on a par with Civil War deaths. Of course, this comparison is not made to lessen the very real pain of Vietnam, but to accentuate the trauma inflicted on an earlier generation. The Civil War inflicted more than ten times the number of military deaths of Vietnam in a quarter of the time.[11] The Civil War alone accounts for nearly half of all American military deaths (47.43 percent).

Trying to come to grips with the social dimension of the soldier dead, one author tried to average the dead among the states, counties, and townships of America. He concluded from his calculations that the war inflicted twenty-one graves per township, "or an average of five funerals a year for the four years of the war." He continued, "there was not a city nor a village, nor a community of any sort, nor yet a family, nor scarcely a single individual, that was not in recent sorrow for some dead soldier." This, combined with the continuing agony of the war's wounded, served as a reminder of the pain of the war, a story "retold until a solemn, heroic, sorrow became the daily food upon which the nation fed."[12] However, to appreciate the dramatic disjunctions that Civil War death produced, we must develop some sense of the antebellum experience of death. From our perspective, having become familiar, if not somewhat inured, to death on a global scale through two world wars that dwarfed even the Civil War, it is difficult to recapture a time when such death was in some ways so painfully new.

Table 1. American Military Deaths, 1773–1974

War	U.S. Population	U.S. Military Personnel	Military Deaths	Deaths per 10,000 of Population	Deaths as a Percentage of U.S. Military Personnel	Deaths as a Percentage of Total Military Deaths
American Revolution	2,148,000	250,000	25,324	117.896	10.13	1.94
War of 1812	8,179,000	286,000	6,780	8.29	2.37	0.52
Mexican-American War	21,406,000	116,000	13,271	6.2	11.44	1.02
Civil War	34,026,000	4,427,000	618,222	181.691	13.96	47.43
Spanish-American War	73,494,000	307,000	5,807	0.79	1.89	0.45
World War I	104,550,000	4,744,000	116,516	11.145	2.46	8.94
World War II	136,739,000	16,354,000	405,399	29.648	2.48	31.10
Korean War	157,028,000	5,764,000	54,246	3.455	0.94	4.16
Vietnam War	204,879,000	8,400,000	57,777	2.82	0.69	4.43
Total Military Dead			1,303,342			

Sources: Columns 1 and 2: Claudia D. Goldin, "War," in *Encyclopedia of American Economic History: Studies of the Principal Movements and Ideas,* ed. by Glenn Porter, 3 vols. (New York: Charles Scribner's Sons, 1980), 3: 935–57. For American Revolution military personnel, I have used the upper limit of the range offered by Goldin. Column 3: Maris Vinovskis, "Have Social Historians Lost the Civil War? Some Preliminary Demographic Speculations," *Journal of American History* 76, no. 1 (June 1989): 37–58. As Vinovskis, who also relies on Goldin's figures, suggests, "the reader should regard some of these estimates as intelligent approximations rather than definitive figures" (36).

Honoring the Civil War Dead

It seems odd to offer evidence of what was once so evident, but historians of death culture have rarely incorporated the Civil War into their discussions of the changes in death-associated ritual and custom over the course of
the nineteenth century.[13] Even historians who encompass the war within their
analysis often give it little emphasis. Phillip S. Paludan complains, with some
justice, that one scholar, "like every other writer on the subject of death, ig-
nores the possibility that the war that took the lives of over 600,000 men might
have had an impact on [the] understanding of the subject." David C. Sloane,
whose masterly *The Last Great Necessity* chronicles more than two centuries
of American cemetery development, asserts that the Civil War "had only an
indirect impact on American attitudes toward death," although he credits the
war with creating "a new category of sacred spot: the war battlefield."[14] However, battlefield preservation was almost always a logical afterthought to the
creation of an adjacent soldier cemetery. By 1890, the federal government had
created seventy-eight national cemeteries to contain the Civil War dead, encompassing nearly 1,500 acres in twenty-two states and the District of Columbia, all before creating the first battlefield park.[15] A primary motivation
for setting aside the fields of war was the preservation of ground made sacred
through blood. Therefore, battlefields have significance because of their association with patriotic death.

Prior to the war, the experience of death and its associated rituals had
been largely personal and highly ritualized. Other than clergy and the church,
institutions only rarely interposed themselves between an individual death
and the deceased's family or kin group. With few exceptions, death occurred
most often in the home. Whether mortality resulted from illness or accident,
unless injury was profound or death sudden, the stricken were taken home
to die. Even if sudden death did occur, the body would be returned home,
for it was there that the corpse was prepared, washed, dressed, and laid out
in a coffin. It was also from the home that the funeral procession began,
wending its way from front door through the streets to a local burial ground.
As a result, the home was the center of death culture in America.[16]

When death occurred in the home, its focus was the deathbed. Over the
past century and more, the deathbed—once so familiar—has become foreign, and the significance of its rituals has been largely lost. In antebellum
America, when death was thought to be imminent, family and friends were
called to support and comfort the dying. These closing moments offered
possible opportunities to resolve relationships and to say good-bye. More than

that, however, the dynamic of the deathbed was a surprisingly dialectical one, for the dying individual lay at the center of a complex set of reciprocal inter-dependencies. The dying gained strength and resolve from those assembled, who in turn watched the death unfold for personal instruction, learning literally how to die. In addition, the quality of death was extremely important in this performance of life's last act. It reflected not only on the life that had been lived, but also on the qualities of the life that would follow death. Those who faced death with willingness, submission, even cheerfulness, were thought to display evidence of salvation, more so than those who died fearfully or in despair. "Good" deaths were those of individuals who—in the company of loved ones—remained conscious until the moment of death, resolute, even eager to submit to the end of life, and in this way gave evidence of an inward saving grace. To die improperly, to "die hard," was to surrender to pain, to express discomfort and fear, and above all to die alone.[17] Educated in the stoicism required to meet these socially defined parameters of a good death—that is, one that could edify through serene acceptance during the deathbed vigil and reassure loved ones that death was to be accepted and even embraced—individuals were, therefore, supremely concerned with the "management" of their own death. The historian Lewis O. Saum emphasizes the significance of the deathbed when he observes that "participation in the ritual of death centered more directly on the deathbed than on the grave. Indeed, to an almost unnerving degree, the imagination, emotion and memory of humble America hovered about that sacrosanct place."[18]

From this social context, both soldiers and civilians confronted the war dead, and were overwhelmed. Virtually every aspect of death associated with the Civil War defied the cultural ideals and rituals that so characterized and constrained death for generations prior to the war. In the first place, the number of the dead was overwhelming. There were no historical referents or even distant memories of comparable national experience to assist in placing Civil War death in any helpful perspective, no large-scale institutions in existence that could assist in coping. But the challenge of the Civil War extended far beyond mere quantity; it attacked in a far more intimate fashion. The rituals of the deathbed were devastated: geographic distance removed for most the possibility of dying at home, within the traditional spheres of friends and families.[19] Instead, even in battlefield hospitals, deaths were all too often attended by strangers, unknown surrogates to whom fell the crucial and intimate rites associated with the closing of life. Even the cultural standards of death were confounded by the war. The painful, profound trauma of battle-field wounds, frequently accompanied by uncontrollable infections and fevers, put a stoic and serene death out of reach for many. On the most intimate and personal level, the war assaulted the most basic and ubiquitous cultural sensibilities; most deaths were lonely, solitary, and anguished, without the comfort of companionship, without the possibility of being "good" deaths.

The Civil War wrenched the nation from its moorings in a thousand ways, but none of its disruptions were as important or as deeply felt as the death it produced. From the distant battlefield to the obscure grave, the death of soldiers affected the nation's citizens for decades afterward. Soldiers and civilians strove to cope with the costs of the war, but the pain of loss could not fail to be colored by the larger context of sectional strife. Both sides, both nations, responded with increasing vehemence to alleged mistreatment of the dead, and perceived atrocities spawned an animus that extended far beyond charges of treason or tyranny. Even though soldiers and civilians began with the same set of cultural references, soldiers' separate experiences of battle, their immediacy to the carnage, necessarily challenged their sensibilities first and forcibly produced innovations among them to supplant the traditional customs and rituals combat so thoroughly violated. Throughout, despite war, both soldiers and civilians sought to reaffirm familiar folkways in the onslaught of overwhelming death and were outraged by the enemy that had exacted that death. Soldiers faced those difficulties first.

Soldiers

Of all the literature devoted to the military experience of the Civil War—or any war—little space is given over to the dead. More certain than victory, combat death is the inevitable result of warfare, and that death must be confronted and reconciled. Military historians have often tallied the number of the dead, but usually only as an indication of damage inflicted or incurred by military units.[20] Yet the dead have more importance than serving simply as an index of fighting strength and require more of the military than their mere replacement by fresh recruits. A balance must be struck between the care of and concern for the fallen and the continuing imperatives of war. The military forces of both nations were unprepared for the quantity of death that soon faced them, and both sides struggled to create policies and practices that served their continuing military needs as well as acknowledged, however scantily, the accepted cultural values associated with caring for the dead.

Soldiers lived in a world bordered on every hand by death. In moments of combat, it surrounded them. In the periods of rest and labor between battles and movements, care for the dead occupied at least some of their hours. They fought on landscapes marked by death; it seems that nearly every battle of any size was at least partially fought in or near an existing cemetery. From Mechanicsburg to Petersburg and more than a dozen places in between, a local "Cemetery Hill" marked the military landscape—the most renowned of which is at Gettysburg—and the passing armies nearly always left behind some of their number in those preexisting civilian burial grounds. Artillery units seemed particularly attracted to cemeteries, perhaps because they were often placed on hilltops or ridges; interment always seemed better allocated to land unlikely ever to see a plow. These eminences often commanded the towns and farmlands across which the armies fought. Additionally, infantry units at times took advantage of the cover provided by the tombstones and the stone walls that often enclosed burial grounds. Late in the war, Union soldiers carried with them the identity and success of Gettysburg's Cemetery Hill, frequently renaming new battlefields in ways that echoed previous combat. While fortifying a hilltop near Rome, Georgia, Brigadier General John M. Corse reported his position as an "eminence to which we gave the name Cemetery Hill."[21] In these ways, death shaped the landscape through which soldiers moved.

What first struck the imagination of soldiers was the sheer number of dead that could result from battle. A soldier recalled of Shiloh: "In places dead men lay so closely that a person could walk over two acres of ground and not step off the bodies." This appearance of a "carpeted" area of bodies was a recurring image. General Ulysses S. Grant repeated nearly the same words after Shiloh: "I saw an open field . . . so covered with dead that it would have been possible to walk across the clearing, in any direction, stepping on dead bodies, without a foot touching the ground." At Antietam, Alpheus Williams was stunned by the sight of an entire Southern regiment, 150 men, lying dead still in line of battle. Elsewhere, he remembered that the dead were "thick as autumn leaves." During the Battle of Fredericksburg, the mounds of the Federal dead were so great before the stone wall at Marye's Heights that they actually impeded the ability of Union forces to advance. Reserve troops, sent forward to reinforce the front lines, had perhaps the clearest notion of the proximity of death, for as they marshaled their resolve to enter combat they were surrounded with its fatal consequences. Moving up to support the Union line on the second day of Shiloh, Daniel McCook wrote of the horrors to be seen on the march to battle: "The disordered hair, dripping from the night's rain, the distorted and passion-marked faces, the stony, glaring eyes, the blue lips, the glistening teeth, the shriveled and contracted hands, the wild agony of pain and passion in the attitudes of the dead—all the horrid circumstances with which death surrounds the brave when torn from life in the whirlwind of battle, were seen as we marched over the field."[22] In such circumstances, soldiers like McCook confronted death prior to battle, in its midst, and at its conclusion. Death on this scale found no parallel in their previous experience around the deathbeds of family and friends.

Moreover, each soldier had died of such terrible violence. Musket and rifle fire consisted of large, soft lead projectiles, which flattened out on impact and caused awful wounds. Artillery fire of case shot and the shrapnel of explosive shell were devastating antipersonnel weapons. It is safe to assert that a portion of soldiers listed as missing were literally destroyed by such weaponry, beyond even the ability to recover a body, let alone recognize the individual who had been so maimed. It was a common observation in battle reports that the numbers listed did not accurately reflect the number killed. Colonel Henry Morrow, writing of the Twenty-fourth Michigan Infantry, recorded, "About 80 of the enlisted men and 3 officers were reported as missing in action. Many of the men have never been heard from, and are known not to be in the hands of the enemy. They were undoubtedly killed, but, not having been so reported, are not included in the above." Among the initial graves at the Antietam National Cemetery, at least three contained nothing but anonymous severed limbs collected from the battlefield and the surgeon's table.[23]

Through this environment of violence and death, individual soldiers moved as parts of larger units. Most soldiers served in troops organized out of communities, often fighting alongside neighbors and acquaintances they had known throughout their lives. This composition certainly lent itself to unit cohesion and generally eased recruitment, but often unacknowledged is the fact that such organization exacerbated the grief of soldier death. Certainly all soldiers form bonds in combat—among friends and strangers alike— but it was difficult to become hardened to battlefield violence when, in addition to their own sense of immediate loss, soldiers knew intimately the impact of that particular death, knew the family would mourn the loss, knew the community that would feel the void. Writing from the battlefield, Brigadier General John E. Smith recognized the impact at home following the deaths at Chattanooga. While "rejoicing at our success over the enemy," he wrote, "we sympathize with the bereaved at home, trusting that the time will soon come when such sacrifice of life for the maintenance of our country and flag will be no longer required."[24] Although the presence of friends might have provided some familiar faces to attend a soldier's death, the exigencies of combat rarely permitted such rituals on a battlefield, and few soldiers could linger with the dying for hours or days beside a hospital cot. Leaving the dying behind to the care of strangers was an all too common experience. The connectedness of soldiers, the bonds of comradery and community, worked generally to intensify, rather than diminish, the pain of death.

The Civil War occurred prior to the twentieth-century innovations within the military—such as "dog-tag" identification, and the Graves Registration Service—that assigned the dead and their needs to specific military personnel. Therefore, the burden of such violence fell first on those ordinary line soldiers who, having survived, had to bury their comrades. Burial was an imperative, the roots of which extend far back into human experience. The overriding concern was for decency. The burial should not simply remove the dead from the immediate, ongoing concerns of the living, but should also accomplish some respect for the dead. Ideally, it should consist of a coffined body laid out with some design of repose and buried deep in a secure location, the identity of the deceased appropriately and permanently marked. Such were the cultural standards of the mid-nineteenth century. But such standards were rarely met in most theaters of the Civil War. Soldiers had great difficulty obtaining either the means to procure a coffin, or the time necessary to construct one, especially in combat situations. They were sometimes able to do so; the ledger book of Cain and Cornelius, a carpentry firm in Nashville, Tennessee, records the sale of coffins dispensed equitably to both Union and Confederate units.[25] However, the only containers for most corpses were their own blankets, with graves shallow and grave markings makeshift and fragile. This became known as a *soldier's burial,* that distinction indicating the distance between what was desirable given prevailing social standards and what was possible in war.[26] Although a wide disparity emerged between the burial of friends and that of enemies, where possible the concerns for decent interment of comrades remained steadfast throughout the war.

Honoring the Civil War Dead

A primary concern of all combatants was the preservation of identity. The first organized response on the part of the Union army to the ever-mounting number of the dead concerned the identity of the lost soldiers, an attempt to humanize and lend order to the chaotic violence of battle. On 9 September 1861, Secretary of War Simon Cameron ordered that the quartermaster general supply registers and forms for recording the identity of each burial and the location of the grave. Additionally, the orders required headboards to be erected over each grave and inscribed with the name and native state of the decedent.[27] The importance of identification stressed so early in the war almost certainly stemmed from the experience of the Mexican-American War. In 1850, Congress ordered that the U.S. soldier dead be collected into an American cemetery in Mexico City. Unfortunately, due to poor records, only 750 bodies—little more than 5 percent of the soldiers killed—were found and reinterred in the new grounds, all of them unidentified. The dead of Zachary Taylor's command were never found.[28] Eleven years later, the first and one of the highest priorities concerning the dead of the Civil War would be meticulous record keeping in service of the preservation of identities.

However, the Union War Department's initial order contained no provision specifying how, when, where, or by whom soldiers were to be buried, but such specification was, ultimately, unnecessary. Soldiers often undertook the work of burial before any order that might be issued by officers in command. For example, among the Federal forces at Gettysburg, General Order No. 33 directed "commanding generals to lay off lots of ground in some suitable spot near every battle-field, so soon as it may be in their power," but, in truth, the work of burying the dead did not often wait for such official designation.[29] If at all possible, soldiers began the work of caring for their own dead almost immediately following the end of combat and sometimes even in its midst. Nightfall, and the cessation of overt hostilities that it brought, provided an excellent opportunity for the burial of fallen comrades. This is particularly true of those units, such as artillery batteries, that were likely to incur casualties at a distance from the enemy lines or those defending entrenched positions, such as the Confederates at Fredericksburg or the Union infantry at Gettysburg. Infantry units that advanced to meet the enemy, fought, and then retired or were driven from the field often left behind their dead and grievously wounded. The first deaths cared for were naturally the closest, men from one's own unit, and they were buried as carefully as the pressures of combat permitted but as quickly as duty demanded. Typically, if circumstances allowed, each army buried its own, as did each unit within those armies.

On the battlefield, graves for one's own dead were as deep as time allowed and were individualized when the dead could be identified. In accordance with standing orders as well as personal inclination, the identification of the deceased was written on or carved into a temporary marker, usually the lid of an ammunition box or other such wooden planking. The activities reported by Joshua Lawrence Chamberlain at Gettysburg seem to be fairly typical of many units: "We returned [after a reconnaissance] to Little Round Top, where we buried our dead in the place where we laid them during the fight, marking each grave by a head-board made of ammunition boxes, with each dead soldier's name cut upon it. We also buried 50 of the enemy's dead in front of our position of July 2."[30] Chamberlain's report accurately reflects the priorities of soldiers: during combat, in the momentary lulls, his men laid their dead nearby; afterward, and after ascertaining that the enemy was not in close proximity, the bodies were buried in individualized, identified graves; only then were any energies expended on interring the enemy dead.

The interment of comrades was as close to the social standards of burial practice as could be accomplished within the limited means available. If possible, this stark military rite was also a religious ceremony conducted by an army chaplain or visiting clergy. As the war lengthened, chaplains grew scarce and it was not unusual for them to move among several units performing services. At Gettysburg, Leman W. Bradley of the Sixty-fourth New York Infantry reported his regiment had "buried our dead and held short religious services, conducted by the chaplain of the One Hundred and Forty-Fifth Pennsylvania Regiment."[31] Religious ceremonies on the battlefield helped reconnect soldiers to their distant homes and communities, as chaplains worked to restore some small portion of a more familiar death culture even in the midst of combat. The notable activities of one chaplain were reported by Colonel Harris M. Plaisted, of the Eleventh Maine Infantry, in command of the Third Brigade during the Richmond Campaign of 1864. Plaisted wrote that, during battle, Chaplain Trumball of the Tenth Connecticut "was conspicuous on this occasion, with revolver in hand, in his effort to stay the crumbling regiment. An hour later he officiated at the burial of our dead, while the skirmish line was still engaged and every moment a renewal of the attack was expected."[32] The performance of a religious burial service in spite of impending attack reveals the significance attached to such rituals.

Honoring the Civil War Dead

Late in the war, as the number of the dead escalated so precipitously, newspaper editors and civic leaders criticized the Quartermaster Department for not ensuring that every burial in the Washington, D.C., area cemeteries included religious services. Quartermaster General Montgomery C. Meigs complained, "It is impossible for the chaplain of hospitals to accompany each body to the grave. It is a daily duty, and the chaplains' whole time would be taken up in its performance." Meigs suggested as a remedy that one of the hospital chaplains be assigned, on a rotating schedule, to the cemeteries every day, and that he "should remain constantly at the cemetery until relieved by his successor." Barring that, he asked that the Quartermaster Department be empowered to hire a minister under the requirements that "he shall live at the cemetery[,] . . . take charge of the whole conduct of interments, and perform appropriate religious services." This, Meigs thought, "would give great satisfaction to the friends of our soldiers."[33]

Ironically, in some circumstances, the religious ceremonies had less significance than the military rites of burial. Later in the war, Chaplain James Peet—assigned to the Fiftieth Regiment of the U.S. Colored Infantry, then encamped at Vicksburg—noted in his monthly report that "in addition to the Religious services, Military Escorts have this month accompanied the remains of the Deceased to the grave, for the first [time] I believe, since the Regiment was organized. The effect, apparently, is most excellent, causing the men to feel that they are regarded *as soldiers.*"[34] African American soldiers, no doubt, appreciated having a permanently assigned chaplain to officiate over burials, but by itself the religious component of such rituals were commonplace, offering no distinction between soldiers and local civilians or laborers. In the significant context of the U.S. Colored Troops and their struggle against prejudicial treatment, it was the military rituals, first instituted by Peet in July 1864, which conveyed to black men in uniform that sense of honor and respect accorded a proper soldier's burial.

Of course, bodies were buried for the same reasons that bodies have always been buried: out of respect for the dead; to prevent desecration; and for the health of the living. But other reasons could become important in war. Counting bodies lying on the battlefield let the enemy forces quantify the damage they had inflicted, yielding potentially vital intelligence in planning the next phase of combat. After the Battle of Brandy Station, Confederate General J. E. B. Stuart reported: "The [Union]'s loss is not known, and will, as far as possible, be carefully concealed by him. . . . Their dead, among whom were several field officers, were buried on different parts of the field before an opportunity was afforded to count them."[35] Stuart's observations of Union burial parties offer another motive for immediate burial of the soldier dead: concealment of potential weakness.

But it was not only in this sense that the military truly utilized the dead for the furtherance of war. Scavenging from the dead was practically a necessity among both Federal and Confederate troops at various points in the war. The dead could be helpful repositories of unconsumed resources, such as food, ammunition, clothing, even money. The Battle of Gettysburg had commenced just after the Union troops had received their pay, and pockets full of Federal currency proved irresistible to Southern and Northern soldiers alike.[36] At other times, the bodies themselves were of greatest necessity. Major General Darius Couch later remembered that, during the frigid December night following the battle at Fredericksburg, "as fast as men died they stiffened in the wintry air, and on the front line were rolled forward for protection of the living." In addition to being used as bulwarks, some corpses were, apparently, propped upright to deceive the enemy. Couch recorded simply that "frozen men were placed for dumb sentries."[37]

In addition, the dead could at times provide the means for brief respites from battle since commanders occasionally arranged for temporary truces to arrange for their care. In the case of Gettysburg, on the second night of battle, 2 July 1863, Adjutant General Lorenzo Thomas reported that "Lee, by flag of truce, asked to bury his dead. Firing ceased at that time."[38] Truces for the burial of the dead and the collection of the wounded were common to most battles or to their aftermaths. After Fredericksburg, two days were required for Union details to bury the dead lying before the stone wall on Marye's Heights. After working from Wednesday, 17 December, to Friday, 19 December, the commander of the detail could finally report that his men had buried 913 soldiers and recovered and removed the bodies of 5 officers. He also noted: "Nearly all the dead were stripped entirely naked by the enemy."[39] Truces were sometimes called for more immediate concerns than respect for the slain. In the siege of Vicksburg, Union troops had fallen quite close to Confederate lines and lay there for some days in the summer heat. S. H. Lockett, the Confederate engineer of the Vicksburg defenses, later wrote: "The dead had become offensive and the living were suffering fearful agonies. General Pemberton, therefore[,] … [proposed] a cessation of hostilities for two and a half hours, so that the dead and dying men might receive proper attention. This was acceded to by General Grant, and from six o'clock until nearly dark both parties were engaged in performing funeral rites and deeds of mercy to the dead and wounded Federal soldiers."[40]

Nevertheless, despite a long tradition, such truces were occasionally refused or not respected. Nineteenth-century military science dictated that whoever controlled the battlefield after combat was the victor of the struggle. Probably the single most frequent reason for denying a truce was to prevent access to the battlefield, either to ensure recognition of victory or to prevent the soldiers on burial detail from gaining valuable intelligence by approaching the lines. In those circumstances, when the dead remained on a battlefield that had fallen under the control of the enemy, the ability to care for the fallen lay at the whim of the opposing commander. If denied, common decency urged that the dead, like the field, would equally fall under his control and responsibility. Wade Hampton, then commanding the cavalry of the Army of Northern Virginia, refused a truce and denied Union forces access to the field of Reams' Station but added, "I have ordered all your dead to be buried."[41] Of course, nothing ensured the loss of identity more than anonymous burial by the enemy.

These responses to the soldier dead acted out on a thousand battlefields were foreshadowed in many ways in the responses of Private Daniel Hough after Fort Sumter, particularly with regard to his burial and loss of identity. Even though a religious funeral ceremony was held while his comrades still remained in the fort, the ground on which he died had become the property of the enemy, and it fell to the Confederates to bury him. Out of respect for the gallant endurance of Anderson's troops, General Beauregard ordered Hough's burial to be performed with military honors. South Carolina's Palmetto Guard, the first Confederate troops to occupy the fort, buried Hough and carefully marked his grave. The commanding officer, G. B. Cuthbert, noted: "A proper respect for the memory of the dead, as well as the desire to put on record a noble act, induces me [to] recount the following fact: Immediately before the departure of the Palmetto Guard [from] Fort Sumter, Sergeant Webb, Corporal Robinson, and Private Mackay placed a neat and appropriate head-piece over the grave of the unfortunate Howe [*sic*]. . . . The performance of this sacred duty did credit to their generous hearts, and proved that Carolina chivalry exists only in combination with a spirit of reverence and magnanimity." Cuthbert's choice of language is instructive. Caring for the dead, even the enemy dead, was a "sacred duty," performed with respect, reverence, and magnanimity by generous and noble hearts. Days later, a newspaper reporter wrote that he had seen a new grave, built of brick, where Hough's body had been moved, marked with a "temporary granite slab a foot square, with the simple inscription upon it—Daniel Howe [sic], died April 14, 1861."[42] It is not clear that the granite slab was the work of the Palmetto Guard, but it is likely. Unfortunately, all the generous acts and magnanimous sentiments that accompanied Hough's burial would be sorely tested as the war progressed and the dead accumulated. As was true for so many soldiers who followed him, and despite the best of intentions, Hough had immediately lost his identity upon burial, laid to rest under an incorrect name by those who had not known him in life. Hough's name was, apparently, pronounced to rhyme with *bough*, as all Confederate sources consistently wrote his name as they heard it, hence "Howe." In later months and years, when there was far more than a single enemy soldier to be buried, identity became even more ephemeral and vulnerable.

In general, the burial of the enemy dead was a far less careful operation than was the burial of comrades. Their bodies were interred in mass graves, often taking the form of long continuous trenches, a chain of shallow depressions with the earth from one excavation filling the grave of the next in line.[43] Because the work of burying the enemy followed only after one's own dead were interred, it was often left undone or only partially completed. Because the Union army retained the field after the Battle of Gettysburg, it was largely the Confederates who were left unburied when orders came to march South. Major General Henry Slocum, discussing the progress of a subordinate commander, reported: "General Geary states that over 900 of the enemy's dead were buried by our own troops and a large number left unburied, marching orders having been received before the work was completed."[44]

Sensibly enough, in the battle and duty reports, it becomes quite clear that an army's own dead received preferential treatment. Because of the Confederate withdrawal from the Gettysburg battlefield, most Southern accounts simply report that their dead and severely wounded were "left on the field." When burials were possible, interments were usually granted to Confederate forces alone: "*Our* dead on that part of the field were buried the next day"; "we interred *our* dead decently."[45] The *Official Records* contains only one account of Confederates burying Union soldiers at Gettysburg. General John B. Gordon reported that "nearly 300 [Union soldiers] were buried on the ground where my brigade fought."[46] Union troops, with the advantage of holding the field, spent virtually all their efforts on interring the Union dead,

Following the battle of Antietam, Union burial details carefully interred the remains of
a Northern soldier, center. Nearby lie the unburied remains of a Confederate soldier.
The image emphasizes a stark reality; throughout the war, each side expended
their greatest efforts on interring their own dead with as much care as time and
circumstances permitted. Only then was any attention offered to the enemy dead.
  Library of Congress

a process hampered by the absence of proper implements. Col. Charles Candy,
of the Sixty-sixth Ohio Infantry, stated: "Owing to the scarcity of tools, few
of the enemy's dead were buried until the morning of the 5th, when pioneer
corps of this brigade, assisted by a detail of over 100 men, buried quite a number."[47] Even with proper implements, the weather could further hamper the
already gruesome task. Burnside's troops at Fredericksburg were well
equipped, but, during the bitter nights, "the bodies of the slain had frozen to
the ground." The trenching for graves required picks to get through a foot of
hardened earth.[48]

Occasionally, the enemy interfered with the process of burial, even of
their own dead. Benjamin Harrison, in command of the Seventieth Indiana

Infantry, reported that Confederate skirmishers fired upon his men as they sought to collect and bury dead Southern soldiers. "After this exhibition of bad faith," he continued, "I made no further effort to reach the rebel dead that could be seen between our lines, and many were left when we moved the next morning unburied, and so remained for several days." Whether the Confederate troops knew that the actions of the burial parties were on behalf of their soldiers is unknown, but this type of confusion occurred between generals as well as soldiers. At Cold Harbor, miscommunication between Robert E. Lee and Ulysses S. Grant contributed greatly to the number of the dead. Messages carried back and forth between the commanders indicate that negotiations for a truce to collect the dead and wounded began early on the morning of 6 June but could not be completed until after 6:00 P.M. on the evening of 7 June. How many died from their wounds during the thirty-six-hour-delay cannot be known, but Grant later reported that only two of the wounded were brought alive from the field.[49] However, outright victory and holding the field did not necessarily mean that the victor would assume responsibility for the enemy's burials. Note that the Union dead at Fredericksburg were buried by Union soldiers days after the battle, under the watchful eyes of the Confederates, who remained in their entrenchments. The only certainty was that, on both sides of the conflict, soldiers buried their own first.

The necessity of burial, sometimes in huge numbers, required long hours of hard and gruesome labor. In addition to the physical strain of digging even shallow graves, the decomposition of the dead made the work nearly unbearable. To avoid touching the dead, picks or hooks made of bent bayonets were sometimes used to drag bodies to their graves. Whiskey helped numb the soldiers to the tasks they faced. Samuel Compton of the Twelfth Ohio Infantry wrote of the burial detail two days after the battle at Fox's Gap: "The squad I saw were armed with a pick and a canteen full of whiskey. The whiskey the most necessary of the two. The bodies had become so offensive that men could only endure it by being staggering drunk."[50] Even when so fortified, the task was horrifying. Small wonder, then, that ready-made tombs became attractive alternatives. One observer noted that the Union burial detail at Fredericksburg laid some 400 to 500 Union dead in an empty icehouse, "where they were found—a hecatomb of skeletons—after the war."[51] At Fox's Gap, a farmer's well made a readily available, if unsavory, grave for fifty-eight Confederates who were tumbled into it.[52]

Honoring the Civil War Dead

Scholar Gary Laderman has asserted that surviving soldiers developed an abiding "disenchantment" with the dead that arose largely out of their overwhelming number and often offensive presence. As a result, Laderman argues, the soldier dead became, in the minds and attitudes of their survivors, inert and meaningless. It was the mission of the military to forget the dead in order to pursue the aims of war: "As the war continued and the death tolls climbed higher, the necessity of crushing the South overshadowed all the humane considerations associated with individual Union soldiers dying in camps and hospitals and on battlefields." So great was the eventual studied "detachment" that a soldier's corpse was reduced to "an inevitable product of war that lost all of its symbolic value as soon as the 'vital spark' had escaped." Burial details, therefore, an "odious charge that aroused feelings of indignation and resentment," merely managed the chaos of the battlefield and removed the dead from the sphere of the patriotic national mission of prosecuting the war. A final indication, for Laderman, of the lack of regard for the dead is the fact that African American soldiers and laborers were, at times, assigned the task of burial duty: "That blacks were involved in the handling of some of the dead when federal forces controlled the field after a battle or when fallen soldiers were reinterred in national cemeteries reflected the *decline in symbolic value* of the physical remains of fighting men for many northern Protestants."[53]

It was certainly the case that burial duty was often "odious," and many in the war must have found a certain emotional hardening a necessary part of performing their duties—soldiers, nurses, physicians, and politicians alike. But to argue that such an attitude indicates a disdain for, or even merely a detachment from, the soldier dead is to misread the evidence available and oversimplify a complex relationship between the living and the dead. In the first place, the dead can and did possess a number of symbolic meanings, but which of these they may have lost Laderman does not specify. There were, perhaps, as many symbols as there were observers, but most can be broadly categorized. For example, military commanders walking the field after combat derived from the dead a number of interpretations, about both the past conflict and any future clash. Bodies scattered across a field could measure the furious tides of battle, the amount of damage inflicted on or by an enemy, the present potential weakness of surviving troops, the strength of a defensive position, or the wisdom or folly of a particular stratagem or tactic. Individual bodies could represent to their comrades personal loss, might invite reflections on one's own mortality, and thus might inspire feelings of fatalism, revenge, bravery, or cowardice.[54] Civilians shared many of these interpretations, especially that of personal loss. Additionally, insofar as the dead could be equated with military success or failure, they could in turn reflect on the purpose, the nature, and even the morality of the war itself, and by extension the nationalist mission that it supported. Laderman has argued that the Northern national government sublimated the dead to the purposes of winning the war, yet the exact opposite may be true for the Union as well as the Confederacy. The staggering number of the dead on both sides surely contributed to the Confederate persistence in the face of increasingly bleak odds after 1863, and the peace platform of the Northern Democrats must have suffered in the presidential election of 1864 from their offer to negotiate a peace that threatened to render meaningless the Northern soldier dead. After committing so much, how could either side simply withdraw from the field? Death remains one of the most significant of human experiences and is therefore never wholly without meaning and symbolic import. That the soldier dead never lost their symbolic value is a major thesis of this work. In fact, following the resolution of the war, that symbolism only grew in strength and meaning for both Northern and Southern Americans.

While Laderman correctly identifies individuals expressing a certain indifference to, if not disdain for, the dead, he does not recognize that it was a purposeful indifference. Callousness in the face of death operated as a defensive psychological shield, meant to protect the individual from the enormity of the pain they confronted, but the totality of responses on the part of the military toward the dead indicate that callousness never equated a loss of meaning. On the first, most rudimentary level, the bodies of the dead retained their symbolic value in that they retained their sectional and political identities rather than merging into an amorphous jumble of corpses. The dead are consistently discussed in terms of "ours" and "theirs," "Yank" and "Reb." Finding a slain enemy at Gettysburg, one soldier remembered, "On the bank near the trench Lye [lay] a large Rebel Sergent[.] One of our miney balls had passed through His Head so quick that it dislocated all the Confederacy there was in it and it was gradually oozing out onto the ground for the flies to Diagnosis."[55] Clearly, although a dark statement of indifference, perhaps even hatred, the dead soldier remained a coherent member of a political and military entity, even of a nation, and this soldier believed that his enemy's fate was a direct result of his convictions. This is not to say that a gallows humor and whiskey were not virtual requirements of sustained burial duty, but when such indifference was directed toward the dead of one's own army, it was inspired less by the dead than by terrible necessity of their care.

Disdain or hostility toward the enemy dead was not simply an extension of combat animosities in the direction of those soldiers who were no longer combatants, although that forms a part of these sentiments. Generally, because the enemy dead were buried last—in itself a symbolic act—the processes of decay and mortification were even more pronounced, making the task of acting decently a real struggle. Some units on both sides sought to have enemy prisoners bury their own dead. Following the Battle of South Mountain, one soldier went to the local provost marshal to obtain Confederate prisoners to work the burial detail. When the marshal would not release the prisoners, he returned and "went at it. Buried 200 Rebs, they lay pretty thick."[56] After the assault on Fort Pillow, the surviving Union soldiers were put to the interment of their comrade dead.[57] But even though burial duty was nearly unbearable and made more onerous when burying the enemy, there is no reason to suspect that a lack of concern prevailed when interring one's own dead. Given the opportunity, an army buried its own in individualized, identified graves from the first of the war to its last days. In a moment rich in symbolism, Union soldiers burying their own in a civilian cemetery outside Fredericksburg, Virginia, took bricks and other materials from the nearby graves of Southerners to mark the graves of their comrades.[58]

Moreover, had the federal government sought to sublimate the dead to the necessity of victory, we should expect to see changes in government or military policy that fulfilled that shift in priority. But no such changes are evident. From beginning to end, while the general disdain for burial duty might have resulted in hasty burials, it did not result in the systematic abandonment of corpses. This is not to suggest that the needs of the dead were not outweighed at times by the demands of sustaining military effort. But neither the Union government nor the military ever countermanded or altered the standing orders issued on soldier burial, nor did they ever withdraw instructions set down to preserve the record of identity and location of each grave. Viewed from the perspective of the military command structure, the emphasis on maintaining the sanctity of individual, decent interments does not diminish but actually expands throughout the war. Given the common understanding of death and death culture shared between soldiers, their officers, and the civilians who supported them, it hardly seems possible for it to have been otherwise.

Civilians

Of course, the response to so enormous a task as caring for the soldier dead could not possibly be contained within the military but inevitably required civilian involvement. Civilians, in some ways, had a more difficult time with Civil War death than did soldiers, for it was the civilian—far removed from the realities of combat—who strived most to maintain and apply the standards of death ritual and custom, almost always unsuccessfully. The great majority of civilians never faced the grimness of war, never saw what soldiers saw, but a few did. As the movements of armies swept homes, farmlands, and whole towns into the conflict, civilians confronted the soldier dead. After the battle, the armies remained mobile and often departed before the burials had been completed. They always left before the last of the mortally wounded had died in local makeshift hospitals, parlors, or barns. Hence, these few came to know the death of the Civil War as soldiers saw it, although not as they experienced it.

Soldiers understood the death of the Civil War in ways that civilians would never fully share. Nevertheless, the war reached out to civilians in new and startling ways. The anxieties caused by the wrenching disruption to familiar cultural practices were only intensified by the ways in which the war was reported. As Phillip Paludan has noted, "The war brought death into the foreground of life. Newspapers, personal letters, word of mouth, brought home to every community the growing mountains of dead that the war was exacting."[59] Telegraphs made distant battles accessible, and new lithographic processes allowed the larger journals to illustrate their narratives with maps and images of war. These tools emphasized the death of soldiers. Newspapers of every size listed the dead and wounded in long, closely printed columns. Family members, who otherwise might not receive a letter of notification for days or weeks afterward, who under other circumstances might not even be aware a battle had taken place, spent anxious, agonizing moments scanning the lists for a familiar name as often as the military units of their state or community were engaged in battle.

Battlefields came to the home front in even more startling ways as the new medium of photography was applied to the theater of war. The lengthy exposure times required by photographers often prevented the preservation of combat scenes and troop movements. The resulting collection of images, therefore, captured particular moments of stillness rather than the sweep of military action. In late 1862, the *Times* of London stated that "the photographer who follows in the wake of modern armies must be content with . . . the still life which remains when the fighting is over." Following in the wake of battle, those compositions often featured the corpses of soldiers. Alexander Gardner's pictures of dead men sprawled in the Bloody Lane at Antietam or huddled amid the rocks of Gettysburg's Devil's Den bore silent witness to the costs of battle.[60]

Through these photographs, civilians now had an almost visceral exposure to the costs of war. A reporter for the *New York Times* documented this response in an extraordinary article chronicling the 1862 opening of a new exhibit at Mathew Brady's New York studio. The photographic display, entitled "The Dead of Antietam," allowed far-distant civilians the opportunity to stand amid the debris of war:

> Crowds of people are constantly going up the stair; follow them, and you find them bending over photographic views of the fearful battle-field, taken immediately after the action. Of all objects of horror one would think the battle-field should stand preeminent, that it should bear away the palm of repulsiveness. But, on the contrary, there is a terrible fascination about it that draws one near these pictures, and makes him loth to leave them. You will see hushed, reverend groups standing around these weird copies of carnage, bending down to look in the pale faces of the dead, chained by the strange spell that dwells in dead men's eyes. It seems somewhat singular that the same sun that looked down on the faces of the slain, blistering them, blotting out from the bodies all semblance to humanity, and hastening corruption, should have thus caught their features upon canvas, and given them perpetuity for ever. But so it is.

The power of these images, captured sunlight reflected off so grisly a scene, brought the results of battle home to noncombatants as never before: "These pictures have a terrible distinctness. By the aid of the magnifying-glass, the very features of the slain may be distinguished. We would scarce choose to be in the gallery, when one of the women bending over them should recognise a husband, a son, or a brother in the still, lifeless lines of bodies, that lie ready for the gaping trenches." Newspapers listed the dead and wounded by name, but photographs *displayed* the violence done to their bodies. However, while newspaper lists referred to individuals, photographic images remained largely anonymous. The failure to find a particular name in the casualty lists resulted in relief. But photographs seemed to create doubt. The spectators at the Antietam exhibit might well have wondered whether their sons or husbands were not listed in the paper because they lay, like the subjects in the photographs, among the unnamed, distorted, and unidentifiable dead. The *Times* reporter observed, "Mr. Brady has done something to bring home to us the terrible reality and earnestness of war. If he has not brought bodies and laid them in our door-yards and along the streets, he has done something very like it."[61]

As important as these aspects of battlefield death were for those who remained and waited at home, they could not hope to match the actual experience of battlefield death. As was true for civilians in many other places, the burden of caring for the dead and wounded weighed heavily on the residents of Gettysburg. Their experiences offer an example of the civilian responses to soldier death and its effect on death culture. But unlike many other towns and villages, the armies never returned to Gettysburg, so the process of civilian care for the soldier dead unfolded with relatively little interference from the continuing war. Also, Gettysburg's fame encouraged the publication of reminiscences by the town's population, in greater proportion perhaps than anywhere else in the war, providing eloquent testimony to their reactions to new circumstances. The residents of Richmond, Petersburg, or Fredericksburg, Virginia, for example, no doubt responded in similar ways, but having to live with recurrent waves of dead and wounded throughout much of the war created overlapping layers of response. The transitions from military to civilian care are more easily discerned at Gettysburg.

Evident within the turmoil of this battle's aftermath are two important aspects of the social response to the soldier dead: first, in the face of these new and daunting circumstances, civilians adopted new practices even while they tried to restore familiar ones; and, second, the bodies of soldiers, although inert and lifeless, provoked in the living a variety of responses built upon the preexisting sectional and national tensions of the war, responses that would, in turn, tinge and influence all future attempts at reconstruction and reconciliation. This latter point is crucial; every invocation of the "bloody shirt," no matter how sincere or how cynical, every cry for Southern redemption, and every gesture toward political and social reunification was colored by memories of battlefields scattered with the soldier dead.

Throughout the night of 3 July 1863, the creaks of wagons and artillery caissons echoed in Gettysburg's narrow streets, giving hope to the farmers and merchants that the war was soon to leave them. Some emerged from their homes on the morning of the fourth, others waited until the fifth, out of respect for the pickets of both armies, who still fired at anything that moved in their vicinity. When Gettysburg residents finally emerged, they found their streets lined with the dead and, as Leonard Gardner put it, "other pictures of destruction which will never fade from my mind." Understandably, the townspeople were completely unprepared for the situation that confronted them. "Dead soldiers were everywhere," remembered Albertus McCreary. "Near a small house lay the bodies of two Confederate soldiers, and on looking into the house I saw two others, one on a bed and the other on the floor." The presence of the dead affected everything, including the environment: "The stench from the battle-field after the fight was so bad that every one went about with a bottle of pennyroyal or peppermint oil." Such circumstances provoked immediate response: "The burial of the dead commenced at once, and many were buried along the line where they fought and fell, and, in many cases, so near the surface that their clothing came through the earth." Interment was the first necessity, but the scope of the task was overwhelming. In addition to those killed outright, the wards of every makeshift hospital continued to lose wounded patients, contributing to the number requiring burial. Outside the United Presbyterian Church, two long trenches were prepared to receive the dying from the church turned hospital. However, one hospital volunteer remembered, "Before these trenches were filled up with ground, rain fell and it was necessary to lay heavy boards over the bodies to keep them down, in place."[62] The relief of the war's departure was more than tempered by such ghastly scenes of battle's aftermath.

Although both armies had accomplished a great deal the two days after the battle, they had by no means completed the task of interring all the dead. Large details of Confederate prisoners were assigned the task of providing hasty covering for the dead scattered over more than thirty square miles, but their work was inevitably makeshift. In addition, the tasks that remained for the local residents were compounded by two new arrivals, both of which tended to subvert the work that the soldiers had already accomplished. Rainstorms arrived on the afternoon of 4 July, washing away in some cases the thin blanket of earth that covered many of the dead. Additionally, relatives and sightseers descended on the town and battlefield like locusts, some disinterring soldiers as they sought frantically for the remains of their kin, others hunting grisly souvenirs. Within days, a significant portion of the armies' work had been undone.

That second invasion of armies of visitors, relatives, and the curious swelled the town beyond capacity. The Globe Hotel "had no lodging for men . . . the women occupied all of the beds [and] we placed blankets and Pillows on the carpets in the Parlors and reception rooms."[63] Homes became hostels and hospitals. Gettysburg resident Sarah Broadhead wrote, "Our house has been constantly full, and every house I know of has been, and is, full. One who called told me that he had sat on a chair in front of a hotel last night, and was glad to get even such quarters."[64] Sightseers wanted souvenirs of the fight, beginning a growth industry among local youths for military gear, expended shot, shells, and other such relics, and the curious from miles around began to scour the fields for anything of value that could be carried off.[65] The Union officer in charge of collecting and preserving Federal and Confederate property, W. Willard Smith, was continually thwarted by the "three to five thousand persons [who] visited the battlefield daily, most of them carrying away trophies." He therefore issued standing orders to have government property returned to the army and posted warnings that violators would be punished by forced labor on burial parties for dead Confederate soldiers and horses.[66] Many, however, had not come to claim souvenirs, but their dead. Mark Hunt, seeking his brother's body, wrote that, after walking the breadth of the bloody field, he had "followed fences as [a local farmer] directed and finally came to an enclosure of rail fence on the edge of the woods." As darkness was falling, he "got over the fence and with the lantern read the little headboards. I found my brother's name cut with a knife. I was satisfied, for I had found what I was seeking."[67]

Following their first impulse, civilians like Hunt sought to mitigate as much as possible the war's disruptions of traditional custom. The dead could no longer be cared for in ways that had been common before the war. Sheer numbers, as well as geographic distance, made the customary ritual and culture of death in America nearly impossible. In order to remedy these disruptions as best they could, Northern and Southern families expressed a great desire to retrieve the bodies of the dead from their battlefield or hospital burial plots and reinter them in a local cemetery or churchyard, in some small way restoring their lost men to the circle of family. Even though, in general, the armies did their best for their own dead, there was great anxiety that battlefield interments were not proper, dignified, or even decent, and publicity about mass burials had only exacerbated those fears. The *New York Times* review of Brady's Antietam exhibition highlighted that concern: "For [burial] trenches have a terror for a woman's heart, that goes far to outweigh all the others that hover over the battlefield." The reporter continued: "How can this mother bear to know that in a shallow trench, hastily dug, rude hands have thrown him. She would have handled the poor corpse so tenderly, have prized the boon of caring for it so dearly—yet, even the imperative office of hiding the dead from sight has been done by those who thought it trouble, and were only glad when their work ended." A powerful consequence of the remoteness of the dead from family was the inability to find emotional and cultural closure through the preparation of the body for burial. The *Times* article emphasized that those responsibilities were unwillingly surrendered by circumstance to others "when, but for the privilege of touching that corpse, of kissing once more the lips though white and cold, of smoothing back the hair from the brow and cleansing it of blood stains," this representative mother "would give all the remaining years of life that Heaven has allotted her."[68]

Occasionally, the desire to retrieve loved ones outweighed any possible dangers inherent in war. Following the combat around Spotsylvania in 1864, Colonel E. Schriver appealed to Assistant Adjutant General Seth Williams to arbitrate the request of civilians who wished to accompany Union burial parties onto the field during truces. Williams approved generally Schriver's desire to be accommodating; however, in the specific case of Spotsylvania, Williams noted that "in the present position of the enemy there are not many of the burial places of the fallen that can safely be visited, except with considerable force." A similar situation faced Grant after Shiloh. He refused a request for Southern men to accompany the Confederate burial parties to "remove the remains of their sons and friends," not out of sectional or military animosity, but because, as Grant wrote, "owing to the warmth of the weather I deemed it advisable to have all the dead of both parties buried immediately. There cannot, therefore, be any necessity of admitting within our lines the parties you desire to send on the grounds asked."[69] Although Grant does not explicitly state the case, in addition to the health concerns to which he refers, it was not possible to retrieve specific bodies of Southerners after Shiloh as they had been buried unidentified in mass graves. Of course, the source of this urge to recover the lost was the desire to reincorporate the remote death within established tradition. But there were simply too many bodies, at Gettysburg and every other battle. In Virginia, the dead from the fields around Richmond were taken to Hollywood or Oakwood Cemeteries, but often they arrived faster than graves could be dug. At one point the local paper reported more than fifty bodies were gathered awaiting burial, the source of a choking odor that hung over several blocks.[70]

But, without a long tradition of institutional services—morticians or funeral homes, for example—interposing themselves between an individual and the death of a loved one, entrusting such highly emotional and personal needs to others sometimes proved very difficult and often overwhelmed logic and economic considerations. One woman from Peasleville, New York, called special attention to her desires in a letter to a minister at the scene of her husband's death: "Concerning my husband's precious remains, if it is possible, how glad would I be to have him buried in the family burial-ground with his dear connections; so that when I am done with the afflictions of this life, I can slumber sweetly by his side. . . . I cannot bear the thought of having him slumber there, away from home and all that was dear to him on earth." Another widow writing at the war's end agonized over the financial costs and emotional benefits of transporting her lost husband to their home in Donegal, Pennsylvania:

> No tongue can express my grief. My friends here are trying to persuade me to leave his body there, as you say he is buried decent; and they tell me I could not see him if I would have him brought home. But, oh, I think it cannot be! But his remains must come home. They tell me it will cost at least an hundred dollars. I am in rather poor circumstances, and know not what to do; but, if you please, see that the board that marks his grave is well put in, so that, after a while, I perhaps can have him home.

While obviously distraught by her husband's death, her inability to reincorporate his death within traditional ritual pathways exacerbates her pain. "I think now, if my dear husband had only been permitted to get home to die, that I would not murmur," she continued. "But this is hard."[71]

These impulses tugged at everyone, regardless of race or cultural background. Martha Wells, a black woman in West Virginia, struggled similarly with the news that her son might have died in distant Texas as part of the U.S. Colored Troops occupation just after the war. After encouraging the officers in Texas to be certain that the soldier was indeed her son, of whom she had recently had more positive news, she stated, "If I am satisfied in my distressed mind that my son is dead I will go to Texas & bring him home." Although she evidently knew little about his location, she sought all the information she could get. "I hope you will give me the name of the Hospital, Doctor, and let me know if I can get him[.] [P]lease let me know the distance to Texas and what it would cost." The difficulties were, evidently, too great for her to overcome, for the government listings of national cemetery burials includes the entry for Augustus Wells, who was buried in grave 312 of the Brownsville National Cemetery, and there seems to be no record that his remains were ever removed.[72] In all these examples, the overwhelming desire is for the comfort of death ritual to be restored, for burial to take place within the circle of family and community. Those desires might be lessened, but never eliminated, with assurances that the interment comported with the standards of decent burial.

Never before in American experience had the mass transportation of the dead ever been contemplated, and within a short span of time the logistical requirements exploded onto the cultural landscape. Patents granted for new innovations in casket design and funereal goods increased rapidly during and immediately following the war. The first body bag, an all-too-familiar feature of later battlefields, was pioneered in the Civil War, although it saw little use. Historians of the mortuary arts acknowledge the significance of the war's influence: "The large scale shipment of bodies back to family homesteads no doubt received its greatest impetus with the mass return to their homes of the Civil War dead, and with the growth of steamboat and rail transportation."[73]

These new circumstances of death required innovations in technology. Thomas H. Holmes, the self-proclaimed father of chemical embalming, remembered that during the war "a complaint was made to General Grant by the railroad companies of offensive odor from bodies on trains going North. An order was issued to Jacob Weaver, Undertaker at Baltimore, to board every train and remove all bodies that were offensive, put them into a vault, or enclose them in tight zinc boxes and notify their friends. . . . Large numbers of bodies which had been dead only two or three days were taken from the trains."[74] The newest mortuary practice, chemical embalming, made the transport of soldiers possible. Techniques of embalming are nearly as old as civilization, but in America prior to the Civil War preservation of the corpse was limited largely to delaying the processes of decay by reducing the body's temperature with ice. This procedure, requiring bulky equipment and quantities of ice, was not possible on the battlefield. Recent innovations proved ideally suited to the circumstances of war. Thomas H. Holmes and others had refined the means of embalming through arterial injection as early as 1856, and dozens of imitators plied this new trade, moving in the aftermath of battle on both sides of the line, offering their services in tents and sheds. As table 2 indicates, the experience of the war and its dead rapidly accelerated the development of a variety of embalming formulas and methods.

In the second year of the war, the ability to preserve the dead had not yet approached the capacity to transport them home. Because of the newness of chemical embalming, older, alternate methods of preservation continued to be advertised, including coffins featuring lids containing "box[es] in which ice can be placed, thus making it possible to take bodies any distance."[75] Another manufacturer advertised that its new "caskets" were "warranted air tight, [and] can be placed in the parlor without fear," thereby hoping to persuade customers by offering the ability to return their lost relations to comforting rituals of a home funeral. If their product lived up to its manufacturer's boasts, the soldier dead could be brought from the battlefield to the train depot, from the depot to the parlor, and then from the parlor to the burial ground, thus providing the illusion that the loss had occurred in the home,

Table 2. Embalming Patents, 1856–1870

Date	Number	Name
1856	15972	J. A. Gaussardia
1860	30576	Warren Iddings
1863	38749	Franklin A. Hutton
1864	44495	John Morgan
1867	6147?	G. W. Scollay
1867	65174	Coffman
1867	67145	Colin C. St. Clair
1867	67170	Edward Granja
1867	69312	L. Brunetti*
1868	74607	C. A. Seely and C. J. Eames
1868	75992	James C. Sickel
1868	81755	Elliot N. Crane
1869	95939	G. W. Scollay

Sources: Robert W. Habenstein and Willima M. Lamers, *The History of American Funeral Directing* (Milwaukee: Bulfin, 1955), 328–29; *Report of the Commissioner of Patents for the Year* [1867–1870].

Note the sharp increase in the years immediately after the war.

*The patent awarded to L. Brunetti is included even though it specifies somewhat cryptically only the preservation of "animal substances."

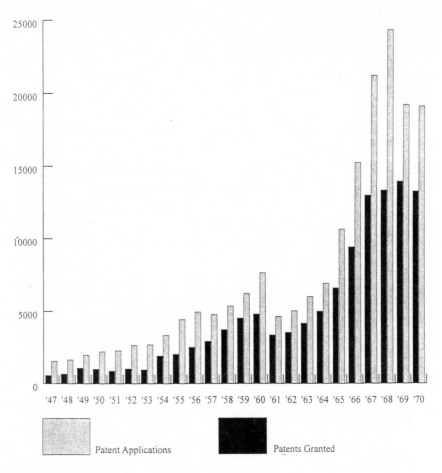

Figure 1. Patent Applications and Grants, 1847–1870

that the body had been prepared and encoffined there, and that death could again be tamed to the social rituals of mourning. Of course, the restoration could not be complete. Few ceremonies could include a display of the body, either because of decay or the violence of death. Writing home, Harry P. Farrow informed his relations of the preparations that he had made in the shipping home of his wife's cousin, killed on the battlefield of Chickamauga: "I suppose it is unnecessary to advise you not to open [the coffin], but for fear that some of the family might desire it done, I would say *don't do it*. He had been buried a week when I reached the grave."[76]

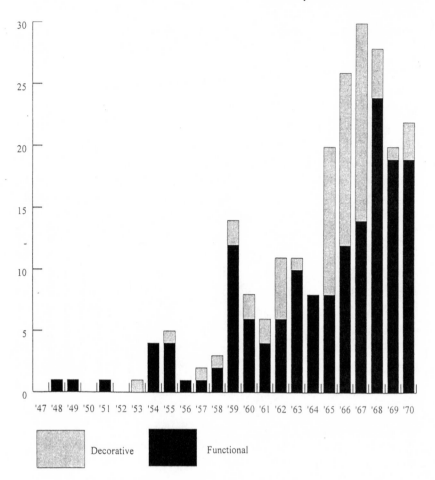

Figure 2. Death-Related Patents, 1847–1870

Figure 1 shows the dramatic growth of patent applications and grants in the years immediately preceding, during, and following the war. This trend is closely paralleled by the expansion of grants for death-related patents as shown in Figure 2, which are defined as patents for materials or processes developed solely for funerary or mortuary purposes. These include both functional and decorative patents, including new casket designs, shipping containers, decorative headstones, and embalming formulas.

Sources: Reports of the Commissioner of Patents for the Year [1847–1870] (Washington, D.C.: [various publishers], 1848–1872). In Figure 2, data for the years 1850 and 1852 are not available.

The logistics involved in the transshipment of so many bodies largely fell to the individuals involved. No provision had been contemplated, either by the military or by the separate national governments, to assist civilians with the task of retrieving their dead. Following the Battle of Gettysburg, New York, Pennsylvania, and Massachusetts all sent state agents to facilitate the transportation home of deceased native sons. But, otherwise, the location, preparation, and shipment of soldiers' bodies were arranged and accomplished almost entirely by the relatives themselves. The residents of Gettysburg did, when possible, assist. After the battle, a citizen recalled, "There were two Embalming rooms in town, . . . [and] at that time a number of our citizens made quite a good thing out of this gruesome business, of taking up the dead for those people and assisting them in preparing them for shipment to their homes." W. R. Cornelius, one of the many itinerant embalmers who followed in the wake of the armies, remarked: "I shipped colonels, majors, captains and privates by the carload some days." He states equitably that "both armies treated me properly and paid me promptly."[77]

George Ryder, who had lost two sons at Gettysburg, contracted with a local farmer, John G. Frey, to locate and ship home their remains. Frey's letter to Ryder is instructive on several points and deserves to be quoted in full:

Dear Sir

I took those bodies today and found the boxes by laying in the Ground so long all bursted so that I was compeled to have 2 new zinc Coffins made and also Rough [outer shipping] boxes which just cost me coffins[,] Boxes[,] taken up and delivery at the depot $32.00 thirty-two Dollars, which would leave just $20.00 owing me which you will please send me by Express[;] for my trouble I make no bill only what it cost me. I should have sent the bodies to morrow morning but I had to get those Coffins made which will prevent me from sending before Thursday morning So they will Start on the 19th from here. I have one Request to make and that is if you have the pictures Send me one of Each of them[,] those small case photographs[.] I have sent fourty [bodies] to different parts and would like to have these pictures[.] I have now already the most of them.[78]

Numerous soldiers found their way home through the assistance given by locals like Frey. Ryder's sons had evidently died in hospital, inferred from the fact that their remains had been boxed when originally buried, something rarely possible on the battlefield. Frey's desire to obtain a picture of each soldier he had returned to relatives gives a startlingly human face to one individual's reaction to death on an immense scale. Frey wished to remember those corpses as individuals, a sentiment that contradicts any suggestion that the bodies of soldiers failed to retain a symbolic value, even after burial. It is not possible to know how many soldiers were returned home through the efforts of nascent morticians and civilians like Frey.

Throughout the war, officers were far more likely to be shipped home than were enlisted men. This may reflect several factors, including a higher level of affluence among men given commissions or an additional bond of fraternity through the experience of command. Officers frequently formed benevolent associations like the Third Army Corps Union, established in 1862 among the officers of the Army of the Potomac. This association had as its main object "to secure funds for embalming and sending home for burial the bodies of officers killed in battle or dying in hospitals at the front." More important, perhaps, than affluence or class, officers were simply thought of differently on the battlefield. Major James Wilson, Third Cavalry, Missouri State Militia, was executed by guerrillas in October 1864. The commander in St. Louis, Colonel J. H. Baker, was ordered to have the body recovered, received at the depot "with proper escort," and buried with military honors. Six enlisted men were executed along with Wilson, yet the orders make no mention of efforts on their behalf. In another example, Confederate Brigadier General John R. Chambliss was killed in battle on 16 August 1864. His remains were coffined and buried by Union troops. Union Major General Winfield S. Hancock wrote that, the next day, Chambliss's remains "were taken out of the grave . . . to be given to his people."[79] At Shiloh and dozens of other battlefields, as burial parties of both sides collected the dead they scrupulously separated out the officers, consigning only the noncommissioned to the mass graves. Rank did indeed have its privileges, not the least of which was the nearly guaranteed retention of identity after death as a result of special handling of the body.

As civilians and soldiers accommodated themselves to the constraint of geographic distance and overcame that difficulty when they could, other facets of death ritual were more difficult to maintain. What remained consistent for many Americans, even in the face of such wholesale death, was the centrality of the deathbed and the necessity of dying properly. A. S. Billingsley, a minister working with the U.S. Christian Commission, comforted many wounded soldiers and attended many of their deaths. He later wrote of the overriding concern for proper, good deaths—concerns expressed by soldiers and their relations alike. Billingsley asserted that such thoughts came immediately on notification of death, "When the messenger of a soldier's death reached the throbbing heart of his bereaved friends, the next question was, '*How did he die?* What were his prospects for eternity?'" By such questions, friends and relations inquired, not about the means of death, but about its manner: "All such questions were proper and natural;" Billingsley continued, "and, when we could, we always answered them with pleasure, and did what we could to console and comfort the bereaved, mourning friends at home. Many of the brave heroes died triumphant deaths, perfectly resigned; and, rising above all doubts and fears, evincing their assurance and preparation in such words as these: 'I am ready.' 'I have no fear of death.' 'The Lord is mine.' 'Tell my wife I died happy,' etc." Of course, Billingsley was aware that not all deaths were good deaths: "To despatch a death notice [following a good death] was not so painful; but when a man died 'without hope,' sacrificing his life for the salvation of his country," Billingsley concluded that "to communicate the sad intelligence was no desirable task."[80]

At times, people hurrying to the battlefield after being notified that a relation had been injured did arrive in time to share in the rituals of the deathbed and gained from the experience in innumerable ways. The Reverend R. J. Parvin of the U.S. Christian Commission remembered one injured soldier, David C. Laird, dying in a Gettysburg hospital. "His father came in time to see him die," Parvin wrote. "When it was all over, I tried to comfort him for his loss, but he put the words kindly aside: 'I don't need any comfort from man, for God has given me so much, in seeing the happy death of my boy, I am perfectly content.'"[81] Laird's father had been among the lucky few who could strike a mediated consolation from the war and its violence.

Billingsley, Parvin, and countless others made the attempt to act as surrogates for absent loved ones, trying to fulfill the cultural imperatives of the deathbed. Nuns traveled to Gettysburg from a local convent to sit with the dying, provide moral instruction, and assist in the death. Afterward, the bedside attendants wrote letters to distant mothers recounting the manner of death, perhaps enclosing a lock of hair. The role of women acting as surrogates is often overlooked, particularly in the light of other roles, like nursing the wounded, that they performed. But their acts as surrogates attending those they could not nurse back to health were as culturally relevant. In 1873, the rather flamboyant Reverend Thomas De Witt Talmadge tried to underscore the significance of women's wartime service. Speaking at Memorial Day ceremonies at Arlington National Cemetery, he asked the assembled crowds to remember "the women who died in the service of the sick and wounded soldiers." Particularly, when he worked to describe their efforts, he asked, "What would these brave fellows have done in the last hour if the women had not come into the hospitals?"

> When the time comes for us to die we want to die at home. The roof may be very humble and the faces that look into one's may be very plain; but who cares for that? Loving hands to bathe the brow, loving lips to read the promises. But these "Boys in Blue" were dying away from home, and what would have become of them had not women in the name of Christ bent over their couch in the hospitals? Men forged the cannon; men fashioned the musketry; men mounted the guns; men unlimbered the batteries; men lifted the wounded into ambulances; but women scraped the lint; women administered the cordial; women watched the dying pillow; women wrote the last message to the home circle; women wept at the solitary burial, attended only by herself and four men with a spade.[82]

In striving to maintain the rituals and values associated with death, civilians and soldiers both worked to overcome the dislocations of war. One of the most difficult obstacles to this process was the nature of warfare itself, the fact that soldiers died while in the service of their nations, either in hospitals or more directly at the hands of the enemy. Because soldier death was not in any way a natural death, it was inevitable that the living project their passions onto the dead. Such projection was a logical extension of the deathbed practice of observing death closely and striving to extract meaning from that process. For most, the pain of loss expanded with the interruption of traditional cultural rituals. Such interruptions provoked an abiding frustration, out of which civilians nurtured an increasing animus directed toward those who had taken the lives of their sons.

Animus

Visitors to almost any battlefield would have seen the conflict reflected in the treatment of the bodies of soldiers. Since wartime burial details rarely transported bodies any farther than necessary, graves often traced the lines of combat. Across the field, collections of individualized graves lay scattered among larger, mass graves—the former more likely along the lines of the victor, the latter the fate of the defeated. Civilians who visited the battlefield of Gettysburg commented on the obvious differences in the burials of Union and Confederate fatalities. A local newspaper reporter noted "a dozen graves of the 20th Massachusetts, near by those of the 137th New York, and close at hand an equal number from the 12th New Jersey. Care has been taken to place a headboard at each grave, with a legible inscription thereon, showing whose remains are resting beneath." Pointedly, the reporter commented, "Some of the rebel dead are still uncovered."[83] Visit any battlefield days later, and the clearest indication of victory could be found in the graves of winners and losers, the distinctions between those graves that were well made and identified and those that were not.

Because soldiers died within a specific military, and therefore political, context, their actions as soldiers, the manner of their deaths, and the construction of their graves could all be interpreted with respect to that context. The bodies of soldiers themselves were interpreted by both their comrades and civilians, the corpses "read" for a variety of reasons, some moral, some political. Even the natural processes of decay were open to the interpolation of regional difference. Unfamiliar with the sight of blackened corpses, one woman believed that the Confederate soldiers had been given a mixture of whiskey and gunpowder before battle, to make them "fight like demons." After death, she said, "they would turn quite black." Some attributed the discoloration to diet; others thought it a sign wrought to point out Southerners' association with slavery. Both sides seemed to assert that only the enemy dead became so discolored.[84] Daniel G. Crotty, a Union soldier walking the battlefield of Williamsburg, noted, "The dead of both friend and foe lie side by side, but it is remarked by all that the pleasant smile on the patriot's face contrasts strangely with the horrid stare of the rebel dead." A Michigan soldier concurred, remarking of dead "rebells" that, even hours after their death, "their traits show how desperate they are and in what situation their conscience was." "Our dead," he thought, "look much more peaceful."[85]

This process of interpretation, of finding distinctions both obvious and subtle, is the point of origin for the meanings attributed to the dead for generations after the war. As soldiers and civilians wrestled with the dislocations to death culture and ritual thrust on them by the war, their efforts were complicated by the larger national struggle. Far from being removed from the field of battle, the dead remained an integral part of that conflict. Not only was each death for a specific cause, it had been inflicted at the hands of the enemy. But beyond that obvious connection, the bodies of the dead became a canvas on which the grief, anger, and animosity associated with war could be projected.

Meaning was faithfully sought from the smallest of signs. Several weeks after the battle at Gettysburg, a young woman named Annie Hollinger was walking the fields south of town where the debris of battle was still plainly evident. From the field she recovered a relic, a severed hand, "dried to parchment so that it looked as though covered with a kid glove." Sharing her discovery, Annie and her sister began to speculate about its original owner. From the "smallness of the fingers," her sister later remembered, "we guessed that it had belonged to a very young soldier or a southerner who had never worked with his hands."[86] Their conclusions are revealing. Because of the size of the hand, only two logical interpretations presented themselves. It was possible that the hand was that of a young soldier, a boy enlisted—presumably—in either army. However, if the former owner had not been a boy, the hand must have belonged to Southerner. No Northern man, in the sisters' calculations, made his living without using his hands. Gettysburg was a farming community, and the young women probably knew few men whose livelihood was not apparent in the calloused condition of their hands. Only Southern men, they imagined, only slave owners supported in effete luxury by the men and women they claimed to own, could prosper without work becoming evident on their hands. In their own way, the Hollinger sisters participated in a process nearly ubiquitous in Civil War America. They sought to understand and interpret the human loss to which they were witness within the larger social and political consequences of war.

At times, even the funeral rituals, shared by Northerner and Southerner alike, had to be abridged because of sectional animosity. Margaret Bissell, a Southern woman, had come to Gettysburg to tend to her wounded and dying husband. After his death, she was able to secure a cemetery plot in a local churchyard and workmen to dig the grave. But, when transporting her husband's remains to the cemetery, she was advised not to walk behind the wagon out of respect to her dead: "I wanted to follow behind the body, but Dr. Richardson objected, thinking that it would give rise to remarks, and admonished us, that we must manifest no feeling."[87] In this instance, even after Margaret Bissell had overcome the obstacle of distance and was able to attend the deathbed of her soldier husband, her exercise of customary death rituals was necessarily curtailed because of the war's sectional passions.

Honoring the Civil War Dead

In addition to the natural resentment of an enemy that had caused the death of comrades or loved ones, and even beyond reading political difference into corpses, tales of atrocities enacted upon the dead outraged civilians and fueled partisan feelings. Suspicion that the enemy routinely and intentionally mistreated the dead was, in some sense, a logical inference readily drawn from the obvious differences apparent in battlefield interment. It was a short and irresistible step from an awareness that "our" soldiers sometimes had to march on before having finished burying the enemy dead to the accusation that "their" soldiers intentionally left the dead exposed and vulnerable. But the enemy was also sometimes accused of having purposefully committed crimes against the bodies of the dead.

In December 1861, the U.S. Congress formed the Committee on the Conduct of the War, a joint oversight committee inspired by the early Union disasters at Bull Run and Ball's Bluff. Four months later, Senator Charles Sumner proposed a resolution that the committee be instructed to investigate "the barbarous treatment by the rebels at Manassas of the remains of officers and soldiers of the United States, killed in battle there." The testimony collected by the committee, widely reported in the press, shocked Northerners with a level of viciousness unimaginable before the war. The indictments horrified civilians: it was alleged that burial was long delayed for Union soldiers, who were often stripped and left naked on the field; that bodies had been levered up out of their graves with long rails in order to remove uniform buttons and emblems as souvenirs; and that, in at least one long trench, Union troops were buried face down. Some of the stories strain credulity. In the depositions taken during the investigation, local witnesses claimed that Southern soldiers took the shinbones of Union soldiers for "Yankee drumsticks"; others asserted that bones were sawn into cross sections to wear as rings and that skulls were taken as trophies. A member of the Louisiana Tigers allegedly took the skull of a Federal officer, intending to have the top removed and mounted so that he could toast from it on his wedding day. Angered at a particular Union officer, Confederate troops purportedly disinterred his remains, cut off his head, dragged his body down into a nearby ravine, and burned it. Some Northern officials even claimed to have disinterred Union bodies that had no bones at all, the corpses having been boiled to separate the flesh from the skeleton.[88]

The veracity of the various witnesses remains hard to ascertain, but the outrage over the alleged violations was unmistakable. Observers clearly noticed the qualitative difference of the graves, even in this, the first major battle of the war. A Union doctor, J. M. Homiston, gave testimony about the care exerted by Confederates in burying their own dead:

> Question. Did they bury their own dead at once after the battle?
> Answer. Some were buried down about Manassas, generally; if there were any friends there, their dead were taken away from the field and buried elsewhere.

Confederates were buried in individual graves, marked with head- and foot-boards. One account asserted that marble headstones were placed at some Southern graves. The committee's questions highlighted the sharp distinctions between the burial of the battle's winning and losing sides. So early in the war, such distinctions were new and startling. But the accusations quickly blossomed beyond the types of burials to include place and manner of burial. General James B. Ricketts, wounded in the battle, testified about the interment of Union soldiers:

> Question. Do you know anything about [the Confederates'] method of burying our dead?
> Answer. I know nothing except about their manner of burial in Richmond. I could from my room overlook the place where they buried our dead. I know they were buried in the negro burying ground.[89]

For Ricketts, and for the committee, there could be no clearer sign of programmatic disrespect for Union soldiers than to bury them among black men and women.

Also unmistakable was the public response. "Not satisfied with the victory won," a Northern minister complained, "to add ignominy to defeat, the rebels buried our men with their faces downward, and took their bones for drumsticks and finger-rings, and their skulls for goblets and punchbowls." The committee report, however, asserted confidently that the acts of the Confederates would garner universal condemnation and would not be emulated by Northern soldiers:

> These disclosures establishing, as they incontestably do, the consistent inhumanity of the rebel leaders, will be read with sorrow and indignation by the people of the loyal States. They should inspire these people to renewed exertions to protect our country from the restoration to power of such men. They should, and we believe they

will, arouse the disgust and horror of foreign nations against this unholy rebellion. Let it be ours to furnish, nevertheless, a continued contrast to such barbarities and crimes. Let us persevere in the good work of maintaining the authority of the Constitution, and of refusing to imitate these monstrous practices we have been called upon to investigate.[90]

In this brief passage, several significant strands are woven tightly together. Clearly, despite the defeat, the committee is still thinking about a short war. The passage that admonishes against the "restoration to power of such men" can only be seeking to establish a foundation for postwar allocation of responsibility and to exclude the Confederate leadership from political participation. The report also seeks to prevent foreign recognition of the Confederacy by exposing these allegations and thereby embarrassing the South before its potential allies. And, of course, the summation of the investigation closely associates the sanctity of the dead with national loyalty through the condemnation of these atrocities. In this light, the committee advocated hewing to a line of "contrast" from these deeds, emphasizing the need to protect "our" nation and the authority of the Constitution from those who would engage in "unholy rebellion."

Accusations of atrocities did not end with Bull Run but persisted throughout the war—although almost never as luridly. At Gettysburg, the Confederate abandonment of Federal corpses, although understandable due to their retreat, fueled a growing animosity among Union troops, who believed that Confederates routinely looted and left the Union dead to decay in the open air. A staff officer of the Second Corps, Frank A. Haskell, asserted that "had the issue of the battle been reversed,—our own dead would have had no burial at all, at the hands of the enemy; but stripped of their clothing, their naked bodies would have been left to rot, and their bones to whiten, upon the top of the ground where they fell."[91] Not only were Confederates accused of stripping the dead of their property, but also of that essential concern, their identity. After walking the battlefield of Gettysburg, the reporter J. T. Trowbridge wrote, "The barbarous practice of stripping such of our dead as fell into their hands, in which the Rebels indulged here as elsewhere, rendered it impossible to identify large numbers. The headstones of these are lettered, 'Unknown.'"[92]

Actually, at Gettysburg the Confederates left many of their own dead unburied in addition to the Union dead near their lines. And, throughout the war, Union soldiers probably scavenged among the dead as much as the Confederates did, although being generally better provisioned they may have had less need for Confederate equipment, shoes, and clothing. In the midst of winter at Fredericksburg, it was the new heavy Union jackets and blouses that the dead were wearing that tempted the thinly equipped Confederates. But, no matter how sincere the need of the living, and despite their own treatment of the enemy dead, soldiers' perceptions of atrocities committed intentionally by the enemy remained undimmed by circumstance or understanding.

Beyond the alleged mistreatment of the soldier dead, disrespect toward the bodies of officers provoked a particular outrage among soldiers and civilians. The deep-seated tradition of special treatment provided a stark demonstration of animus when disregarded. Even when burial was afforded the officer dead, a failure to recognize what was thought to be the proper respect was a consistent point of contention. This is particularly emphasized in the memoir of W. W. Lyle, a chaplain who accompanied troops late in the war to Chickamauga and Chattanooga. Returning after several weeks to the battlefield of Chickamauga, Lyle asserted that Union soldiers discovered that Southern troops had committed atrocities upon their dead comrades. "Ghastly skeletons, lying exposed to the winds of heaven, bare and bleached, could be seen as fearful witness of rebel inhumanity," he wrote. Lyle reported the recovery of one soldier's corpse "with both ears cut off" as well as "several bodies from which the heads had been removed" and "set up on stakes and rails of the fences." In the midst of recording these dramatic examples of disdain for the enemy, the chaplain also took special pains to note depredations of an entirely different order, those committed upon the body of an officer. A grave, "probably an officer's, was honored with a flat stone, on which was marked, 'A damned Yankee nigger-thief lies here to rot and pollute our soil.'"[93] Although tradition worked strongly enough to ensure a burial accomplished with some care, protected with a large, flat stone—therefore "probably an officer's" grave—the expression of animus, the insult, in an otherwise respectful interment caught Lyle's attention, despite the more grievous examples of atrocities actually done to the surrounding bodies of soldiers.

Although Lyle's experience is instructive, violations of the long-standing traditions dictating the special treatment of officers seem to have been only rarely committed. However, two notable examples perpetuated animosity between the societies at war with a particular vehemence.

In February and March 1864, Colonel Ulric Dahlgren, the son of Union Admiral John A. Dahlgren, commanded a small cavalry force, working as part of General Judson Kilpatrick's larger cavalry raid against Richmond, Virginia. Dahlgren's objective was the city's prisons—Belle Isle and Libby Prison—to liberate the Union prisoners they contained. However, his raiding party never managed to enter Richmond, and Dahlgren was killed from ambush by home guards outside the city. Conflicting interpretations have since emerged as to the raid and its purposes, but Confederates believed that Dahlgren, acting on express written orders allegedly found on his body, intended to free the prisoners, then incite them to arson, riot, and the assassination of Jefferson Davis and other political officials. The documents, released by the Confederate government and published in local newspapers, inspired a swarm of bitter recriminations against Dahlgren and the North. Incensed by what they perceived as violations of proper military conduct, Confederate officials and officers condemned the orders and sought to ascertain their validity. The correspondence eventually involved Confederate Secretary of War James Seddon and his Union counterpart, Edwin M. Stanton, Union Generals Benjamin Butler and George Gordon Meade, and Confederate Generals Robert E. Lee and Braxton Bragg.[94]

However, even before the contents of the reputed orders were widely known, the local militia had stripped Dahlgren's body, severed a finger to obtain a ring, and removed his artificial leg (Dahlgren had lost his right leg below the knee after Gettysburg). His corpse was left in the road, and the Union soldiers captured from Dahlgren's troops were forced to march past it. The body remained in the road until roaming pigs took an interest in it, when it was dumped over a fence out of their reach, then unceremoniously buried.[95] As outrage grew with the publication of the orders, Jefferson Davis personally ordered that Dahlgren's body be disinterred and sent by train to Richmond. At the York River Station, crowds circulated in and around the boxcar containing his opened pine-board coffin. Shortly thereafter, Davis again intervened, personally ordering an artillery officer in the local defenses, John W. Atkinson, to bury Dahlgren in an anonymous grave known only to Atkinson and the burial detail. The *Richmond Whig* reported that "the corpse was removed from the depot and buried—no one knows, or is to know, where." Recognizing the breach of normal practices associated with officers, the *Richmond Examiner* related, "It was a dog's burial, without coffin, winding sheet or service. Friends and relatives at the North need inquire no further; this is all they will know."[96]

Since Dahlgren was an officer, the retrieval of his body should have been relatively easy to arrange, but under these circumstances the process occupied the tortured diplomatic channels between both nations for weeks. General Benjamin Butler contacted Robert Ould, Richmond's Agent for Exchange, to inquire about the possibility of recovering Dahlgren's remains. In his letter, Butler argued that such a recovery was the normal state of affairs and complained about the mistreatment of Dahlgren's body: "As remains of officers have been forwarded to their friends in this manner I trust this request may be granted; specially so, because I see by the Richmond papers that some circumstances of indignity and outrage accompanied the death." Butler chided, "You do not war upon the dead as these papers imply."[97]

Significantly, Atkinson remembered that Ould visited him personally, seeking the burial site of Dahlgren. Under direct orders from Davis, Atkinson refused to divulge his secret even though, he later wrote, "Admiral Dahlgren . . . promised if his son's body was delivered to him that he would have General Grant's order forbidding all exchanges of prisoners revoked." Grant, in early 1864, had closed the exchange cartel, preventing the Confederacy from replenishing its regiments with soldiers returned from Northern prisons. No corroboration has been found that such high stakes were ever offered in exchange for Dahlgren's corpse, but Atkinson remembered that, when Ould's agent returned with written permission from Davis to exhume Dahlgren, the president's instructions had stated that the "return of the body would be of material advantage to the South." According to Atkinson, therefore, the Confederacy agreed to return Dahlgren, not for reasons of military propriety, as in the case of all other officers, but because it stood to profit materially by doing so.[98]

Whatever the Confederacy's intentions—and it seems unlikely that a restoration of the prisoner exchange cartel was ever seriously offered—the South found that it could not return Dahlgren even when it wanted to. As the negotiations had progressed, a collection of Union sympathizers in Richmond had stolen Dahlgren's body and relocated it to a farm nine miles outside the city. This final bizarre turn of events embarrassed the Davis administration—because it pointed out the strength of Unionist elements in the capital—and frustrated Admiral Dahlgren's efforts to recover his son. On 11 April 1865, just two days after Lee's surrender at Appomattox, Secretary of War Edwin Stanton ordered the local Union commanding officer to finally recover Dahlgren's remains. Unfortunately, since it was thought inadvisable to move a body during the warm summer months, Dahlgren was not finally reburied in Philadelphia until 30 October 1865, twenty months after he had been killed.[99] Whatever the nature of his raid, Dahlgren's postmortem career made him, for the South, a potent symbol of Union barbarity and, for the North, a notorious example of Southerners' disdain for the Federal dead.

But whatever outrage accompanied the treatment of Dahlgren, no matter how his corpse polarized antipathy between North and South, the public outcry paled by comparison to the mistreatment of Colonel Robert Gould Shaw of the Fifty-fourth Massachusetts earlier in the war. Commanding the first volunteer black regiment formed in the North, in July 1863 Shaw led his troops in the first assaults on Battery Wagner, a key element in the Union's plans to retake Charleston, South Carolina. Although Shaw's men performed with exemplary valor and successfully seized and held a portion of the fortification for nearly two hours, the lack of support from other Union regiments compelled them to withdraw from the assault. The costs of the attack were brutally high; 45 percent of the regiment were casualties, with Shaw numbered among the dead.[100]

The following morning, throughout the predawn hours, Union troops watched as Confederate burial details hurriedly cleared the dead from the approaches and escarpments, hurrying the bodies into large trench graves dug into the soft sand. Under a flag of truce, soldiers from several Northern units, including the Fifty-fourth, approached the battery. According to custom already well established by this time in the war, they requested the bodies of their officers, in particular Shaw. Two other officers killed in the assault had been buried in separate graves, and at least one, Colonel Haldimand S. Putnam, was returned at this time. However, referring to Shaw, a Confederate officer replied brusquely, "We have buried him with his niggers."[101]

The Confederate insult was intentionally twofold. In the first place, no special care had been extended toward an officer who had died in an audacious and unquestionably valorous attack against an entrenched enemy position. The special treatment of officers, even enemy officers, had been so widely accepted by July 1863 that there is really no parallel to such disregard to be found on any other battlefield. Although Dahlgren's corpse was mistreated, it was considered separately from the other deaths in his unit in a way that was not true for Shaw. James Henry Gooding, a corporal in the Fifty-fourth, wrote of the soldiers' response to the news: "We have since learned . . . that Colonel Shaw is dead—he was buried in a trench with 45 of his men! not even the commonest respect paid to his rank." Gooding later noted that "The men of the regiment are raising a sum to send the body of the Colonel home, as soon as Fort Wagner is reduced. They all declare that they will dig for his body till they find it. They are determined that this disgrace shall be counteracted by something noble."[102]

Of course, the second insult was in many ways more pointed, for Shaw was buried among black men. The insult implied by the Southern soldiers and officers who buried Shaw is clear. Jefferson Davis and the Confederate military had recently adopted strict measures toward black soldiers and their white officers, the former to be sold into slavery, the latter to be executed on the antebellum standard of having incited black men to armed insurrection. In this context, and with the understanding that examples of integrated burials at public cemeteries were so rare as to be essentially nonexistent throughout both the North and the South, indiscriminately dumping a white officer's body in a mass grave of black volunteer soldiers represents the greatest display of disdain that the Confederacy could muster toward the dead.

Significantly, the Northern public and press responded with impassioned outrage, indicating clearly that Northern racial sensibilities were also violated by the action. Infuriated Northerners immediately worked up plans for an expedition to the Carolina coastline, in force if necessary, with the intent of rescuing Shaw's discarded corpse. The firestorm did not abate until Shaw's parents publicly indicated that they would not support any such efforts and, in fact, expressed their opinion that there was no fitter place for their son to rest than among the men he led into battle. Shaw's father, Francis G. Shaw, wrote the local Union commanding officer, General Quincy Adams Gillmore, asking him to "forbid the desecration of my son's grave, and [to] prevent the disturbance of his remains or those buried with him." Shaw's parents believed simply that "a soldier's most appropriate burial-place is on the field where he has fallen." Drawing on their thoroughly abolitionist background, the Shaw family with this act reminded Northerners that their anger, at least in part, stemmed from sharply problematic racial perceptions. Even those who objected on the grounds that Southern actions represented disrespect to an officer found it hard to argue from Shaw's death onward that an officer should resent being buried with his own troops. Although such sentiments did not alter the essentially distinct treatment of officers, they did plant seeds for how future developments, namely the National Cemetery System, would be imagined. Shaw remained in his mass grave until after the close of war, when many of the Union soldiers killed at Wagner were recovered from their vulnerable, sandy graves and removed to more suitable grounds. If Shaw's body was among those recovered, he now lies among the unknown dead of Beaufort National Cemetery.[103]

The specter of race clearly compounded the issues of officer burial in Shaw's case, foreshadowing the extreme difficulty that black soldiers, as a group, faced in securing the most meager of burials at the hands of Southerners. In March 1865, the men of the Fifty-fifth Massachusetts Regiment returned to the scene of a North Carolina battle they had fought eight months previously. On that earlier occasion, they had been forced from the field, leaving behind their dead. Months later they returned to find that their dead had apparently been ignored by the Confederate troops; the regimental historian later wrote: "Within the rebel lines, on an island, held solely, except during short expeditions, by their forces, by the side of the road over which their cavalry must have passed daily, the dead of the Fifty-fifth had lain for more than eight months unburied, where they fell. Several were recognized by their position, and the remnants of their clothing; but, among bones of nine bodies, there was not to be found a single skull!" Bodies remaining unburied while in such close proximity to the living suggests a sentiment strong enough to outweigh even the concerns of health, and it is tempting and logical to assume a racially motivated disdain. The historian noted, "So far as could be judged, the bodies of the white troops who fell, had been buried by the enemy."[104] Why the skulls of these men were missing was never explained, and even the unit history does not hazard a guess.

The animosity directed toward the living enemy was easily extended to the enemy dead. It could be magnified and intensified by perceptions of the enemy's mistreatment of one's own dead. Such animus was not quickly dispensed with after the war. Long after veterans of both sides were able to embrace each other, the memories of the dead remained sharp and bitter. For the soldiers who had seen so much death and the society that endured its burden, the memory of the dead and the need to honor and commemorate them proved to be among the longest and most rending legacies of the war.

At the beginning of that long, painful conflict, the deaths of Daniel Hough and Edwin Gallway typified the majority of soldier death in the Civil War. Where possible, soldiers were buried by their own, usually in identified graves. Hough, killed on a battleground that changed possession, was buried by the enemy. As a result, his identity became vulnerable and was eventually lost. Gallway, mortally injured, was carried to his enemy's hospital where he later died. However, he lived long enough to speak of himself and his family;

Gallway's remains were buried in a local Charleston cemetery and later re-trieved by his relatives for burial at home. For Gallway's relations, the dis-ruption of cultural practices could be overcome after time, through significant expense, and with the help of others. The spontaneous surrogates of the hos-pital and itinerant embalmers and morticians were the first steps toward erect-ing what Lewis Saum has called *an institutional shield* between families and death.[105] That process was completed when the national government became the guarantor of a proper interment in the national cemeteries as compensa-tion for national service. However, before that time, Gallway became one of untold thousands of soldiers, retrieved by anxious and grieving relations, trav-eling on hundreds of trains toward a final reunion with family. In the hills of Pennsylvania, Rebecca Harding Davis witnessed a moment enacted repeat-edly at railroad yards and depots throughout the war: "Nobody was in sight but a poor thin country girl in a faded calico gown and sunbonnet. She stood alone on the platform, waiting. A child was playing beside her. When we stopped, the men took out from a freight car a rough unplaned pine box and laid it down, baring their heads for a moment. Then the train steamed away. She sat down on the ground and put her arms around the box and leaned her head on it. The child went on playing."[106] In ways that both exemplified and transcended the example of so many tableaux like this one, the war's end would be marked forever by the most renowned funeral train in American history.

"A Heroic, Eminent Death":
The National Dimensions of
Lincoln's Assassination

Coffin that passes through lanes and streets,
Through day and night with the great cloud darkening the land,
With the pomp of the inloop'd flags with the cities draped in black,
With the show of the States themselves as of crape-veil'd women standing,
With processions long and winding and the flambeaus of the night,
With the countless torches lit, with the silent sea of faces and the unbared
    heads,
With the waiting depot, the arriving coffin, and the sombre faces,
With dirges through the night, and the thousand voices rising strong and
    solemn,
With all the mournful voices of the dirges pour'd around the coffin,
The dim-lit churches and the shuddering organs—where amid these you
    journey,
With the tolling tolling bells' perpetual clang,
Here, coffin that slowly passes,
I give you my sprig of lilac.
    —*Walt Whitman,* When Lilacs Last in the Dooryard
    Bloom'd *(1865)*

O N 14 APRIL 1865, Robert Anderson stood once again within the confines of Fort Sumter. Its walls had been shattered by months of Union artillery, pounded into masonry rubble studded with "innumerable" cannon shot heaped at the base of its walls, the parapets of which were "ragged as a saw-edge." Anderson stood on the parade of the ruined fort, surround by four thousand soldiers, dignitaries, and well-wishers, including his wife and children. They had all come to bear witness to a great symbolic act; after a few brief remarks, Anderson pulled at the halyards in his hands, and the American flag that he had been forced to lower in surrender four years earlier once again flew over the entrance to Charleston's harbor. As the flag reached its zenith, the cannons of the fort roared again in salute, one hundred rounds. By order of Secretary of War Edwin Stanton, the cannonade expanded to become "a *national* salute from every fort and rebel battery" that had attacked the fort four years earlier. As the noon hour traveled westward, the salute was echoed in almost every military post and camp from Washington, D.C., to Nashville and beyond, a rolling thunder celebrating the principle of Union. More than most events at the close of war, this was a reassertion of dominion, of national authority, and the guns echoed across the countryside. As Anderson stood again in the midst of artillery fire, did he think of that earlier April and Daniel Hough? Did he look about the rubble of the parade for his grave, unsuccessfully? There is no record that any of the orators—the ministers, Anderson, or the keynote speaker, Henry Ward Beecher—made mention of Hough, but it was his anniversary as well. Later that evening, Anderson toasted the absent president, commenting on the universal appeal that Lincoln had won in the last months of the war. Although he was threatened after his first election and entered Washington cautiously, he had won the favor of his people. Now, Anderson said, Lincoln "could travel all over our country with millions of hands and hearts to sustain him." But, within the hour, a thousand miles away, the hands supporting Lincoln were carrying the president to his deathbed.[1]

As the war had been unprecedented in every aspect, one last violent act on the verge of peace stunned the people of the North, who had for a few days allowed themselves to think of the future without war. News of Lee's surrender had arrived in Washington, D.C., on 9 April, Palm Sunday, and the guarded optimism that had been building over the previous six months since the fall of Atlanta burst forth into hosannas of celebration for the triumphal entry of victory into the nation's capital. For five mornings, the North woke to peace, and the celebrations began anew. There was only a slight lessening of the celebratory enthusiasm as the culmination of the holy week, Good Friday and Easter, approached. But on the night of Good Friday Abraham Lincoln was assassinated, and on the sixth morning the president was dead. Later, some remembered that the moon that night had darkened to the color of blood. As the minister Wilbur Paddock somberly observed, "The deed itself spoke in thunder tones to the hearts of the people."[2] From that moment on, in ways extraordinarily difficult to appreciate fully now, the memory of the war was forever melded with the death of Lincoln.

Honoring the Civil War Dead

As Joyce Appleby has observed, "There is nothing so hard to discover in the past as that which has subsequently become familiar."[3] To date, there has been a general tendency to view Lincoln's death merely as the closing punctuation of the Civil War. Of course, the proximity in time of Lee's surrender and Lincoln's death makes such connections obvious, but they should not be unquestioned. Although Lee's surrender was hailed as the end of the war, contemporaries knew that Confederate armies still marched, particularly in the West, where Texas remained defiant and largely immune from federal authority. Despite the week of elation following the surrender of the Army of Northern Virginia, the finality of peace seemed less certain after Lincoln's death. But the events of April 1865 have become so familiar, so well-worn in our historical consciousness, that we find it difficult to appreciate the events as they were lived and experienced. The nation had been rent apart by an unthinkable war; both sides had lived for long periods during that conflict with anxiety and despair as defeat seemed assured; at the moment that one side emerged with apparent victory, its president was assassinated. The challenge lies in reducing any sense of inevitability from the sequence of these events, to understand this particular death, the funeral that followed, and the oceanic grief that they inspired, as contingent, improvisational events.

From that perspective, two areas of social response to Lincoln's assassination become unique forums for understanding Northern Americans' understanding of themselves, the conflict through which they had just passed, and their uncertain future. First, the public responses to Lincoln's death, and the uses made of that death, can be understood only within the context of the vast expanse of the war's soldier dead. Many of the same tensions that arose during the war between traditional death ritual patterns and the innovations required by war were evident in Lincoln's death and mourning. Hence, if civilians longed, but were largely unable, to restore the centrality of the deathbed in the rituals marking their personal loss, then Lincoln's deathbed would capture the imagination of the North. If custom decreed that bodies be brought home when possible, then Lincoln's body—as it made the grandest and most spectacular journey home of them all—would become for the public an opportunity to mourn as a nation, at least in imagination. If soldiers dying on the battlefield were thought of as martyrs for a greater, national cause, then Lincoln would be identified as the greatest of martyrs—as Moses, as Christ—and would come to symbolize the sacrifice of all for the life of the nation itself.

These close associations between Lincoln's death and nationalism are also obvious yet, again, accepted all too often without critical analysis. Although most Americans had spent many months trying to imagine the conclusion of the war and its effects on the United States, only Northern thinking had focused on concerns for reuniting the divergent sections of the country. Most Southern thinking, and even that of some Northerners, had been preoccupied with imagining the future relationship between two separate nations. Therefore, Lincoln's assassination must also be understood within the second context of Northern nationalist thought. When people grieved for Lincoln, they grieved the attacks on their nation as well, at the moment when the nature of that nationality was most in flux. In part because of its close proximity to the war, Lincoln's death called the nation itself into question, more so than any subsequent presidential assassination. Drawing on a historical imagination informed by religious sensibilities, Northerners erected an explanatory myth to consecrate the tragic elements of war and murder to a collective future, expanding a single death mourned by a section of the country into the sanctification of the national whole. In addition to the grand sweeping influences of Lincoln's life on American history, it was his death that catalyzed the American nation.

The bullet that killed Lincoln crashed into his left occipital some three inches behind his left ear, tumbled forward through his brain, and came to rest just above and behind his right eye. Slumped in his chair, Abraham Lincoln died. An army surgeon attending the play, Dr. Charles Leale, resuscitated the president on the floor of his theater box but immediately pronounced the wound mortal. Despite his certainty that the president would not recover, Leale decided it would be too hazardous to risk transporting him to the White House. Lincoln was, instead, carried out and across the street to a small back bedroom of a boardinghouse, a ten-by-fifteen-foot room in which America's most famous deathbed vigil was kept.[4]

Throughout the night, Lincoln's friends and associates, members of his cabinet, and other political and military figures came and went, filing into the small room to stand in clusters for a few minutes or for several hours, watching this momentous death unfold. The calm eye of the storm, that small, crowded room anchored a swirling chaos, for as news of the tragedy spread few could resist being swept up in its turbulence. Lincoln was not the only victim that night, and after the news of the attack on Secretary of State William Seward became widely known, rumors ruled the night: the fleeing leaders of the Confederacy had ordered the cabinet killed; the government was without leadership; Grant had been assassinated; the war was to be renewed, Appomattox repudiated; rebel troops were even now marching on Washington. The fears of that night have been almost completely forgotten. The minister Charles Brigham asserted to his congregation, "We need not disguise our sense of the great danger which [the assassination] brings upon the land."[5] The dawn brought little relief: after a long and anxious night, Lincoln succumbed to his wound and died at 7:22 the next morning.

Lincoln's death and protracted public funeral became a crucial influence in the ongoing evolution of American death culture. The events surrounding his death present in sharp relief the preservation of traditional practices as well as the tides of innovation. The aspect of Lincoln's death that was most traditional was his deathbed, and that tableau remained central among the various ways in which Lincoln was mourned publicly, even though most of the rest of the nation came to know the deathbed only after the fact. Hundreds of Washingtonians had heard the alarms from Ford's Theater, followed the commotion, and stood unbelieving on the street through the long, cold night, joining in the deathwatch, albeit at a distance. But the vast majority of Americans learned of Lincoln's death from newspaper accounts of his final hours; in New York City, Walt Whitman later wrote that he and his mother "got every newspaper morning and evening, and the frequent extras of that period, and pass'd them silently to each other."[6] And it was the Lincoln deathbed, more than any other single image, that captivated American sensibilities.

When viewed against the ideal, however, this vigil differed from the desired norms in several ways. The death was not by contemporary standards a good death: Secretary of the Navy Gideon Welles described the last minutes as "the death struggle." Lincoln himself never regained consciousness and so was incapable of "managing" his death or of participating in the reciprocal acts of support and comfort that characterized the deathbed. Matthew Simpson, a longtime friend who gave Lincoln's Springfield, Illinois, eulogy, noted the difficulties resulting from the manner of his death, suggesting: "Had he died on a bed of illness, with kind friends around him; had the sweat of death been wiped from his brow by gentle hands, while he was yet conscious; could he have had power to speak words of affection to his stricken widow, or words of counsel to us ... how it would have softened or assuaged something of the grief!"[7] These remarks communicate well the cultural requirements of death as well as a sense of what was lacking.

Additionally, not all of Lincoln's family were present at the deathbed. His eldest son, Robert, was the only relative to stay throughout the vigil. Lincoln's youngest son, Thomas, or Tad, remained at the Executive Mansion, even in an age when small children were routinely incorporated into death rituals. Mary had requested his presence, saying, "Oh! that my little Taddy might see his father before he died!" But this was deemed "not advisable" by Lincoln's doctors, perhaps because they assumed that it would only increase Mary's ordeal. So overwhelming was her grief that she visited the bedside for only brief periods throughout the long night until, startled by a loud, stertorous breath from Lincoln, she "sprang up suddenly with a piercing cry and fell fainting to the floor." At that point, she was peremptorily ordered out of the room by Edwin Stanton.[8]

Stanton's actions have traditionally been interpreted as evidence of his imperious nature, but his response might reveal disappointment in how poorly Mary performed within the socially circumscribed rituals of the death-bed. Far from stoic in her demeanor at the bedside, Mary pleaded with her dying husband, tugged at him, and her wails no doubt sounded much louder in the small confines of that quiet, tomblike room. As Lincoln remained unconscious throughout, Mary no doubt longed for some interaction with her dying husband. But Stanton's actions indicate his assuming a role of protector, not of Mary, but of the dying Abraham, a role that he maintained throughout the next several months, acting to protect the dignity of Lincoln's death and funeral. Since the First Lady and Stanton never really got along, it seems quite likely that Stanton's sensibilities were offended by Mary's inability to conform to social norms.[9]

Biographer Jean Baker makes a similar observation about Mary Todd's life in general: "As a widow and thrice-bereaved mother, she violated the nineteenth-century rules of submission to the decrees of Providence. . . . Disobeying every rule of the anonymity expected of ladies . . . she was seen as lacking the self-control of the pious female." Mary later expressed sentiments that echoed what thousands of wives and mothers had, no doubt, felt for their lost husbands and sons: "I often think it would have been some solace to me and *perhaps* have lessened the grief, which is now breaking my heart—if my idolized had passed away, after an illness, and I had been permitted to watch over him and tend him to the last."[10] For Lincoln and the vast majority of the soldier dead, the circumstances of their deaths had injured them and their loved ones beyond calculation.

Instead, as was true for most Civil War soldiers dying on the battlefield, the task of mediating Lincoln's death fell to those outside the circle of family, to friends, strangers, and professionals. From the tone of their reminiscences, it seems that these surrogates understood this fact and accepted their expanded roles. The doctors in attendance, who could do little except monitor Lincoln's deteriorating condition, wrote scrupulous notes as to the medical progression of his death. Even here, however, there are notations that have little to do with medicine. Charles Leale recorded that Lincoln was "serene," his face "untroubled." Leale continued, "[My] knowledge that frequently just before departure recognition and reason return to those who have been unconscious caused me for several hours to hold his right hand firmly within my grasp to let him . . . know, if possible, that he was in touch with humanity and had a friend."[11] In this way, those attending Lincoln's death tried to fulfill the traditions of death. They sought lessons of faith and stoicism from an unconscious man and tried to return what comfort they could. They were surrogates in this process, and their later accounts of the vigil proved to be a point of great attraction for many who had during the war lost sons and brothers whose deaths were also attended by surrogates.

The description of Lincoln's deathbed was picked up by and relayed in the popular press. In its coverage of the president's death, the *Chicago Tribune* announced on its front page, "Complete Details of the Great Calamity; The Last Hours of Abraham Lincoln; the Death Bed of a Great and Good Man." The *Cincinnati Daily Enquirer* informed its readers: "The countenance of the President [at death] was beaming with that characteristic smile which only those who have seen him in his happiest moments can appreciate, and except a blackness of his eyes his face appeared perfectly natural. He died without a struggle, and without even a perceptible motion of a limb. Calm and silent, a great and good man passed away." While fully within the traditions of nineteenth-century preferences, these comments were more imagination than reporting. Lincoln's physicians and other observers in the room noted a prolonged death struggle, marked by periods of irregular, labored breathing, culminating in the peculiar respiratory phenomenon known as the death rattle. Yet a biography published just months later described Lincoln's passing as a "good" death, relating that there were "no indications of suffering" during the vigil and that, at the moment of death, "there was no convulsive action, no rattling in the throat, no appearance of suffering of any kind—none of the symptoms which ordinarily attend dissolution and add to its terrors."[12]

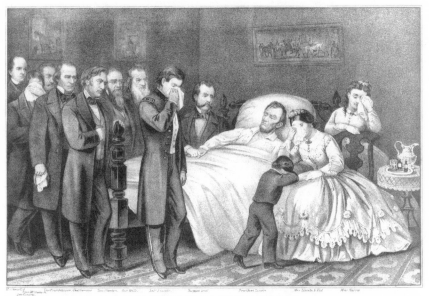

DEATH OF PRESIDENT LINCOLN.
AT WASHINGTON, D. C. APRIL 15TH 1865.
THE NATIONS MARTYR.

This Currier and Ives engraving is but one of numerous deathbed prints created to satisfy public demand for mementoes of the national tragedy. Reflecting the social expectations for a "good death," Lincoln is portrayed surrounded by family, with his eldest son, Robert, standing just left of center in his military uniform. The youngest son, Tad, although pictured here with Mary, remained at the White House and was never present during the vigil. The violence of Lincoln's death is muted, any physical manifestation of his wound eliminated, suggesting a more genteel, peaceful and perhaps even submissive death.

Library of Congress

Similarly, images of Lincoln's deathbed served as representative images for the collective death of the war. Prints and engravings depicting the dying president at the center of a small group of participants huddled around his bed became a popular trend in graphic arts publishing. The popularity of these images suggests that they are a particularly useful means for exploring the social norms and values associated with the scene of death. In them, Lincoln's countenance is always calm, at rest, nearly beatific, any evidence of his wound usually having been eliminated. The gathered witnesses, Robert included, are usually stoically composed. In several early prints, young Tad is depicted with his mother at Lincoln's bedside. In only a few are there hints of emotion:

occasionally Mary was portrayed prostrate across Lincoln's body; less frequently Robert was illustrated in profound grief; in Alexander Gardner's photomontage and John H. Littlefield's engraving, both produced in 1866, the eldest Lincoln child is turned away, averting his contorted face in the shoulder of a friend, almost entirely hidden from the viewer. Wrenching grief is muted, directed away from the observer's point of view. Nowhere is there any representation of the flood of emotion that so injured Stanton's sense of deathbed propriety. Uniformly, the scenes portraying Lincoln's passing show typical responses to a stoic, good death.[13] Surprisingly, at a time when photography was having such an important influence on the portrayal of battlefield death, only one photograph of Lincoln in death is known to exist. Purportedly, the ever-protective Stanton ordered all such pictures destroyed. The one extant, of Lincoln lying in state in Albany, New York, was found among Stanton's papers after his death. So great was the desire for such photographs that several photographers manufactured faked Lincoln deathbed photographs for the briefly flourishing market.[14]

At 8:30 the morning of 15 April, about an hour after Lincoln's death, his body was taken to the White House in a plain coffin draped with the American flag. The hearse moved slowly through the drizzly streets, surrounded by a mounted military escort and followed by silent crowds. Once at the White House, Lincoln's body was subjected to a brief autopsy, during which his brain was removed, dissected to determine the path of the bullet, weighed, and replaced. Like many of the Union's soldier dead, Lincoln's remains were chemically embalmed in anticipation of an extensive public display, then dressed in the suit that he had worn on the morning of his second inauguration. When his casket—lead lined, faced with mahogany, and embellished with silver studs—had been prepared, he was moved to lie in state in the East Room.[15]

The newly sworn-in president, Andrew Johnson, decreed a national day of mourning to coincide with the state funeral to be held on Wednesday, 19 April. Like the rest of Washington, and like most of the North, the East Room was heavily draped in black, with the heavy coffin on a large, canopied bier dominating the room. On Tuesday, the White House opened its doors to thousands, who moved silently past the body. A reporter noted, "It required waiting not less than six hours to get in[,] . . . and the line, four deep, extended for blocks." The next day, Wednesday, all official Washington attended the funeral services—except Mary Lincoln, who remained upstairs in the White House, still too emotionally distraught to attend, and Tad, who remained by his mother's side. The day was a mournful one throughout the North, and churches of all denominations opened for special services. The next day, newspapers reported that sanctuaries had been packed beyond capacity, and hundreds of sermons from special Wednesday services were reprinted in dense, black-bordered columns. Bells tolled throughout the Northern states, as in Harrisburg, Pennsylvania, where the mayor requested that the town's church bells toll for the half hour preceding the national services and for an hour afterward. The universality of the occasion, the breadth of simultaneous ceremonies even at great distances, made possible by telegraphic communication, amazed those involved. "It is a new thing," a minister reminded his Philadelphia congregation, "this *actual participation* of a whole nation in the funeral obsequies of its fallen chief."[16]

At the conclusion of the White House services, the body was lifted from the bier and carried outside to an immense hearse, elaborate in its black draperies. At the heart of a vast procession, Lincoln's remains were escorted to the Capitol building, where they would lie in state under the building's newly completed iron dome. Thousands of Union soldiers accompanied the body, as did five thousand government employees, church groups, Irish and German fraternal organizations, schoolchildren, wounded soldiers from local hospitals, all marching to dirges played by thirty bands. At the rear, thirty-eight ranks of black businessmen, laborers, community leaders, and members of benevolent societies, more than four thousand men, marched in honor of Lincoln. The sidewalks were packed with throngs of thousands more who had come to witness the measured passing of the coffin, as cannons from the city's defensive forts thundered and shook the ground. Having arrived at the Capitol, Lincoln's remains were placed in state on a catafalque built for the purpose. All the next day, crowds solemnly endured the often-wet Washington spring to file slowly though the Rotunda and past the open coffin.[17]

Many observers were especially sensitive to the grief of black Americans. As a Chicago paper recounted: "The most conspicuous among them all . . . was the procession of colored women which marched two by two along the avenue to join their friends in front of the mansion. Over 200 women were on foot, their heads white with the frosts of age, and dressed in garments exhibiting all hues of the rainbow, some clad in handsome tints, some in mourning, some in red, white and blue calicoes. Some wore handsomely trimmed bonnets, and some . . . covered their heads with handkerchiefs. They were followed by a long string of colored urchins. The sight was novel." The report went on to comment that, a mere four years earlier, such an assembly "could no more have passed unmolested along the streets of the National Capital than it could have passed over Long Bridge from Virginia . . . without passes from their slave driving masters." In a particularly ironic twist, Lincoln's funeral procession had been inadvertently led by black soldiers. So thick were the crowds lining Pennsylvania Avenue that the Twenty-second U.S. Colored Infantry—which had been scheduled to march in the rear of the procession but had arrived at the rail station late—could not make its way to the organization area. The commander ordered the regiment into the street and into formation, but as he and his men marched toward the White House they realized that the cortege was already under way and headed in their direction. Wheeling smartly about, a black infantry unit thus came to lead the procession to the Capitol.[18]

The solemn and expressive ceremonies in Washington marked only the initial strains of a solemn cascade of emotion that engulfed the North. The extraordinary arrangements made for Lincoln's transportation back to Springfield, Illinois, provided the opportunity for a vast number of Northerners actually to participate in what would become the most elaborate funeral in American history. Even as visitors filed past the bier in the muted halls of the White House, the details of the journey home were being finalized. Many in Washington had assumed that Lincoln would be entombed in the vacant crypt that lay beneath the Capitol's Rotunda, prepared originally as a resting place for George Washington, who had instead been laid to rest in the family crypt at Mount Vernon. Alternately, several papers reported that Lincoln would be temporarily interred in the Congressional Cemetery, at least until a final disposition could be determined. The minister Leonard Swain told his congregation that Lincoln would be laid in a "grave beneath the shadow of the Capitol." Mary, however, had other ideas. She recalled that on a recent carriage ride, she and Lincoln had paused in a wooded glade. He had remarked that he was older than she and would certainly precede her in death. He requested that he be laid to rest in a similarly green and quiet place. Even then, Washington was never quiet, and rarely had it been kind to Mary throughout her tenure as First Lady. Virtually shunned by high society, she had lost a son to illness in Washington and then witnessed the murder of her husband there. She would return eventually to Illinois, and she would not accede to leaving her husband or her son behind. On Friday, 21 April, Lincoln's body—alongside his son William's—was placed on an ornate funeral car to begin the long trip home to Illinois. Like so many of the soldiers and officers who had served under him, Lincoln was carried homeward in a last journey, as part of a protracted national funeral that simultaneously exemplified and transcended all such processions before.[19]

Lincoln's funeral train wound its way back to Springfield, following nearly the same route, in reverse, that he had traveled four years earlier as president-elect. By order of the War Department, the railroads became military roads for the duration of the funeral. A pilot engine, festooned in black, preceded the funeral train by ten minutes, restricted to a speed of twenty miles per hour to preserve solemnity and safety. Keeping to a strict timetable, the funeral train moved somberly through six states (see table 3). In eleven major cities, the ritual was the same: Lincoln's coffin was brought off the train and transported with much ceremony to a central location for a public funeral. There, the coffin was opened and the body prepared for viewing. Balancing the numerous requests for funeral ceremonies against the goal of returning to Springfield in a reasonable time span meant that each city's schedule for public rites and viewings had to accommodate the funeral train's inflexible schedule, rather than the reverse. In Philadelphia, a private viewing for dignitaries was held from 10:00 P.M. until 12:00 midnight on 22 April, followed by a public viewing from dawn the morning of the twenty-third until 1:17 A.M. on the twenty-fourth. After traveling all the rest of that morning, Lincoln lay in state in New York City from 1:00 P.M., 24 April, through noon of the next day. The train then moved on to Albany, where it arrived late the night of the twenty-fifth, and then the remains were again on view, from 1:15 A.M. until 1:30 P.M. of the twenty-sixth. Silently, mournful crowds filed slowly by in almost unceasing flows, 120,000 in Philadelphia, 100,000 in Indianapolis. The largest funerals were in New York City and Chicago, with the estimated attendance exceeding one million combined. Finally, because of the relentless imperatives of the train schedule, the doors to the hall would be closed, the coffin resealed, and the body returned to the train to continue its journey westward.

At each of these funerals, the incidents of mourning nearly defy description. In Harrisburg, the skies poured rain on the nighttime procession from the train depot to the state House of Representatives, illuminated by the stuttering glare of chemical lights. A local reporter wrote: "A terrific deluge ensued, with lightening and thunder, shaking heaven's firm masonry and illuminating at intervals the deep pall which nature had spread over the scene. In the midst of this storm, the line marched on, solemn and steady, the

Table 3. Lincoln Funeral Train Timetable, 18 April–4 May 1865

Location	Arrival	Public Viewing	Departure
D.C., White House		9:30 A.M.–5:30 P.M., 18 April	2:00 P.M., 19 April
D.C., the Capitol		8:00 A.M.–9:00 P.M., 20 April	8:00 A.M., 21 April
Baltimore	10:00 A.M., 21 April	1:00 P.M.–2:30 P.M., 21 April	3:00 P.M., 21 April
Harrisburg	8:35 P.M., 21 April	9:30 P.M.–12:00 midnight, 21 April; 7:00 A.M.–9:00 A.M., 22 April	11:15 A.M., 22 April
Philadelphia	4:30 P.M., 22 April	5:00 A.M., 23 April–1:17 A.M., 24 April	4:00 A.M., 24 April
New York	11:00 A.M., 24 April	1:00 P.M., 24 April–11:50 A.M., 25 April	4:15 P.M., 25 April
Albany	11:00 P.M., 25 April	1:15 A.M.–1:30 P.M., 26 April	4:00 P.M., 26 April
Buffalo	7:00 A.M., 27 April	9:00 A.M.–8:00 P.M., 27 April	10:10 P.M., 27 April
Cleveland	7:00 A.M., 28 April	11:00 A.M.–11:00 P.M., 28 April	12:00 midnight, 28 April
Columbus	7:30 A.M., 29 April	9:30 A.M.–dusk, 29 April	8:00 P.M., 29 April
Indianapolis	7:00 A.M., 30 April	8:00 A.M.–10:00 P.M., 30 April	12:00 midnight, 30 April
Chicago	11:00 A.M., 1 May	5:00 P.M., 1 May–8:00 P.M., 2 May	9:30 P.M., 2 May
Springfield	8:40 A.M., 3 May	12:00 noon, 3 May–10:00 A.M., 4 May	Interment

Total: 12 Days, 1654 miles

Sources: Victor Searcher, *The Farewell to Lincoln* (New York: Abingdon, 1965), passim; John Power, *Abraham Lincoln, His Life and Public Services, Death and Great Funeral Cortege* (Chicago: H. W. Rokker, 1889); *Harrisburg (Pa.) Patriot and Union*, 22 April 1865, 2; *Cincinnati Daily Enquirer*, 19 April 1865, 2; *Chicago Tribune*, 20 April 1865, 1; Philip B. Kunhardt Jr., Philip B. Kunhardt III, and Peter W. Kunhardt, *Lincoln: An Illustrated Biography* (New York: Alfred A. Knopf, 1992), 386; and Ida M. Tarbell, *The Life of Abraham Lincoln*, 4 vols. (New York: Lincoln History Society, 1923), 4: 94–106.

explosion of guns answering the muffled tolling of bells, the lightning of heaven revealing the sadness of many thousand faces." In New York City, as Lincoln was moved up the steps of City Hall, where he was to lie in state, he was carried through the midst of a nine-hundred-member German choir singing hymns. Cleveland had no structure large enough to accommodate the expected crowds, so the city built an outdoor pavilion in the park, and two lines moved past the open coffin at the rate of 180 mourners a minute.[20] It seemed that everywhere it rained, and everywhere the sounds of the funerals were bells and cannons and the hushed murmurings of large, grieving crowds. The throngs passing in review of the coffin were described by another Harrisburg observer: "Strong men bowed in reverence, repressing their emotion; fair women tremblingly gazed on the face of the slain, as they paid the purest tribute of their sex in tears, while children looked with wonder on the occasion, and caught the impression of a scene which will be distilled by them to the generation whose destinies they will control, as a spectacle second only to that which once shrouded the world in darkness, rent in twain the temple, opened the jaws of death, and bid the occupants of the grave walk forth among the living on earth."[21] These sentiments express what would become a familiar and often-repeated pattern; Americans seeking to understand, to give scale to the immensity of these dramatic events ultimately understood them best in a religious context.

Other than the eleven scheduled stops, the funeral train kept its schedule, halting only for fuel and water. Along the route linking the funeral cities, residents gravitated toward the rails simply to witness the passing of the train and the relic that it carried. Charles A. Page, a correspondent accompanying the funeral train, observed, "Nearly all the farm-houses on the way displayed flags bordered with black, and always the people came down to the road, and stood uncovered as we passed." Regardless of time or weather, at small-town depots or in the midst of farmlands, people congregated to honor the passing dead. The 142 miles between New York City and Albany seemed crowded with displays and tableaux, enactments of symbolic mourning: here an open grave around which women in white cast flowers; there a personification of Columbia prostrate in grief before Lincoln's portrait. Twenty-five thousand residents of Utica, New York, and surrounding areas met the train in a chill midnight rain when it stopped for water. Thirty-five thousand were on hand in Syracuse, simply to view the train standing briefly in the station. At night, everywhere bonfires and torches pushed back the darkness to make the black-cloaked train easier to see. Mary Borland remembered that some two dozen neighbors clustered together at the small Williamstown, Pennsylvania, station to watch the train pull through. "The train went pretty fast," she recalled, "but did not whistle and everything was solemn." Borland believed that every man, woman, and child was affected by the spectacle and recorded that "all wept as it passed." Towns along the route erected arches over the tracks, heavily draped in black, with banners expressing the mournful sentiments of the day. These larger constructions became more evident in the towns farther along the route, which had had more time to prepare. Such expressions also intensified as the funeral train carried Lincoln closer to home. One reporter noted arches at the successive small towns of Richmond, Cambridge, and Dublin, Indiana, observing, "This State is plunged in the depth of grief." In Chicago, Sergeant Luther Buick noted that, although the train was met by a very large crowd, everything was still.[22]

Lincoln scholar Lloyd Lewis described the outpouring of emotion in this way: "At every stop . . . delegations of thirty-six town belles in white, with black scarfs over the left shoulder, bore onto the train flowers and flags, spoke, sang, wept, recited tributes, enacted little dialogues and departed leaving morbid mottoes; the thirty-six girls representing the thirty-six States of the Union." Church choirs sang while "at the coffin mothers twisted babies downward so that their eyes might focus on the dead face" and children were lifted high or shaken awake by parents late at night, "anxious that they should remember always the sight of the funeral train."[23]

The desire to participate expanded beyond the funerals themselves. In Baltimore, where the viewing was limited to a mere ninety minutes, officials reopened the Mercantile Exchange after the funeral train had departed from the city, and thousands filed past the empty bier where Lincoln's body had so briefly rested. In Philadelphia, the hall where Lincoln had lain in state remained open to the public for another five days, still draped in black, the ornamented hearse parked in front. In Indianapolis, the memorials remained on display for thirty days. Smaller mementos and expressions of mourning proliferated in private homes as well. Prints and engravings wrapped in black crepe and collections of mourning badges, buttons, and other souvenirs became small shrines. A writer for the *Pennsylvania Daily Telegraph* noted the commercial aspect of the funeral in Philadelphia: "They are making fortunes out of it—by selling Badges of Mourning with Mr. Lincolns Photograph— also Cards with dates of Birth and Account of his birthplace—besides his 'life and Public Services.'" In a culture that often braided flowers and wreaths from the hair of the deceased, at least one woman created such a token from hair taken from Lincoln's horse, which had been led without rider in the Springfield funeral procession.[24]

Finally, after the longest serial funeral in American history, after traveling 1,654 miles over twelve days with eleven formal funerals and viewings, Lincoln's body was laid to rest in a temporary vault in Oak Ridge Cemetery outside Springfield. Town officials hoped to erect a large tomb in the center of the city. They received a telegram just five days before the body's arrival asserting Mary's insistence that Lincoln be taken to that quiet glade she imagined Oak Ridge Cemetery to be, or she would inter her husband in Chicago. After the last public funeral, Lincoln was entombed on 4 May 1865.[25] Over the course of that funeral, an estimated one million people personally viewed the body, and another 7 million participated in some memorial observance, out of a national population of approximately 32 million, a figure that includes the millions of Southerners who expressed little interest in participation as well as the millions of freedmen and freedwomen who had no means to travel the distances involved. Lincoln's funeral remains without parallel in American history.[26]

The scope of participation and the myriad manifestations of grief and mourning were immediate responses to an enormous personal sense of loss. In addition, coming hard on the end of a war that had been so devastating, Lincoln's death was inevitably tied to the nationalist context of that war in myriad ways. That it was, for example, immediately, and correctly, attributed to an avowed Southern sympathizer contributed to the perception of the crime's relation to the sectional crisis. Clearly, the war and Confederate defeat were uppermost in the assassin's mind; he had shouted the Virginia state motto—*Sic semper tyrannis*—from the theater's stage, giving voice to Southern perceptions of Lincoln as tyrant. From this foundation, it required no great leap to imagine this act as the result of a conspiracy involving Confederate leadership at the highest levels, to see this act of political murder as the last desperate act of the war.[27]

Those who had escaped the war untouched personally by the experience of death were now touched by Lincoln's death. One minister mourned, "How deep and pungent the national sorrow! Although it is caused by one man's death, yet the impression is so deep, it seems as though there was one dead in every house." Wilbur F. Paddock concurred, suggesting that "in every house

Honoring the Civil War Dead

The first mourners in Chicago stream into the Cook County Courthouse to view the president's remains, as thousands still line the streets in the background. The Chicago ceremonies drew the largest crowds, with an estimated half million mourners at this penultimate stop in the nation's most elaborate funeral.

Library of Congress

there was, as it were, one dead; and that one—a father."[28] Lincoln's death had the effect of broadening and renewing the impact of the Civil War's soldier dead. For individuals who had already experienced death as a result of the war, Lincoln's death and funeral served as a reminder of that pain. Seventy-five years ago Lloyd Lewis observed: "Coming at the end of four years of war, Lincoln's funeral gave the Union population an opportunity to express *en masse* the sorrow and grief that it had been accumulating all along as the death lists grew. Dramatically, the funeral released the people's pent-up passion to signally honor their war dead."[29] Lincoln's death became symbolic of the individual death, even death long past. This time, however, the pain was a common pain, for those who had not experienced the death of the war personally were, nonetheless, affected by Lincoln's death. As Morris Sutphen told his Philadelphia congregation, "It is no wonder that the death of the nation's

Chief Magistrate sends a tide of sorrow over the land, and that houses hitherto uninvaded by the desolations of this desolating war, are now filled with grief."[30] And so, for those who had and those who had not experienced loss firsthand, Lincoln's death came to symbolize all soldier death. Although dominated by a simple, almost irresistible logic, within the complex strands of thought with which the Civil War and Lincoln's death were woven together may be found threads that were the result of highly imaginative, even irrational processes. The contours that such connections assumed in the commemoration of the war, of the war's dead, and of Lincoln himself demonstrate the particular needs of those who had survived four dynamic and terrible years of national trial only to be faced with yet another seemingly insuperable calamity. The resolution of the crisis of presidential assassination might have taken any number of forms but was found largely through evoking a Northern myth of American nationalism, a resolution ensuring that every event, no matter how potentially disruptive to the continuity of American destiny, fell safely within providential designs for American prosperity and future aggrandizement.

The sense of nearly universal mourning shared largely among Northerners alone intensified and shaped the connections drawn between Lincoln's death and the war. As Southerners had killed Union soldiers, so had Southerners killed the president. But at this point the connections reached beyond similarity of circumstance—death through violence—and contemporaneity. The reflexive questions that such a sudden and prominent death prompted came to encompass the meaning of both the war and Lincoln's death. One author remembered that "masses of the people came together by a spontaneous impulse, to look in each other's faces, as if they could read there some hint of the meaning of these dreadful deeds—some omen of the country's fate."[31] The assassination endangered the peace and made many people question whether the war was in fact over, whether Union victory had been truly secured. Beyond that initial anxiety, Lincoln's murder also cast doubt on the assumptions that accompanied victory.

First, Northerners had come to follow the president's providential formulation of the war, especially as expressed in the Second Inaugural Address. The war would continue, Lincoln had said, "if God wills that it continue, until all the wealth piled by the bond-man's two hundred and fifty years of unrequited toil shall be sunk, and until every drop of blood drawn with the lash, shall be paid by another drawn with the sword, as was said three thousand years ago, so still it must be said 'the judgements of the Lord, are true and righteous altogether.'"[32] Yet there was nothing in such a divinely ordained trial that seemed to answer for the president's own demise; in fact, national victory seemed hollow if a defeated enemy could still inflict such a profound blow.

Second, Northerners questioned openly whether union was possible with a people who could commit such a dastardly act. For the few so foresighted as to imagine the conclusion of the sectional war, victory bestowed on the North the necessity of creating a national identity that must further the traditions and history of the revered past but that must also, eventually, extend that identity to include former Confederates. The satisfaction of national Union required it. Union was so powerful a drive, and the need to realize the battlefield victory so intense, that the most strident internecine struggles of Reconstruction wrestled with the ramifications of incorporating, not one, but two alien peoples into the national whole. In a very real sense, the burdens of supporting the aspirations of former slaves and elevating them to full citizenship was mirrored by the requirements of supporting and reelevating Confederates to social equality within the nation as well.

In the hours and days following Lincoln's assassination, these concerns— the attempts to understand the divine plan underlying recent events, how presidential murder altered the meaning of the war, and whether Southerners, indicted as a whole for an individual act, could be reconciled to the nation emerging from the war—all found expression in a variety of forms. But these questions themselves were rarely recorded explicitly. Instead they must be deduced from the flood of public utterances that poured from pulpit and editorial pen, from legislatures, civic clubs, labor organizations, and other social groups. The consistency of themes among such diverse sources implies a uniformity of needs to which the events of war and death—the deaths of seemingly innumerable soldiers each affecting a particular family, and a single murder affecting millions—must be made to answer.

Overwhelmingly, these expressions were religious in nature, in part, because there were providential concerns at stake. It was also because Americans were, in the nineteenth century, an essentially religious people. Furthermore, as is true at almost any time in American history, great tragedy seems to invite, almost require, explanations greater than those that can be found within the human compass. But, in the main, the efforts to confront the issues raised by Lincoln's assassination at the end of four years of terrible war rise from the circumstances of that death. Because the president was shot on Good Friday and died the next day, Americans received news of his death as they prepared for Easter. Other than newspapers, the Sunday-morning sermons, originally written to celebrate the resurrection of the nation in tandem with the anniversary of Christ's own resurrection, became the first public interpretive moment, the first time that hundreds tried in any organized way to assuage the grief and explicate the loss. Newspaper commentaries were also abundant, but the didactic nature of sermons made them the forerunners in the interpretation of the event's meaning. When individuals flocked to church with questions uppermost in their minds, ministers across the North struggled to find answers. Some congregations were so intent on receiving this type of instruction that, for example, when the Reverend Mr. Massey of the Baptist Church in Medway, Massachusetts, made no mention of Lincoln in his Easter sermon, his parishioners gave him fifteen minutes to get out of town. The centrality of this quest for meaning prompted another minister, Phillips Brooks, to council his congregation: "After the first trembling horror, [after] the first outburst of indignant sorrow has grown calm, these are the questions which we are bound to ask and answer."[33]

One of the most immediate impulses demonstrated in the sermons as well as the secular literature is to find some historical comparison for the recent trauma. But the American context permitted no real comparison, for there had never been a successful political assassination of this magnitude.[34] Two previous presidents—William H. Harrison and Zachary Taylor—had died while in office, but few references were made to their deaths. The manner of Lincoln's death, its criminal and violent nature, seems to have precluded drawing on those previous examples as grounds for more comforting allusions. Additionally, in those earlier deaths no specter of national disruption attended the smooth transition of power from the dying president to the vice-president, so that while they had been occasions to mourn, they carried little of the anxiety that accompanied Lincoln's death. Therefore, instead of American examples, ministers and others drew the majority of their historical analogies from both classical and biblical references, relying most heavily on the latter.

Of course, ministers had long demonstrated a facility for viewing national and political events within religious contexts, and Lincoln's death seemed particularly suited to this practice. Parke Godwin succinctly married the religious connotations to the eventual national political needs: "Within a

week—the Holy Week, as it is called in the Rubrics of our churches—we have
had our Triumphal entries, amid the waving of the palms of Peace; we have
had our dread Friday of Crucifixion; we have had, too, in the recently renewed
Patriotism of the Nation, a resurrection of a new and better life!"[35] Throughout the day Saturday, ministers who had expected to celebrate the most joy-
ful day of the Christian calendar hastily composed sermons of a much more
somber tone. George Briggs of Salem, Massachusetts, later remembered that
on that day, "smitten, pierced with anguish, the nation bent at its altars beneath a passion which the consoling, triumphant promises of that Easter
morning had scarcely the power to calm." Lincoln's funeral procession
throughout the Northern states was, likewise, the subject of religious constructions. Recalling biblical precedent, one minister likened it to "the passage of the herald-corpse of Jacob from his death-bed to the field and cave of
his fathers." Another referred to the railways carrying Lincoln back to Springfield as a "*via Delarosa.*"[36]

But even ostensibly secular expressions found the need to resort to religious metaphors to make plain their sense of recent tragedy. Shortly after
Lincoln's murder, the City Council of Baltimore—like numerous other city
councils—met and passed resolutions expressing its grief as well as its sympathy for the bereaved family and providing instructions for the civic observances of mourning. In them, council members lamented that Lincoln had
"been removed from his sphere of influence." Yet, even in death, they asserted,
Lincoln would continue to exert great influence over the nation and its reconciliation. At least this seems to have been their intent, since the resolutions
began, "We bow with resignation to this sad calamity, and trust to the inscrutable wisdom of Providence to bring light out of darkness, and sanctify
this deep affliction to the welfare of the nation."[37] This tragedy that removed
the president personally from the sphere of influence over the living might
still be "sanctified" to the nation's benefit, through a wise, although inscrutable, Providence. The Decatur, Pennsylvania, council of the United American Mechanics passed a resolution stating "that we regard him as our political
Moses."[38] In this civic setting, such words provide a glimpse into a general
pattern of social response, representing a blending of sacred and secular motifs
that renders sharp distinctions impossible, and perhaps meaningless.

Lincoln's name was most often linked with the figures of Moses and
Christ, although these were only the most popular of a host of biblical analogies. Even while Lincoln lived, Abraham, patriarch of the Hebrews, was the

source of many such comparisons, as in the popular recruitment song "We Are Coming, Father Abra'am, Three Hundred Thousand More." At a wartime camp meeting among laborers at Gettysburg, a white woman observing the services noted: "They prayed with all their souls, as only black men and slaves can, for themselves . . . and for 'Massa Lincoln,' for whom they seemed to have a reverential affection, some of them a sort of worship in which confused Father Abraham and Massa Abraham in one general call for blessings. Whatever else they asked for, they must have strength and comfort and blessings for 'Massa Lincoln.'" Some ministers recalled Cyrus, deliverer of the Hebrews from their Babylonian captivity.[39] But the biblical analogies that had the most impact, aside from the many allusions to his personality and character, were those that illuminated Lincoln's death. The parallels to Moses had both foundations: In the first place, through the Emancipation Proclamation, Lincoln had delivered a persecuted people from generational bondage; in the second, like Moses, he had died after leading his people through their greatest trials but before entering fully into the promised land of peace and national restoration. David Belden, in Nevada City, drew this portrait for his audience: "A martyr in triumph, like Israel's Law-giver, to him it was given to lead his people through the Red Sea of conflict, and the wilderness of suffering, but to find his own grave at the very gates of the promised land, which he was indeed suffered to behold but not permitted to enter."[40]

Although occasionally apologizing for risking blasphemy, ministers made allusions to Christ as often as to Moses, and with greater effect. Christine analogies were multifaceted. Some orators drew parallels between Lincoln's rhetorical style and that of Christ, emphasizing the use of parables. John McClintock of New York, for example, observed, "How Christ-like he was in dying!" pointing largely to the anniversary of the Crucifixion. The analogies could also characterize Lincoln as Christ through indirect association. Treadwell Walden of Philadelphia asserted that "treason and rebellion had taken a Judas shape" so that "all day yesterday [Saturday, 14 April] it seemed, as it did to the disciples of old, that all was over; that our cause had been committed to hopeless burial." To many ministers, Lincoln's frequent utterances of conciliation and charity toward the defeated South—particularly at the close of the Second Inaugural Address—demonstrated a forgiving attitude toward those who had killed him, and so he died, as one minister suggested, "whispering as he ascended, 'Father, forgive them, for they know not what they do!'" John Chadwick, a pastor in Brooklyn, New

York, even predicted a resurrection, albeit a sentimental rather than a corporeal one, in the hearts of loyal Americans: "So shall it come to pass, that he who died upon the day when Christ himself was crucified afresh in tearful memory shall rise again, as Christ himself arose in the new life of such as loved him, and obeyed his word."[41]

The vast scope of what was possible in these comparisons found expression in an extremely comprehensive sermon of Henry Deming's arguing that individuals of great social worth never really die:

> The good of the present live in the future, as the good of the past are here with us and in us to-day. The great primeval law-giver, entombed for forty centuries in that unknown grave, in an obscure vale of Moab, to-day legislates in your halls of State, and preaches on your Sabbath in all your synagogues. . . . [T]he dead Justinian issues in your courts the living mandates of the law—the dead Martin Luther issues from your press the living oracles of God—the dead Napoleon still sways France from that silent tomb in the Invalides—the dead George Washington held together through wrangling decades this brotherhood of States, and the dead Abraham Lincoln will peal the clarion of beleaguered nations and marshal and beckon on the wavering battle lines of liberty, till the last generation of man.[42]

Throughout this passage, the significance of the dead resounds as far more than colorful analogies; Deming argues passionately that the dead can and do provide a spiritual service with social and nationalist dimensions. Such constructions demonstrate the very real needs of the living that the dead could be made to serve. Yet, significantly, the religious similes were often political metaphors as well. The image of Father Abraham evoked not only reverence but alluded to Abraham's position as the founder of his people, a religious as well as a political leader. Similarly, associations with other biblical figures shared this mixture of meanings. Ministers frequently drew allusions from biblical assassinations or notable deaths that were usually political murders as well, demonstrating on that metaphorical level the significance of such death to a polity as well as being a manifestation of God's role in a nation's life. With wonderfully creative imagery, orators and ministers shaped the event of Lincoln's death to the needs of their congregations. As Lloyd Lewis reminds us, "Very human, very complex forces were shaping the words of these leading clergymen—and others like them—as they explained to the people why Lincoln had been so mysteriously taken away."[43]

Crucially, every allusion had repercussions, for ideas do not exist independently of a social context. The most powerful and logical conclusion to be drawn from religious allusions was that, as God had required the deaths of Christ and Moses, so he also required the death of Lincoln. A few ministers felt incapable of explicating the mystery of the tragedy, as indicated when one exclaimed, "Wonderful life! More wonderful death! Who but God can unlock its inscrutable meaning?" However, in general, ministers were not at all shy about asserting what God's reasons might have been. More typical was the assertion of Gordon Hall, who said, "Furthermore, we know that *Mr. Lincoln's continuance in office would not have been so favorable to God's plan as his removal.* How do we know that? Because God removed him. This proves it." The logic was inescapable. But just because God had "done this deed," as Morris Sutphen put it, that did not mean that it was without pain. Divine authorship "does not go a hair's breadth toward changing our feelings . . . concerning our common bereavement and its utterly wicked cause." Still, parishioners, Americans, must take comfort in the certainty of providence. Charles S. Robinson of New York urged his congregation to "be alert now for the discovery of some new purpose. The infinite plans of the Almighty are shifting their phase for some disclosure that will relieve our embarrassment. It is expedient that even such offences as these should come. There can be no doubt that God means to make good out of this evil."[44]

The overarching themes of God's authorship reflected entirely the North's anxiety about the war's aftermath. Like Moses, Lincoln had finished his work—the salvation of the Union. But, beyond that rather simple Mosaic analogy, many asserted that Lincoln's usefulness to the nation had also come to a close along with the war. Hiram Crozier described Lincoln as "patient with all . . . differences, silent under all attacks, forgiving to a fault as a child." Daniel Rice characterized the president's heart as "tender as that of a woman." John McClintock said, "Oh! What an epitaph—that the only fear men had was that he would be too tender, that he had too much love." The not-so-veiled assertion was obvious enough; Lincoln was not capable of handling the rigors that the nation faced in Reconstruction. Most ministers who made this observation thought Lincoln too magnanimous, too gentle hearted, "not stern enough," to mete out justice to traitors. Therefore, logic dictated, Lincoln died to make room for Andrew Johnson. In particular, Johnson played Joshua to Lincoln's Moses. As the minister Cephas B. Crane asserted: "Andrew Johnson is the Joshua whom God has appointed to consummate the work which our dead Moses so nobly commenced."[45] As Lincoln was not permitted to see the promised land of national peace and Union triumphant, it fell to Johnson to lead the chosen people. Speakers pointed out that Johnson was a Southerner, had grown up amid the depravity of the South, knew intimately its dangers. His own comment that "treason must be made odious, and the traitor must be punished and impoverished" convinced many of his intentions.[46] But Johnson was, prior to Lincoln's death, no one's choice of leader. Several sermons commented on his apparently drunken state at Lincoln's second inauguration, or, as the Massachusetts minister Charles Brigham put it, "his defects in habit and his lack of culture." But with the assassination, Johnson needed to be reconfigured under the designs of myth to be God's anointed, indeed, the very reason that Lincoln was allowed to be murdered. Brigham concluded: "While Abraham Lincoln was the choice of the people, Andrew Johnson was the choice of God. God is wiser than we are."[47]

The creativity displayed when faced with the daunting task of making sense of the seemingly irrational act of presidential murder was remarkable. P. B. Day expressed the hope of many when he stated that "as painful as the event of our President's death is to us, we think we can see the divine hand in it." Ministers asserted at times that Lincoln had been removed by a jealous God: "Was not the President's death *necessary* to the nation's life? Were we not leaning upon an arm of flesh, forgetful of the ever-living God, indulging—though in a different form—the very sin of idolatry which brought upon us the woes through which we have passed?" Thus, Lincoln's death served the purpose of admonishing the nation to remain focused on God's role in the recent crisis, not on the acts of any one human participant. God's designs were larger than the human tools used to accomplish his purpose.[48] George Putnam, speaking before the Atheneum Club of New York City, seemed to plead that such lessons were available in this otherwise inexplicable tragedy: "May it not prove that there was a danger of too much leniency and forbearance to traitors, and that God would teach us that Justice must not be wholly superseded even by benignant Mercy?" But, for all the striving to understand God's role in Lincoln's death there were some who cautioned that these ready explanations were not to be taken up lightly, for cries for vengeance belonged to another. Samuel Crocker warned his Boston congregation, "Let us not too hastily deduce the moral of his death. Let us not, in our just indignation, read in it a lesson at variance alike with every principle of our religion. . . . Having

been successfully bourne through the fiery furnace of this protracted conflict, under the mild and Christian sway of our late chief magistrate, let us
not, in our final triumph, initiate a harsh and vindictive policy towards a dis-
armed and helpless opponent."[49]

But most cried out in pain and bitterness for retribution, both human
and divine. Samuel T. Spear spoke with considerable venom and advocated
a death sentence, sanctioned by God, for all traitors. The Reverend L. Clark
Seelye was reported to have asserted, "We are united in the determination to
hang every traitor who deserves it."[50] And so these most Christian of men,
ministers all, asserted from the pulpit that Lincoln's death had been permitted in order to cast the Southern evil into the harsh light of Northern animosity. Indeed, many ministers took the extraordinary position that Lincoln's
death was required by God as an instruction to Northerners in the depravity
and evil of the South. According to Presbyterian minister Charles Robinson
"There was, perhaps, needed one more proof of the unutterable sin of treason." Some ministers argued that Lincoln's death was required if the nation
was to learn the evil of slavery. That such a lesson was required after decades
of sectional tensions, after four years of horrific conflict, after the deaths of
more than half a million soldiers, strains credulity, yet this was apparently
the case. O. H. Dutton told his Holyoke, Massachusetts, congregation:

> We needed, I say, to have this truth forced upon us. . . . We denied,
> and still deny, that the rules of ordinary warfare were violated; that
> wounded men were butchered; that captured men were subjected
> to the terrible torture of a slow starvation, which could end only in
> idiocy or death. We forced ourselves to doubt these things, till the
> truth of the awful tale was thrust upon us by concurrent, irrefragable
> testimony; by the tottering return to us of brothers and friends, ru-
> ined by no wound of the battle-field; and by those sun-pictures which
> cannot lie, and which are so dreadful we hide them from our wives
> and daughters in pure mercy.[51]

In this way, the deaths of soldiers and Lincoln were, again, married in thought.
Lincoln's death heightened the significance and sharpened the pain of the
soldier dead.

While working to explicate the instructional elements of one particular
death—Lincoln's—ministers found increased leverage for their condemnation of the South by drawing on the numerous deaths of Union soldiers. At
the Columbus, Ohio, commemorative ceremonies, the Honorable Job E.

Stevenson "declared that conciliation of those who had murdered Mercy was condemned by the cries to heaven of thousands of soldiers murdered in rebel prisons—by bereaved homes in all loyal States." Henry Badger decried against a feeling of forgiveness that he detected: "But the people, happy with victory and the promise of peace, . . . lauded Robert Lee, and were ready to receive him with a hero's honors, instead of a traitor's infamy." But the dead of the war could not allow it. "Individuals cried out against it. Mourning households protested against it, as an outrage on the memory of their patriot dead. They whose hearts lie buried at Antietam or Gettysburg; who weep over Malvern Hill or Fair Oaks; whose kindred lie . . . in the nameless graves at Richmond; . . . these all protested against such unseasonable mercy to traitors, as unfaithfulness to our country's future, and to the memory of our dead."[52]

Was the North ready to be forgiving until Lincoln's death? Some thought so. "In the exultation of victory," said Francis Abott, "the nation betrayed marks of a good-natured weakness, of a criminal magnanimity; and God may have suffered this appalling blow to strike us, to waken us to our duty, and startle us into obedience." The Congregationalist minister Leonard Swain remarked, "There was an alarming tone in some of our public journals, and some of our public addresses, which indicated that we might be going to shrink, as a nation, from the great final duty to which we had been brought by the victorious termination of our conflict." The North had proven its superior might, he told his congregation, and victory invited magnanimous feelings. "Now let us show [the South] that we can afford to be generous," he continued, and, after a "gentle token" of Northern disapproval, "then, forgiving and forgetting what is past, shake hands in reconciliation and receive him once more to our fellowship." But, Swain concluded, "All this is brought to an end at once and forever by the dreadful event which hangs all the sanctuaries of God in mourning to-day." Even in a more secular setting, the sentiment was clearly evident. "Before his death, peace was possible," read a resolution passed by citizens of San Francisco. "All the atmosphere was filled with generous emotions and kind sympathy—but now peace means subjugation or annihilation! God have mercy on the souls of the rebel chiefs!"[53] However, historian Thomas Reed Turner cautions against the belief that it was the assassination alone that quenched magnanimous exuberance following Lee's surrender. As Turner carefully observes, "It seems more realistic to view such conciliatory expressions as merely a first outbreak, with the understanding that the nation would have been faced with harsher realities before long, even if the assassination had not occurred."[54] But the assassination did occur, and even if such sterner sentiments were inevitable, Lincoln's murder focused such antipathies at a particularly early and specific moment.

The outrage of a specific act of vengeance was quickly attributed to the whole, and cries for a sterner justice were plentiful. The violence of the Southern war effort was recounted in sermon after sermon, a litany ranging from the combat deaths of Northern soldiers to the accusations of atrocities that had circulated widely during the war. Such crimes were now compounded by the assassination of Lincoln, again conflating the death of soldiers with that of their president. In one window of Miller and Matthew's, a stationery store on Broadway, a sign reading "Justice Not Revenge" seemed by itself to urge caution in dealing with the South. But the next window held another sign reading "Massacre at Lawrence, Andersonville Prison Pen, Mining Libby Prison, Murder of the President." Grouped together, the animosities developed during the war were renewed and refreshed in the highly emotional response to assassination, and few were willing to discriminate between the actions of war and political murder. In fact, presidential assassination seemed to overshadow all else. Reverend Billingsley, of the U.S. Christian Commission, asserted: "The murder of Caesar in the Roman senate was atrocious; hanging Union soldiers by scores for their loyalty in North Carolina was barbarous; the wholesale, cold-blooded massacre at Fort Pillow was fiendish; starving to death thousands of soldiers in Andersonville was horrible beyond description; but these most shocking crimes, culminating in the diabolical murder of President Lincoln and attempted national assassination, are second only to the crucifixion of Jesus Christ upon Mount Calvary!"[55]

Billingsley pointedly compared Lincoln's murder to the attempted assassination of the nation itself. Such close identification was at the heart of Northern national mythic constructions. The renowned orator George Bancroft told his New York audience, "The blow aimed at him, was aimed not at the native of Kentucky, not at the citizen of Illinois, but at a man, who, as President, . . . stood as the representative of every man in the United States." Henry A. Nelson of Springfield agreed: "Our horror of that murder was not merely for it as the murder of a fellow-man; we knew that the blow was struck at him in his official and representative capacity."[56]

Two particular formulations rise from this close identification, the first accentuating Lincoln's role as a *representative* figure of the nation both in life and in death, the second emphasizing a true *correlation* between the nation and Lincoln. In Swampscott, Massachusetts, an individual who had greeted the news of Lincoln's assassination with three cheers was seized by a mob and tarred and feathered. He was then placed in a small boat and dragged through the town on display, forced to hold an American flag high over his head. In order to gain his release, he had to promise to purchase an American flag and keep it on display at half-mast throughout the mourning period for Lincoln.[57] The Massachusetts mob made the unstated, unthinking assumption that this individual could properly expiate his insult through the display of the national symbol. The only obvious reference to Lincoln is that the flag is to be flown at half-mast, an acknowledgment of Lincoln's representative role, but the initial punishment—holding aloft the national symbol while being publicly humiliated—speaks directly, but un-self-consciously, to the correlation between man and nation.

In the thought and rhetoric of the pulpit and the press, Lincoln's death was ordained for specific reasons. All of them served to bolster the providential interpretation that God had taken an active role to ensure the continued elevation of the United States. The Reverend N. L. Brakeman brought the entire spectrum to bear in his sermon to Union troops stationed in Baton Rouge:

> [Lincoln] may have been thus taken, that the lessons of his life and God's word might be more deeply impressed upon the nation's heart. We may have needed the revelation it has given to the true character and the diabolical spirit that sought the nation's life. Perhaps he would have been too lenient with that spirit and was removed that justice might be dealt—dealt with a sterner hand. We may have needed the unprecedented trial to teach us, *as a nation and others also*, how much we could bear and yet survive. We had felt one common thrill when first the tocsin of war sounded; we felt bound by a common sympathy in the hour of gloom and despondency; we had witnessed the triumphs of patriotism over party at his re-election, and felt *we* were strong; a mighty triumph, twice told, had just awakened and united the nation in a common joy. Did we need another tie to bind us in a closer union?[58]

Brakeman's was a significant and, in this context, poignant question. Most ministers touched on it—to a greater or lesser degree—in their explication of Lincoln's assassination. That question, and all the others that ministers tried to answer, probed the relation between the death of Lincoln and the American nation. But there is a large assumption at the heart of Brakeman's assessment; he assumes to know and speak for the totality of the American people. His language is inclusive: "we felt"; "we had witnessed." But could all Americans feel "united . . . in a common joy" following Lincoln's reelection or Lee's surrender? Clearly, only Northern Americans would be so included. Brakeman seems aware of the problem—hence his awkward formulation "as a nation and others also"—but still suggests the nation could be bound together, North and South, through the assassination of the Northern president at the hands of a Southern sympathizer. Brakeman was not alone in his confusion; nearly every aspect of the eulogistic explications spoke confidently of a providential design for the nation while at the same time making it clear that God was a Union man.

These verbal and rhetorical complications are the starting point of Northern national mythmaking. Careful exploration reveals that Northern orators used such inclusive, general terms as *United States, American, the American people,* and, especially, *nation* and *national* in ways that generally excluded Southerners. This subtle but particular use of language has been largely overlooked yet remains an important characteristic of the words that flowed from presses and pulpits following Lincoln's death. That Northerners would mourn Lincoln more than Southerners was obvious, but needed stating nonetheless. Henry Badger asserted that, "Never went a man to the grave, so loved and mourned as Abraham Lincoln,—so followed by the tender sorrow of twenty millions of his fellow-men." Of course, given a national population of roughly 32 million, Badger can be referring only to the Northern portion of that population. Interestingly, Badger also seems to be excluding the 4 million former slaves, perhaps because he did not consider them to be "his fellow-men." Similarly, another minister observed that "yesterday morning five million families waked from their slumbers to find themselves orphaned," again too small a number to include all Americans.[59] Southerners, who had sought to secede from the Union and for whom the murder was carried out, could not be imagined as having been victimized by Lincoln's assassination, just as an attack on Jefferson Davis could not have been considered an injury to Northerners. These distinctions are usually subtle, but not always consistent. Indeed, contradictory statements can often be found on the same page, sometimes even in the same paragraph. One orator in Baltimore began by speaking in terms that seem inclusive of all in the country: "We all feel of one family, . . . mourning the loss of one to whom we all looked as to a parent.

Honoring the Civil War Dead

. . . Our brothers and sisters all over the land mourn with us this day. We are tendered by affliction, and all our differences forgotten, for the hearts of all are desolate, and our nation mourns." Yet he goes on to enumerate the groups to whom he refers: "We mourn for ourselves, we mourn for our common country, but most of all for those who wandered off from the family altar, and turned their backs in anger upon us." In other words, we feel grief for ourselves, the land, and those others, who were of this family but are no longer. Significantly, the imagery is of an altar, implying that Northerners continued to tend the true faith, Southerners having turned away in apostasy. But the inclusive sense returns: "Throughout our wide domain the lightning has flashed the terrible truth, and to-day thirty millions of people have one common thought and one common cause for sadness. . . . [A]nd universal sadness pervades our land from the forest bordered streams of Maine to the waters of Mexico." Other speakers were well aware of the distinctions that they were drawing: "The parricides have murdered the father of *their* country as well as of ours, for his generous and loving heart embraced them as well as us in its longing for friendly and fraternal restoration to the blessings of a common country." But, as would remain true for the next several decades, these assertions of unity and common spirit would remain the most elusive and presumptive aspect of the Northern myth of American nationalism. Richard B. Duane, a New Hampshire minister, thundered, "We have a country. God being our helper, we mean to have one still."[60]

Despite the inclusive confidence of a nation in mourning, it seems unlikely that a significant number of former Confederates mourned Lincoln's death. However, the scope of the Southern reaction to the assassination has been difficult to gauge. Much of the South was firmly in Union control, occupied by Federal troops. With or without justification, many Southerners felt constrained from expressing their opinions concerning the murder freely. Most urban centers that supported presses and newspapers were under federal authority and felt pressures to refrain from free expression, even if publication were possible. An exception was Texas, which remained free of Union military occupation until June 1865, and there the sentiments were predominantly celebratory. A Houston newspaper pointed to the difference between Northern and Southern perceptions: "Some will regard [Lincoln's murder] with all the horror of the most wicked assassination, others will feel it to be that righteous retribution which descends direct from the hand of God upon the destroyer of human liberty and the oppression of a free people." In the

South, too, divine intervention in the political affairs of the nation was acknowledged and expected. The *Galveston Daily News* exclaimed that Lincoln's death was "one of the inscrutable decrees of Providence." And the earlier Northern logic that the removal of the president must be within the plan of God was echoed in Dallas—"God Almighty ordered this event or it could have never taken place"—but no doubt with a certain Southern twist of meaning. Lincoln's removal was a judgment of divine will, although somewhat friendlier to Southern values.[61]

Southerners, too, sought historical comparisons. Texan Kate Stone wrote simply, "Caesar had his Brutus, Marat his Charlotte Corday, and Lincoln his Booth." Also, Southerners seemed to delight in pointing out the ironic turn of Lincoln's vaunted eloquence from the Second Inaugural Address: "How prophetically the lines, which he applied to the South, refer to himself: 'It must needs be the offences come. But woe to that man by whom the offence cometh.'" These sentiments were echoed in Galveston: "The very words that he had used in the exultation of his inauguration were prophetic of his own fate. 'But woe to the man by whom the offence cometh!' Out of his own mouth he was condemned."[62] Southerners relished a double irony: not only was the Bible verse that Lincoln had quoted turned back on him, but like Pharaoh, his doom came from his own utterances toward the persecuted people of a new Israel. Both North and South, then, claimed themselves to be the chosen people, and as God could be interpreted by many as a Union man, others could see in him a genuine Southerner.[63]

The Southern pulpits also held back because of the Federal presence. Even when seeming to lament the president's death, Southern expressions of sympathy were suspect. Alfred S. Patton, a Baptist minister in New York, denounced Southerners from his pulpit: "Tell me not that the leading men of the South disapprove these acts. Tell me not that they mourn for the death of Lincoln—it is what they have wished for, and as their barbarous spirit led them to applaud the cowardly [Preston] Brooks, so, in their secret souls, they to-day approve the miscreant murderer Booth." In this atmosphere, most Southern ministers stepped carefully. A collection of Lincoln eulogies published in 1865 contains the unusual contribution of a Natchez, Mississippi, minister which, although employing eulogistic tones of loss and remorse, never once makes explicit reference to Lincoln's name or to the war.[64]

On 1 June, the day set aside by Andrew Johnson in response to Lincoln's death as a National Day of Humiliation, as Northern ministers were once again calling to mind the evil that Southern slavery had wrought, a very few voices called out in defense of the South. Expounding upon Proverbs 17: 5, "He that justifieth the wicked, and he that condemneth the just, even they both are an abomination to the Lord," the Reverend J. L. Burrows sought to point out that many in the South had abjured and condemned Lincoln's murder. Nevertheless, the real crimes that concerned him were those committed against the Southern people: "In the language of the day, fraud is called shrewdness—blasphemy, free speech—falsehood, invention—perjury, equivocation, and robbery, appropriation." Spoken from a Richmond, Virginia, pulpit, Burrows's words were clearly aimed at the Northern military and civilian occupation of that town since war's end, where doubtless many such "appropriations" were made in the interests of the victors. "The whole black catalogue of outrages perpetrated by maddened armies, which authority and discipline are often too weak to restrain, and which are condemned alike by the law of nations and the law of God—we sometimes hear palliated and defended."[65]

Even in Burrows's sermon the qualified language of separate national identities can be discerned. Burrows continues: "We are called upon to-day, by the President of the United States, to assemble in our churches, and give expression to our condemnation and grief, for the terrible crime which has shocked the nation, and hurled the chief of a great people from his high position by an assassin blow. We respond to the invitation, join the nation in its mourning, record our detestation of the crime, and our sympathy with those who suffer." This language is that of a people apart from the moment of the day, looking on and joining in by invitation. The blow has shocked *the* nation, not *our* nation. Johnson's invitation seems required; this church might not have participated without such a call. The formal construction of the last sentence—"we" respond, "join" the nation of which we are not normally a part, record our detestation, and sympathize "with those who suffer"—implies that there are none who suffer within this congregation.[66]

This message becomes clearer as Burrows warms to his subject. The core of the sermon is a counterstrike at Northern pulpits that condemned the South as a whole for the assassination: "I would not transcend the limits of *allowed* liberty of speech, I would not awaken emotions that are inconsistent with the solemnities of the day, but surely *it may be permitted* us, while we lament the calamity that has bowed *a* nation in mourning, to repel the charge uttered from many a religious paper pulpit, that we are involved in the guilt that has wrought this calamity and awakened this mourning." This passage shows evidence of the social and political pressures brought to bear on Southern expression; Burrows was careful in his defense of the South. Immediately after the assassination, however, his tone had been slightly different. In a sermon preached 23 April, Burrows reacts to a "terrible event" that has "shocked and thrilled the hearts of the people of *this* country." Special consideration must apply to this crime against leaders, "[whose] lives are more sacred, because they belong not merely to themselves, but to the nation." This oration seems inclusive, whereas Burrows's comments from June seem to distance his congregation. His April address continues: "It is an outrage upon the rights, and interests, and affections of a whole people. Committed by a subject of the government, of which the victim is the representative and head, *as in this case*, it associates with it all that is foul in treason with all that is base and revolting in murder."[67]

This passage can be read in two ways: either Burrows is trying to point out that, the war being effectively ended, Lincoln had once again assumed his place as the representative head of state for all Americans, or he is trying—as he does elsewhere—to place special emphasis on the fact that a Northern (Maryland) criminal killed the Northern political leader. In April, Burrows is arguing in a more politically inclusive fashion than he will in the months to come; in June, he has effectively separated the South from the crime and from Northern interpretations of it. Circumstances in Richmond over those two months probably pushed him from the first reading to the second. In addition, far from being that stern representative of an outraged North, Andrew Johnson had been remarkably conciliatory to the South, having just days before the National Day of Humiliation issued his 29 May Proclamation of Amnesty and Pardon, a measure that many Northerners found appalling in its generosity. Burrows's 1 June sermon clearly celebrates and defends the South. In a phrase that rallies a flagging Confederate nationalism, Burrows reminds his audience that "among the noblest and purest men, morally, the world has ever seen, have been many who have been denounced, condemned and executed for treason and rebellion, and yet from the scaffold their pure spirits, justified through the righteousness of Christ, have ascended to receive the smiling approval and blessing of their infinite Judge and Father."[68] Hence, as Northern pulpits formulated the essential elements of the Northern myth of nationalism, the Southern pulpits countered with the foundations of the Lost Cause, in this case, victory drawn out of defeat. And, at least in Burrows's case, as Lincoln's death hardened Northern sentiment, it also made Southern expressions far more defensive than they might otherwise have been.

Many wondered what effect Lincoln's death would have on reunification. Immediately after the crime, the *Washington National Intelligencer* commented, "The deed will discourage and retard pacification and reconstruction which was the benevolent aim of the late President. *The assassins have murdered the peace!*" Hiram Sears fell back on Bible verse to express his foreboding: "Tell it not in Gath, publish it not in the streets of Askelon, lest the daughters of the Philistines rejoice, lest the daughters of the uncircumcised triumph." George P. Putnam, speaking in New York on 19 April, the day of Lincoln's Washington, D.C., funeral, asked his listeners, "Can we again welcome to honorable citizenship, the men who either directed or countenanced the doings at Fort Pillow, at Lawrence, at Salisbury, and Andersonville?" Charles Robinson of New York seemed to answer: "He cannot be brother of mine, he belongs to no race of mine, who, in the foul cause of human bondage, fights with a rural massacre, makes war with midnight arson, and crowns his unmanly barbarity with stabbing a sick man in his bed, and shooting an unarmed husband in the very sight of his wife!" Peter Russell of Eckley, Pennsylvania, hoped that Southerners would respond appropriately. "God forbid," he preached, "that any considerable number of our Southern people should assume the guilt of this crime and make it their own, by applauding it, approving of it, and boldly proclaiming that it is just what they desired and counseled. Alas for them if generals and governors, and congressmen, and legislators, and papers, and public meetings should justify it! If this be so, I tremble for what may follow."[69]

Although, at least in this case, Lincoln's death may have sharpened the sectional division, not a few thought that it might eventually have the opposite effect. In Albany, William Wilson told his congregation that perhaps Lincoln's death was permitted "to deepen our devotion to our country. . . . It would seem that the nation must grow as does the church, from the seed sown in the martyr's blood." Hiram P. Crozier hoped that "his blood, shed by unnatural and wicked hands, may cement the union of these States." Many ministers explicitly extended Lincoln's death, occasionally his corpse, as the basis of reunion. Methodist minister Cephas Crane asserted that Lincoln's role was identical to Christ's, in that, as Christ had died to reconcile man and God, Lincoln died to reconcile North and South: "When God would bring an apostate humanity into reconciliation with himself, the sacrifice of his only and well-beloved Son was requisite to the realization of his purpose and desire." Crane continued the parallel, "So, when our national government would bring back to allegiance to itself its millions of apostate subjects, it was requisite that he who was dearest to all loyal hearts should be offered in sacrifice."[70] Again, the assertion of a Northern nationalism—"our" government, "loyal" hearts—is readily apparent.

George Dana Boardman, a Baptist minister, spoke broadly of the role that Lincoln's death played for the nation: "Even so, the nation's triumph and greatness may spring from Abraham Lincoln's death." Had Lincoln not been murdered, in retirement we would have treasured him, but he likely would have been in distant Illinois, where "he might have abided alone, fructifying into no national harvest." Away from the central focus of national politics, Lincoln might have faded from importance: "We should still have revered him, as we revere all of God's great ones; but no nation would have been born of him." Boardman's formulation suggests that while in life Lincoln had saved the former Union of states, in death he forged a nation. "Even here," Boardman continues, "in the cause of Liberty, as in the cause of the Church, it shall be found that the blood of the martyrs is the seed of the Republic. Take courage, then, my countrymen: for even now I see springing from the tear-wet bier of Abraham Lincoln the green and tender blades which foretell the birth of an emancipated, united, triumphant, transfigured, immortal Republic. Even so, Father! For thus it seemed good in Thy sight!"[71] The images of birth, growth, and death are powerful and render Lincoln's death a metaphor of the organic, natural expansion of the nation.

The mythic perspectives on Lincoln's assassination were larger than the religious sensibility that informed them. Lincoln's death was the catalyst for the Northern myth of American nationalism. The need for national regeneration lent the mourning for Lincoln its particular character and scope. The security of the goals won on the battlefield, of the Cause Victorious, was the touchstone from which the Northern nation could launch its profound outpouring of grief and memory, an oceanic response, not just to Lincoln's death, but to the war in its entirety. Out of this sharp punctuation of trauma, which exploded outward to encompass all that Northerners had individually suffered throughout the war, these central elements of the Northern myths and metaphors were erected to stave off the uncertainties of their tumultuous present and to dispel the shadows that the war and Lincoln's death had cast on their providentially ordained future. The noted orator George Bancroft concluded succinctly:

> The grave that receives the remains of Lincoln, receives the costly sacrifice to the Union; the monument which will rise over his body will bear witness to the Union; his enduring memory will assist during the countless ages to bond the states together, and to incite to the love of our one undivided, indivisible country. Peace to the ashes of our departed friend, the friend of his country and his race. He was happy in his life, for he was the restorer of the republic; he was happy in his death, for his martyrdom will plead for ever for the Union of the states and the freedom of man.[72]

This confident statement was made even as Confederate and Federal troops still opposed each other in combat, even as men still died. Arthur G. Thomas told an audience gathered at Philadelphia's U.S. General Hospital that "we needed all this—these draped cities—this drooping of the flag—our joy-bells muffled. It was meet that one so exalted in the affection and confidence of the people, should die for the nation. We needed this crucible of affliction to chasten the national spirit, and to fuse us as the heart of one man; and in God's way it has been done."[73] To argue among the wounded and maimed that the horrors of war had merely been prelude to the "crucible" of Lincoln's murder demonstrates starkly the necessity of interpreting that tragic war within the Northern nationalist myth.

The varied sources of myth all spoke with the same essential voice: they reveled in a hard-won peace; assumed the spoils of national authority that victory assured them; asserted a reunified national existence that did not really yet exist, especially as it included, albeit uncomfortably, those who had tried to separate from it; and incorporated a brutally destructive war and the first assassination of a president within the projected expansion of global influence that was the rightful legacy of God's chosen people on earth. The country's greatest sins were made necessary stepping-stones to a larger destiny, the nation's most severe trials made into ordeals of humiliation, repentance, and salvation. Despite that mythology's illusory nature, which became quite apparent immediately after the war and Lincoln's death, the North would spend the next several years augmenting its strength and setting about making myth become reality, fulfilling the national prayer expressed by the minister who prayerfully asked, "May God make us worthy of the memory of Abraham Lincoln."[74]

3

"One Interminable Grave-Yard": Northern Dominance in the Commemoration of the Dead

Sons of the Dark and Bloody Ground,
Ye must not slumber there,
Where stranger steps and tongues resound
Along the heedless air.
Your own proud land's heroic soil
Shall be your fitter grave:
She claims from war his richest spoil—
The ashes of her brave.
. . .
Rest on, embalmed and sainted dead!
Dear as the blood ye gave;
No impious footsteps here shall tread
The herbage of your grave.
    —*Theodore O'Hara,* The Bivouac of the Dead *(ca. 1848)*

I N NOVEMBER 1865, Winslow Homer, who had spent much of the Civil War illustrating the conflict for *Harper's Weekly,* first exhibited his most poignant and symbolically powerful painting of the war, *Veteran in a New Field.* This is a work of deceptive simplicity, ostensibly a response to one of the most dramatic social dynamics of the short seven months since the war's end. With a rapidity unimaginable just a year before, the enormous Union armies had almost completely disbanded, hundreds of thousands of soldiers returning home to take up their peacetime pursuits. By December 1865, more than 80 percent of the largest armed force ever assembled on the North American continent had traded the status of soldier for that of veteran. *Veteran in a New Field* focuses on that transition to civilian pursuits; a single figure, facing away from the viewer, has begun harvesting the wheat in an overgrown field perhaps neglected throughout his long absence. He has just returned from the war; his canteen and uniform jacket lie almost hidden in the wheat stubble behind him. The painting is stark and simple; comprising only the pale sky, the tall golden wheat, and the white-shirted figure of the veteran, swinging his scythe through the grain. It conveys great peace and solemnity, but Homer intended to portray far more than a soldier's return to agriculture.

When *Veteran* was first shown to the public in an Artist's Fund Society exhibition, it drew praise for its vigorous if impetuous execution. The *Evening Post,* for example, praised Homer's "largeness of manner" and his "very happy superiority to the conventional." But Homer's work, the critics thought, was not without flaws. The *Post* hoped for more "delicate" execution in future works, but it was Russell Sturgis of the *Nation* who most sharply pointed out its errors. Sturgis complained of the roughness of Homer's manner—a "headlong piece of work," of "slapdash execution"—but he also thought the painting inaccurate. The tool chosen for harvesting was outdated by 1865, so "we are inclined to quarrel with the veteran for having forgotten, in his four years or less of campaigning, that it is with a cradle, and not with a scythe alone, that he should attack the standing grain." "And such grain!" Sturgis continued, "six feet high are its shortest stalks." Apparently stung by generally positive but specifically critical reviews, Homer altered the painting after its exhibition, most obviously by shortening the height of the wheat.[1]

Although long dismissed as an early and immature expression of Homer's later artistic power, *Veteran* was more significant than the critics of 1865 or many since have realized. Although Sturgis complained of inaccuracies, Homer did not err in his portrayal. Both the single-bladed scythe and the too-tall grain served his artistic impulse. Despite the array of symbolic readings that critics have developed over the years, only recently have any noticed the power with which Homer handles the subject of death in this work. Homer's veteran is in a new field, to be distinguished from the field he has recently left, the battlefield of fatal violence. The scythe—consciously chosen by Homer—is the traditional weapon of Death incarnate, harvesting lives as farmers harvested grain. But the grain itself, once painted the same height as a man, makes obvious Homer's intent. This veteran, although in a new field, is taking up his old occupation. It is metaphorically the same labor, the same actions, despite the newness of the field. Although this soldier, and thousands like him, had escaped the war, battlefield death has followed him home, haunting his peacetime pursuits and coloring his perceptions of life and livelihood.[2]

THE VETERAN IN A NEW FIELD.—FROM A PAINTING BY HOMER.

An engraving of Winslow Homer's *Veteran in a New Field*, published in *Frank Leslie's Illustrated Newspaper*, 13 July 1867. The image preserves characteristics of the original painting, which was later altered by Homer in response to his critics. In particular, he reduced the height of the wheat. This version gives greater emphasis to the symbolism of Death, with the veteran performing the same task in the new field with a scythe among the man-sized grain as he had performed with his rifle—now discarded—on the field of battle.

Library of Congress

By November 1865, just seven months since Appomattox, since the assassination, the results of war seemed too much in doubt. Andrew Johnson had issued his proclamation of amnesty to all but a few former Confederates, an act of generosity ensuring that black Americans would remain economically disadvantaged through the elimination of any real possibility that land reallocation would occur in the South. He had also initiated the process of re-creating Southern state governments, with the result that, by the end of the year, the former rebellious states had reconstituted themselves and selected representatives to the national legislature. With few exceptions, the political leadership of the postwar South looked much the same as it had in 1860. In November, Mississippi created a new body of law designed to replicate the social control of black Americans that had been unquestioned under slavery. Similar "black codes" would emerge in various forms in every Southern state. Not surprisingly, Northerners shared a discontent over Southern responses to the war's conclusion. When this discontent intersected with Northerners' concerns for their interpretation of the war's meaning, when it conflicted with the Cause Victorious, there was no hesitancy in exercising the greatly magnified powers of the federal government.

In December 1868, veterans of four of the Union's armies—the Army of the Tennessee, the Army of the Cumberland, the Army of the Ohio, and the Army of Georgia—gathered together for a reunion in Chicago. General Charles Cruft, formerly of the Army of the Cumberland, stood before the assembled veterans to give voice to, as he entitled it, "The Teachings of the War." Among the facts "settled by the war," he said, "was the mastery of the Federal Government." Essentially preaching to the choir, Cruft continued, "The war determined the Federal Government as the great central controlling power which shall, for all time to come, regulate, within the limits of the written Constitution, the various States of the Union." Cruft noted that before "the Rebellion," most citizens had little contact with the government, nor possessed much awareness of its functioning. "They knew that Congress held annual sessions," he said, "that a President was elected every four years, the Cabinet changed, that the Government transported their letters, and that it held a court in their State." But beyond that, Americans did not interact with the federal government personally: "Comparatively few, away from the seaboard or the larger cities, had ever seen a customs-house, light-house, navy-yard, man-of-war, file of soldiers, or any thing else, except the national flag, which represented the physical being of the General Government." However, Cruft concluded, "The war . . . taught our people the existence of a federal power, and its ability for self-protection, and the general defense."[3]

The federal power that Cruft celebrated made itself felt in myriad ways following the war, encompassing virtually every aspect of American life,[4] but particularly significant to our concerns here are its exertions on behalf of the dead. The postwar actions of both Northern and Southern politicians, civilians, and veterans moved simultaneously toward the shared goal of commemorating the war and their dead and, through that commemoration, toward the construction of a social interpretation of the war and its necessity, even if that goal was not always expressed consciously in those terms. In this process, Northerners had a tremendous advantage. Unlike Southerners, their memories had been legitimated by victory, not called into question by defeat. With the strength of government and the justification of national triumph, Northerners expended enormous energies on honoring their soldier dead and protecting their vision of the war's meaning. In a way, whether former soldiers or not, all were veterans of the Civil War, and they worked together to reshape their new fields of peace ever conscious of the dead.

As the foundation of the war's commemoration, the first order of business was to ensure Union soldiers a decent and honored interment. What had been done in haste under the exigencies of war could now be done with propriety and due respect. The often hurried and unceremonious wartime burials could be rectified in the peace that followed through the expansion and formalization of a national cemetery system that sought to guarantee each Union fatality an eternal rest in ground sanctified to the national mission. The creation of the national cemeteries arose within the military experience of war, but was ultimately the product of both military and civilian authorities. The transition of a loose collection of burial grounds into the National Cemetery System was the result of three related but largely independent actions.

First, the federal government acted to provide the logistical concerns that soldier burials might require. After the War Department issued its orders in 1861 and 1862, which charged commanding officers with the responsibility of establishing burial sites for their men, it became increasingly apparent that the grounds that commanders might select for cemetery purposes were almost always privately owned. This does not seem to have been a concern of Union commanding officers conducting operations on Southern soil during the war; lands needed to bury their dead were simply seized for the purpose. On Northern soil ownership proved a problem, but not an insoluble one. Congress attached a provision to an omnibus bill, passed 17 July 1862, granting the president authority to purchase land for cemeterial purposes where necessary. As a result of this legislation, fourteen existing cemeteries were designated as national cemeteries by the end of 1864. For the most part, these grounds were in Northern states and near troop concentration points. At Alexandria, Virginia, a new cemetery replaced the overburdened burial grounds at the Soldiers' Home Cemetery as the repository for soldiers mustering in and around Washington, D.C. Although closed to further burial, the Soldiers' Home grounds were also incorporated for administrative purposes. Two pre-existing army post graveyards, at Fort Scott and Fort Leavenworth, Kansas, were expanded for troop burials, and the troop

concentration centers of Danville, Indiana, New Albany, Illinois, and Philadelphia were all included. However, the designation of these burial grounds
as national cemeteries did little to change the way they operated individually, but merely indicated federal ownership more than anything else and provided only a loose administrative connection between them.[5]

Second, the impetus toward a more expansive understanding of soldier
burial originated within the military. During the war, battle commanders had
done remarkably well in the organization and implementation of the burial
orders handed down by the War Department. However, on Christmas Day,
1863, Major General George H. Thomas, commanding the Army of the
Cumberland, issued his General Order 296, which directed that "a national
cemetery be founded . . . in commemoration of the battles of Chattanooga,
fought November 23, 24, 25, 26, and 27, and to provide a proper resting-place
for the remains of the brave men who fell upon the fields fought over upon
those days, and for the remains of such as may hereafter give up their lives in
this region in defending their country against treason and rebellion." He further ordered that upon its completion, the bodies of "all now buried in and
around the town [be] removed to that place." In addition to the collection
and interment of the dead, Thomas also proposed "to erect a monument upon
the summit" of the hilltop cemetery, to be made of locally available materials, and that all work on the cemetery and monument "shall be exclusively
done by the troops of the Army of the Cumberland." By this order issued in
the midst of the war, Thomas emphasized the desire to commemorate his
soldier dead as well as ensure their proper, honored burial—two trends that
would dominate all cemetery construction after the war. Thus, national cemeteries moved from a strictly administrative and logistic concern to a commemorative one. Less than a year later, he created another such cemetery on
the battlefield of Stones River.[6]

Third, civilian organizers at state and local levels also exerted themselves
on behalf of the soldier dead. While the government and the military were
largely, but not exclusively, concerned with administration and logistics, from
the beginning civilians had additional concerns beyond the practicalities of
interment. In two places, Gettysburg and Antietam, the activities of civilians
laid important foundations for the Northern postwar commemoration of the
war dead. Pointedly, the different geographic and political contexts of those
two sites pushed the development of these cemeteries in similar, but distinct,
directions. The efforts at Gettysburg were begun and largely completed dur-

ing the war and were therefore shaped by the sensibilities attending that open and continuing conflict. Although conceived during the war, the creation of the Antietam cemetery languished, because of entanglements over title and deeds, and was not really begun until after the war's close. The differences between the efforts of civilians in a Northern state in the midst of war and those in a border state during a contentious peace are reflected in the cemeteries that they created. However, the similarities exhibited by both cemeteries are a testament to the power of Northern interpretations of commemoration and its importance.

Among the many visitors to Gettysburg in the week following the battle was Pennsylvania's governor, Andrew G. Curtin, who was dismayed by the numbers of dead still unburied or only partially buried. The wounded naturally commanded the greater part of all efforts of Gettysburg residents and the numerous volunteers clustered in the small town, including the U.S. Sanitary Commission. It was clear, however, that the community by itself was simply not capable of assuming full responsibility for the soldier dead. The town had possessed only a few small churchyards and but one village burial ground, Evergreen Cemetery, before the war. As soldiers died in the various hospitals, they were buried in small scattered plots. Some were taken to Evergreen for burial, but the keeper of the town's graveyard was away in the war. Still, the president of the Evergreen Cemetery Association ordered the excavation of scores of graves for the soldiers, the work to be done primarily by the keeper's wife, Elizabeth Thorn, and her elderly father. "Yet for all the foul air we two started in," Mrs. Thorn later recalled. "I struck [measured] off the graves and while my father finished one, I had started another." Temporary laborers came to help but quickly fell ill from the noxious air. "And then father and I had to dig on harder again. They kept on buring [*sic*] the soldiers until they had the National Cemetery ready, and in that time we buried one hundred and five soldiers." The toll taken by such labor was high—all the more so for Mrs. Thorn, who had been pregnant throughout the ordeal. "So you may know that it was only excitement that helped me to do all that work, with all that stench. And in three months after I had a dear little baby. But it was not very strong, and from that time on my health failed and for years I was a very sickly woman. In my older days my health has been better, but those hard days have always told on my life."[7] The "excitement" of those days demanded the allocation of most efforts on behalf of those still living. But the demands of the dead were insistent and concern for their well-being uppermost in the minds of many.

Honoring the Civil War Dead

Governor Curtin and others sought solutions to the problems posed by the dead, especially by those soldiers still buried out on the battlefield. The greatest concern was the impermanent nature of grave markings and even of the graves themselves. The battlefield was farmland, and the workings of weather and cultivation were likely to eradicate either the identity of the dead through the loss of grave markers, or the graves themselves. Massachusetts and New York dispatched agents to assist in the care of their soldiers, wounded and dead. Those agents reported the same threats to the identity of the dead that had distressed Curtin. John F. Seymour, the New York agent and brother of the state's governor, delegated an army surgeon, Theodore Dimon, to act as his representative. Among his other duties, Seymour charged Dimon with the improvement of the markings on the headboards of New York soldiers' graves. Dimon responded that he was much concerned about the future safety of these graves. He noted that while Pennsylvania had offered free railway freight for the removal of its sons from the battlefield—thereby minimizing their responsibilities—New York had found that option prohibitively expensive. Still, Dimon recounted, "It seemed wrong to leave the soldier buried like a dead horse, when in another year all marks of his grave would be obliterated by the owner of the soil. It occurred to me as practicable to have a piece of ground purchased for a burial place on or near the battlefield, to which the dead bodies of all our soldiers should be removed and there buried by regiments and states and their graves permanently marked."[8]

At an informal meeting of state representatives and agents, probably held in late July 1863, Dimon recounted the idea. It was seized by David Wills, a local attorney and Governor Curtin's agent on the battlefield. Wills communicated the plan to Curtin, who agreed to its soundness. Under the governor's aegis, Wills negotiated on behalf of the state of Pennsylvania for the purchase of several acres adjoining Gettysburg's Evergreen Cemetery and proposed the other Union states whose sons had been killed assist in the funding and maintenance of a cemetery for the Union dead. The state purchased seventeen acres from David McConaughy for $2,475.87. McConaughy, like Wills a local attorney, served as president of the Evergreen Cemetery Association and had purchased the land as a planned extension to the town's burial grounds.[9] On 15 October 1863, a call for bids was issued on two contracts, the first for the disinterment of the Union soldiers buried on the battlefield, the second for their subsequent reburial in the new cemetery. A Gettysburg resident, F. W. Biesecker, won both contracts with a bid of

$1.59 per body. Removal began 27 October, but an early winter froze the ground, interrupting the work. Hence, the cemetery was scarcely half complete when Lincoln and other dignitaries arrived to dedicate it in November. Completion of both contracts was not reported until 18 March 1864, by which time Biesecker had disinterred and reburied 3,564 soldiers. This number does not represent all the Union soldiers killed in the battle, as many had been shipped to other locations for reburial and some had already been interred in the existing Evergreen Cemetery.[10]

This new cemetery, originally known as Soldiers' National Cemetery, established many precedents for the national commemoration of the dead. Carried out while the war still raged, the civilian efforts that shaped it naturally reflected the concerns of the Union states that funded them. The cemetery at Gettysburg was to be a cemetery for Union soldiers. It was stipulated in the burial contracts that Biesecker would "exhume all bodies designated by the person in charge, and none others; and when ordered, he shall open up graves and trenches for personal inspection of the remains, for the purpose of ascertaining whether they are bodies of Union soldiers, and close them over again when ordered to do so."[11] The name of the cemetery therefore conveyed the same exclusive definition of *national* that had become prevalent in Northern rhetoric, and even preceded those rhetorical patterns later exhibited in the oratory of Lincoln's funeral. The cemetery was *national* in the sense that the states of the Northern Union had funded it and that it was intended for the interment of Union soldiers—those who had died loyal to the nation—alone.

Lincoln certainly recognized this. Although Garry Wills is correct in the emphasis that he places on the Gettysburg Address as a transformative influence on Northern views of the meaning of the war, he underestimates the partisan nature of Lincoln's speech. Wills asserts that "despite verbal gestures to 'that' battle and the men who died 'here,' there are no particulars mentioned by Lincoln—no names of men or sites or units, or even of sides (the Southerners are part of the 'experiment,' not foes mentioned in anger or rebuke)." Yet Lincoln spoke in a particular place at a particular time, specifically in an unfinished cemetery of "*these* dead"—the recently reburied Union dead. No Confederates rested near the speaker's podium. When Lincoln exhorts the rebirth of the nation so that "*these* dead shall not have died in vain" he cannot be speaking of the Confederate dead.[12] Such a rebirth would, in fact, render their deaths futile. Military victory, including the deaths of the enemy, was necessary so that the nation—the Northern perception of that nation—might enjoy such a rebirth. Wills is correct that sectionalism plays no part in the Gettysburg Address, and certainly no vindictiveness can be discerned in Lincoln's speech there, or scarcely anywhere else. Yet the unspoken result of Union victory was Confederate defeat. Spoken in the cemetery grounds, Lincoln's words gave meaning to the deaths of Union soldiers alone. The place of Southerners within the "experiment" was that of a hindrance to be overcome on the way to fulfilling the Northern sense of national destiny.

Samuel Weaver, a local physician and the appointed superintendent of the recovery and reburial process, supervised personally the exploration of nearly six thousand graves on the Gettysburg battlefield. Those identified as Union soldiers were taken up, coffined, and removed to the cemetery. Those identified as Confederate were reburied where they lay. In his report on his activities, Weaver acknowledged the importance of making accurate identifications:

> It may be asked how we could distinguish the bodies of our own men from those of the rebels. This was generally very easily done. In the first place, as a general rule, the rebels never went into battle with the United States coat on. They sometimes stole the pantaloons from our dead and wore them, but not the coat. The rebel clothing is made of cotton, and is of a grey or brown color.... The clothing of our men is of wool, and blue; so that the body having the coat of our uniform on was a pretty sure indication that he was a Union soldier. But if the body were without a coat, then there were other infallible marks. The shoes of the rebels were differently made from those of our soldiers. If these failed, then the underclothing was the next part examined. The rebel cotton undershirt gave proof of the army to which he belonged.

"In no instance was a body allowed to be removed which had any portion of rebel clothing on it," Weaver assured the committee. He had executed his charge with "infallible accuracy." "And," he concluded, "I most conscientiously assert, that I firmly believe that there has not been a single mistake made in the removal of the soldiers to the cemetery by taking the body of a rebel for a Union soldier."[13] Weaver's painstaking description of the process of identification, along with his claim of infallibility, indicates the power of the need to segregate the loyal from the disloyal dead.

Hired laborers disinter the remains of a Union soldier under the supervision of Samuel Weaver, right. Once encoffined, the bodies removed from this cemetery were transported to the newly established Soldiers' National Cemetery on the Gettysburg battlefield. Taken in early 1864, this image documents the process that most of the Union dead would undergo during the creation of the seventy-three national cemeteries established by the federal government between 1861 and 1870.
PictureHistory

In all, there is very little record of any dissent to this seemingly automatic assumption that the cemetery would be for Union soldiers alone. In another context, Winthrop Jordan has called such a response an "unthinking decision," the reflexive, automatic certainty that comes from a predisposition of mind. The wrenching pain of war created such predispositions. There was some evidence of concern for the enemy dead, but no suggestion that they should lie in the Soldiers' National Cemetery. Early in 1864, an unsigned article in a local paper observed that "there appears to be considerable feeling in and around Gettysburg, that a place be set apart for the burial of the Confederate dead who are now buried promiscuously over the battlefield, or in the vicinity." The effects of weather and the impending cultivation of fields threatened to erase the grave markings. The appeal was made to "common humanity," but not without qualifications; the removal should be to "some spot, not in or around *our* own National Cemetery," and "*our* state should not make the purchase, nor should it be expected." "But," the writer concluded, "if Southern people should express the desire and would carry it to completion, we should say—let it be done for the sake of *our* common humanity."[14] As it did in the Lincoln funeral sermons, the possessive *our* confounds the overt intent—on behalf of *our* common humanity (North and South), Southern soldiers should be decently interred, but not in *our* national cemetery. Of course, what part of this suggestion stemmed from sympathy for the men killed and what part from farmers simply wishing their lands cleared of the war dead is unknowable.

Several years later, General George Meade, who had commanded the Union forces during the battle, uttered similar sentiments at the dedication of the monumental centerpiece of the Soldiers' National Cemetery. Despite the fears expressed five years earlier, the Confederate graves were apparently not erased so quickly from view. "When I contemplate this field," Meade said, "I see here and there the marks of hastily dug trenches in which repose the dead against whom we fought. . . . Why should we not collect them in some suitable place?" Meade, like the author of the newspaper item, carefully defined what he intended: "I do not ask that a monument be erected over them; I do not ask that we should in any way endorse their cause or their conduct, or entertain other than feelings of condemnation for their course; but they are dead! They have gone before their Maker to be judged. In all civilized countries it is the usage to bury the dead with decency and respect, and even to fallen enemies respectful burial is accorded in death." But the issues of respect were complicated, for Meade and virtually everyone else, by the war's memory and by Northern perceptions of Southern intractability in Reconstruction. Suggesting that decent interment be provided raised the questions of responsibility, expense, and whether decent interment could be interpreted as homage. Meade tried to specify his intentions: "Some persons may be designated by the Government to collect these neglected bones and bury them without commemorating monuments, simply indicating that below sleep misguided men who fell in battle for a cause over which we triumphed." He also recognized the scope of the problem, stating, "I earnestly hope that this suggestion may have some influence throughout our broad land, for this is only one of a hundred crowded battle fields."[15]

A key element in Meade's comments, and in those of others expressing similar concerns, is the association of proper, decent interment with the possibility that such burial implied honoring the dead. While there is nothing intrinsic in the act of interment that suggests doing honor to the dead, Northerners embarked on an aggressive campaign of securing the proper and honored interment of the Union dead immediately following the war's end and throughout a period lasting more than five years. Throughout that process, Northerners certainly expressed the idea that caring for the dead, even years later, involved honoring their sacrifice. In this context, the disinterment, relocation, and reburial of the Confederate dead was, in many people's minds, equated with that very kind of honor that both the newspaper article and Meade were quick to deny. These careful definitions of intent were necessary in a cultural and social environment where the burial of the dead had become the act of commemorating and interpreting the war that had exacted their deaths.

An article on the Gettysburg burial ground published in the December 1865 issue of the veteran's periodical *Hours at Home* reveals the process of interpretation as it unfolded and suggests the significance that would eventually be laid on all national cemeteries:

> None but loyal soldiers of the Union lie here; and would all that such who fell upon this high field of the nation's honor might have been gathered into this most honorable sepulchre! About a thousand, however, had been removed by friends to distant burial places before the plan of a National Cemetery was suggested. But none who should look upon this peaceful and well-ordered cemetery would now desire to remove a soldier-friend from its hallowed associations. . . . This intermingling of States in the ashes of their dead, without regard to sectional divisions, is itself a symbol and a prophecy of the reality and perpetuity of that Union which was here redeemed and sealed by so much precious blood. No fratricidal hand can hereafter efface from our history the memory of Gettysburgh.[16]

At this point, months after war's end, old and new perceptions of the nation mingle. In this author's mind, the new nationalism is represented by the separate sovereign "States" of the North allowing the "intermingling" of their sons in death. Since "none but loyal" Union soldiers are buried at Gettysburg, the "sectional divisions" of which the author speaks can only refer to the Northeastern and Western states, sections of industrial and agricultural production. With the interment of the dead, the old concept of sovereign states within the nation gives way to "a symbol and a prophecy of the reality" that the war has produced: a federal union of states subordinate to the nation, one redeemed through blood and sanctified by death. In an entirely secular context, the providential covenant has been secured through the deaths of soldiers and symbolized by their burial. But, although dedicated to the nation as a whole, it was a burial without Southerners.

Nothing seems to have come of the sentiment to reinter the Confederates on the field of Gettysburg, not even serious discussion. The Southern dead were left in their mass trench graves for several years following the battle. Earlier, in 1866, the Evergreen Cemetery Association had set aside a portion of their field for some Confederate interments yet reserved the right to prohibit "improper" monumental inscriptions. The number and locations of those interments are now lost.[17] In sum, the drive toward honoring the lives and deaths of Union soldiers seems to have necessitated, perhaps understandably, the neglect of the Confederate soldier dead at Gettysburg. Although this separatism also dominated the organization of the Antietam cemetery, in Maryland the tides of controversy were much stronger. While no significant protest emerged in Pennsylvania over the segregation of the Union and Confederate dead, in Maryland—which had supplied troops to both sides of the war and had a long history of sympathy and support for Southern causes and the Confederacy—the issue haunted the development of the cemetery for years.

The battle of Antietam on 17 September 1862 remains to the present day the single bloodiest day in American military history, yet the establishment of the cemetery was delayed for several years, due in part to a clouded title to a portion of the proposed site.[18] Despite the legal entanglements, in 1864 the Maryland State Legislature made appropriations for the cemetery and incorporated its Trustees. Section 2 of that enacting legislation states, in part, that "the bodies of those in the army of General Lee who fell, shall be buried in said cemetery in a separate part of the cemetery from those of General McClellan's army who fell." A year later, apparently because of administrative difficulties not anticipated in the original law, a second, revised version of the act redefining the Antietam National Cemetery Board of Trustees was passed, superseding the first. Still, the provision for Confederate burial remained. Section 2 of the revised law stated that the cemetery was "for the burial and final resting place of the remains of the soldiers who fell at the battle of Antietam or at other points North of the Potomac river during the invasion of Lee." In case of ambiguity, section 4 stipulated that "the remains of the soldiers of the Confederate army are to be buried in a part of the grounds separate from those of the Union army."[19] On this basis, Maryland appropriated $7,000 for the purchase of the land and for the erection of a stone wall enclosure. As at Gettysburg, monies were solicited from the other Union states whose soldiers had fought at Antietam, in amounts proportional to their representation in Congress. Two local residents, Aaron Good and Joseph A. Gill, had recorded the burial sites scattered across the battlefield's acreage, and their information was invaluable to the planning of the future cemetery.[20] With title finally perfected in 1865, the land was purchased and the stone wall constructed. The next step was to remove the bodies from the field and inter them in the cemetery. On the basis of a plot plan designed by Augustin B. Biggs, who served as general superintendent of the cemetery and trustee from the state of Maryland, burial parties from the War Department began the arduous duty of collecting the Union dead from the Antietam battlefield and reinterring them within the cemetery. As work progressed, the project was enlarged to include the corpses from surrounding battles, such as South Mountain and Fox's Gap. By July 1867, nearly five thousand reburials had been performed under the watchful eye of the superintendent, who reported to the trustees that he personally "held the tape over every coffin, and recorded in his book the number, name and date of death before the first spade of earth had been replaced."[21] With the cemetery apparently nearing completion, although not yet landscaped, the trustees decided to dedicate their efforts on 17 September 1867, the fifth anniversary of the battle.

The ceremonies were well attended by notable dignitaries—President Andrew Johnson and members of his cabinet, Generals Grant, McClellan, and Burnside, the chief justice and other members of the Supreme Court, senators, representatives, governors, and mayors. It was almost certainly the richest assembly of government officials since the close of the war. Other than residents of Maryland, no Southerners seem to have been invited or to have attended. The governor of Maryland, Thomas Swann, welcomed the assembled guests. He pointed out that after Maryland's initial efforts toward a cemetery, "our sister States [were] invoked to lend their aid in throwing around it a national interest." He pointed out that the "flag which floats over us to-day is the flag of our Union. . . . The star of this great Republic is again in the ascendant." The soldiers who had died "sacrificed their lives for their country, and are sleeping upon this field."[22] The now-familiar theme of a possessive qualification of nation and nationalism was again readily apparent. As had Lincoln, Swann dedicated a cemetery containing only Union dead, despite the requirements of the enabling state legislation. Apparently Maryland too had disowned its relations to other Southern states, at least rhetorically, for they could not be included among the "sister States" who had contributed to the cemetery and lent to it "a national interest."

Swann's predecessor, former Maryland Governor A. W. Bradford, continued this theme in his keynote address. He recalled that a note of thanks from some unionist Maryland citizens had been forwarded to General McClellan after the battle. Bradford remembered that in his reply, the general had expressed the hope "that no Rebel army would again pollute our State." Governor Bradford quickly added his own hope that the wartime "passion or policy" of sectional animosity that had inevitably been produced by the war, "if they still linger, . . . should find no place on such an occasion as this." Nevertheless, in his remarks at the dedication Bradford spoke consistently of "loyal hearts" and "patriot soldiers," of "departed patriots" and "*our* soldiers' [*sic*] dead." He said that "no people and no party that ever ventured" to express sentiments contrary to the Constitution "could, unless blinded by insane passion, have foreseen aught but ultimate ruin and annihilation." The cemetery and its monuments would communicate to future generations the "spontaneous and unaffected gratitude and devotion of the people." "Thus in our hearts would we enshrine the memory of the Union soldiers." But, Bradford cautioned, "Think not for a moment, my friends, that I am about to desecrate the solemnity of such an occasion by any discussion of the partisan topics of the day." He continued: "May not imagination, as it seeks to portray the future of this great American Republic, without any overstraining of its powers, see the coming time, distant it possibly may be, but none the less desirable or certain, when her sons from every State shall seek this little hamlet for its hallowed memories of the past, and coming from the South as well as the North, reunited in fact as well as theory, in affection as well as formality, shall stand here together as pilgrims at a common shrine."[23] This appeal for a future when, out of "affection" for their "hallowed memories of the past," Southerners would gather reverently at a Union cemetery is as expansive a statement of the Cause Victorious as can be found.

In the introductory remarks to the volume published to commemorate the ceremonies, the anonymous author recounted how all civilized nations set aside "suitable resting places" for their dead and how it was not just a privilege but a duty when the dead, "with unselfish disinterestedness, have rendered the offering of their lives as a sacrifice on the altar of their country." The author continued: "Animated by such sentiments as these, as well as by the dictates of a common humanity, the originators of the Antietam National Cemetery relaxed no efforts in the accomplishment of their design, to locate on this *Aceldama,* which is truly a bloody field, a suitable spot for the establishment of this national Necropolis."[24] These remarks are extremely suggestive. The stressed reference to *aceldama,* Hebrew for "bloody field," held powerful resonances for a people well schooled in biblical verse. According to the Book of Matthew, Judas attempted to return the thirty pieces of silver that he had taken for the betrayal of Christ. When he was rebuffed, Judas cast the silver to the floor of the temple and left to his own self-destruction. The priests collected the money but were unable to place it within the temple's treasury because it was tainted by blood. So they used it to purchase the field of a potter for use as a cemetery, "to bury strangers in" (Matt. 27: 3–10). Scripture relates that this field was well known to all in Jerusalem (Acts 1: 19).[25]

With this simple reference, about an ostensibly nonpartisan dedication, the associations that the writer called forth were pointed ones. Antietam had certainly been a bloody field, yet that it was purchased, metaphorically, through betrayal, much as the original Aceldama had been purchased through the betrayal of Christ, placed a particular emphasis on the ceremonies of the day and on the dead that they honored. The commemoration was, despite its avowed nonsectional bias, pronounced over the dead of the Union army alone. Cast in the role of Judas Iscariot, rebel soldiers sacrificed their own lives on the bloody field that they had metaphorically purchased through their rebellious betrayal, much as the Bible relates that Judas metaphorically "purchased a field with the reward of iniquity; and falling headlong, he burst asunder in the midst, and all his bowels gushed out" (Acts 1: 18). It is tempting to speculate on the further associations that readers might have recalled, remembering the close identification of Lincoln and the nation, of Lincoln and Christ.

President Johnson's brief closing comments seemed to sense the general tenor of the day's orations. He would not speak at length, he said, but hoped that "we may follow the example which has been so eloquently alluded to this afternoon, and which has been so clearly set by the illustrious dead. . . . Would to God we of the living could imitate their example, as they lay sleeping in peace in their tombs, and live together in friendship and peace."[26] This was of course impossible, despite the endorsement of the ideal; the designs of the trustees had given many months' effort to ensure that the Union and Confederate dead did not sleep side by side. The Union soldiers lay within stone walls, in neatly arcing rows; the Confederates remained scattered across farmland and churchyard. The example to be taken from the dead was continued sectionalism.

The minutes of the Board of Trustees meeting that had preceded the dedication ceremonies make no mention of the provisions originally set out to bury Southern soldiers, nor does the board president's report of the same date.[27] Those provisions were, however, the first order of new business at the first meeting after the dedication, on 5 December 1867, almost certainly inspired by the contrast between intent and actuality highlighted during the dedication. Thomas Boullt, from Maryland, called the attention of the trustees to section 4 of the 1865 revised incorporating act and urged that some action be taken to carry it into effect. With this opening, John Jay, from New York, took the opportunity to read a letter from his governor, Robert Fenton, reviewing the legislative history of the cemetery, emphasizing the important provisions, and raising some mitigating circumstances. Because the trustees had solicited and relied on War Department burial teams for the reburial process, Fenton acknowledged, the federal government was responsible for the selective reinterment. Throughout the five years following the war, the U.S. Quartermaster Department had detailed burial squads to facilitate the identification and relocation of Union soldiers throughout the country. As a cost-saving strategy, the Board of Trustees had requested the Quartermaster's assistance with the relocation of bodies at Antietam, but, as the federal government's burial squads concerned themselves only with the Union soldiers throughout the nation, they relocated only Union soldiers at Antietam. Still, Fenton chided, the trustees had made no effort to solicit government assistance in carrying out their charge to inter both Union and Confederate soldiers. It was true, he noted, that "the States recently in rebellion had not . . . assumed their share of the necessary expenses," but Maryland and West Virginia had, as both had contributed native sons to the Confederacy. It was, for Fenton, a matter of good faith toward Maryland, especially, for the trustees "to effectuate as far as lies in their power the known intent of the [1865] act."[28]

Fenton summed up by admitting it was true that "a strong local and individual feeling in the neighborhood of Antietam and other parts of Maryland, naturally engendered by the invasion, may have created some indifference in regard to the confederate dead and an indisposition to see them buried side by side with those who died in defence of our nationality. But it is confidently believed that no such feeling pervades the breasts of the American people, or the surviving officers and soldiers of the Union Army."[29] Fenton's impression that there did not exist any widespread antipathy toward the Southern dead is striking, especially given the recent months of work and organization at Antietam. Such a sentiment recalled the words, if not the intent, of Governor Bradford at the dedication three months earlier: "To-day nothing perhaps could sooner reawaken a national spirit in the heart of the South, than the thought that representatives of the Northern States were gathering the remains of its fallen sons for interment in our National Cemetery; and in future days when our country is one, not alone in its boundaries, but in spirit and affection, . . . the Cemetery at Antietam . . . will have a common interest for descendants of those who died' on either side, in that sad and memorable civil war." Such sentiments were commendable in their generosity, but they may have been poor descriptions of the mood of the board or the states. After reading Fenton's letter, John Jay then offered a resolution to the assembled board, asserting that the Confederate dead would be buried in "the Southern portion of the grounds not now occupied, and separate from the ground devoted to the burial of the Union dead." Three of the assembled board members—representatives of West Virginia, Minnesota, and Ohio—voted to table the motion, but were defeated. In the resulting vote, the resolution passed nine to two, with only West Virginia and Ohio voting against it.[30]

The resolution did not go unnoticed. The *Washington Chronicle* reported the board's intention, commenting that the "Northern States having dead interred in the cemetery have made liberal appropriations for the purpose of beautifying the grounds, and it is now expected that some of the late rebellious states will make similar appropriations." The response from New Jersey was more heated. Governor Marcus L. Ward retorted, "The National Cemeteries are consecrated to the loyalty of the nation, and those who died for their country should not, in my opinion, share a common grave with those who would have destroyed it." Another newspaper commentary said that the trustees intended "to inter side by side with loyal men who perished to save the Government the traitors who sought to destroy it." In support of his opposition to such burials, the anonymous writer raged: "It is not out of place to state that when the same cemeteries were first set apart, rebels residing in the locality covertly and maliciously violated the graves of Union soldiers, ploughed up and carried their bones to dust mills to make manure, and offered every indignity which their deviltry could invent to insult the upholders of a victorious Government." Once again, the perceptions of atrocities against the dead continued to fuel the animus of sectionalism. The *Hagerstown (Md.) State Guard* reported that "If the commissioners . . . should decide to insult the memory of the loyal dead in burying rebels by their side, . . . the commissioner of Pennsylvania will recommend to the Legislature of that State, through Governor Geary, the justice of removing the bones of all Pennsylvanians buried at Antietam to the battle-field of Gettysburg."[31]

Of the Northern states contributing funds to the cemetery, Vermont, New Hampshire, Delaware, Illinois, Michigan, West Virginia, and Iowa had not yet forwarded their appropriations to the board by the time of its next meeting, 6–7 May 1868. In response to Jay's resolution, Michigan refused to pay at all, and Pennsylvania held back its next installment. The board sent those states' legislatures copies of the original incorporating legislation, the basis on which those appropriations had been first solicited. Maryland even promised another $5,000 for the additional burials. But the matter was growing more problematic, not less. At the 6–7 May meeting, the president of the board, Augustin Biggs of Maryland, reported that the space enclosed by the stone wall was insufficient to bury the Confederate dead. With further contributions unlikely, less than $1,500 remained in the treasury. The board voted to halve the salaries of the president and the secretary/treasurer and then passed a second resolution defining its intent to purchase additional grounds adjoining the cemetery for the interment of the Southern dead outside the existing walls.[32]

Meanwhile, Union veterans weighed in on the issue, approaching, not the board, but Washington. A group of Union veterans petitioned Congress for relief from the provisions of the Maryland state charter that insisted on the burial of Confederates within the cemetery. In reply, the Committee on Military Affairs ultimately reported that the originating laws were quite specific, and "whether the States [solicited for funds] were deceived or not your committee have no means of knowing, but if they were deceived it must have been through inexcusable negligence on the part of their authorities, as full and explicit notice was contained in the charter." The matter was tabled and the committee excused. Its most telling comment was perhaps its first: "The cemetery at Antietam is not and never has been, except in name, a national cemetery."[33]

By now, the board was completely mired in the problem, with no easy solution in view. When the trustees met in Philadelphia, Colonel W. H. Grimshaw of Delaware successfully urged that the matter be postponed. A second meeting three weeks later in Washington, D.C., brought support for the idea from an unexpected source. A letter from seventeen former Union officers expressed their belief that "the act of collecting the remains of the rebel dead and giving them decent interment, *in a separate enclosure,* would be in harmony with our feelings[;] it would not, in our opinion, be conferring honor on the rebel dead, or desecrating the honored memory of our fallen comrades who now sleep on those fields." New York representative John Jay, now president of the Board of Trustees, suggested that the matter of Southern burial was open to discussion. The ensuing conversation was not recorded, but, "after a full and free exchange of views," the matter was unanimously postponed once again.[34] On 2 June 1869, another attempt was made at enacting the resolution to purchase separate grounds for Confederate reburial, but a substitute resolution offered by G. L. Cranmer of West Virginia was tabled without recorded comment on the motion of John J. Bagley of Michigan.

The board continued to languish financially because of withheld funds and seemed unable to take direct action of any significance on the issue. A delegation was dispatched to the governor of Pennsylvania, who gave his assurances that as soon as the burial of Confederates had been resolved, presumably to Pennsylvania's liking, he would hasten the remaining amount of the appropriation due the board. A letter sent shortly thereafter urging that the payments be made informed the governor that the matter had been "settled practically, in opposition to their burial in any portion of the Cemetery and in opposition to the purchase of additional grounds." It is unclear on what basis these presentations were made, for at the next meeting the issue was again addressed as if nothing had been settled. A proposition that Maryland be asked either to alter or to repeal the offending portions of the 1865 law went down to defeat, as did a third attempt to resolve the purchase of additional land for the cemetery.[35] Although there is no record of further discussion or action, the issue continued to haunt the board.

What is so surprising is the tortured nature of the dispute. The problem of Confederate burial space could hardly have been unanticipated. Augustin Biggs, who served as both general superintendent and first president of the board, had laid out the original plot map and had "held the tape" over every coffin as it had been buried. Even before the first body was interred, the Board knew an approximate number for both Union and Confederate burials from the records maintained by local residents after the battle. This foreknowledge seems to have had little effect on the configuration of the burials. While pleasing to the eye, the arrangement of Union graves was hardly space efficient. Additionally, when the board sought a resolution to Confederate exclusion, the only position ever suggested for the Confederate graves was the southern portion of the field, but the arc of Union soldiers was placed closest to the southern wall, making this unlikely from the first interments. There may have been enough room for the Southern burials along the northern wall, but this would have placed the Confederates closer to the main entrance than the Union soldiers. If this was discussed at board meetings it was not recorded, but the result of such action may have been unacceptable to many. Finally, Governor Fenton's earlier point was cogent: the Board had solicited the assistance of the War Department to provide the labor for the relocation process, and that labor, at Antietam and everywhere else, was on behalf of Federal soldiers alone—a fact the board must have known before seeking their help. Consciously or not, it seems that the board had acted from the first, despite Maryland state law, to neglect Confederate burials. By the time it became a publicly disputed issue, the matter was really beyond remedy. No Confederates were ever buried at, or even near, Antietam National Cemetery. As the years passed and the Confederate graves deteriorated, Maryland again prevailed on Aaron Good, this time with the assistance of Moses Poffinberger, to catalog, remound, and if possible identify the graves of the Southern soldiers who remained on the field. In 1870, in response to the "persistent refusal of the Trustees of the 'Antietam National Cemetery'" to bury Confederates, the Maryland legislature acted to create a second, separate cemetery some miles away. On the assumption of the Antietam burial grounds within the National Cemetery System in 1875, it was quietly noted that the Confederate dead had been removed from the battlefield and "buried near Hagerstown."[36]

The efforts of the federal burial details at Antietam represented the merest fraction of the largest and most intensive government peacetime efforts following the Civil War. With the advent of peace, new concerns about the dead arose in the halls of the War Department, which continued to act on its orders to ensure the decent interment of Union soldiers. Officers of the Quartermaster Department, into whose jurisdiction fell the disposition of the soldier dead, began in 1865 to assess the conditions of Union burials throughout the country and plan for their improvement. In October 1865, long after Gettysburg's cemetery was completed, but before Antietam's burial grounds had really been begun, Quartermaster General Montgomery C. Meigs called for his officers to investigate and report on the "*localities* and *condition* of *cemeteries,* with reference, especially, to their exact *location,* condition, place of deposit, and condition of records, with recommendations of the means necessary to provide for the preservation of the remains from desecration; and whether the *site* should be continued, and the land purchased, or whether the bodies should be removed to some permanent cemetery near."[37] The execution of this order revealed the terrible extent of the dead strewn across the American landscape.

Union investigators were confronted with 300,000 Union deaths scattered across the Eastern United States, from New York to Florida and as far west as Oklahoma and Texas. There did exist natural points of concentration: notable battlefields, like Shiloh and Fredericksburg; the grounds surrounding long-established hospital sites, like those around Washington, D.C.; and the landscape of the yearlong siege of Petersburg and Richmond. Between these points, however, bodies were dispersed—in small groups, by ones and twos, clustered in someone's farmyard, huddled together in a corner of a civilian cemetery, at the foot of a notable roadside tree. Undaunted, the Quartermaster Corps continued to operate under its wartime directive to "lay off . . . some suitable spot" and to gather the dead together.

The motivations to collect and reinter the Union dead were similar to the concerns expressed by civilians in Gettysburg and Antietam. In the first instance, the hasty burials that prevailed throughout the war resulted in graves that were vulnerable to decay. The fragile headboards that marked most identified graves consisted usually of only a bit of planking with pencil markings and would not endure through much weather. Also, as at Gettysburg and Antietam, farmers needed to work their lands, and even with the best of intentions graves could be obliterated. But the work of the Quartermaster Department indicates that another motivation held sway over even these concerns. The fear was, not just of inadvertent loss, but also, as Meigs's order indicates, of the intentional desecration of Union graves in the South.

Rumors of grave desecration ignited a furor of activity on the part of Congress and the War Department. In the spring of 1866, Congress ordered the investigation of the rumored violation of Union graves in the vicinity of Atlanta. The answering report reveals the Quartermaster Department already in place and meeting the challenges of proper interment. As of 18 April 1866, the commanding officer in Atlanta reported that "all Union dead remain where they were buried," continuing: "No graves have been ploughed over so far as can be ascertained. An order from General Thomas forbidding this desecration has been distributed throughout the district; and all parties seem disposed to preserve what records remain." Additionally: "It is thought that there need be no apprehension that full justice will not be done to the graves of our soldiers in Georgia."[38] The anxieties in the War Department, in Congress, and throughout the military itself, clearly stemmed from fears for the deceased, and their efforts were expressly motivated by the desire to protect them from those who might wish to obliterate their graves. The graves of American soldiers had been collected and protected in Mexico a decade before the Civil War. For the exact same motivations, the War Department and Congress acted after the Civil War to protect the Union dead from another hostile, foreign people—Southerners. From 1866 through 1868, officers and work crews from the Quartermaster Department fanned out across the South. Their efforts began with the difficult task of locating the myriad graves scattered across the countryside, often on private land. E. B. Whitman, an officer with the Army of the Cumberland and afterward attached to the Quartermaster Department, tried to relate the scope of his activities to those veterans who had assembled in Chicago at the meeting of the four armies in December 1868. "To be of practical value," he said, "for the purpose designed, it would require not only a minute examination of every battle and skirmish ground, but a thorough, systematic exploration of all the various routes of our armies, their places of rendezvous, and of encampment; the locations of hospitals, public and private burial places, door yards, gardens, orchards, fields, and woods, from the Mississippi river to the Atlantic, and from the Ohio to the Gulf."[39]

On 1 March 1866, Whitman and his ten-man team set out from Nashville, on horseback with pack mules, to scour the countryside for Union graves. Over the next nine months, their investigation ranged from Fort Donelson, Vicksburg, Corinth, and Shiloh east to Atlanta, Andersonville, and other locations along Sherman's March to the Sea. As an example, Whitman described his crew's activities at Shiloh:

The entire party formed in manner of skirmish line, at short distances from each other, passed and repassed in line over the entire extent of the field, sweeping it in belts or swaths, pausing at every appearance of a grave, to notice its location, and to copy the inscription, if any. Seven days were thus occupied by the whole party on this field alone. No less than four hundred miles of travel for one man were accomplished, resulting in the discovery of one thousand eight hundred and seventy-four graves, of which six hundred and twenty were identified at the time. These graves were distributed in one hundred and seventy-eight localities, of which twenty-nine were regimental groups.[40]

Similarly, Captain Jason M. Moore performed much the same tasks on the battlefields of the Wilderness and of Spotsylvania Courthouse, although he took as his task to inter properly any soldier's remains his crew came across. As he and his men combed the landscape, "the remains of all soldiers, both Union and rebel, [were] interred, and headboards, with the name, rank, and regiment, placed at each grave, (with some exceptions in cases of rebels,) when it was possible to identify the deceased." Although this selective treatment sounds harsh when stated so bluntly, Moore also reported that "it was no unusual occurrence to observe the bones of our men close to the abatis of the enemy; and in one case several skeletons of our soldiers were found in [the enemy's] trenches." Movement from these battlegrounds had been swift, and apparently no local civilians had worked to inter the Union dead. But despite the circumstances the discovery of so many neglected remains no doubt inspired the antipathy of the workmen. "The bones of these men were gathered from the ground where they fell," Moore continued, "having never been interred; and by exposure to the weather for more than a year all traces of their identity were entirely obliterated."[41]

Every avenue was exploited. Circulars were distributed and reprinted in the newspapers asking for any information that would direct the work crews to the graves of Union soldiers. In the Shenandoah Valley, local residents were paid a bounty for bodies that they disinterred and brought to federal authorities. Jennie Friend, who lived in the vicinity of Petersburg and Poplar Grove, Virginia, remembered, "The summer of 1866 was a time of searching through the country for the Union dead, to place in the cemetery. Five dollars was given for every collection of bones with a skull." As bounties were successfully received on the presentation of only the long bones and skull and sometimes the skull alone, many wartime burials remained in place to be discovered

Honoring the Civil War Dead

years later by archaeologists who puzzled over the headless corpses.[42] How many Southern skulls were turned in for the cash award and now lie identified only as "Unknown" in a national cemetery is impossible to ascertain. In Fredericksburg, Virginia, one resident recalled: "[Federal officers] inquire[d] as to the burial places of the Federal soldiers whom I had found dead upon my lot and in my house after the battle. I told him that I had found one Federal soldier stretched on one of my beds. In my parlor, lying on the floor, was another whose entire form left its imprint in blood on the floor,—as may be seen to this day. . . . I had all these bodies, and five or six others found in my yard, buried in one grave on the wharf."[43]

Thousands of Union soldiers were in like manner found, disinterred from their original graves and reburied within central locations that would eventually be subsumed under the National Cemetery System. This process was very specific, disinterring and collecting only the Union dead, to honor and protect only their graves. As a result of these efforts, virtually every Union soldier buried in the South was disinterred, coffined, and reinterred in a national cemetery. Each cemetery sat at the center of a collection circle, with spokes radiating outward to touch distant burial sites. Whitman reported that the cemetery at Knoxville contained remains from 174 other separate locations, Nashville from 251, Shiloh from 565, and Marietta from a staggering 1,970.[44]

Because during the war combat was concentrated in Southern states, and because these were the areas of most concern to those worried about proper respect being paid to Union soldiers, the great majority of burial efforts took place in the states of the former Confederacy. But the efforts to create cemeteries in the South for Union soldiers alone were often troubled. Southerners were at times resentful of the efforts expended on Union but not Confederate soldiers. In his survey trips through Mississippi, Whitman remarked that resistance to government actions increased the further north in the state he traveled: "The state of feeling is such, in Northern Mississippi, that the results of my investigations on the routes of the roads to Grenada, are given with some doubt, as to their entire accuracy. At all places we visit, it becomes necessary to seek more or less aid and information from resident citizens; but in the region alluded to, there seemed to be no disposition shown to render any assistance or to furnish any information." The former slaves were, according to Whitman, the "only reliable source of information" concerning the location of the Union dead; few other Southerners were helpful. "At Holly Springs," he wrote, "the person whom I sent down to make investigations, was openly insulted in the street, and it was only by exhibiting his weapons and showing a disposition to use them, if necessary, that he was allowed to pass unmolested." Whitman had little better luck in Oxford, Mississippi, a town about thirty miles south of Holly Springs that had been occupied briefly by Union forces in December 1862: "At Oxford, the seat of the State University, the elegant buildings of which were spared by Genl. Grant, and which is now in full operation, with some two hundred (200) students and with chairs filled by Ex rebel officers[,] the Post Master said that he knew of no Federal graves; and if he did, he should not dare to be seen pointing them out. In explanation, he stated that although for nineteen years a resident of that place, all of his old friends had deserted him on account of his having taken the *oath* required to enable him to hold his office; and that recently, he had received a letter requesting himself and family to absent themselves from *Church.*" Even without the postmaster's assistance, Whitman located at least thirty-five Union soldiers, buried in the university's Civil War cemetery or in the vicinity of the town.[45]

In addition to a general reluctance on the part of local citizens to assist in the process, burial efforts were also hampered because government agents often found it difficult to procure suitable land. This was largely due to the fact that, after President Johnson's 29 May 1865 order of general amnesty, even formerly disloyal Southerners retained their property. Several military officers requested the authority to seize "the burial grounds *used during the war* as PRIZE OF WAR." An interesting alternative was the proposal that Andrew Jackson's Hermitage be commandeered to serve as a cemetery for Union dead. Only its remoteness made the plan unworkable: "Otherwise . . . there would be a certain fitness in the homestead of Jackson being the resting-place of those who laid down their lives to perpetuate the Union."[46]

Not all Southerners were disinclined to assist the burial details and surveyors. Whitman made special note of a young woman, Emma Williams of Jackson, Tennessee, "who, although the daughter of a rebel father, devotes herself to the care of the graves of our fallen soldiers, replacing the fallen headboards, and scattering bouquets and fresh flowers upon the graves." Whitman also noted that Williams, "when in a pensive mood," had once requested of her mother, "'When I die bury me where the Union soldiers lie.'" In another notable example, local citizens objected to the process of removing bodies from their midst. In the inspection report of the National Cemeteries for 1869, the inspector recorded that it was the intention of the Quartermaster Department to remove the 124 Union soldiers from Baxter Springs, Kansas, to the national cemetery at Springfield, Missouri. However, "the citizens petitioned the government to let them remain, as [the soldiers] were generally citizens of Kansas, belonging to the body-guard and band of General Blunt, which was attacked by the rebel Quantrell." The petition was granted, and the local residents of Baxter Springs set aside land for the burial, conveying it without charge to the government, and in so doing preserving their connection, geographic and symbolic, with their dead.[47]

The work of the Quartermaster Department documented the worst imaginings of the Northern people. As Whitman reported from near Vicksburg, Mississippi: "I have counted as many as seven skeletons heaped promiscuously together in one pile, which had at different times been turned up by the ploughshare of the farmer, more eager to realize bales of cotton than regardful of the claims of humanity, or in awe of military orders to be enforced before civil tribunals." At Millikin's Bend, he wrote, "As I have been informed, a planter by the name of Jones has levelled an entire grave yard to enlarge the area of his cotton patch, and in the immediate vicinity of Vicksburg a race course has been constructed over the graves of Union soldiers." In his field reports, Whitman continued to find fault with Southerners who impeded his work, but he also tried consistently to praise any assistance that he received. With heavy irony, he recorded that "I have noted many instances tending to show, that the tender mercies of those lately in rebellion, towards our dead, partake much of the spirit that prompted those acts of barbarism at Andersonville, Fort Pillow and [Tishomingo] Creek." But he did admit, "Many individual exceptions to these remarks I know to exist."[48] Whitman had obviously contributed a great deal personally to the government's goals of securing and honoring the Union soldier dead. Years later, in his remarks before the Army Reunion, he stated more generally that the work of the burial details "revealed the sad fact, and brought it to notice, that the entire country over which the war had extended its ravages, was one interminable graveyard, and it early deepened and extended the conviction already felt by many, that it was the duty of Government to assume, without delay, the place of friends and relatives, and with tender care collect together and afford proper protection to the remains of those who had fallen in so noble a service, beyond the reach or care of friends."[49]

But the goal of government interceding on behalf of family had not been anticipated in the Omnibus Bill of 1862. Indeed, much of the work of the

Quartermaster Department had been done without executive or congressional approval, in advance of any positive order from the federal civilian authority. Additional legislation would be required to transform the administrative lattice that connected the various military cemeteries into a national cemetery system. Congress took the first steps toward this end in an act passed 13 April 1866. Its purpose was clear: "That the Secretary of War be, and he is hereby, authorized and required to take immediate measures to preserve from desecration the graves of the soldiers of the United States who fell in battle or died of disease in the field and in hospital during the war of the rebellion; to secure suitable burial-places in which they may be properly interred, and to have the grounds inclosed, so that the resting-places of the honored dead may be kept sacred forever." Within a year, on 22 February 1867, Congress passed legislation that would shape the nature and appearance of the national cemeteries throughout the United States, An Act to Establish and Protect National Cemeteries. The law stipulated that the secretary of war was to maintain the cemeteries, enclose them with a "substantial stone or iron fence," and mark each grave. Furthermore, the law provided for the employment of superintendents and the construction of their lodgings on cemetery property, levied penalties for the willful destruction of cemetery monuments, headstones, or landscaping, and required an annual inspection of the grounds.[50]

Pointedly, the original draft of the legislation uniting all these Union cemeteries and establishing the National Cemetery System was clearly aimed at the unreconstructed South, targeting as it did "the States lately in rebellion."[51] Presumably, the authors of the bill thought that loyal states would assume the responsibility for burying their own dead, perhaps inspired by the committees at work at Antietam and Gettysburg. But the law exempted from the centralized administration the national cemeteries already begun throughout Northern states, from Iowa to New York. After further debate, the wording was revised, and the bill passed as a truly national system, that is, one effective throughout the United States.[52] Even so, despite the universal character of the wording, it was apparently understood that the *national* burial of soldiers continued to apply only to those who had died loyal to the Union.

Today, the national cemeteries are familiar to virtually everyone as grounds set aside for the interment of America's veterans and their spouses. Decent, honored burial has become a guaranteed benefit accruing to those who enter military service, whether death comes on the battlefield or long after retirement from active duty. But this system evolved into its present form only after decades of development. The present system is not what was envisioned by the military officers who anticipated its necessity or the legislators responsible for its creation, as their concerns and practices show. As originally conceived, the cemeteries would contain the fallen Union soldiers who had died on the field, in hospital, or in prison. No further interments were contemplated. When the task had been completed, the cemeteries were to be closed to further burial. And not for many years to come was the term *national* meant to include those who had not died loyal to the nation. Including Confederate soldiers was beyond the pale of anyone's thought; hence, *national cemetery* is best thought of as a synonym for *Union cemetery.*

The initial motivations governing the creation of national cemeteries were born of the hostility of the war. Normally, veterans of wars between nations have the luxury of being able to remember their war in the absence of the enemy and the enemy dead. For veterans of civil wars, however, this was impossible. The patterns discerned earlier of partisan and sectional passions being read into the bodies of the dead on the battlefields of the Civil War were made permanent in the approaches to their sepulture. The protection of the scattered Union dead from the kinds of depredations and atrocities, real and imagined, that had become notorious during the war remained paramount. No Confederates who died while under arms opposing the Union were interred in any of the national cemeteries. Only those who had died in Union custody—while prisoners of war or in Union hospitals—were interred in grounds that eventually became a part of that system. About thirty of the original Civil War cemeteries contained plots devoted to the Confederate dead. For example, the cemeteries at Elmira, New York, and Sandusky, Ohio, accommodated the inmates of those prisons. In other cemeteries, smaller Confederate plots or individual graves were contained within the walled national cemeteries, although almost always relegated to a separate corner of the field. In this manner, the prisoners at Point Lookout, Maryland, and Jefferson Barracks, St. Louis, Missouri, were interred in separate sections. In some instances, as at Shiloh, Tennessee, and Vicksburg, Mississippi, a small number of Confederate soldiers were buried among the Union dead. But so completely ingrained was the notion that national cemeteries, by design, honored and protected only the loyal dead that one contemporary writer could state un-self-consciously that "the total number of bodies of United States soldiers reported throughout the United States is 316,233."[53] Clearly, what he means is the number of Union soldiers within a specific geographic nationality, yet, by conflating two different senses of *United States*, he communicates something quite different. This is a partisan statement, one in accordance with the Northern national myth without seeming to be so on the surface. The segregation was complete.

Significantly, black soldiers were routinely included in the national cemeteries. As Congress debated and enacted new definitions of citizenship during Reconstruction, the army was effectively testing the equality of treatment won on the battlefield by black soldiers. Racially integrated burial grounds were rare at the time of the Civil War. When Republican leader Thaddeus Stevens died in 1868, his insistence on being buried in a racially integrated cemetery challenged society's sensibilities, his epitaph emphasizing his choice of resting places: "I repose in this quiet and secluded spot / Not from any natural preference for solitude / But, finding other Cemeteries limited as to Race by Charter Rules / I have chosen this that I might illustrate in my death / The Principles which I advocated through a long life / EQUALITY OF MAN BEFORE HIS CREATOR."[54]

The conspicuous burial of black servicemen in the national cemeteries makes them among the first publicly funded integrated cemeteries in American history. Of the numerous cemeteries reviewed in the inspection reports of 1869 and 1871, at least sixty-two separate cemeteries contained the remains of black soldiers. The cemetery at City Point, outside Richmond, Virginia, reported over 1,300 U.S. Colored Troops burials, as opposed to approximately 150 "rebel prisoners of war." In addition to the more than 400 black soldiers buried in Arlington National Cemetery, the remains of 3,235 "contrabands" were to be found in the grounds that would become the most sanctified of the national cemeteries.[55] Racial integration occasionally took time at some of the national burial grounds, and veterans of the U.S. Colored Troops were occasionally relegated to separate portions of the burial field. Six African American veterans of World War I were interred eventually in Antietam National Cemetery, although in a distant, southern corner of the field that once had been the proposed burial site of Confederate soldiers. U.S. Colored Troops veteran Henry Gooden is the only black American interred in the Gettysburg cemetery. Gooden died in 1876 and now lies between two white soldiers along the arcing ranks of the U.S. Regular Troops.[56] Overall, the legacy of black interments in the national cemeteries is a mixed one, complicated by the tensions between the ideals that many thought implicit in the successful prosecution of the war and the Northern society that formed the context for those ideals. But, on the whole, the color line of segregation that pertained in the nation's cemeteries was between blue and gray, not black and white.

The creation of the national cemeteries represents the greatest single expression on the part of the federal government about the war and its importance to the national existence. By March 1870, bodies of 309,225 Union soldiers had been found and collected into the national cemeteries, at a cost of $3,112,209. The allocation of such financial resources and manpower to locating, disinterring, collecting, reburying, and protecting every Union fatality throughout the Southern states remains in that context a national effort unparalleled in our history. Contemporaries like E. B. Whitman recalled comparisons with Greece and the honors that nation paid to its dead as well as with France, which, "in her triumphant period, made a feeble and partial effort to gather up for honorable burial" the remains of its soldiers. But the relocation of the Union dead accomplished from 1866 to 1870 outstripped history. "Such a consecration," Whitman wrote, "of a nation's power and resources to a *sentiment*, the world has never witnessed."[57]

The rise of various fraternal organizations of Union veterans did much to further the commemoration of the war dead and expand the importance and social influence of the national cemeteries. Ironically, the first such organization, the Third Army Corps Union, was formed during the war specifically in response to the death of Union officers.[58] The officer staff of the Third Army Corps organized themselves into a burial assurance group; survivors would contribute to have fallen officers embalmed and returned home for burial. Although the union later took on the semblance of other fraternal organizations, its first purpose was cemeterial in nature. In the months following the close of the war, dozens of fraternal veterans' associations organized across the North. The Military Order of the Loyal League of the United States, the individual societies of the various armies (for example, the Cumberland, Ohio, Tennessee, and Georgia), officer corps societies, even local groups like the Returned Soldiers' Club of Brighton, Massachusetts, all organized to cement the bonds of wartime acquaintance and experience, to petition and act in their members' political interests, and to remember those who no longer stood beside them and their widows and orphans.[59]

Of course, it was the Grand Army of the Republic (GAR) that spoke with the loudest voice in postwar America on behalf of veterans. Although its founding charters and constitution say little about the dead—focusing instead on those relatives who had survived the fallen soldier—the GAR soon chimed in on the various issues attending the formation of cemeteries and the National Cemetery System. During the height of controversy at Antietam, Comrade E. Y. Goldsmith of Maryland introduced the following preamble and resolution at the GAR's second national encampment, held in Philadelphia on 15 January 1868:

> Whereas, arrangements are being perfected by State legislation and otherwise to inter in the Antietam National Cemetery the remains of those rebels who were killed in the vicinity of said cemetery; and,
>
> Whereas, we feel that respect to our fallen comrades requires us to oppose any such movement, and to protect their ashes from insult: Therefore, be it,
>
> Resolved . . . That we demand from Congress such legislation as will forever prevent the burial, in any of the national cemeteries of any person other than the deceased soldiers and sailors of the Republic for whom they were intended.[60]

Although Congress never made such a specification in law, it seems to have been universally adopted in practice. From then on, the national cemeteries became a recurrent topic for the GAR. The political activism that the GAR demonstrated on behalf of living veterans or the survivors of the dead is well documented.[61] However, its efforts for the commemoration of the dead are as significant. At its third national encampment, the group resolved to "earnestly urge upon the citizens and legislators of those States where no provision has been made, to take immediate steps to fulfill the obligations imposed upon them by the casualties of the late war."[62]

Veterans, led by the GAR, campaigned strenuously and successfully for an expansion of the national cemeteries to something far beyond what had been originally intended. So successful were they that the cemeteries became sacred spaces, so sacrosanct that many were suspicious of the first movement to expand interment privileges. National legislators came to fear that Union veterans dying in poverty would not receive the honored interment that they themselves had rendered to the battlefield dead but would instead be consigned to anonymous burial. On 1 June 1872, Congress extended the grant of guaranteed interment in the national cemeteries to indigent Union soldiers and sailors. However, the GAR responded angrily, fearing that the national cemeteries would regress to disdained potter's fields. On receiving the reassurances of Congress and the War Department, the GAR retracted its opposition, and veterans who gathered into fraternal organizations in order to maintain relationships forged in battle began to think of renewing relationships with those who had died long before.[63] It became the fond wish of many to be buried with the war dead of their old regiments and divisions and the desire of family and friends to see the veterans who had died in peace honored in a manner commensurate with that accorded the soldier dead.

But the continued burial of war veterans, beyond the indigent already considered, had not been anticipated by legislators, who at first resisted it—an ironic reversal of roles. In Arkansas, local veterans had been informally interred alongside their former fellow soldiers for several years. When this practice was discovered by the administrators of the cemetery system, it was halted at once, and the recent burials were ordered exhumed and removed. This brought a storm of outrage and protest from the GAR and relatives. Congress quickly passed further legislation that enlarged the interment privilege to any honorably discharged soldier, sailor, or marine who had served in the Civil War. Signed on 3 March 1873, the act ensured that the "graves shall receive the same care and attention of those already buried." The law, however, applied specifically to veterans "dying subsequent to this act."[64] While Congress moved to honor the veterans, it did not at that point want to contemplate another round of Quartermaster burial details, surveying, recovering, and reinterring the veterans who had died in the eight years since the end of the war.

The development of the cemeteries progressed, therefore, from wartime necessity to become sacred sites after the war, from the resting place of those killed in the war to a dignified alternative for the indigent and, finally, the last repose of any soldier who had served honorably in the armed services of the United States. This evolution bypassed Confederate soldiers. Their sons, some of whom went off to fight in the Spanish-American War, were eligible for burial. But for at least thirty-five years, no Confederate soldier who died while under arms resisting Federal authority was ever buried in a national cemetery.

The most significant act performed by the GAR and other veterans' societies on behalf of their dead comrades—and the interpretation of the nation that they sought to perpetuate—was the institutionalization of Memorial Day. Numerous conflicting tales cloud the origins of that holiday's regularized observance. One legend has the commemoration rising spontaneously at Gettysburg, where the widow of one soldier and the mother of another met while laying flowers on the last day of May in 1864. General John B. Murray claimed to have organized local veterans to decorate the graves of the fallen in Waterloo, New York, on 27 May 1866 and to have suggested this practice to John A. Logan, guiding light in the creation of the GAR, at a reunion. Similarly, T. C. Campbell of Cincinnati organized a parade of GAR posts for decorating ceremonies in 1867.[65] The official story finally sponsored by the GAR was that an anonymous comrade had written to Norton P. Chipman, then serving as the GAR's adjutant general, saying that in his native Germany it was customary to gather in cemeteries in spring and strew flowers on the graves of the dead. Chipman, thinking the idea a good one, drafted a general order and submitted it to Logan, then commander in chief of the organization, who added several paragraphs and released it as General Order No. 11 on 5 May 1868, urging all GAR posts to set aside 30 May as a day dedicated to the memorialization of their soldier dead. This date was selected to allow for the last blossoms of spring in most areas of the United States while hoping for early blossoms in the most northerly states. The order spoke of the duty owed to "our heroic dead, who made their breasts a barricade between our country and its foes." Additionally, the order also recounted the central elements of the Northern nationalist myth: "Their soldier lives were the reveille of freedom to a race in chains, and their deaths the tattoo of rebellious tyranny in arms. We should guard their graves with sacred vigilance. . . . Let no wanton foot tread rudely on such hallowed grounds. . . . Let no vandalism of avarice or neglect, no ravages of time, testify to the present or to the coming generations that we have forgotten as a people the cost of a free and undivided republic." Robert B. Beath, the historian of the GAR, observed that there were those who, in the first place, "doubted the wisdom of instituting" such a holiday for fear that it would "unnecessarily keep alive memories of the war, and foster animosities that should be buried in oblivion." Secondly, some thought the money that went to decorations and ceremonies better spent on the living. In reply, Beath wrote: "The Grand Army has answered this latter [concern] by increasing its benefactions year by year, and no *good* citizen has at any time had reason to observe any force in the first objection"[66]

In response to the order, Sunday, 30 May 1868 became the first "nationally" observed commemorative day, although some GAR posts scheduled their ceremonies a day earlier to avoid any potential violation of the Sabbath. Reports from the many posts of their activities poured into the GAR national office, which were then collected and printed under the aegis of Congress for the edification of those who had not participated. The ceremonies and rites from more than two hundred locations, mostly in Northern states, were collected as a record of the national observance. In most every location, processions to local cemeteries preceded orations, prayers, and hymns, as young women and children scattered flowers on the graves. At Loudon Park, Maryland, seventy children from the Union Orphan Asylum sang "Hail, Columbia" and "Come to Me," before being shepherded through the rows of graves to scatter their blossoms. The Charleston, South Carolina, Unionists held extensive programs, even though the war dead had been removed to Beaufort National Cemetery and there were, therefore, no Union graves in Charleston to decorate.[67]

David Blight champions the memorial observances at Charleston's "Race Course" cemetery, organized and conducted largely by black Southerners on 1 May 1865, as the primary inspiration for the creation of Memorial Day.[68] Although it is not clear from his account whether the ceremonies were intended to be annual observances, Blight's argument is convincing, bolstered as it is by the fact that Memorial Day ceremonies were observed there three years later, after the Union dead had been removed to Beaufort. Ultimately, however, as will be argued in the next chapter, it may be less important to identify the holiday's first observance than to understand how profoundly the large number of claimants to its origin indicates the ubiquity of the impulse, North and South, white and black, to commemorate the dead.

Of course, some of the observances in Southern locations were sparsely attended. Writing of the national cemeteries, journalist Charles Cowley remarked on one reason: "Some of them are in secluded situations, where for many miles the population is sparse, and the few people that live near them cherish tenderer recollections of the 'Lost Cause' than of that which finally won." At Culpeper, Virginia, there were few local white participants, the rites observed only by "two ex-soldiers of the republic and the loyal colored people of the place." The African Americans were students of Mrs. A. P. McNulty's "colored school," and the religious offices were fulfilled by "Rev. H. Blair, the colored Baptist clergyman of this place." An observer of the Winchester, Virginia, ceremonies reported that, despite bad weather on the day before, Memorial Day "was beautiful, to the great disappointment of the rebels, who had predicted us a bad day." More important, this anonymous observer related the social consequences of the commemoration of Union soldiers: Despite the prediction of a poor turnout by local "rebels," "the crowd was so great that everybody was astonished. Thus, not only was the letter and spirit of General Logan's order fulfilled, but it was most pleasing to all the Union people, because it was the first 'social' (if I may so style it) gathering of the loyal people of this town; and besides showing us 'who was who,' it will greatly tend to remove many little previous jealousies, etc., and bring them closer together for the furtherance of the Union cause."[69] Hence, for the first time since the end of the war, nearly three years past, the "Union people" of this Southern town gathered and expressed solidarity, learned who was loyal and who was not, and consciously understood that the perpetuation in memory of the Union dead could affect the local condition of American nationalism.

Such awareness was evident at Hampton, Virginia, where as late as 1876 the students of the Hampton Normal and Agricultural College were forbidden to participate in the memorial exercises for Union soldiers and compelled to attend Confederate memorials later the same day. A reporter for the black newspaper the *People's Advocate* noted: "In the afternoon, the patriotic Gen. S. C. Armstrong with his teachers and students marched in double rank and file to the cemetery, to take part in the exercises with the Southern nobility. The first to speak was Gen. Armstrong, who denounced the entire body of colored people who had decorated [Union graves] in the forenoon. Then followed half a dozen Southern gentlemen who espoused the 'lost cause' and declared they fought justly to save their homes and firesides—they should have said slaves too." In a commentary on these events, a minister is quoted as observing, "While our children are learning letters, they are also learning to accept degradation."[70] The power of the dead to invoke the most passionate of emotions within the context of their commemoration worked throughout the period to emphasize the lessons of the war.

At the national GAR encampment of 1870, Commander Logan observed that "ours was the first and only organization to institute an annual commemoration to the departed heroes of the war; and to us, by common consent, appears to be committed the mournful and pleasing duty of perpetuating it." At Logan's suggestion, Memorial Day observances were adopted as article 14, chapter 5 of the order's rules and regulations.[71] From these beginnings, the GAR sought to make Memorial Day a literally national holiday, urging Congress to pass such legislation as was necessary to ensure its observance throughout the country. Most Northern states readily adopted such legislation, among them New York in 1873, Connecticut and Pennsylvania in 1874, Wisconsin in 1879, California in 1880, Illinois in 1881, and Kansas in 1886.[72]

The enactment of an annual day of graveside commemoration naturally furthered the GAR's concerns for the developing national cemeteries. When the government had difficulty acquiring land for cemeteries in the South, the GAR responded in 1870 by declaring, "We trust that the general Government will not fail to exercise, under the *war power,* its sovereignty over such of those hallowed resting places of our departed comrades as are in that section of the country which they bravely aided in conquering, and *not ask the permission of the conquered,* that the soil thus consecrated may be the nation's forever."[73] The invocation of the war power—which grants the president extraordinary authority only during times of rebellion—five years after Appomattox is telling. Northern frustrations with the South as it stood in 1870 naturally flared over the issue of Union graves in the "conquered" section of the country. Resolutions for national legislation to expand the protection of cemeteries arose again in 1871. Additionally, during Memorial Day ceremonies in previous years, it was a common observance that while such rituals were taking place throughout the North there was no one to scatter flowers on the distant Southern burials.

In his first year as commander in chief of the GAR, General Ambrose Burnside took personal action to ensure the commemoration of Union graves in the South. Burnside thought that planting flowering shrubs on the graves themselves would perpetuate the central idea of Memorial Day even in the absence of veterans to decorate them. In 1873, the GAR moved to ensure the decoration of Union graves in distant Georgia, at the Andersonville and Marietta cemeteries. In 1882, it continued to urge the observance of Memorial Day, hoping that "not a single grave of a *union* soldier or sailor shall be unvisited."[74] So successful was the campaign that by 1891 the quartermaster general, R. N. Batchelder, institutionalized the decoration of Union graves by making it the responsibility of the national cemetery superintendents: "In order that the decoration of Soldiers' graves in National Cemeteries may not be neglected in any part of the country . . . in all cases where Grand Army Posts or other organizations neglect or omit to seasonably provide for the decoration of such graves, the Superintendents of National Cemeteries shall see that these graves are appropriately decorated, and shall assume charge of the decoration ceremonies upon the day designated for such observance, and shall confer with and invite comrades and religious societies and other organizations in the vicinity to participate in the ceremonies."[75]

Throughout their creation and development, the national cemeteries existed for two reasons. In the first place, they served as a sanctuary from a hostile, foreign people. The initial and most consistent motivation to collecting and reinterring the Union dead was to protect them. In the second place, the national cemeteries became the repositories of the honored, heroic dead, uniformly and properly interred. But, just as the grounds were designed to honor the dead, so too were they designed to instruct the living. The Rural Cemetery Movement had long held grass lawn and ornamental cemeteries to be places where the living could return, to mourn, but also to gain intellectual and spiritual inspiration. As modified by the National Cemetery System, burial grounds would become forums of nationalistic inspiration and instruction. Such purposes behind that effort, most of it by necessity expended in the South, were consciously enacted and plainly evident. As E. B. Whitman asserted, "To a considerable extent in Southern soil, and in the very presence where bold Treason reared its ungrateful head, they shall teach the children, whose fathers sought to dismember and destroy the Republic, to cherish its institutions, and to seek its honors and rewards. *That Nation which respects and honors its dead, shall ever be respected and honored itself.*"[76] The sanctified grounds of the national cemeteries were dedicated both to the past and to the future: for the past, they honored and commemorated the dead, providing them in exchange for their lives a protected, proper burial; for the future, they held out the ultimate example of service to the nation, a didactic lesson in marble stones and manicured landscapes. The institution of Memorial Day gave annual reinforcement to the messages of national loyalty and sacrifice. Northern individuals, veterans' groups, and government agencies expended great energy in perpetuating the commemoration of the Civil War, guaranteeing that its communication through the generations would retain a distinctly Union flavor. Nowhere is this more dramatically apparent than in the serried rows of gravestones in any national cemetery.

Southern states could not hope to match the funds or manpower poured into the effort of remembering and honoring a national interpretation of the war, even if they had been allowed to do so. Nevertheless, Southerners also committed their perceptions of the war to monument, myth, and ritual. And, like their more powerful Northern counterparts, they too sought in the years following the war to control the commemoration of it, at least as far as they were able. Although impoverished, defeated, and disenfranchised, their creativity and perseverance in the commemoration of their soldier dead remain one of the most remarkable stories of the war and the beleaguered peace that followed.

4

"Death in a Far-Off, Stranger's Land": Southern Creation and Commemoration

> Sleep sweetly in your humble graves,
> Sleep, martyrs of a fallen cause;
> Though yet no marble craves
> The pilgrim here to pause.
> In seeds of laurel in the earth
>
> The blossom of your fame is blown,
> And somewhere, waiting for its birth,
> The shaft is in the stone!
>
> Meanwhile, behalf the tardy years
> Which keep in trust your storied tombs,
> Behold! your sisters bring their tears,
> And these memorial blooms.
>   —Henry Timrod, "Ode" (1867)

L IKE THEIR UNION COUNTERPARTS, Confederate soldiers were lost to grieving and distant families. Writing shortly after the end of the war, the Reverend A. S. Billingsley notified a Montgomery, Alabama, family of the loss of their son. The soldier's sister replied:

> We had already received the bitter intelligence; but are none the less indebted and thankful to you for your note. Although you are an entire stranger to our once happy, but now gloomy, household, on behalf of the entire family allow me to return to you our most *heartfelt* thanks for the attention and care you bestowed upon the deceased. And although in the busy struggle of life our paths may never meet, rest assured, my dear sir, that under whatever suns, or upon whatever seas, it may please an all-wise God to cast *us*, we shall never, never forget you, who pointed the soul of him we loved so well to

the brightly-beaming star of Faith and Hope. The day we received your sad, but comforting letter, because it bid us "Be of good cheer," "It is thy Father's will," was the anniversary of the third year since last he was with us. *Then*, in the prime of his young, but noble manhood, he left us—*now*, poor boy, he sleeps the quiet sleep of death in a far-off stranger's land. Pardon me for these ebullitions of private grief.[1]

As should be expected, many elements of antebellum death culture and ritual are present in this Southern example. Billingsley's original letter no doubt tried to reconstruct the hospital deathbed scene for the absent family, who in turn thanked him for the religious counsel offered their lost son. In many ways, this letter underscores what was shared by all Americans in their experience of death. But there are also elements that are distinctly and uniquely Southern. The unidentified woman writes plaintively of the uncertainty her family faced in common with all Southerners following the war, of places "under whatever suns, or upon whatever seas," God may cast "*us*," her emphasis marking the recognition of the indefinite future stemming from losing a long and bitter war, of the difference between a national destiny and a sectional one. No matter how much comfort the belief that God foreordains all direction to human endeavors, the future for Southerners was clearly cast along a track different than they had anticipated. Moreover, although both Northern and Southern families thought of relations lying in far-off lands, and although both may even have described that land as belonging to "strangers," Northern mythology required the reincorporation of Southern lands into the American nationality. Southern myths preserved a sense of separateness in defeat that always characterized Northern lands as foreign lands. This was the marked distinction between commemorative efforts: Although both sides commemorated only their own dead, Northerners did so within a memorial rhetoric that invoked a broad, inclusive nationalism, while Southerners followed the dictates of a separate mythos predicated on difference and distinctiveness.

The circumstances of defeat and the early confusion of Reconstruction gave rise and impetus to Southern myths. The Lost Cause is clearly an explanatory corpus of myth that sought primarily to explicate acceptable reasons for Confederate defeat while reinforcing the righteousness of the Southern enterprise.[2] Bewildered by the collapse of the Confederacy, and looking toward an uncertain future within a restored Union, Southerners faced the prospect of abandoning the ideas and beliefs that had nourished the war effort only to adopt others resulting from their defeat. In the years following Appomattox, the most common explanation for military defeat was that the South had not so much lost as it had been exhausted by the North's superior numbers and capacity for the industrial production of war matériel. This solution accomplished much for the South: it permitted the unspoken assumption that had the resources of war been more evenly distributed the success of the Confederate forces would have been assured; it asserted that the North had not so much won as outlasted a handicapped opponent, thereby robbing Union forces of any pride in victory; and it permitted the redemption of every Confederate military leader by casting them all as brilliant, gentlemanly tacticians and strategists, while condemning their Union counterparts as simply butchers grinding out the last years of the struggle without regard to the niceties of civilized combat or the value of their own soldiers' lives.

Of course, such an advantageous intellectual construct was not without cost. At best, it represented the repudiation of the early and consistent boast that, since any sturdy son of the South was more than equal to any ten corrupt Northern wage slaves and immigrants, the manpower advantage was meaningless; at worst, it cast doubt on the abilities of Southern officers and soldiers to fulfill that boast. But, in this and many other ways, the mythos of the Lost Cause shaped Southern perceptions of the war to meet the exigencies of defeat. Everything became centered on the need to bolster this myth, for without it Southerners could not explain defeat.[3] The mythology was readily extended to embrace the dead, for if men had died to perpetuate the Cause then the sanctification of their deaths lent sanctification to it. Therefore, following impulses very similar to those that shaped Northern commemoration, Southern efforts to codify a particular interpretation of the war necessarily began with their dead.

But the domination of the Lost Cause in the commemoration of the war and the preservation of it in memory was not immediate. The mythos took time to find full expression and did not reach maturity until the 1890s. For many of those early years, it was expressed, of necessity, in a covert language. Southern commemorative patterns are generally less accessible than their Northern counterparts, given the political environment of Reconstruction and military occupation, the devastation of Southern state economies, and the relative paucity of presses in the postwar South. But the overall pattern is clear: in contrast to Northern memorialization, which crystallized immediately on Lincoln's death and grew steadily in strength and coherence from that point onward, Southern commemoration began haltingly in the shadow of a forced acquiescence to national authority, soon found exemplars from which to grow and flourish, but did not finally mature as a national expression until the last decade of the nineteenth century and the first decade of the next.

In addition to bearing the onus of rebellion, Southerners as a whole shouldered a multitude of additional crimes. Lincoln's assassination was widely characterized as the product of the social environment and political rhetoric that all Southerners dwelt within and may have quashed a sense of magnanimity in Northerners toward the South immediately following Lee's surrender. Additionally, many in the North were dismayed by a sudden apparent resurgence of the Slave Power, most clearly seen in the figure of President Andrew Johnson who—despite his avowals of making "treason odious"—had generously pardoned former Confederate leaders and hastily sponsored the reestablishment of state governments in what was interpreted as a precipitous retreat from a more desirable, and firmer, stance on Reconstruction. Finally, a wider circulation of earlier congressional investigations into the desecration of Union graves and the postwar revelations of the relatively poor treatment of Union prisoners further eroded sectional relations. The trial of Henry Wirz, superintendent of Andersonville Prison and the only Southerner executed for war crimes, scandalized the North with its revelations of abuses visited upon captive soldiers. In this atmosphere, the North viewed with hostility any action on the part of former Confederates or their sympathizers that might be interpreted as a celebration of the Rebellion.[4]

Given the way Southern obstructionism so successfully undermined Reconstruction, it may seem difficult to credit that Southerners felt the weight of any restrictions because of military occupation. Certainly none seem evident in the early imposition of the "black codes" or the later political terrorism of the Ku Klux Klan. In fact, the Northern institution of the Freedmen's Bureau operated frequently as a willing accomplice in the shuttling of freedmen into contracted labor situations that, in their most abusive forms, restricted rather than facilitated the freedom of black workers in the South.[5] Yet no contradiction exists: the Northern military commanders of the occupation, who might not have objected to the exploitation of black Southerners and who may even have cooperated in the process, would nevertheless have objected strenuously to any act that exalted the rebellious, treasonous Confederate dead. That is, the social dimensions of the postwar South were less pressing to them than the military and political dimensions. While they were conflicted on issues of race and racial policy, they emerged from the war crystalline in their clarity about the nature of the Confederacy.

In a manner that underscores this point, and indicates its prevalence, on 4 June 1866, Representative Thomas Williams of Pennsylvania offered a resolution in Congress designed to investigate reports that "the memories of the traitor dead have been hallowed and consecrated by local public entertainments and treasonable utterances in honor of their crime, which have not only been tolerated by the national authorities, but in some instances approved by [their actions]." Williams's legislation was aimed directly at Andrew Johnson and forced him to garner reports from the heads of the various executive departments on whether any government authorities—and Williams had specified "national authorities"—had indeed tolerated "honors to rebels."[6]

In such a climate, the commemoration of the Southern dead had to be carefully and cagily managed. Because honoring the war's soldier dead always possessed a political dimension, the duty of commemoration fell in the South to those whom society considered politically irrelevant—women. Like women in many other places, times, and cultures, Southern women assumed much of the responsibility for honoring and caring for their dead. But they did so in a political context completely dissimilar to that of any other women, particularly their Northern counterparts, for the act of commemoration itself constituted a political statement in its often-explicit endorsement of the cause for which the honored dead had died. Since they had no political life to protect, Southern women assumed the task of honoring Confederate veterans, not by default, but by strategy, and they took up their duties, quite literally, with a vengeance. For example, women of Georgia proposed erecting a monument to their dead in Athens. A newspaper article remembered, "The ladies eagerly seized the suggestion but the men discouraged it. They said they were under parole and were pledged not to aid or encourage any movement of that kind. The women said they were under no parole, so they began to have entertainments such as bazaars, May parties, plays, etc. [in order to raise the necessary funds]."[7]

In part, this explains why Southern men are much less outspoken just after the war in the cause of commemoration than are Northern men of the same period. Northern men tended from the first to dominate the rituals and ceremonies of commemorating Union soldiers, or at the least took the most credit for those memorial acts. Of course, women in the North and the South were always central to the rituals of death and deathbed and the preservation of memory, but in very real ways Southern women became the custodians of the Lost Cause at a time when that role was inexpedient for Southern men. Thus, at the laying of a monument's cornerstone in 1875, former Confederate General Clement A. Evans declared, "It is not man's privilege, but woman's to raise these memorials throughout the land. The fitness of things commands us to yield to her the foremost place in this pleasing duty. Her smile encouraged our ardent youth to put on the armor of war. Her voice cheered them into the thick of battle. Her sympathies followed them like angels through the dreary toils of camp and march and siege; her hands bound up their wounds, and her tears fell upon their cold, pale, bloody corses. And before the smoke of battle had fairly cleared away, she stood up in Georgia, first of all, and said, 'We will build monuments to our fallen men.'"[8]

While Southern women's vital contributions to the war effort would be celebrated for decades to come, few have acknowledged the service that they performed on behalf of the dead and, by extension, on behalf of the Cause.[9] The distinctions between the socially derived and highly gendered attributes of Southern men and women were highlighted by former General R. E. Colston in an address of 1870: "While some men who once did gallant service in the Southern armies have, alas, turned false for filthy lucre, where are the renegades among Southern women? Even we who have preserved our truth unstained, have we not grown colder and more forgetful? Had it depended on us [men] alone, is there not much reason to fear that our brothers' bones would still lie unheeded where they fell? Not that we have grown indifferent or estranged, but the claims of the living and the anxieties of misfortune have absorbed our attention." Of course, there may well have been "renegade" women, but without a more prominent place in social or political leadership their heterodox inclinations might never be noticed. Still, in the depths of congressional Reconstruction, Colston chose his words carefully. Men were preoccupied with the public sphere of the "living" and weighed down by "the anxieties of misfortune." Southern women certainly knew misfortune, but Colston seemed to imply a kind of public or political misfortune that did not involve women directly. Reinforcing the religious connotations that both Northerners and Southerners perceived in the Civil

War, he likened the efforts of Southern women to sacred precedent: "Unwearied by their labors and self-sacrifice during four years of war, they were, like Mary, the first at the graves of their beloved dead."[10]

The commemoration of the Confederacy and the war dead would occupy white Southern women well into the next century, forming a crucial avenue by which they entered into social activism. In the beginning, they drew on the multitude of impromptu organizations that had arisen to support the Confederate war effort, simply redirecting the original aims of those groups to serve the needs of the postwar South. Organizing themselves, Southern women moved deliberately and as forcefully as their limited circumstances allowed toward the memorialization of their lost soldiers. Years later, a popular magazine celebrated these first steps and in doing so emphasized the special contribution of women: "For the past thirty years the women of the South have been solicitous and tender in their care for our dead, and will not call on any alien hand to decorate and care for the graves of their fallen heroes. Devoted as the men of the Confederacy were to our holy cause, their devotion is excelled by the women of our Southland."[11]

The first organized efforts to commemorate the Confederate dead were personal and local. As in the North, there are in the South numerous accounts of the origins of Memorial Day, each with its own traditions, but all with a particularly Southern perception of the ceremony's beginnings. A favorite version of Memorial Day's Southern origins involves the local Soldier's Aid Society of Columbus, Georgia. During the war, the women of the society "nursed the sick, fed the hungry, and buried the dead" at the local hospital. They performed the surrogate's deathbed tasks of writing "letters to distant and sorrowing soldier mothers, [and] sent locks of hair to far away sweethearts of those whose dying hours they soothed." Following the war, like much of Southern society, the Soldier's Aid Society found itself without real direction. Its secretary, Lizzie Rutherford, and several other of its women took it upon themselves to maintain the soldier graves in the local cemetery. Rutherford, like many Northerners, was inspired by German custom, of which she learned from a romantic novel, and suggested that the society set aside a similar day for the commemoration of the soldier dead in its custody.[12] The adoption of this idea transformed the Soldier's Aid Society into the Ladies Memorial Association, which observed its first Memorial Day on 26 April 1866, the anniversary of the last Confederate army's surrender.[13]

Mrs. Charles J. Williams, the association's secretary, had written other women's groups and newspaper offices throughout the South so that the occasion might be more universally observed. In her letter, dated 12 March 1866, she observed some of the restrictions that militated against more substantive commemorative activities: "We cannot raise monumental shafts and inscribe thereon their many deeds of heroism, but we can keep alive the memory of the debt we owe them. . . . Legislative enactment may not be made to do honor to their memories, but the veriest radical that ever traced his genealogy back to the deck of the Mayflower, could not refuse us the simple privilege of paying honor to those who died defending the life, honor and happiness of the Southern women." The exact nature of the strictures she does not recount, but, in addition to impoverishment, she is almost certainly referring to congressional concerns over the possibility of "honors" being paid to rebels when she uses the phrase "legislative enactment." Pointedly, Williams sought to defuse criticism, not only by having the women of the South assume the tasks of commemoration, but also by making the protection of women the reason that soldiers had died in the first place, thereby justifying their memorial activities. Perhaps in response to the Union reburial efforts already under way in many parts of the South, she also expressed concern for "the thousands who were buried 'with their martial cloaks around them,' without Christian ceremony or interment." To the decoration of graves she urged the addition of "a eulogy on the unburied dead of our glorious Southern army." Her appeal to set apart this day of commemoration from "the Potomac to the Rio Grande" demonstrated her understanding, not only of the particular sectional appeal of her design, but also of the fact that what little could be done by the South should be done.[14]

The history of the Ladies' Memorial Association of Wake County, North Carolina, was far more specific as to the restrictions placed on its commemorative activities. The Federal army had moved north from South Carolina, taking possession of Raleigh and its Pettigrew military hospital. According to local tradition, the officer in charge of the occupation wanted to inter the Union soldier dead in the nearby hospital cemetery. He therefore notified the town fathers that the Confederate dead already buried there must be evacuated in two days or "be thrown in the road." The citizens rallied and the men of the town began the task of removing their dead to another plot of land, donated by a local resident. Mrs. Garland Jones later wrote her account of that "labor of love": "They came with picks and wheelbarrows, determined never to cease until the body of the last Southern soldier was removed to a place of safety." She also noted the special role that women played: "They were assisted in this work by our faithful women, who, walking by their side, cheered and encouraged the men as they trudged the weary distance between the two cemeteries under a scorching, summer sun. One good woman, seeing them almost overcome by their task, begged a cask of beer, and, walking by their side, gave it out as she saw they needed it." But this forced removal was not the end of alleged Union restrictions on the Southern dead. The residents had selected for their first Memorial Day 10 May, the anniversary of Stonewall Jackson's death, but "at this time our City was under martial rule, and no public observance of the day was allowed," Jones remembered. "Indeed," she continued, "the threat was made that if the women went to the Cemetery in a procession, they would be fired upon without further warning. So, quietly and unobserved, these loyal and devoted women gathered in groups of not more than two or three at the different street corners, each one bearing their crosses and wreaths, and wended their way to the Cemetery, closely followed and watched by a Federal officer, to see that no procession was formed."[15]

A single iconic image combined the dominance of women in the commemoration of their dead and the restrictions that many felt were placed on those activities. First as a popular poem, then more broadly as engraved prints of a painting by William De Hartburn Washington, *The Burial of Latané* served as an important cultural touchstone in postwar Confederate memorialization. Both poem and painting honored a celebrated incident of the war. In June 1862, Robert E. Lee first assumed command of the Army of Northern Virginia, just as Union General George McClellan's vast army threatened the Confederate capital. To provide much-needed military intelligence and a welcome diversionary demonstration against the enemy, J. E. B. Stuart, Lee's cavalry commander, conducted a daring raid around the entire Union force, discovering weaknesses in its dispositions and disrupting as much as possible its supply and communication lines. Although more important for its morale-boosting effect than any material advantage gained, the raid was accomplished at the cost of only a single Confederate, Captain William D. Latané, killed as he led his men against a Union force defending the road. Latané's body was carried to a nearby plantation, Westwood, the home of Mr. and Mrs. William Brockenbrough. The white men of the household were

This iconic image, *The Burial of Latané*—as popular in the South as Lincoln deathbed images in the North—spoke to former Confederates on a number of levels, but particularly evoked the wartime interruptions of death ritual and custom, as well as affirmed the centrality of women in matters of death and commemoration.
Virginia Historical Society, Richmond

all away at the war, but the women agreed to provide a fitting burial for the fallen captain. After the departure of Stuart's forces, a slave was sent to bring a minister back to conduct the services but was turned back to the plantation by Union pickets. Left to their own devices, the women conducted the services themselves, with Mrs. Brockenbrough's sister-in-law—Mrs. Willoughby Newton—reading the Episcopal service.[16]

Widely reported soon after in Richmond newspapers, the incident inspired a local literary figure, John R. Thompson, to write a eulogistic poem. Thompson emphasized Latané's bravery and martyrdom and the fate that he shared with almost all fallen soldiers, to die far from family: "A brother bore his body from the field / And gave it into strangers' hands . . . Strangers, but sisters, who with Mary's love / Sat by the open tomb and, weeping, looked

above." But the central stanza of the poem recounts the restrictions placed
on the services:

> No man of God might read the burial rite
> Above the rebel—thus declared the foe,
> Who blanched before him in the deadly fight;
> But woman's voice, in accents soft and low,
> Trembling with pity, touched with pathos, read
> Over his hallowed dust, the ritual for the dead!

Thompson's verse later inspired Washington, a local artist, to paint his in-
terpretation of the incident. Significantly, Washington—a student of Emanuel
Leutze, most famous perhaps for his painting of Washington crossing the
Delaware—chose to depict, not a Homeric image of Latané's tragic fall in
battle, but the quieter heroism of the women who accomplished his burial.
Seizing on the funeral tableau, Washington demonstrated how powerfully the
Southern imagination responded both to the disruption of burial ritual and
to the restrictions imposed by the enemy.[17]

The imagery associated with Latané's death and funeral, communicated
so effectively through poetry and art, found widest expression in A. G.
Campbell's engraved reproduction of Washington's painting. With white
women and children arrayed to one side and faithful slaves standing on the
other, Latané's open grave dominates the center, his corpse lying nearby on
top of his coffin, hidden from view by his rough cavalry cloak. At the head of
the grave, Mrs. Newton stands holding the Book of Common Prayer, her eyes
cast piously upward. Other scholars have noted the importance of the
engraving's elements—the docile, faithful slaves, the emphatic testimony to
women's self-reliance in the crisis of war, and of course the centrality of
women in Confederate commemoration.[18] But what is not depicted is evoca-
tive as well. No member of Latané's family is present; he was buried—no
matter how lovingly—by strangers. In this fashion, the thousands of Southerners who displayed this print in their homes could see something of their
own lost loved one's burial. Also, although tradition holds that slaves produced a coffin for the captain, the engraving leaves the viewer with the distinct impression that he will be buried simply in his cloak, as were so many
soldiers of both sides, the coffin in this case seemingly acting merely as a platform. Finally, the lack of clergy in this civilian setting denotes subtly but distinctly that Union forces had prevented Latané from receiving a proper burial.

Although capably done, this funeral is improvisational and incomplete. The Southern imagination could detect in it, not only the sentiments of common loss and the crucial role of women in rising above that loss, but also the cruelty of others in restricting a proper display of respect for the Confederate dead.

Ultimately, however, the nature and scope of restrictions placed upon the commemoration of the Southern dead are difficult to assess. Clearly, in some regions, like North Carolina, the military forces in residence sought to control such activities by positive order, although no record of such orders has yet been found and what actions were taken may subsequently have been exaggerated by local indignation. At least since the days of Major General Benjamin Butler, who during the Union occupation of New Orleans threatened any woman violating his order of curfew with an arrest for streetwalking, Southerners had resented bitterly the presence of Federal military authority. Despite the lack of evidence, Southerners acted as though restrictions were commonplace, perhaps because they had been communicated by military officers through means other than formal orders, for example, through intimidation.

Regardless of such restrictions, real or imagined, Southerners kept their own Memorial Day. There was confusion about its origins, just as in the North. It was later claimed that the custom had originated in Richmond, Virginia, the contribution of the Reverend Charles Minnegrode, who, in the parlor of Mrs. Charles G. Barney, recalled his German ancestors' practice of strewing flowers on All Saints' Day. Minnegrode's idea, it was claimed, also gave rise to Richmond's Ladies Hollywood Memorial Association, which took as its special charge nearby Hollywood Cemetery and mounted its first memorial observance there on 31 May 1866.[19] Southern observance tended more than that of Northerners to drift from date to date, perhaps because there were so few dates marking the end of the war that invited fond memorialization and no multistate organization, like the Grand Army of the Republic (GAR), to enforce uniformity on states that had not always acted uniformly even during the days of the Confederacy. As had the North Carolina women's groups, the Memorial Association of Charleston, South Carolina, usually settled on 10 May, the anniversary of Stonewall Jackson's death. North Carolina maintained that date of observance into the twentieth century.[20]

Southerners also took great delight in pointing out their belief that Northerners had adopted their holiday.[21] Long after the men of the GAR had codified their creation of Memorial Day, an 1898 history of the Southern origin of Memorial Day provided three notarized affidavits of women present at the adoption of the resolution and announced quite plainly that "the North looked on, thought the custom good, took it to herself and has hallowed it as she does her Thanksgiving obligation. April was too early for her flowers, hence she set apart May 30th." Another account recorded that Mrs. John A. Logan, the wife of the commander in chief of the GAR, gave her husband the idea for Memorial Day after a visit to a Virginia churchyard. She had noticed that several of the graves were marked by flowers and "small flags of the dead Confederacy." "The sentimental idea so enwrapped me," Mrs. Logan remembered, "that I inspected them more closely and discovered that they were every one the graves of soldiers who had died for the Southern cause." When her husband met her at the train station on her return to Washington, she related the experience to him, whereupon he immediately pledged to order the GAR to follow the Southern example.[22]

Mrs. Logan's version has no place in the official story adopted by the GAR, which apparently subordinated her role and substituted an anonymous veteran's suggestion as the origin of the fraternity's ritual. Whatever the truth of these and numerous other claims, in all likelihood the impulse to decorate and remember the war dead arose nearly simultaneously in countless locations, in both North and South. Such ubiquity points out the essential nature of the need to commemorate and, by extension, the need to understand and interpret. The desire throughout the United States to claim Memorial Day's origin bears eloquent testimony to the importance of the dead in the structure of sectional interpretations of the war and its meanings. Moreover, especially in the South, the day served as a reminder of more than the dead. Looking back after nearly half a century, Mrs. John T. Sifford of Camden, Arkansas, remembered, "Each one of these fifty years has carried us farther from the war, farther from the desolation it wrought, farther from the prejudice it engendered." But, she continued, "The first Memorial Days were times of tears, of revived bitterness, of re-awakened resentment. The heart of the south bled anew at each recurrence of the day of decoration, and not all the flowers of all the seasons sufficed to hide the scars and rents of the conflict."[23]

An 1868 Confederate commemoration in the former border state of Kentucky—just two years after the general adoption of Memorial Day exercises throughout much of the South—offers an interesting glimpse into that state's relationship with the war and the nation. The unnamed speaker, who identified himself as one who "loved the Cause—I would have given my life to it," began by reminding his listeners: "We come here to make no eulogy on the Cause for which they were martyrs. We come to weep, not praise; to mourn, not defend. *They are our dead*—loved with passionate idolatry, mourned with an unutterable agony." Although he spoke with high praise of Southern military chieftains and the "privates and subalterns" of the Confederate army, the Northern mythology of national union permeated his text. "We are all Americans," he wrote, "we are citizens of a common country, in whose destinies are involved those of our children." Both Union and Confederate soldiers lay in the Lexington cemetery, he indicated, and they will arise together on Resurrection Day: "Religion, patriotism, the love we bear our children, alike appeal with eloquent earnestness for the return of the day of good feeling and brotherly love."[24] In this way, although he had reiterated the Northern assertion that "we are all Americans," he also pointed out that citizens from both sides had yet to see the "return" of the prewar national fraternity.

Of course, the events that inspired and shaped this unnamed speaker's discourse, the collection and protection of the Union soldier dead, prevented his oratory from fully embracing the ideals of unity that he espoused: "I believe I utter the sentiment of those who hear me, when I say that we trust the day may come when such a peace will bless our land that all the living will lovingly do honor to *all* the dead." His comment calls attention to the federal collection process that had transformed the cemeterial landscape of Lexington the year before. He and his audience stood amid a Confederate lot containing some ninety-seven soldiers. Not far away, the federal government had recently reinterred 822 Union soldiers. The dichotomy was underscored as the speaker posed a simple rhetorical opposition: "To the dead, I have no enmity—to the heroic dead, I have no feeling but of respect." We can only speculate on the gestures that accompanied these words, gestures that may have indicated first the Federal graves and then the surrounding Confederate dead. But the distinction between "the dead" and "the heroic dead" is telling.[25]

Still, in some Southern states, thoughts of distant Confederate soldiers did inspire concerted action.[26] In the main, such relocation efforts became the charge of local government, the Ladies' Memorial Associations, and other social organizations. By 1877, the town of Winchester, Virginia, had gathered the Confederate soldiers from within a radius of twenty miles. In that year's Memorial Day exercises, the common grave of 829 unknown soldiers was decorated at the central mound of the Stonewall Cemetery.[27] Elsewhere, just as Northern postwar efforts had largely concentrated on the vast number of soldier dead in the Southern states, so too did the energies of the South eventually focus on the states of the North. By far, the great majority of Confederate dead in the North—having died in military prisons and hospitals—had been at least decently interred. While the graves themselves at times might suffer from neglect, at least the soldiers had been interred in individualized graves and, for the most part, with their identities intact.

The glaring exception to this pattern in the North was the Confederate soldier dead of Gettysburg. The Soldiers' National Cemetery had been completed in 1864, and it was in design and execution a cemetery for the Union dead alone. No Northern effort to reinter the Confederates was ever made. Dr. Samuel Weaver, who had been so instrumental in the location, identification, and removal of the Union dead to the Soldiers' National Cemetery, had in the course of that work become quite familiar with the location of Confederate soldiers' graves, and he was the logical contact for the Ladies' Memorial Associations of Virginia and other Southern states. Weaver's list of soldier graves was the best, really the only, comprehensive compilation of such information on the Confederate dead. Although Weaver agreed to assist the women of the South in their recovery of their dead, he himself died before work was begun. It fell to his son, Rufus B. Weaver, also a physician, to carry out the work of identification and exhumation.[28]

From 1870 to 1873, Rufus Weaver and his small crew of workers traversed the battlefield, opening graves, and boxing their contents for shipment. Weaver, with his knowledge of anatomy, insisted on sifting the graves himself. Remains were removed from at least ninety-six separate locations, ranging from hospital burial grounds to farmers' fields. In many cases, the soldier's home state could be identified even if his identity had been lost. So, in 1871, 74 sets of remains were shipped to the Ladies Memorial Associations of Charleston, South Carolina, 101 sets to Savannah, Georgia, and 137 sets to Raleigh, North Carolina. Over the next two years, six separate shipments containing a total of 2,935 remains were sent to the Ladies Hollywood Memorial Association of Richmond. Most were boxed together as sets of multiple skeletal remains. In some few cases, the graves remained well identified enough to make individual removals: Weaver forwarded 73 identified soldiers to those four Southern cemeteries. The loss of identity where graves had once been marked was especially painful, and many of the reburials in the South were necessarily in mass graves. For example, of the remains shipped to Georgia, only 2 were reburied in individual graves. The other ninety-nine were interred in eight mass graves. But they were no less honored for being anonymous, and it was enough for some that Southern soldiers no longer lay neglected in Northern soil. Such emotional ties were strong. The Ladies Memorial Association of Wake County eventually removed 107 North Carolinian soldiers from the cemetery at Arlington, already by 1883 beginning to be identified as the preeminent national, and therefore Union, cemetery.[29]

In at least one instance, Southern commemoration prevailed over Northern memorial aspirations. The Battle of Franklin, Tennessee, had been brief but terrible. On the afternoon of Wednesday, 30 November 1864, General John Bell Hood committed his infantry to an assault on nearly equal numbers secure behind extensive fortifications. With the winter sun slanting down on their left, the Southern soldiers marched into murderous combat. Half the Confederate regimental commanders in the battle, fifty-four officers, were killed or wounded. Six generals died in the battle, including Patrick Cleburne. The fighting continued even as the shadows lengthened into night, the soldiers firing at their enemy's gun flashes in the darkness. By the time the Northern army withdrew to continue its march toward Nashville, the Confederates had lost seven thousand men, more than Grant had lost at the disaster of Cold Harbor. The Confederates had advanced into the outer trench works on the Union left and spent hours there unable either to withdraw or to advance, all the while under a withering, enfilading fire. One soldier remembered his commander, General O. F. Strahl, calling on him: "I rose up immediately, and walking over the wounded and dead, took position with one foot upon the pile of bodies of my dead fellows, and the other in the embankment, and fired guns which the General himself handed up to me until he, too, was shot down." The next morning, he returned to his position to find that "Colonel Stafford was dead in the pile, as the morning light disclosed, with his feet wedged in at the bottom, with the other dead across and under him after he fell, leaving his body half standing, as if ready to give command to the dead!"[30]

The commitment of so many lives against such impossible odds made the battleground of Franklin a place particularly resonant with the Lost Cause mythos. After the battle, a local couple, Mr. and Mrs. McGavock, offered some acreage in their orchard, and the bodies were carefully transferred into this makeshift burial ground. More important, the McGavocks became the custodians of more than the bodies of the dead; they had adopted the legacy of interpreting and remembering the battle itself. Long afterward, although grown infirm and elderly, Mr. McGavock conducted tours of the battlefield's prominent positions, retold the valor of the Confederates, and carefully preserved the identity of the dead in the cemetery. So important was this legacy that, when the federal government considered placing a national cemetery in Franklin, the proposal drew considerable protest. The officer in charge of the military investigation reported that "the citizens of Franklin will do everything in their power to defeat the locating of a cemetery there, and will not sell land to the government at any price. In case a location is taken forcibly, a guard of twenty (20) men will be necessary to prevent desecration."[31] No Union cemetery was located in Franklin.

Since the close of the war, the South's commemoration of its war, its cause, and its soldiers was most forcefully expressed—albeit still in muted tones—in the commemoration of its dead. Southern memorialization remained local and diffuse, a result of both federal government curtailment of public honors for former Confederates and economic hardship. During this period of intense Northern commemorative activity, the South persevered on its own memorial pathways. Significantly, as had been the case in the North, a single death—Robert Edward Lee's—provided the great spur to organized memorialization throughout the South.

After Appomattox, Lee had largely withdrawn from the active public role that he had filled during the war, but such was his importance to the South that he never fell into total eclipse. On 24 August 1865, he accepted a position at modest Washington College, in Lexington, Virginia, and passed his last years as its president. Gracious in defeat, he seemed to desire nothing more than quiet acquiescence to federal government authority and counseled others to accept the arbitrament of war and the realities of a reunited nation. He remained a powerful presence in the South and was often consulted on the various plans and dreams of Southern commemorative activity. He gave his blessing to the Ladies Memorial Associations' retrieval of the Southern dead from Gettysburg, commenting that "if the southern people are prepared to receive them then it is fitting that they should reside here." Yet on other occasions he opposed such activity. Former Confederate General Bradley Johnson approached him in early 1870 about the possibility of forming a fraternal organization of former members of the Army of Northern Virginia, no doubt in response to similar organizations proliferating throughout the North. Lee opposed the plan, thinking such activism "inexpedient." On 12 October 1870, Lee died quietly after a lingering illness.[32]

Ironically, although Lee was keenly aware of the "inexpediency" of celebrating the Confederate past, his death provided the occasion for collective Southern memorial activity in ways that would have been impossible otherwise. Following his death, a local organization—the Lee Memorial Association—formed around the idea of honoring the Confederacy's greatest military champion. Its members acted largely on behalf of Lee's family and Washington College, planning the general's funeral, a statue to be placed on the Washington campus, and the entombment of Lee in the college's chapel. To cement the relationship of the college to the Lee name, Lee's son Custis was invited to continue in his father's position as president, and the name of the school was changed to Washington and Lee. Agents fanned out across the South, soliciting funds and donations for the proper commemoration of Lee.

However, as soon as the news of Lee's death spread, other Southerners sought to commemorate Lee in a grander fashion than a modest tomb in Lexington. A rival organization arose in Richmond, headed by Confederate General Jubal Early and calling for Lee's interment in Hollywood Cemetery in Richmond, among his fallen troops, so that, as one veteran commented, "when the first flush of the resurrection morn tinges the skies, may their unsealed eyes behold the grand figure" of their former commander. The rapid organization of this second group—the Lee Monument Association—indicates the power of the need to commemorate the Confederate effort and its greatest champion. Eventually, the two associations negotiated the distribution of commemoration, with Lexington retaining the tomb of Lee while Richmond was ceded the right to erect a grand equestrian statue to Lee's memory.[33]

Significantly, at the first meeting of the Richmond association, Bradley Johnson offered to the group the idea of the fraternal veterans' organization that Lee had discouraged just months before his death. Jubal Early issued a call for veterans to assemble, and in early November former Confederate officers and soldiers met to praise Lee and to organize the Association of the Army of Northern Virginia. Although this association was based in Virginia, it represents the first attempt at a multistate commemorative society in the South. Much as Lincoln had been linked to the Union dead as their representative, Lee too was placed among his fallen soldiers. Former General John

B. Gordon, newly elected president of the organization, remarked, "As he thought of the loss of the cause—of the many dead, scattered over so many fields, who sleeping neglected, with no governmental arms to gather up their remains, sleeping isolated and alone beneath the tearful stars, with naught but their soldier blankets about them—oh! as these emotions swept over his great soul, he felt that he would fain have laid him down to rest in the same grave where lies buried the common hope of his people."[34] More organizations followed—the Confederate Survivors' Association of South Carolina, blessed with the same acronym that had adorned the Confederate government, CSA, and later the Association of the Army of Tennessee. Two influential journals also sprang up to carry the Confederate message to the myriad of local and regional groups. The first was a conscious effort to prevent the victors from writing the history. In January 1876, the Southern Historical Society began publishing its *Papers.* That publication was joined later by the *Southern Bivouac,* launched in 1882.

Lee's death ushered in a new period wherein the larger-scale, organized commemoration of Lee and the Southern cause became possible. It was possible then, and not earlier, largely because of the character and reputation of the man whose death spurred the activity. Lee's comportment after the war—his apparent acceptance of the war's resolution—had gratified Northerners. Military leaders of both armies had come to respect, if not admire, Lee's generalship. As historians Thomas Connelly and Alan Nolan have noted, the Lee image created by the commemorative activities may not always have corresponded closely to the man, yet that figure reflected both Southern and Northern needs. Given Lee's demeanor, it was a fairly simple act to interpret him as an individual dedicated to the war aims of the Confederacy yet still avoid vilifying him as a rebel and a traitor. At the unveiling of the sculpture of a heroic, recumbent Lee in the Washington and Lee Chapel, the orator of the day, John W. Daniel, asserted that "Lee had nothing in common with the little minds that know not how to forgive. His was the land that had been invaded; his the people who were cut down, ravaged and ruined; his the home that was torn away and spoliated; his was the cause that perished. He was the General discrowned of his mighty place, and he the citizen disenfranchised. Yet Lee forgave, and counselled all to forgive and forget."[35]

Still, from another perspective, Lee had himself "invaded" the homeland of others, his soldiers had "cut down" a considerable number of Northern sons, and he had violated his prewar officer's oath to the U.S. Constitution, a treasonable offense to some. But emphasizing Lee's "forgiveness" nicely avoided the issue of whether he had been forgiven for his role in the events that Daniel described. Southerners, whether out of emotional need or political savvy—and perhaps both—saw in Lee the archetypal example of the Lost Cause, the gentleman called reluctantly to battle who performed his grim task with grace, intelligence, and consummate skill and sacrificed all for Southern independence. Northerners saw, primarily, a Southern man who had accepted the Northern myth of American union.

In this manner, Lee's longest lasting service to the South probably stemmed not from the battlefield, but from his role as the exemplar upon which reconciliation of North and South could be modeled. In the public response to Lee's death, a new perception of the war and its soldiers first found widespread expression. Much to the South's benefit, the living soldiers would be remembered—as was Lee—for the manner in which they had approached war, not for the underlying motives for which they had fought. The commemoration of Lee set a standard whereby soldiers could be distanced from the reasons they wore a particular uniform, celebrated instead for their élan, their valor, and the power of their convictions. This formulation was not new in 1870, but it had never been carried off with such effect before. This transmutation was also not completed with Lee's death, but that event established the terms on which the national memory of the war would be negotiated in the coming decades. Most importantly, Northerners and Southerners took different inspiration from Lee's example, just as they interpreted the war itself in different ways. Northerners found comfort in his messages of conciliation and cooperation and, after his death, interpreted Lee as a palimpsest upon which they could record a paragon of Southern acquiescence to the Cause Victorious. Conversely, Southerners who had long cherished Lee interpreted Northern postmortem praise of their general as approbation of their cause. At the very moment when Northerners' anxiety over preserving their hard-won war aims began to ease, however slightly, Southerners found new vitality in contesting "national" interpretations of the war and its meaning.

At this particularly significant moment in American history—as the nation approached its centennial, the South its Redemption, and black political power faced its eclipse—Southerners took up in earnest the process of carving out a Southern space within the Northern myth of the Cause Victorious. In part, this process pushed forward the burgeoning desires for reunification. But it also sought to manipulate the Northern myth to secure a new vitality and legitimacy for Southern memory. Where soldiers were concerned, however, the reunification of the nation did not require the perpetuation of memory, but instead sought the balm of forgetfulness. Southerners suggested that it would be far better to concentrate on the personal rather than the political motivations that induced soldiers to fight. This new interpretation would turn public memory away from thinking about armies as enforcers of sectional difference and toward remembering armies as exemplars of military tradition and honor, away from soldiers as conscripted political agents challenging government power through violence and toward soldiers as individuals banding together voluntarily in service of greater truths and ideals. Most important, it involved the turning away from accusations of treason and rebellion toward celebrations of ennobling attributes like dedication, self-sacrifice, and patriotism. This latter point was crucial, for the difficulties of Reconstruction had added to the sins of the South a recalcitrance to embrace the national authority with anything like sincerity, let alone ardor. Southerners wanted to demonstrate that patriotism had never been lacking in the South; it had simply been expressed through opposition to the federal government.

A Southern invention, the focusing of memory on the valor of individual soldiers, became the fervent argument of former Confederates for a good while before being adopted, at first tentatively, by many Union veterans. Gerald Linderman has argued that in many respects soldiers of opposing armies had more in common with each other than with their respective home fronts. It was the experience of combat, of the hardships endured together, that formed a strong and lasting bond between soldiers of both armies.[36] Certainly, there are numerous examples on both sides of respect for and even appreciation of the enemy or his conduct throughout the records of the war. The tenor of the "Battles and Leaders" series published in the pages of *Century Magazine* seem to illustrate such filial sentiments expressed by veterans toward their former foes,[37] just one example within a proliferation of published reminiscences and personal accounts of military service ushered in an era in which the war could be discussed in terms of strategy, logistics, and tactics.

Recently, historian Carol Reardon has pointed out the value of such literary venues: "In many cases for the first time, interested readers could balance familiar Southern chronicles of [Pickett's Charge] with graphic and detailed Northern accounts of its repulse." As a result, Reardon suggests that "these essays helped Northerners and Southerners find mutual respect and common ground for open dialogue."[38] This open dialogue permitted Union and Confederate veterans to speak with one another about their shared experiences of battle without having to touch on the social and political struggles that had necessitated their service. It was later characterized as the tradition of the "American soldier" by an orator speaking at a Memorial Day observance in Jackson, Mississippi, in 1913: "This Confederate soldier we may claim for the South first and foremost, but we must concede to the American people the achievements of his arms as an American soldier. This happily for the South as well as for the whole country, is the sentiment of the men who wore the blue, and it is the sentiment that is reuniting the whole people of the North and the whole people of the South in the bonds of a common patriotism."[39] These public interactions isolated war from its matrix and prove to be the best examples of the transition from a war fully remembered to a war selectively forgotten.

It was in this period, between the death of Lee and the death of Reconstruction, that the defense of the Southern soldiers and the Confederate cause expressed in Memorial Day services took on a new aggressiveness. In 1874, at the reinterment of soldiers who had died in Jubal Early's 1864 raid on Washington, D.C., the first speaker, A. Y. P. Garnett of Maryland, commented on the "sacred duty imposed upon" the living by the sacrifices of the dead and the necessity of honoring those acts: "Whilst the power and resources of this great Government, aided by the wealth of States, and the willing cooperation of a grateful people, have contributed to bestow conspicuous honors upon the fallen dead of the one side, shall we with timid hands and subjugated spirits silently and coldly perform this last ceremony of affection over those we are here to represent? God forbid." Garnett's address, just two years shy of formal Redemption in the South, begins to demonstrate a more dissonant tone in dealing with issues of commemoration: "I congratulate you, my friends, that the period has at length arrived in the history of this unhappy strife and alienation of the two sections of our country, when we are permitted here, under the very shadow of the Federal Capitol, and almost within hearing of the chief magistrate of these United States, free from molestation by any political power, or hostile expression of private animosity, to perform these sad offices of sympathy and love to our fallen brethren."[40] The manner in which Garnett expressed his thoughts is significant. "The period" that had "at length arrived" was not a period of reconciliation or nationalism. It was simply a period when such a sectional observance could be tolerated even "under the very shadow" of the federal, not national, Capitol. But Garnett's purpose was not strictly eulogistic. Or, more precisely, he eulogized more than the dead soldiers surrounding him. He eulogized the South itself, as the plural pronoun in "these United States" makes clear. "In the execution then of this duty which we owe to the dead," Garnett continued, "and in vindication of the truth of history," it was necessary to point out the legitimacy of the Southern cause. Displaying a pattern very similar to that employed in Northern commemorative activities, this funerary and memorial exercise becomes interlaced with justifications of the actions of the living: "We of the South have been charged with inaugurating that war; we have been denounced as traitors and rebels; the vials of wrath have been poured upon our heads; the curse of God has been invoked to wither us and sweep us, with a besom of destruction, from the very face of the earth." Yet, Garnett asserted, the Southern cause of self-government was constitutionally justified and honorable.[41]

From this point, Garnett proceeded through a lengthy justification of Southern motivations, but at last he returned to the dead. After proving to his satisfaction the virtues of the Lost Cause, he asked, "Who dare apply to these Southern soldiers, whose lives have been sacrificed upon the altar of their country's honor, and whose whitened bones now lie before us, the odious appellation of traitors and rebels?" But in a nod toward the Northern nationalist sentiment—perhaps to demonstrate his reasonableness—Garnett concluded, "Let us then return thanks, with grateful hearts, to an all-wise Providence that the contest is ended, and, resting upon the teachings of history, console ourselves with the happy belief that the day is not far distant when, as a united people we shall regard the heroic deeds of both sides, as a precious heritage of a common country."[42] Clearly, for Garnett that day had not yet come, and whenever speaking of the dead was a necessary component of commemorative exercises it remained an elusive dawning for decades to come.

Also in 1874, Judge J. A. P. Campbell introduced his Memorial Day remarks with a justification of the commemorative impulse. "It is right to keep alive," he said, "the spirit of patriotism which inspired our Southern movement." Campbell continued: "This is not inconsistent with our present relations to government, but only shows a just appreciation of that spirit of patriotism which animated our people, and will ever inspire them under any government." Campbell's purpose seemed to be that of demonstrating that no one need have reservations about the resurgent sense of pride in Confederate commemorations: "Fond recollection of the dead implies no want of affection for the living. Fidelity to the Confederate government by its citizens in trial and danger, is an earnest of the same to another. He, who being of it was not loyal to the Confederate cause, may well be doubted in his profession of fidelity to another." Under Campbell's formulation, Northerners should encourage the celebrations of the Confederacy as proof that Southerners have the capacity for loyalty. But it did not take into account that, while fidelity in times of war might be praiseworthy, fidelity in defeat to a failed rebellion is unacceptable. Campbell concluded his remarks that day by warning his audience that "recreant . . . will the survivors of the sad contest be, if the time shall ever come when the dead heroes of the struggle shall be forgotten, or their memory permitted to be tarnished with the uncontradicted slanders of ignorance or *hate*."[43]

Three years later, the noted Southern orator Alexander Boteler sounded a seemingly more modest position at the Memorial Day exercises in Winchester, Virginia. Celebrating those who had "volunteered without bounty, fought without pay and died without murmur," Boteler asked his audience to strike for the way of reconciliation: "It is particularly incumbent upon us now, as American citizens, to do what we properly can to promote that better feeling of justice, liberality and fraternity which is beginning to prevail amongst many of our influential men in high position." "Both sections," he continued, "are learning to do justice to the modifications of honest opinions on all political questions, and the really representative men of each no longer regard those of the other with the jaundiced eyes of local jealousy from the low level of their prejudices. They are recognizing the fact, and, what is still better, *they are publicly admitting it*, that all good Americans do not live on the same side of the Potomac, and that all bad people do not belong to the same political party." Still, in spite of the conciliatory words to all "Americans," Boteler felt compelled to note the existence of "motives which prompt me to refrain to-day from all discussion of the issues of the war."[44] Amid the dead, he felt confident that his characterization of the progress toward reconciliation was accurate, but apparently not strong enough to bear the weight of recalling the underlying reasons that had exploded into war and exacted the deaths being commemorated.

A year later, in 1878, Charles C. Jones Jr. stood among Confederate graves and had no such compunctions. He stated baldly that "for the past we have no apologies to offer, no excuses to render, no regrets to utter, save that we failed in our high endeavor; no tears to shed except over withered hopes and the graves of our departed worthies." Although caution still prevailed in many corners even after Redemption, Jones challenged, "In open day, and in the face of the world, we here protest that so far being 'rebels against legitimate authority and traitors to their country,' our Confederate Dead were 'lovers of liberty, combatants for constitutional rights, and, as [exemplars] of heroic virtue, benefactors of their race.'"[45]

These excerpts demonstrate the persistence of Southern memory of the war and the lasting importance of Memorial Day oration as a vehicle to honor the dead as well as the cause for which they had died. Orations tended to be pulled in two sometimes contradictory directions. As Reconstruction waned, orators tended to become more vehement in their defense of the Southern gamble for independence. Yet, as Boteler's comments demonstrate, the lure of reconciliation—including the promise of national participation and economic rehabilitation—encouraged conciliatory remarks. Still, as the words of Charles C. Jones remind us, the passions of indignation were never very far below the surface.

Northerners, looking on from a distance, satisfied themselves that, following the death of Lee, at least one component of the Cause Victorious— that of Union and the supremacy of the national government—was more secure than it had seemed at any time since the war began. As the rhetoric of veterans shifted to terms of mutual admiration and respect, the former Confederate rebels seemed less rebellious than they once were, more willing to accept the outcome of the war. Of course, the new sense of reconciliatory sentiment came at a high cost. The other war aim—the destruction of slavery—had been the most obvious immediate result of the war, but freedom had proven difficult to define to everyone's satisfaction, especially those who had been formerly enslaved. During the period of greatest resistance to federal authority in the South, many Northerners were willing to define freedom broadly, to include citizenship and the exercise of the franchise among men at the very least. But, after Lee's death, just as Southerners seemed more acquiescent, Northerners demonstrated a willingness to accept narrower definitions of freedom. Clearly, Northerners' priorities after the war centered on their first and most persistent war goal, that of Union. Despite the increasing assertiveness of Confederate rhetoric in the 1870s and 1880s, no serious threat to that national unity emerged. The threats that did emerge—those endangering the freedom of black Southerners—sought to reestablish, socially and economically, the social control inherent in slavery without ever resurrecting the institution explicitly. Therefore, Northerners essentially found it possible to relinquish social justice for black Americans in exchange for satisfaction that the North's war goals of Union and abolition, however narrowly defined, remained secure. This process of negotiation within the larger compass of the Cause Victorious proved so seductive that it survived the full blossoming of Confederate militancy in the 1890s, when another Southern death invigorated the Lost Cause with a vehemence unimaginable at war's end.

As the North had marshaled its nationalist interpretations of the war around Lincoln's death and funeral, the South reacted in much the same way in 1889 to the death of Jefferson Davis. Davis's death held a special poignancy for many Southerners. The long-suffering president of a country that no longer existed became in many ways the living symbol of the Lost Cause. He had absorbed first the condemnation of the North for his leadership of the rebellion and then, in large measure, the condemnation of the South for that rebellion's failure. In the decade before his death, however, Davis—like the South—was redeemed, at least in the sense that his service to the Confederacy took pride of place over his failings as its president. In many ways, as long as Davis lived, so too lived the lost Confederacy. His resurgence was at its peak when he died, and his death felt like the symbolic death of the Confederate cause itself. In mourning Davis, the South mourned itself.[46]

As Lincoln's deathbed had become an important focus of his funeral and Northern mourning, Jefferson Davis's deathbed fulfilled similar needs for Southerners. Most accounts of his death took pains to emphasize the characteristics that it shared with the traditional good death, even when the events did not lend themselves to such an interpretation. Two separate accounts of the deathbed appeared and were reprinted in the nation's major newspapers. An obituary that seems to be the earliest account—appearing in the *New Orleans Picayune,* among other places—recounted that Davis "lost consciousness" at the onset of his last decline "and never sensibly recovered his faculties," remaining in a "comatose condition" until death. The *Augusta (Ga.) Chronicle* reported: "Mr. Davis remained in a comatose condition and the attendants could see no signs of consciousness. Mrs. Davis said she occasionally felt a return of the pressure of the hand she held, although he could neither speak nor make a sign." Alternately, perhaps because this manner of death so disappointed those still clinging to the death rituals and values of the previous generation, a second—contradictory but "better"—death account also appeared. The *Times-Democrat* noted that, from the onset of his last illness, Davis had been in "brave and even buoyant" spirits, the picture of "Christian resignation." This second obituary account continued, remarking on "those gathered around his bedside who had been watching and noting with painful interest" and stating that Davis "never for an instant seemed to lose consciousness. Lying peacefully upon his bed and without a trace of pain in his look, he remained for hours." Some papers, like the *Columbus (Ga.) Enquirer-Sun*, reprinted both accounts of the deathbed, although the Columbus paper compromised somewhat with the headline: "Like a Babe Falling to Sleep He Dies." Even the *Picayune* made the effort to assure its readers of his good death, emphasizing that his face was "always calm and pale," and his wife, Varina, saying that she "occasionally felt a return of the pressure of the hand she held" and confidently relating that "the departure of the spirit was gentle and utterly painless." In a concluding notice that was far more commonplace than the similar notice for Lincoln had been, the *Picayune* reported that Davis's remains were to be embalmed early that morning, 6 December.[47]

There were several points at which Lincoln's deathbed could be compared, to a disadvantage, with Davis's. Of these, the most important is that in the second, alternate account, the emphasis on Davis's remaining alert and resigned contrasted with Lincoln's never having regained consciousness. This allowed for his last words to be recorded, an important custom of the day. Toward the end, as physicians tried to induce him to take medication for his failing condition, Davis refused, saying simply, "Pray, excuse me." These simple words were seized upon by Southerners, who read into them larger meanings associated with Davis and his last years. Davis had never applied for or accepted a renewal of his U.S. citizenship, thus always remaining resolutely a Confederate. Imagined to be gentlemanly to the end, his final words were interpreted as statements of a firm but genteel refusal to be readmitted within the nationality that had defeated his cause.

Davis's funeral was held in New Orleans; businesses closed, and citizens of the city draped their homes and shops with black crepe. J. Wm. Jones, former secretary of the Southern Historical Society, noted that "the draping was so general as to make its absence an occasion of adverse criticism." Davis lay in state in City Hall, in a council chamber quickly inundated with floral displays. In the center of the room, Davis's coffin lay slightly inclined, the top third of the lid made of glass so that the remains would be readily visible. The *Atlanta Constitution* reported that the body was "surrounded by emblems of peace, emblems of war, emblems of the confederacy, and emblems of the union." The mourning was reportedly universal among the town's populace: "Negroes, as well as whites, and grand army men, as well as confederate veterans, lingered over the dead hero with the same manifestations of respect." After lying in state, Jefferson Davis was entombed in the Army of Northern Virginia monument recently constructed in Metairie Cemetery, just outside the city. These arrangements were temporary since his widow had not yet made a determination about a final resting place.[48]

Because of the distance in time that had grown between the war and Davis's death, those two events could not be connected with the same electric immediacy that had pertained in Lincoln's case. But Davis's passing served as a catalyst for ideas long dormant, or at least long held in quiet reserve. Its stimulating effect on Confederate nationalism can be found in the reports of Davis's New Orleans funeral. In the initial descriptions of Davis's lying in state, the reporter for the *New Orleans Picayune* noted only two flags in the room— the regimental flag of the Fourteenth Louisiana, torn and tattered by combat, and "the colors of the United States." These were crossed and against the wall, behind the catafalque. The reporter also described decorations of bunting and examples of "the national colors." But nowhere in the seemingly exacting account is a Confederate flag of any sort mentioned. Nor do the few photographs of the room give much indication of Confederate symbols or emblems, despite the report in the *Atlanta Constitution*. However, in accounts of the first flood of mourners, who stood in long and mournful lines to take one last solemn look at the former president, Confederate flags were noted as being in abundance. One account quotes the *Picayune* as stating: "The Confederate flag, which plays a prominent part in the decorations, was much admired. Some of those present had never seen one."[49]

The flood of telegrams of inquiry and condolence received by the Davis family expressed almost exclusively Southern sympathy. Just as Northern sentiment had largely excluded Southerners from the grief associated with Lincoln's assassination, Southern grief now largely excluded Northerners. Telegrams and other sentiments of bereavement frequently expressed the selective nature of this loss. W. L. Cabell wrote Varina Davis, "Myself in common with all Confederates in Texas mourn the death of your illustrious husband." Governor Daniel Fowler expressed similarly defined sentiments:

Honoring the Civil War Dead

The remains of Jefferson Davis, lying in state in the Council Chamber, New Orleans City Hall. This photograph, by an unknown photographer, gives evidence of the relative lack of Confederate symbols and decorations, the lone exception being the regimental flag of the Fourteenth Louisiana, above and to the right of the casket.
Jefferson Davis Funeral Album, Louisiana Division, New Orleans Public Library

"North Carolina mourns with you the death of the greatest & most beloved of the sons of our south land." Another telegram spoke of "the sorrow of every southern heart today in whatever clime," while many spoke of a South "united" in sorrow and "whole" in grief and of "loyal Southerners" who expressed their love of their lost chieftain. Therefore, as had Lincoln's, Davis's death encouraged many statements about identity, about those included within the circle of mourners and those who stood apart. From St. Joseph, Missouri, Robert A. Hope and a group of "ex-Confederates" sent word that "although we display no outward badge here our hearts are bereaved over the loss of our Chieftain & we mourn with his family." The *Atlanta Constitution* observed, "Messages of condolence come from all parts of the globe, but it is generally known in the city that none have come from the north, except from southern men."[50]

An immense crowd thronged the streets of New Orleans on the day of Jefferson
Davis's funeral. His remains, just appearing between the central columns of City Hall,
are being carried down to the waiting hearse for the journey to Metairie Cemetery.
Note the complete lack of any Confederate flags or symbols, suggesting that Davis's
death provided the foundation for a greater and more visible resurgence of Confederate nationalism, much as Lincoln's death and funeral had provided for the North
twenty-five years earlier.
Jefferson Davis Funeral Album, Louisiana Division, New Orleans Public Library

In addition to the customary statements of bereavement, Varina Davis
received several communications taking up the issue of her indecision. At least
five states asserted a claim on the Confederate president's final resting place,
including Tennessee, Virginia, Georgia, Louisiana, and, perhaps most ardently,
Mississippi. Robert Lowry, the governor of Mississippi, wrote a telegram asking, "Will you kindly make known to the family that Mississippi, the State he
loved so well, will claim the honor of being the resting-place of the patriot, statesman, and nobleman, whose great name is indissolubly linked with her own?"
On behalf of Richmond, Mayor J. Taylor Ellyson had written Varina Davis
directly, and in her reply she expressed at length the difficult nature of her
decision: "If gratitude for the manner in which the people of Richmond sustained him during the war, his affection for her citizens and pride in the calm
fortitude of her men and women under crushing defeat, were to be the moving cause only, I might lay him there unquestioned—But the State of his

birth—Kentucky; the State of his adoption, which showered every honor upon him within her gift—Mississippi—The State where the Confederacy first unfurled her flag[—]Alabama—The State in which his parents spent their early life and where his Father was born, and where my Husband has received many honors—Georgia[—]The State in which we found friends and home, and where our dead repose, Tennessee—and last, not least, the State which now gives him sepulture amidst the tears and plaudits of her people—Louisiana—All these have put forth claims so strong that I cannot choose among them, and have decided to wait perhaps a year before making a selection." Although she would take nearly two years to make the decision, Varina Davis was already aware of the powerful lure that Richmond offered. "To rest in the same soil with your immortal Heroes—Genl Rob't Lee and Stonewall Jackson, is a privilege fully appreciated, and I would be the last to undervalue the boon." Still, there were the other claimants to be considered. Finally, Mrs. Davis simply requested that Ellyson and the others "have patience with me for a season."[51]

The immediate tendering of so many offers of a final burial site, many of them almost frantic in tone, gives emphasis to the effect of Davis's death on the former states of the Confederacy, especially considering the relative inattention accorded Davis and his wife in their declining years. Shortly after her husband's death, perhaps to escape the weight of Southern symbolism, Varina Davis left the South—still undecided as to the issue of a final resting place—and lived the rest of her days in New York, to the consternation and puzzlement of many she left behind.[52]

Of course, nothing could so solidify a defensive adherence to Davis and all that he was now imagined to represent as a dismissive attitude among Northerners. Aside from newspaper notices, there was little response to Davis's death in the North. Although Davis had once served as Franklin Pierce's secretary of war, none of the customary traditions were observed on his death: the flag at the War Department in Washington did not lower to half-mast, his portrait in the hall went unadorned by badges of mourning, and there was no general announcement to the troops. Redfield Procter, the current secretary of war, gave a curt reply to a group who inquired why the War Department flag had not been lowered in respect. Procter's initial response was that he had received no official notice of Davis's death. After receiving such notice the next day, Procter's response was simply "that Jeff Davis, secretary of war, had been dead to the United States government since 1861." Pressed by other reporters for more substantial commentary, Procter clarified his position: "I see no occasion for any action, whatever. It would subserve no good purpose that I can see. It is better to let the matter rest in oblivion—sleep, if it will and to relegate it to the past, than to do anything that would revive memories thus forgotten." Despite the widespread reprinting of these comments, Proctor later wrote to the family in explanation, "In refraining from any official action . . . I would not and hope I do not add to the great sorrow of his family and many friends. It seems to me the right course and the best one for all. You will, I am sure, understand that its adoption is prompted also by a sincere wish and purpose to act in the spirit of peace and good will which should fill the hearts of our people." Alone among the men who had served as secretary of war, Davis's death went unacknowledged.[53]

Many Northerners agreed that Procter had acted appropriately, arguing that Davis's refusal to apply for or accept citizenship demonstrated a marked indifference to the nation. The *Newport (R.I.) Mercury* observed, "Had Jeff Davis died a loyal man, even after his leadership of the confederacy, he would probably have received some token of respect from the War Department, over which he once presided. The flag of the department would have at least been put at half-mast, and orders to do the same would have been issued to all the army posts in the country. But he remained obdurate to the last. He would not accept American citizenship, nor would he apply for pardon nor amnesty for his offences. It was therefore fitting that the department should ignore his existence, as the government which he had attempted to destroy had long done, and perhaps this contemptuous indifference is the severest punishment he could have received."[54]

Such lack of recognition did not prevent Southerners from extending every courtesy, of course. Louisiana and other Southern states lowered the national flag to half-mast on hearing the news. At a funeral oration in Augusta, Georgia, the noted Lost Cause champion Charles C. Jones Jr. condemned Northern behavior, stating, "Although no Federal Flag be displayed at half-mast, or Union guns deliver the funeral salute customary upon the demise of an ex-Secretary of War, we may regard with composure the littleness of the attempted slight, and pity the timidity, the narrow-mindedness, and the malevolence of the powers that be. The great soul of the dead chief has passed into a higher, a purer sphere uncontaminated by sectional hatred, wholly purged of all the dross engendered by contemptible human animosity."[55]

Moreover, the oratorical and literary expressions associated with Davis's death seemed to adopt a decidedly more belligerent tone than had been obvious before. What had been expressed in bold but still guarded terms after Lee's death emerged with new aggressiveness after Davis's. In Norfolk, Virginia, in a sermon recounted in Richmond's newspapers, Methodist minister W. G. Starr frankly told his congregation that he "would be ready to pick up his gun for the same cause at any time." Southern papers also noted the stir caused by a woman residing in Washington, D.C., who decorated her home in crepe and mourning symbols in honor of Davis. "It was suggested to her by one of the newspaper men who called on her this morning that some one might try to tear the mourning emblems down. If any one entertains such an idea he only need first see Mrs. Fairfax as she appeared when that suggestion was made. He will at once abandon his project." The most significant aspect of the incident was the neighborhood in which it occurred. "A number of colored people gathered on the sidewalk opposite the house," the paper continued, "and loudly criticized the action of the inmates, but they went no further, and at a late hour this afternoon the dismal drapery and the red, white, and red rosettes were still in place, fluttering in the cool breezes and reflecting their colors in the windows of the Lincoln school building, which happens, curiously enough, to be precisely opposite [the home]." Richmond Mayor J. Taylor Ellyson told local reporters: "The southern people loved him because he suffered for them. They are prepared to protect and guard his memory from the fierce future winds of prejudice in saying to all those who hated him and whose hearts are consumed at this hour by sectional animosities, 'If this be treason make the most of it.'"[56] Such expressions indicate that Davis's death served the same nationalist function that Lincoln's death had served. In reflecting on the life lived, Davis's death provided a foundation for a particularly aggressive resurgence in Southern rhetoric and commemorative activities.

While direct links are difficult to establish, the period of increased commemorative activity that immediately followed Davis's death has no parallel in the postwar history of the South. In 1889, the United Confederate Veterans (UCV) was established. Structurally organized into small units much like the posts of the GAR, the UCV eventually incorporated hundreds of the small, local veterans' groups throughout the South as "camps" named in honor of notable Southern war heroes. As postwar mobility had carried veterans across the Mason-Dixon line, many Northern states hosted active UCV camps, just as many Southern states hosted GAR posts. But unlike its Northern counterpart, the UCV was the only multistate Confederate veterans' organization.

Moreover, its political power was minuscule compared to that of the GAR. Political activism therefore remained only a small part of its functions. Finding most of the political fruits garnered by the GAR—pensions, interment of spouses in national cemeteries, preferential hiring for government positions— beyond its reach, the UCV focused instead on fraternal support of Southern veterans and commemoration of the war. Of course, Southern women had blazed that path since Appomattox. But, with the abandonment of Reconstruction and the resumption of white-supremacist rule in the South, former Confederates could again become politically and socially active—albeit in a far more modest way than the members of the GAR could—without suffering serious repercussions.

However, the rise of the UCV and the surge of Southern men into commemorative activity did little to abate the continuing commemorative activity of Southern women. Even though most reburial movements had been completed by the 1880s, Ladies Memorial Associations across the South mostly carried on undeterred. Many simply broadened their activities beyond the maintenance of local cemeteries and the observance of Memorial Day to include the care of ailing and indigent veterans and their families, the monumentalization of the landscape, and the preservation of Southern history. These goals were tackled piecemeal and independently by women's groups throughout the former Confederacy, through the establishment of soldiers' homes and hospitals, fund-raising for everything from memorial statuary and columns to stained-glass windows, and the publication of histories, local and sectional, espousing the particularly Southern vision of the war and its aftermath.[57]

In 1890, the women of Nashville organized and chartered with the city the Ladies' Auxiliary to the Confederate Soldiers' Home. Two years later, at a dinner hosted by the auxiliary, the president and founder of the organization, Mrs. M. C. Goodlett, proposed that the name of the organization be changed to reflect their broader benevolent concerns and to honor the daughter of Jefferson Davis. Southerners had become quite proprietary of all the Davises: in 1886, the family friend and staunch defender Jubal Early introduced Winnie Davis to an admiring audience as "the Daughter of the Confederacy." Although Southern papers howled when she accepted marriage to a Yankee who was the grandson of abolitionist Reverend Samuel J. May, taking Early's cue Goodlett proposed that the new name of the group be the Daughters of the Confederacy. Within two years of Goodlett's proposal, all

Southern women's groups merged, and the national organization that eventually coalesced was incorporated as the United Daughters of the Confederacy (UDC) in 1894.[58] The two parent organizations—the UCV and the UDC—were joined by the Sons of Confederate Veterans in 1896 and the Children of Confederate Veterans in 1898, organizations that sought to marshal the efforts of subsequent generations of Southerners.[59] For all these groups, the commemoration of the war dead remained a consistent priority.

The 1890s proved to be the high-water mark of Southern commemoration. Not since the war had so many individuals and so many resources been overtly committed to the Southern cause. Sparked by the death of Lee, and nurtured by Redemption, the cause of Southern commemoration received its greatest impetus from the death of Davis. Ironically, the symbolism of that death was strengthened by a funeral train that in sentiment and effect could not equal, but certainly echoed, the funeral train of Lincoln. Almost four years after his death, the decision about a final resting place for Davis still weighed heavily on his widow. After his passing, she bore much of the attention that had centered on her husband, representing so many Southern widows, bearing the loss of their husbands taken so long ago. As Lincoln's death had brought the death of the Civil War to so many Northern homes, Davis's death renewed the personal loss of the South. It was common knowledge that the tomb in New Orleans was a temporary one: over the years Mississippi, Virginia, Tennessee, Alabama, Kentucky and Georgia had all continued to make overtures to Varina Davis for the honor of holding permanently Davis's remains. Finally, in 1883, she declared that Hollywood Cemetery in the former Confederate capital of Richmond was the fittest place for her husband to rest. So, with less fanfare than had been accorded Lincoln, and certainly with less notice in the Northern papers, Davis was removed from his tomb, placed on a train, and carried east to Virginia.[60]

As Lincoln's death and westward funeral train procession throughout the Northern states served as a powerful catalyst for Northern commemorative patterns—indeed, as a spur to the Northern myth of American nationalism—Davis's eastward but similar procession had an identical effect on Southerners. On 29 May 1893, a train and its escort left the New Orleans station headed east (see table 4). The train slowed through towns and villages but except for three state capitals—Montgomery, Atlanta, and Raleigh—made few stops along the way. In each of the capital cities, the remains were removed from the train and carried through streets thronged with onlookers to lie in state

Table 4. Timetable of Davis Funeral Train, May 1893

	Arrival	Public Viewing	Departure
New Orleans	Disinterment, 27 May		7:50 P.M., 28 May
Montgomery	6:00 A.M., 29 May	[8:30–10:30 A.M.], 29 May	11:30 A.M., 29 May
Atlanta	4:30 P.M. 29 May	[5:30]–7:00 P.M., 29 May	[8:30 P.M.], 29 May
Raleigh	1:05 P.M., 30 May	[1:30–3:00 P.M., 30 May]	3:40 P.M., 30 May
Richmond	3:10 A.M., 31 May	Dawn–3:00 P.M., May 31	Interment

Total: 55 hours, 1,200 miles

Sources: Edison H. Thomas, "Story of the Jefferson Davis Funeral Train," reprinted from *L. & N. Magazine* (February 1955); Michael B. Ballard, "Jeff Davis' Last Ride," *Civil War Times Illustrated* 32, no. 1 (March/April 1993): 32–39; *New York Times,* 28–31 May 1893.

Note: All times are local time, and brackets indicate approximations. Although two hours were allotted for each viewing in Montgomery, Atlanta, and Raleigh, frequent delays and stops adversely affected the planned timetable. Unlike at Lincoln's funeral, Davis's corpse was never on display to the general public.

for two hours. The train slowed near Beauvoir, in Biloxi, Mississippi, the Davises' last home, where children had strewn the tracks with flowers. At Montgomery, Alabama, the Confederate flag that had flown above the Southern occupation of Fort Sumter was resurrected to fly over the statehouse as his body was carried into the capitol through the same portico where he had taken his oath of office.[61] At West Point, Georgia, a large floral archway spanned the tracks, similar to the dozens that had decorated Lincoln's westward journey.

On 30 May, ironically the Northern observance of Memorial Day that year, Davis's body was carried from the train to lie in state in the capitol at Raleigh, North Carolina. The history of the local Ladies Memorial Association recalled the train's appearance in that city: "At the South gate of the Capitol Square, Gov. Elias Carr and his staff, in full dress uniform, met the procession. Church bells tolled and all Raleigh seemed to be in mourning. Public buildings and stores were closed and those along the line of march were draped in black, and with Confederate flags. . . . Over the casket was laid the bullet-torn flag of the Fiftieth North Carolina. Many beautiful floral designs were placed around the catafalque. Designs of the Confederate flag, made of flowers, were sent from nearby towns . . . The State colors were at half mast at the Capitol."[62] The "full dress uniform" worn by the governor and others was certainly gray in color, and the notation that the state flag was at half-mast invites the reader to think about the national flag that was not. Throughout this procession, almost in contrast with Davis's first funeral, Confederate flags and symbols were plentiful. Finally, the train arrived in Richmond at about 3:00 A.M. on 31 May, and, after a day of processions, orations, and grieving, the president that the other half of the nation mourned was laid to rest.[63]

The death of Davis heralded the rise of the most overt expressions celebrating the Lost Cause and the Confederate dead. These expressions were possible, not only because the South had emerged from the restrictions that had haunted its commemorative impulse in the quarter century since the war's end, but also because it had negotiated throughout that span with the North for a national memory of the war. The advantage that the South maintained throughout that process centered on the necessity of the North finding a way to reincorporate the once-rebellious and now newly resurgent Confederates. The precepts of the Cause Victorious demanded it. But the process of reintegration so necessary to securing, finally, the victory of the battlefield was a difficult one, requiring Northerners to confront, not only white Southerners, but black Americans as well. The resolution of the thesis of Northern national demands and the antithesis of the Lost Cause was found in the uneasy synthesis of reconciliation.

"Something Like a National Act":
The Uneasy Synthesis of American Nationalism

Brave hearts! brave Ethiopia's dead
On hills, in vallies lie,
On every field of strife, made red
With gorey victory.
. . .
The land is holy where they fought,
And holy where they fell,
For by their blood, that land was bought,
That land they loved so well—
. . .
Fair Afric's *free* and valient sons,
Shall join with Europe's band,
To celebrate in varied tongues,
Our *free* and happy land.

Till freedom's golden fingers trace
A line that knows no end,
And man shall meet in every face,
A brother and a friend.
   —Sarah Shuften, *"Ethiopia's Dead"* (1865)

O N THE SPRING MORNING OF 14 APRIL 1876, three delegations of the American people gathered to acknowledge the importance of Abraham Lincoln in their respective national lives. The first delegation included Ulysses S. Grant, president of the United States, members of his cabinet, congressmen, Supreme Court justices, and diplomats. The second delegation was led by Frederick Douglass, the keynote speaker at the day's festivities, as well as John Mercer Langston and Bishop John M. Brown of the African Methodist Episcopal Church. The second group was, for the most part, easily distinguishable from the first—by color. The sitting Forty-fourth Congress contained but eight black congressmen from six states. They could not know, but perhaps suspected, that their numbers represented the zenith of black congressional representation and that things would remain so for nearly a century. But the third delegation present that morning had for several years worked diligently to eclipse the second. Its members represented the resurgent political might of the South, returning to the halls of influence in numbers completely unanticipated in 1865.[1]

All those assembled had come to honor publicly the individual who had most significantly affected their mutual nation, Abraham Lincoln. On that April morning, the eleventh anniversary of Lincoln's murder, those citizens—white, black, Northern, and Southern—gathered to unveil a monument to his memory and his legacy. The Freedmen's Memorial Monument to Abraham Lincoln depicts the metaphoric moment of emancipation. A standing Lincoln gestures beatifically to an enslaved black man crouching before him, posed in the act of rising from his knees, his shackles broken and fallen from his ankles. While Lincoln looks down paternally, the rising freedman looks straight ahead and upward, toward the horizon of his future, which, by 1876, many perceived to be already clouding.[2]

In his dedicatory remarks, Frederick Douglass noted that the impulses motivating the dedication of the Freedmen's Monument were identical to those motivating the commemoration of the war dead. That day, Douglass proclaimed, he and the others in attendance were responding to an outpouring of "the sentiment"—including the desire to memorialize "great public men"—"from which year to year adorns with fragrant and beautiful flowers the graves of our loyal, brave, and patriotic soldiers who fell in defense of the Union and liberty. It is the sentiment of gratitude and appreciation, which often, in the presence of many who hear me, has filled yonder heights of Arlington with the eloquence of eulogy and sublime enthusiasm of poetry and song; a sentiment which can never die while the Republic lives." Douglass's rhetoric was that of the Cause Victorious, employing such delimiting terms as *loyal,* and brooking no possible misinterpretation with his clarification of the deaths incurred "in defense of the Union."[3]

But for Douglass that sentiment was subordinate to a more significant nationalist message. The importance of the monument lay in its nature as an expression of black memory, of black commemoration: "For the first time in the history of our people, and in the history of the whole American people, we join in this high worship and march conspicuously in the line of this time-honored custom. First things are always interesting, and this is one of our first things. It is the first time that, in this form and manner, we have sought to do honor to any American great man, however deserving and illustrious. I commend the fact to notice."[4] Standing in Washington at the highest point of black political power and representation since Emancipation, Douglass employed the possessive language familiar to Northern orators since Lincoln's assassination, but for a separate purpose. For the divisions that Douglass noted between "our people" and "the whole American people" were predicated, not on sectional animosities, new and old, but on prejudices, deep-seated and ancient. The object of "high worship" was, of course, Lincoln, but, as Douglass noted, the day of commemoration was as significant as any act of Lincoln's, for it represented the action of black Americans, as a people and as members of the American polity, an act worthy of notice.

That black men and women were Americans, legally fully imbued with citizenship, partners—albeit junior partners—in the continuing experiment, was one of the most revolutionary aspects of the war and of the Cause Victorious with which Northerners interpreted that conflict. Douglass had opened and closed his oration with congratulatory remarks on the fitness of the dedicatory exercises. But his careful eye noted that sectional variations in political and social adherence to the American nation still reigned nearly unfettered:

> Let it be told in every part of the Republic; let men of all parties and opinions hear it; let those who despise us, not less than those who respect us, know that now and here, in the spirit of Liberty, Loyalty, and Gratitude, . . . we, the colored people, newly emancipated and rejoicing in our blood-bought freedom, near the close of the first century in the life of this Republic, have now and here unveiled, set apart, and dedicated a monument of enduring granite and bronze, in every line, feature and figure of which men of this generation may read— and those of after-coming generations may read—something of the exalted character and great works of Abraham Lincoln, the first martyr President of the United States.

"Nowhere else in this great country . . . ," Douglass asserted, "could conditions be found more favorable to the success of this occasion than here. We stand to-day at the national centre to perform something like a national act."[5] While we cannot now be certain of the reasons why Douglass qualified his statement, allowing that the commemoration of emancipation could be only "something like" a national act, his words indicate that despite the Northern myth's assertion of the nation as whole and undivided, the reality of a unified people within that nation remained elusive, as it would for many years to come.

The Cause Victorious required the incorporation of two alien peoples within the perceived membership of the nation, and in neither case was incorporation easy. Emancipation required that property become people, but people of uncertain and ill-defined status within the body politic. Union required that former rebels, traitors, and insurrectionists be again embraced as fellow citizens, but citizens of an equally uncertain status. Both movements toward drawing foreign elements into the American nation challenged all previous definitions, customary or legal, of what it meant to be an American. Therefore, as the definitions were challenged by war and its consequences, the "imagined community" of Americans was similarly redefined.[6] Struggling with the deeply rooted suspicions of race prejudice as well as with the animus inspired by a horrible war, Northern Americans crafted a myth of unity even as they struggled with its implications.

No action challenged so dramatically the Northern public's perception of black men in America as their enlistment into the Union army. Northern civilians who had followed the Union army south to the coastal islands of South Carolina and Georgia were among the first outside the military to face the contradictions in racial thought revealed in black military service. One of these civilians, Robert Steward Davis, wrote of the military actions around Charleston. Discussing the storied Massachusetts Fifty-fourth Regiment, the first black regiment formed in the North, Davis described its deportment during its first battle as noble and heroic, "the gallantry and bravery of this regiment, vindicating beyond a doubt the colored man of the North as a man of patriotism and courage." But, in the next paragraph, Davis revealed his difficulty with his own portrait of black soldiers. In telling the story of a black sergeant bringing in a tall Confederate prisoner, Davis presented him as a minstrel character—"a ludicrous sight; the little negro with expanding eyes, large mouth, ivory-glistening," "[a] stunted negro who could with ease have walked between the legs of his prize." Davis, praising and denigrating with nearly the same breath, reflected the deep-seated susceptibility of Northerners to racial stereotype. In the next installment of his memoirs, Davis wrote of the extraordinary assault on Fort Wagner led by the men of the Fifty-fourth. Davis asked, "Who fight more valiantly than the 54th Massachusetts, as they struggle in the midst of this darkness and death to indicate their race?"[7] The ease with which Davis shifts his descriptions of black soldiers, from images of minstrelsy to awe-inspiring heroism, reveals how deeply conflicted whites were in their interpretations of black military service. In the war, black men sought to "indicate" their worth as soldiers, individually and collectively, with acts that reflected inevitably on their worth as men. In accomplishing this, however, their actions fell completely outside the prejudiced expectation of white officers and soldiers. Thus, Davis must ask his question, even within a social and military context where nothing was more apparent than race.

Emancipation may have been the most significant event of the war, fully investing the Northern war effort with a moral as well as a political imperative, but translating slaves into freedmen through law produced few obvious and immediate alterations in the relationship between those who had been enslaved and the nation that had enslaved them. Now free, African Americans would have no constitutional standing as citizens until the ratification of the Fourteenth Amendment, still several years away. However, clothing these men in national uniforms, arming them and training them to use those arms, deploying them alongside white soldiers on the same nationalistic mission—all these changes forever altered the relationship of black Americans to white society. But, as Davis's text demonstrates, whites' perception of black soldiers proved to be deeply conflicted. For more than two generations, men and women on both sides of Mason's and Dixon's line had been thoroughly enmeshed in an intellectual context asserting the inferiority of Africans and their descendants in America. The hesitancy to embrace black Americans as soldiers "can only be explained," according to *Harper's Weekly,* "by referring to the extraordinary manner in which for forty years slavery had been warping the heart and mind of the American people. A generation of men had grown up in awe of slavery, and in unchristian contempt of the blacks. And that generation declared that it would not have negro soldiers."[8] Through this perceptual lens, Northerners had great difficulty accepting men who became a living denial of such racialist concepts. However, an even greater challenge to the Northern perception of black soldiers arose in the need—the desire—to commemorate the contributions of black men to the successful prosecution of the war.

There were, unfortunately, numerous opportunities to mourn black soldiers, for the nature of their service often exposed them to greater risks than their white counterparts. These greater risks were almost entirely the product of racism. Thomas Wentworth Higginson referred to the "astonishing blunder of organizing the colored regiments of half-size at the outset," a measure "however agreeable it might have been to the horde of aspirants for [officers'] commissions, was … based on the utterly baseless assumption that they required twice as many officers as [white soldiers]."[9] These half-sized regiments often went into battle undermanned, top heavy in command, yet lacking in effective strength, ironically often serving in combination with other half-strength regiments that had fallen to that status through the attrition of combat.

But the dimension of military racialist thought that produced the most devastating effect on black troops was the military's perception of disease and sickness. The proportion of whites who died of disease in relation to those who died in combat or from wounds was approximately two to one, the proportion of blacks approximately eight to one. In proportion to the number of soldiers enlisted, one in seven black soldiers, but only one in fifteen white soldiers, died from disease.

The awareness of the problem, during the war and immediately after, was widespread. In 1869, Benjamin Apthorp Gould assembled a statistical review of Union soldiers based on the records of the U.S. Sanitary Commission. In his study, Gould noted "the inordinate mortality and singular susceptibility to fatal disease exhibited by the colored troops" but declined to review the matter "since our materials are inadequate for the proper investigation of the subject." An article appearing in the *Chicago Tribune* and reprinted widely frankly acknowledged the "extraordinary mortality among the colored troops from disease." Unlike Gould, the *Tribune* author was willing to conjecture about the cause of such high rates of death: "These figures indicate conclusively that the negro, in the condition in which the war found him, was less capable than the white man of enduring the trials, physical and moral, of military service." The causes of fatal diseases among blacks, the article continues, were almost certainly of a "psychological character," demonstrating that "the great susceptibility of the colored man to disease arose from a certain lack of mental activity and buoyancy of feeling, and that a higher moral and intellectual culture would diminish the effect." "This view," the *Tribune* asserted, "is sustained by the professional opinion of medical authorities."[10]

The need to explain these rates of disease incidence rationally involved the *Tribune* author in a number of errors. Blacks were characterized as less able to endure the physical strain of military service, but nearly every commander in the field praised their endurance, particularly at physical labor, often at the expense of white soldiers. In addition, the assertion that blacks were less "buoyant" cut against the grain of nearly every white assessment of black mental character. Uneducated black men could, perhaps, justly be accused of being without mental complexity, but then so could uneducated white men. Further, when the *Tribune* author was confronted with difficult statistics pertaining to white soldiers—for example, disease incidence was particularly high among Iowa soldiers, as high as 114 deaths per 1,000—he concluded, not that disease bore no relation to innate qualities, but that "the variations of mortality from disease resulted in part from the nature of the respective services required of troops drawn from different localities." This explanation was not applied to black soldiers, whose death rate—more than 140 per 1,000—was much higher even than Iowa's. Thus, the source of black disease was located *within* black men, while white disease was more often attributed to environmental stress.[11]

Yet the environment played a crucial role in the perpetuation of high disease rates among black soldiers. It is clear from army records that black soldiers were often intentionally exposed to disease—at times expressly to prevent the exposure of white soldiers. In 1865, Major General J. M. Schofield specifically instructed a subordinate officer in North Carolina to "use the colored troops as you think best, so as to relieve the white troops from duty where they would be exposed to disease." Of course, American medicine was largely ignorant of germ theory or the vectors that influenced communicability. As James McPherson has noted, the Civil War occurred at "the end of the medical Middle Ages."[12] But it is also clear that, during the war, evidence was mounting that the presuppositions of black immunity were incorrect.

In November 1863, the medical inspector for Arkansas forwarded to the Surgeon General his observations based on research into the specific contention that "negroes have been found to enjoy comparative immunity from miasmatic diseases." Among white soldiers in the area, about 84 percent of all illnesses were the result of miasmatic disease, as were eight of fourteen deaths (a mortality rate of 57 percent). In the same period, only about 51 percent of diseases among black troops were miasmatic in nature, although the mortality rate of blacks—twenty-five of fifty-two deaths (or 48 percent)—was roughly similar to that of whites. Still, among black civilians, "contrabands," treated at the hospital, 75 percent suffered from diseases of the same class, but their mortality rate approached 68 percent (twenty-five of thirty-seven deaths). From these data, the inspector concluded that "These facts[,] it seems to me[,] clearly show that negro soldiers do not enjoy immunity from what has proved to be the great scourge of our armies—malaria." Additionally, in considering the incidence of all illness and mortality in a broader context, the inspector's analysis showed that, while sickness rates were fairly similar among white and black troops (15 and 12 percent, respectively), there was a startling disparity in overall mortality rates: for white soldiers fewer than one death per hundred (only 0.89 percent), but among blacks over four deaths per hundred (4.17 percent), a rate nearly five times as high. The inspector closed his recounting of these stark figures by observing: "White and negro troops are called upon to perform precisely the same kind of duty. Both are fed[,] clothed and treated alike and have equally good quarters[,] and the medical supplies are the same for each[.] [U]nder these circumstances I can only come to the conclusion that negro soldiers are nearly or quite as subject to miasmatic diseases as are white soldiers and further that when once brought down by these diseases that they do not so readily recover as do whites."[13]

Despite this evidence, medical officers and military commanders were slow to recognize its importance. Officers continued to make decisions about troop assignments on the basis of their perception of race and the relative health risks posed by particular areas. The combination of ignorance and racialist determinism had tragic consequences for black soldiers assigned to high-risk areas. Those consequences were at their worst during the postwar occupation of Texas, a disaster that reflected the racial prejudice, ignorance, and disdain that plagued any attempt to incorporate black men within the Cause Victorious.

Just after the end of the war, in June 1865, the Union army began demobilizing while at the same time selecting key ports for occupation. In addition, the Johnson administration continued Lincoln's practice of keeping a watchful eye on the French engagements in Mexico. Acting on a request from the president, Henry W. Halleck detached two army corps, the all-white Fourth Corps and the all-black Twenty-fifth Corps, to Texas for occupation detail. The creation of the Twenty-fifth Corps in December 1864 itself reflects the conflicted relationship between Union officers and their black subordinates. Historians have traditionally emphasized the corps as the pinnacle of black military organization. Dudley Taylor Cornish, for example, remarks that it is "unique in American military history, . . . an entire army corps made up of Negro regiments, thirty-two in all." Another historian refers to the Twenty-fifth as "the largest concentration of black soldiers engaged in any one theater during the war."[14] Much rarer is the acknowledgment that the Twenty-fifth Corps was created through the process of segregating white and black regiments who previously had served together in the Eighth and Tenth Corps. While the Twenty-fifth is a notable achievement for a military service that only reluctantly admitted black men barely two years earlier, the motive behind its formation is a shabby one—the desire of white officers and soldiers not to have to interact with black soldiers.

Whatever the impetus for creating the Twenty-fifth, the motivations for sending it to Texas were clouded by prejudice. The man seemingly most responsible for the assignment was Halleck. Despite the success that the Twenty-fifth had demonstrated in the field, Halleck grew increasingly disdainful of his black army corps. Within two weeks of Lincoln's assassination, he wrote Secretary of War Edwin Stanton about ridding himself of it: "[The Twenty-fifth] is reported to me as being poorly officered and in bad discipline, and altogether unfit for the military occupation of Virginia. Would it not be well to send this corps to the Rio Grande, in Texas . . . ?" The next day, 29 April, Halleck opened the subject with Ulysses S. Grant: "General Ord [a subordinate of Halleck's] represents that want of discipline and good officers in the Twenty-Fifth renders it a very improper force for the preservation of order in this department. A number of cases of atrocious rape by these men have already occurred. Their influence on the colored population is also reported to be bad. I therefore hope you will remove it to garrison forts or for service on the Southern coast and substitute a corps from the Army of the Potomac."[15]

Halleck's postwar tenderness for the Virginians in his area of influence remains unexplained. His statements, however, invite speculation. None of the white army corps under Halleck were singled out for this kind of criticism, and several were certainly as lacking in discipline. The emphasized reference to "atrocious" rape suggests that Halleck is, perhaps unconsciously, making a distinction with a lesser category of sexual violence. It seems likely that Halleck complains of assaults on *white* women by men of the Twenty-fifth, not black women, thereby making the attacks "atrocious" in a way that he might not have expressed had the circumstances been otherwise. Indeed, Halleck's only concern for other black men and women in the area is that the presence of thirty-two regiments of armed black soldiers was having a "bad" influence on the former slaves in the region. Again, although not stated specifically, Halleck's reference is almost certainly to the inspiration that the local black population must have taken from the presence of the Twenty-fifth

Corps, a palpable and obvious power composed entirely of people whom white Virginians once strived to render powerless. A brief note survives from General Ord to Halleck, informing him of the impending court-martial of a single member of the Twenty-fifth, accused of rape, but there is no other evidence to support Halleck's description of a "number of cases." Ultimately, had the Twenty-fifth been an all-white unit, no single act by an individual would have condemned the entire corps to the fate that Halleck designed.

The corps was ordered out of Halleck's jurisdiction, assigned to garrison and post duty along the coast of Texas from Indianola south to Brownsville and extending as far up the Rio Grande as possible. The Fourth Corps, an all-white organization, was sent to Texas at the same time, but its zone of assignment was central Texas. The placement of the two corps was intentional and specifically concerned with disease. General Philip Sheridan, the military commander in the region, directed in his orders that the Twenty-fifth Corps "will be required along the Gulf Coast" while the Fourth "can be put at points further from the coast *where it is healthier.*"[16]

In Texas, as in other regions in which the war was conducted, disease was the primary killer, but there it approached a virulence seldom seen elsewhere. The Gulf Coast presented a strange combination of desert and bayou. The chaplain of the Fifteenth Ohio Volunteer Veterans wrote vividly of the "rebel mosquitoes" plaguing Indianola and of the water in the town's cisterns thickly contaminated with their larvae, or what he called the "wiggles."[17] In addition to these indigenous vectors of disease, occasionally regiments already infected with a variety of communicable illnesses were stationed alongside other, uninfected troops. More than a year before the arrival of the Twenty-fifth Corps, the commander at New Orleans was instructed to house an incoming shipment of black soldiers apart from other military units and civilians: "Two contagious diseases have broken out among them (mumps and measles), [and] the commanding general does not desire to send them among the troops in Texas until the diseases shall have run out."[18]

Also contributing to the high fatality rates from disease was poor logistic support on the part of the military. Historian Joseph T. Glatthaar has noted that the army was not prepared to supply food to the numerous troops suddenly deposited on the Texas coastline and that what rations were available were sadly deficient in essential nutrients. As a result, scurvy and other nutritional deficiencies further weakened and sickened the troops, making them more susceptible to the ravages of the diseases that they encountered. Similarly, hospital and medical supplies were also lacking. The nearest hospital, an eighty-bed facility located in Brazos Santiago, was overwhelmed with more than five hundred cases on the arrival of the Twenty-fifth. Many of the ill had to be transported as far as New Orleans, and eventually a second hospital was established at Brownsville, where men died at the rate of ten a day.[19]

B. R. Catlin, the chaplain for one of the regiments assigned to the Texas occupation, tried to convey the difficulties faced by the men in his charge. With the exception of two brief two-day stops at Mobile Bay and Fort Jackson, Louisiana, the regiment had been on board its transport vessel from 26 May until landing in Texas on 26 June. During that long, oppressive voyage, Catlin had been able to provide church services three times and had presided over three funerals. He lamented that "the circumstances of the voyage were very unfavorable to the work of a chaplain. The men were necessarily confined to close, dark quarters, without active employment and many of them sea-sick. There was therefore little opportunity for instruction, nor could much be done to promote their cheerfulness and fortitude." But, as difficult as the circumstances on board ship were, it was the nature of their assignment that most weighed on the soldiers in his care:

> And it may be added that they were very much disappointed in being ordered to Texas. For many of them allege that at the time they were mustered into the U.S. Service promises were made them—that they should have a furlough at the end of six months service—that they should be discharged at the end of the war and—that if they continued in the service they should have sixty days furlough each year. These alleged promises encouraged them to hope for a speedy return to Kentucky, where the Reg't. was recruited. Those men having families were especially disappointed when they learned that their destination was Texas.

In its first month on the Texas coast, Catlin reported, the regiment lost "two officers . . . and five privates by death from disease." Catlin also revealed that he shared the mistaken impression that attitude and cheerfulness might provide immunity against the rigors of life in Texas. "The men manifest improved spirits, though the cherished hope of soon returning to their homes in Kentucky continue to operate against their cheerful and hearty adoption of a soldiers trials and duties." However, in September, Catlin quietly noted the effect that environment could have on the regiment: "A Company which had been detailed at an earlier date to cut timber in an unhealthy location has returned with a loss by death of about twenty five per cent. of the number it brought to Texas."[20]

The death of Union soldiers in Texas, as elsewhere throughout the Southland, forced the creation of cemeteries that would eventually be incorporated into the National Cemetery System. Black soldiers were regularly buried in the national cemeteries, but their inclusion was not without racialist dimensions. The burial squads frequently reinterred black soldiers in segregated plots, often located in the more undesirable areas of the proposed cemetery grounds. Additionally, the graves of identified black soldiers were often dispersed in areas of the cemetery otherwise allocated to the interment of unidentified remains. Corinth National Cemetery, for example, has only a handful of U.S. Colored Troops interments, but their conspicuous headstones are seemingly randomly scattered among the small numbered blocks of unknown soldiers in the southeastern corner of the cemetery. While examples of such segregated burial can be multiplied easily, the clearest evidence of at least some racial determinism in national cemetery construction comes from the example of Texas and the Twenty-fifth Corps.

In 1866, apparently both as a function of the developing National Cemetery System and as a part of an ancillary project undertaken by the Quartermaster Department to publish a "Roll of Honor" listing the names and locations of as many of the Union dead as could be identified, Assistant Quartermaster Jason M. Moore coordinated a survey of the Union dead in Texas. The survey revealed to others what was already evident to those already there, the high mortality rate among the arriving occupation troops. The survey recorded Union burials in twenty-six separate cemeteries: 358 of white soldiers in fifteen different locations and 840 of black soldiers also in fifteen different locations. Although the survey indicates that the dead were "interred . . . during the Rebellion," almost all the dates of death listed indicate the soldiers died after war's end and that, hence, almost all were among the occupation troops sent to Texas beginning in June 1865.[21]

The segregationist policies that resulted in the geographically separate assignments of the Fourth and the Twenty-fifth Corps are evident in the distribution of their dead. In what became known as the Eastern District, centered on the northern Gulf Coast by Galveston, 54 white soldiers were buried in 4 locations and 9 black soldiers in a single location. In the Central District, anchored on the coast by Port Lavaca and Indianola but extending inland as far as San Antonio—the assignment of the Fourth Corps—154 white soldiers and officers were buried in 8 locations and 114 black soldiers in 6. Finally, in the southernmost district, which ranged from Corpus Christi south to Brazos Santiago, then up the Rio Grande to Brownsville and beyond to the Ringgold Barracks at Romo, 160 white soldiers were buried in 3 separate locations, 717 black soldiers in 8 locations.

Moore's initial survey seems to be something of a feasibility study, for at this early point no movement or collection of the dead in Texas was attempted or apparently contemplated—despite the fact that in other regions the bodies of the Union dead were being concentrated into central cemeterial locations. Moore commented, "Scattered as these places are over a large extent of territory, it was not considered advisable to disinter the remains and remove them to a central cemetery."[22] While the distances involved in working in Texas were, at times, considerable, burial details at work in the central and eastern parts of the American South did, nevertheless, collect and transport bodies over distances as great and even greater.

Despite the initial disinclination to create national cemeteries in Texas, three were eventually established in the primary administrative centers of the three military districts, Galveston, San Antonio, and Brownsville. Again, because service assignments among the three regions had been segregated, the collection of the dead into the national cemeteries naturally reflects that separation. Soldiers of the Rio Grande District, mostly black men, were buried in the largely black cemetery at Brownsville. Similarly, Galveston became a predominantly white cemetery. By itself, of course, this tendency tells us little about the practices of the Quartermaster Department squads in Texas. Only when taking the disposition of bodies in the Central District into account does a different story emerge. Few of the Central District burials listed in Moore's 1866 survey seem to have been relocated to inland San Antonio, their logical destination, presumably because access to both of the other two cemeteries was more easily accomplished by sea. Hence, most of the burials in the Central District were sent to either Galveston or Brownsville, and it is in that relocation that a clear racial bias becomes apparent.

The coastal burial grounds of the Central District were clustered around the towns and settlements of Victoria, Green Lake, Lavaca, Indianola, and, thirty miles up the coast, Matagorda. Significantly, although the burials reported in these areas in 1866 were, when considered together, fairly balanced racially—154 white to 114 black interments—the U.S. Colored Troops dead were located in only 2 of those locations (110 in and around Indianola and

3 in and around Matagorda). The other cemeteries contained only white soldiers: 85 in Victoria; 11 in Green Lake; and 13 in Lavaca.[23] Only one cemetery,
in Indianola, was integrated (11 white soldiers buried with 107 black soldiers).
While, like the burials in the other two districts, these reflect the segregated
nature of assignments given to the living, the collection and relocation of these
dead show no such logical rationale. A volume of the *Roll of Honor,* compiled by the Quartermaster Department in 1868 to document burials in the
new Texas national cemeteries, bears this out. Galveston, with a total of 383
burials, contained only 36 "colored" soldiers. According to the description
of the cemetery in *Roll of Honor,* "One hundred and fifty bodies interred [in
Galveston] were removed from Lavaca, Green Lake, Victoria, [and other lo-
cations]." Similarly, the description of the Brownsville cemetery—which
contained 206 known white and 720 known black interments—points out
that the grounds had not yet been completed and that more reinterments were
expected from "Indianola and vicinity."[24] In other words, the soldier dead in
the three largely white burial grounds were transported north to Galveston,
those in the sole largely black burial ground shipped south to Brownsville.

Such a disposition cannot be simply a matter of coincidence. Certainly,
the distances involved militate against any other explanation than racial bias.
Victoria, Green Lake, and Lavaca are all located further inland than Indianola,
so all bodies transported by ship must have passed through either Indianola
or nearby Port Lavaca to gain access to the sea. A straight-line ocean course
from Indianola to Galveston covers a distance of approximately 120 miles. A
similar direct course from Indianola to Brazos Santiago, at the mouth of the
Rio Grande, is nearly 190 miles, at which point the transport vessel would still
have had to travel another 30 miles or more upriver to reach Brownsville.
There seems little logic in transporting black soldiers nearly twice as far as
white soldiers, unless racial bias provided the illogical rationale. More than
anywhere else, the Texas national cemeteries reflected the difficulties associated with the end of slavery and the extension of citizenship to black men.
Such difficulties were not restricted to distant Texas alone.

Although the fact is not obvious now, Arlington National Cemetery was
first developed, at least in practice, if not in planning, as a segregated cemetery. During the war, the federal government seized and purchased the Alexandria estate of Mary Custis Lee, the wife of Robert E. Lee, on the basis of an
1862 law imposing a tax on "insurrectionary properties." As government property, the mansion and surrounding grounds at first served as military hous-

ing, the southern end of the estate as a haven for escaping former slaves. Although safe from slavery in this small but significant community, many men and women died, from disease, the rigors of their earlier enslavement, or the hardships of escape. As they died, these "contrabands"—eventually numbering more than thirty-two hundred—were interred along the northernmost edge of the Arlington property. On 15 June 1864, when it became obvious to Quartermaster General Montgomery Meigs that space in the existing military cemeteries in and around Washington, D.C., was soon to be exhausted, he recommended that the Lee estate be declared a military cemetery, with Secretary of War Stanton's eager approval. In point of fact, Meigs had already begun the interment of soldiers on the estate grounds, and more than a dozen were buried there by the time Stanton approved such actions.[25]

According to Meigs's surviving reports and correspondence, those first soldier burials were also made on the northernmost edge of the Lee estate, but after gaining Stanton's approval, Meigs wanted to focus future burials in the area immediately adjacent to the Lee family's home. However, Union officers living in the mansion redirected the workers to that northernmost plot of ground, away from the house. Once he discovered his orders had been thwarted, Meigs took steps to ensure that the home would be surrounded by graves; in August 1864, he personally supervised the reburial of twenty-six Union soldiers around the perimeter of what had been the rose garden adjacent to the house. Thereafter, officers and soldiers were buried on the western flats behind the house, and in 1866 more than two thousand unknown Union soldiers were moved to a mass grave placed in the center of the rose garden. As the war progressed, Union burials crept south across the grounds in the ranks and files familiar throughout almost all the national cemeteries. But, even after Meigs's design of the developing cemetery had prevailed, the bodies of black soldiers continued to be interred in that distant northern section of the estate alongside the "contraband" burials.[26]

On Memorial Day 1871, the distinctive difference in treatment of the black and white dead became glaringly apparent. The ceremonies at Arlington were impressive—a main speakers' stand richly garlanded, provisions for appropriate music from the Marine Band, flags, grand orations, and the strewing of flowers on the graves of the fallen. President Grant, members of his cabinet, congressmen and senators, all contributed to the dignity of the occasion. But, after the conclusion of the ceremonies, a group of notables and "a large number of colored persons" traveled down the hill to the separate graves of black soldiers. As reported in the black-owned *Washington Daily Morning Chronicle*, "On arriving there they found no stand erected, no orator or speaker selected, not a single flag placed on high, nor even a paper flag at the head boards of these loyal but ignored dead." Representatives were dispatched to bring the situation to the attention of the day's organizers, and a remedy of sorts was offered— "a half dozen (perhaps more) rosettes, and a basket of flower leaves." Needless to say, "deep was the indignation and disappointment of the people."[27]

Resentment grew as the story circulated among the nation's black-operated newspapers. In New Orleans, the *Semi-Weekly Louisianian*, the newspaper edited by the black political leader P. B. S. Pinchback, characterized the ceremonies as "hypocrisy" and "farce": "If any event in the whole history of our connection with the late war embodied more features of disgraceful neglect, on the part of the Union whites, or exhibited more clearly the necessity of protecting ourselves from insult, than this behavior at Arlington Heights, we at least acknowledge ignorance of it." The following week, the paper demanded a more balanced commemoration of the dead on two grounds, the service rendered by black soldiers during the war and the service expected of black voters in Reconstruction: "If the assistance of our race in the late war was of any account, we ought to secure a recognition from our white friends who, however strong and determined, could not have won the victory without us. And even if it were of no account, the pretensions to political equality made by the white Republicans towards living negro voters, ought to leave no room for evidences of contempt towards the negro dead in these cemeteries, which are visited with such enthusiasm when white graves are to be decorated." The *Shreveport South-Western* further suggested— surprisingly so in Reconstruction Louisiana—that "had the result of the war been reversed, and the Southern people been called upon to decorate the graves of their dead, . . . her colored slain would not have been neglected."[28]

The issue of inequitable commemoration of the soldier dead permitted black Americans to express their concerns about the Cause Victorious and their place within it. And Memorial Day 1871 was not the first time that the black soldiers buried at Arlington had been neglected. The year before, Washington's *New Era* documented a similar neglect, noting that, after the Grand Army of the Republic (GAR) called for national memorial observances in 1868 and 1869, "the order was cheerfully responded to by the colored people." However, "What was our astonishment, grief, and indignation to find that the Committee of Arrangements had made no provision to deco-

rate the graves of the colored soldiers!" Perhaps the notice of the 1871 incident was thereby highlighted in that similar neglect had been so prominently
noted the year before. But the *New Era* also pointedly commented on the
burial patterns at Arlington and raised issues that would again be raised the
following year: "It is true that the bodies of both the white and colored soldiers are within the limits of the same cemetery, but separated by the distance
of a mile, in an undesirable portion of the grounds; while, with strange in-
consistency, rebel soldiers are buried with the [white] Union soldiers."[29]

The Southern soldiers buried on the grounds, near the mansion, had been
prisoners of war, and, in the years subsequent, all would be removed, recovered by their native states. But the contrast between their presence in 1870
and 1871 and the distance between the white and black Union burial plots
found no easy answer in the minds of black observers, including the *New Era:*
"We demand as an act of justice, that during the coming year an exchange be
made, that the Confederate soldier have his place by the paupers of the State,
among whom the colored soldiers now sleep, and the Union dead be placed
side by side." That the difference in burial was entirely attributable to race
was obvious, as was the conclusion to be drawn about the issues of the war:
"Because forsooth the rebel skin was pale while living, does it serve to atone
for his rebellion when dead?" Just like observers of commemorative practices
elsewhere, black Americans in general, and the *New Era* in particular, made
the almost visceral connection between the dead, the cause for which they
died, and the circumstances confronted by the living:

> Let those whose spirits went up from Fort Wagner, where fell the
> heroic Colonel Shaw . . . see that we are still pressing on for freedom
> always remembering those whose blood has partially purified this
> land. [Is it] possible that Port Hudson's, Fort Pillow's and Olustee's
> heroes are to be ignored? Is it possible that we as Americans must
> submit to our own degradation? That those men who imperiled their
> very existence to give to this country a whole and perfect union, are
> to be considered unworthy to occupy a grave in company with their
> white brethren. . . . Oh, the blindness of prejudice! It truly follows
> us to the grave.

The solution seemed self-evident: "I do not say let our resentment follow a
man into the grave, but I do say when an obscure portion of the cemetery
must be filled with graves, there, in that obscurity let the country's enemies
sleep."[30]

Perhaps as a result of the recurrent nature of the neglect at Arlington, an "indignation meeting" was arranged in the midst of the cemetery during the 1871 memorial observances. At that meeting, there among the dead, black citizens of the Washington, D.C., area appointed a committee of representatives—including John M. Langston, F. G. Barbadoes, and Frederick Douglass—to confront the secretary of war on the issue of separate burial locations for white and black soldiers within Arlington. When contacted by the committee, the secretary requested Montgomery Meigs—the man most responsible for Arlington having become a national cemetery—to provide any information on the committee and its purpose. Meigs responded that he had no information on the committee itself but supposed, "It is probably the Committee appointed on Decoration Day by colored citizens, who, it was stated in the public prints, objected to the interment of colored soldiers in the North eastern part of the grounds at Arlington, near the lodge and gate on the main road nearest to Georgetown."[31]

The separate burials, Meigs explained, were simply a consequence of the cemetery's development. The first burials had been made in the northern portion of the grounds, with white soldiers buried in a plot separate from black soldiers who had been interred with black civilians: "Great numbers of colored refugees from Virginia and other Southern States came to Washington in 1863, [186]4 & [186]5, and the Quartermaster's Department was called upon to provide for them and to bury many of them who died in hospital or in camp, or in employment of the Department as teamsters or laborers, &c." But the placement of soldiers in this area had been an error. "Had my intentions been distinctly understood and carried out," Meigs stated, "no interments would have been made in this quarter of the cemetery, all would have been buried on the hill and nearer to and encircling the mansion. Not to do this was an error which I corrected as soon as I discovered it." But Meigs's own report indicates that the "mistake" had not, in fact, been corrected: "A few whites only, I think, had then been interred in [that northern corner], and . . . these few were removed to repose with their comrades." However, the black soldiers had not been removed, perhaps because Meigs did not regard them to be comrades. As Meigs explained, "The colored soldiers appear to have been left where so large a number of their own race had been interred, and thus this part of the ground was generally devoted to the colored people, soldiers and refugees."[32]

The black delegation wanted the U.S. Colored Troops burials moved to a position among the other Union soldiers. But Meigs demurred: "As for the disinterment and removal now proposed I think that there are objections to it in sentiment as well as in the expense, but all care for the dead is for the sake of the living, and, if the colored people generally prefer to have their comrades, who fought for them, taken up again and scattered among the whites—it can be done." However, despite having admitted that at least some of the white soldier burials had already been moved, he continued, "I always regret to move a body [once] interred in National Cemetery, believing that the dead once decently buried should have rest." Ultimately, Meigs argued that the black soldiers should remain in their separate graves and that such an arrangement should be agreeable to all: "These [soldiers] are buried among their own people[;] the whole of the colored persons, buried at Arlington, were urchins of the strife which brought freedom to their race in this country, and I believe that hereafter it will be more grateful to their descendants to be able to visit and point out the collected graves of these persons, than to find them scattered through a large cemetery and intermingled with another race."[33] The first members of the U.S. Colored Troops buried in Arlington were so profoundly segregated out of consideration—not for any white officer's racial sensibilities, Meigs's included, but for what he felt black Americans would want.

The issue of these separate burials was raised again two years later, but this time by white veterans. An executive committee of the Department of the Potomac, GAR, passed a resolution in 1873 requesting the removal and reinterment of "the bodies of all white and colored Union soldiers now buried in the lower or colored cemetery at Arlington, to the cemetery proper." Apparently, Meigs had been mistaken earlier, for he now acknowledged that 404 U.S. Colored Troop soldiers and "about" 1,000 white Union soldiers had been buried in that northern section near the "contraband" graves. Whether the GAR resolution was provoked by outrage over white soldiers being buried near black civilians is unknown, but it did include "colored Union soldiers" within its purview and argued for their removal as well, to lie in places adjacent to other Union soldiers up on the slopes south of the mansion. Again Meigs argued against the request. "My own opinion in the matter," he wrote, "is that the soldiers once buried within the limits of the National Military Cemetery at Arlington should not be disturbed." Furthermore, "The whole enclosure is a National Cemetery." But here Meigs has broadened his approach—he suggests that moving black soldiers might diminish the significance of their memory: "The colored soldiers buried now together give evidence of the death of many of their race in the struggle for their freedom, while scattered among the white soldiers, their number being comparatively small, they would be comparatively unnoticed."[34]

All Meigs's reasoning, however interpreted, seems less satisfactory in the light of precedent and a long-held understanding of the effects, if not the intent, of the segregation at Arlington. In the last months of the war, in nearby Alexandria, the issue of black soldiers and civilians being buried in the same grounds had already risen and found resolution. Agents of the Quartermaster Department inquired about the propriety of a cemetery that had developed near a local Union hospital for former slaves. The director of the project, A. Gladwin, explained that, when the need for a cemetery arose, there were no black soldiers in the hospital and that it was only later, after the first such death, that the situation had been carefully considered and the decision made to bury black soldiers in the same cemetery as black civilians, although in a separate section of the grounds and with full military honors. Gladwin explained: "With regard to the burial of soldiers in this ground, selected on purpose for colored people, no invidious comparisons have arisen with the colored people or their friends."[35]

However, the inquiry from the Quartermaster's Department implied that plans were being made to transfer the bodies of the soldiers into the national cemetery at Arlington. To this alternative Gladwin was staunchly opposed. It was, Gladwin asserted, an issue of segregation. Apparently aware that the bodies of black soldiers were buried in a section of Arlington separate from white soldiers, Gladwin preferred that his soldiers remain where they were: "But were they now to be removed from where they have been quietly lain to the Soldier's Cemetery, and still be interred in a place, separate and apart from the white troops, the question of distinction would at once, and almost necessarily arise; and I feel quite sure that it would not contribute to any good result." Pointing out, in addition, that such a removal would be an unpleasant task and a needless labor, Gladwin underscored the issue of honorable commemoration:

> If the question of military honor, so richly due to all our fallen soldiers could rise above all distinctions of race among those who have nobly proffered their lives for the defence of our imperiled country, and it were designed to bury them in the order in which their deaths should respectively occur, and the minds of the people were best answered in that way, I would not raise an objection to the removal

of those already buried, and the interment there of those who shall hereafter decease in their vicinity.

But with the understanding which I now have of the matter, I should beg leave to request that there be no move made in that direction.[36]

Gladwin's reluctance to have the soldiers removed from a civilian cemetery was predicated on his understanding that their services could never be honored equally with that of the white soldiers if they were buried in a segregated fashion. Better to leave them with black civilians, where no whites were buried, so that the contrast would not be injurious to the sensibilities of the living.

Both Gladwin and Meigs opposed the reburial and relocation of black soldiers, preferring instead to leave them buried with black civilians, but interpreted the meaning of segregation differently. Gladwin acknowledged that soldiers should be interred separately from civilians, a segregation he endorsed, but rejected the further separation of black soldiers from white soldiers, which he felt would only invite invidious comparisons. Conversely, Meigs resisted the intention to bury black soldiers alongside their comrades-in-arms, choosing to keep them separated and interred with black civilians. Segregating soldiers from soldiers was not a disparaging act, Meigs argued, but instead was necessary in order to give import to the particular sacrifices of black soldiers. So broadly did Meigs make this argument that he even reinterpreted the black civilians buried at Arlington in a similar manner. Meigs asserted confidently, "I do not suppose that any of their [the black soldiers'] friends deliberately approves of certain complaints which have come to my notice against the present location[,] on the ground that others of their race, equally sacrificed in the attempt to obtain freedom, but many of them feeble from age or sex, who died and were buried by the United States during the war, lie in the same part of the grounds. All these were victims of the struggle."[37]

In this last, most subtle and duplicitous reworking of the Cause Victorious, Meigs imagined the broadest possible conception of the black struggle during the Civil War. All black Americans—men and women, soldiers and refugees, even the aged and infirm—contributed to the national struggle to secure the two Union war aims. All fought to preserve the Union and destroy an immoral institution. Through this convoluted argumentation, Meigs asserted the right answer for the wrong reasons. In order to prevent the movement of those early burials, Meigs concluded that the presence of black soldiers and civilians—men, women, and children—in a common plot within the preeminent national cemetery would remain mute but powerful testimony to the contributions of a people to their, and their nation's, freedom. A separate section south of the Lee house was in later years dedicated to the burial of black soldiers, but despite the protests of the 1870s, the first interments of U.S. Colored Troops soldiers were never relocated, and the insincere, yet completely appropriate, interpretation that Meigs had derived remains largely unacknowledged.

These examples make it clearer how difficult it was for the nation as a whole to accept and incorporate black men and women within the understanding of American identity emerging from the Civil War. Black citizenship was never embraced by most white Americans, being regarded simply as a consequence of emerging victorious from the Civil War and preserving victory thereafter. For most, the original war aim of slavery's destruction did not encompass civil rights for those freed from bondage. Some few politicians and activists claimed that freedom could be maintained only through the granting of civil rights, but as Southern recalcitrance persisted throughout Reconstruction, it became increasingly easier to accept the limited victory of mere emancipation. Such a concession did not improve the plight of black Americans, but neither did it violate the prevailing Northern interpretation of what Union soldiers had died to achieve.

The issue of emancipation may have remained narrowly defined and therefore secure; the issue of Union, however, remained stubbornly abstract. Since the death of Lee, the efforts of Southern veterans and politicians to move the terms of discussion to issues of valor, fortitude, and military prowess had successfully blunted the efforts of Northern veterans and politicians to promote a harsher line of interpretation based on causation. There was a good deal of complicity in the process on the part of Northerners; after all, the fruits of victory seemed secure. From the position of strength, comforted by the Cause Victorious, Northern veterans and others could tolerate and even participate in the literary explorations of the war. But, following the death of Davis, the rising tide of rhetoric among Southerners asserting the legitimacy of their cause provoked increasing discontent among their Northern counterparts. Union veterans faced the difficulty of countering the resurgent Confederate commemorative activism without threatening the tenuous rapprochement of the preceding decades. By the 1890s, at the very time when sectional tensions seemed at their lowest since the war, Northerners faced the dilemma of either vigorously defending the Cause Victorious or embracing reconciliation with a white Southern populace that seemed increasingly adamant about the virtue of a failed rebellion. As terms once agreed upon began to shift and blur, the dead remained a resolute component that had to be incorporated into any new interpretation.

In 1895, the ex-Confederate Association of Chicago hosted a reunion to honor the Confederate dead of Camp Douglas with the erection of a towering monument in Oakwoods Cemetery. Many Northerners objected to the reunion and especially its purpose. The *Confederate Veteran* reported: "Some Commanders of State Departments Grand Army of the Republic have been unkind enough to denounce [the reunion]. . . . The Department of Illinois has expressed serious disapproval because the date named is May 30—*National* Decoration Day—It is singular that that date was selected. The VETERAN has ever been conservative, and it expresses sorrow rather than annoyance at the expressions of disapproval."[38] As the *Veteran* pointed out, the *national* Memorial Day seemed a "singular" choice, enough so that it provoked the anger of Union veterans. The Department of Illinois GAR was objecting to the activities commemorating dead Southern soldiers—at least on that particular day—thirty years after the war had ended.

The organizer of the event, John Underwood, collected and published transcriptions of the ceremonies, including after-dinner orations, so that the example of that reunion and the messages of national fraternity would reach and influence many more than those who had crowded the dinner hall. In his own introduction to the book, Underwood illustrated the foundation that served as the basis of reunion, for that one evening and—in a larger sense—for the reunification of the nation. It was not said in so many words, nor were the ideas expressed uniquely his. But he did point out how significant the soldier dead remained to the process of reconciliation, just as the Illinois veterans' protest pointed out how significant they remained to those who sought to undermine that process.

Underwood began as war veterans often do, by telling war stories. In June 1864, during the war of position and maneuver in the valleys of Virginia, Union General David Hunter turned his forces toward the town of Lexington. The resistance as he approached was light but annoying. Moving into the village proper, the Federal troops soon came upon the buildings and grounds of the Virginia Military Institute, sometimes called the West Point of the South. The alumni of this academy had provided significant service in the war, from the adolescent cadets who had assisted in the rout of Union troops at the Battle of New Market, to no less a warrior than Thomas J. "Stonewall" Jackson, who before the outbreak of war had been a professor at the Institute. Hunter ordered it burned to the ground.[39]

It was this act, and dozens more like it, that earned Hunter a special measure of hatred in many Southern hearts. The general relentlessly burned private property if he thought it had any connection to the frequent outbursts of guerrilla activity that assailed his forces. Moreover, he held the reins on his troops lightly, and pillaging was common and profligate. All in all, he might seem a curious choice for reminiscence, but Underwood had carefully selected Hunter to make his argument all the more pointed. The Union armies had remained in Lexington for two days, awaiting word from outlying troops and the arrival of a supply train. On 14 June, Hunter ordered his men to assemble and march toward nearby Lynchburg, a direction that would take them by the Lexington cemetery. As Underwood told the tale, when the general and his staff reached the small burial ground, Hunter ordered his men to halt and remove its fence palings. With all obstructions thus removed, Hunter then ordered the march resumed with arms reversed. In this manner, according to Underwood, the Union soldiers paraded out of Lexington, paying military respect to the remains of a fallen enemy, Thomas J. "Stonewall" Jackson, whose grave lay just inside the small roadside cemetery.[40]

Two aspects of Underwood's recounting of this tale are significant. First, through these actions he reiterates what had become the hallmark of Southern postwar rhetoric concerning the conflict. As they sought to reconcile themselves with their own defeat and Northern victory, former Confederates and their supporters deftly transformed the vocabulary used to discuss the war. A key element of that transformation was the assertion that, although divided on a great many issues concerning the war, veterans of either side could agree that their enemies had fought well. After noting that Confederate General Jubal A. Early—two weeks later and without knowledge of Hunter's actions—likewise saluted Jackson's grave by removing the fence palings and reversing arms for the march, Underwood commented, "These citations clearly indicate the axiomatic truth that all enlightened and just people admire fortitude, bravery and determined purpose under reputable circumstances, without regard to the right or wrong of the political or other cause which provided the opportunity that enabled the display of opposing deeds of heroism."[41] Of course, the implied negative was intentional; thirty years after the war, those who could not agree on this "axiomatic truth" were neither "enlightened" nor "just." In this statement, Underwood succinctly expressed the culmination of Southern labors to win concessions within the Northern myth of American nationalism.

Second, so important was the mutual respect between combatants within this sectional negotiation that, to paraphrase Voltaire, if it did not exist, it was necessary to invent it. Underwood's war story, consciously or not, exaggerated Hunter's acts at Lexington. In fact, there is no good evidence to suggest that Hunter's salute to Jackson's grave ever took place. Hunter's chief of staff, Colonel David H. Strother, records that several officers and soldiers visited the grave during their stay in Lexington. But he does not mention Hunter doing so.[42] Nor is such a visit or gesture of respect mentioned in Hunter's own reports. Hunter's approbation of Stonewall Jackson's valor, so crucial to Underwood's purposes, seems not to have taken place. Underwood's exaggeration, or invention, of the incident clearly delineates the importance of gaining recognition of Southern valor from Northern sources, particularly from a Northern source as hateful, and hated, as Hunter. Not only do the acts of commemoration reveal the passions locked up within this negotiation, but how these acts were interpreted and occasionally embellished reveal the long-standing needs of this process, even after reunification had, supposedly, taken place.

This kind of distinctive rhetoric blossomed throughout the 1890s, a period during which sectional feelings had, supposedly, eased sufficiently for the beginnings of a genuine reconciliation to emerge. Historians have generally asserted that the reunion of the sections was accomplished relatively quickly. James McPherson has written, "By the 1880s, passions were cooling. . . . Parades replaced processions. Commemoration gave way to celebration."[43] And historians have for some time tried to date the process of reunification with precision. Almost all point toward the moment when Southern and Northern sons fought side by side in the Spanish-American War as evidence that the nation had put sectional conflict in its past.[44] Ken Burns's recent documentary epic ends on such a conciliatory note—aged veterans clasping the hands of equally ancient enemies across the stone wall at Gettysburg.[45] Historian Paul Buck has thus far offered the subject perhaps its most positivist affirmation: "Thirty years after Appomattox there remained no fundamental conflict between the aspirations of North and South. The people of the United States constituted at last a nation integrated in interests and unified in sentiment.... The controlling influences which shaped national destiny operated in one section as freely as in the other. The interlocking of economic dependence had completed its mastery over particularistic trends.... The memories of the past were woven in a web of national sentiment which selected from by-gone feuds those deeds of mutual valor which permitted pride in present achievement and future promise." Such actions, Buck wrote, produced a "national solidarity hitherto unknown in American life. The reunited nation was a fact."[46] Of course, with respect to memory, that process of selection was as significant for what was excluded as for what was included.

With few, mostly recent, exceptions, historians have rarely made explicit the cost of reunification while celebrating its benefits. This has been true as long as there has been a historical profession. The greatest allies to both sides were the nascent professional historians, particularly those who were the historians of Reconstruction and the war. Usually writing from the assumed position of the nonparticipant, and self-imbued with the ideal of objectivity, they constructed a national history that satisfied both Northerners and Southerners. Blazing this trail was John W. Burgess, a Tennessean born into a slaveholding family who later fought in the Union army. Burgess established a graduate program at Columbia that attracted some of the most able minds in the nation. Although William A. Dunning became the best known of the Columbia graduates, it was the second generation—predominantly Southern by birth—that was committed to researching and analyzing Reconstruction with a critical eye. The process was entirely conscious, historians adopting, as Peter Novick has indicated, "the great task of national reconciliation, healing the wounds of the Civil War and Reconstruction, [and] repairing and deepening national unity." Those tasks suited the intellectual needs of professionalism and scientific history: "A truly national historical profession would be created—and historians would simultaneously be contributing to the great task of reconciliation."[47]

Novick's position echoes John Higham's earlier conclusion: "In the 1870's and 1880's ... a mood of sectional reconciliation was softening the acerbities of the mid-nineteenth century.... Accordingly, the leading patrician historians ... took as a dominant theme the forging of national unity and power in a crucible of sectional diversities." Higham characterized the resulting perspectives: "Turbulent and unlovely as the post–Civil War years were, they could be shaped to the evolutionary pattern of national progress if one endorsed their final outcome: the reunion of North and South through the overthrow of military despotism and the restoration of white supremacy. Thus [William A.] Dunning, like [James Ford] Rhodes and the vast majority of American historians, ratified the results both of the Civil War and its aftermath."[48] They did so, of course, in ways that fulfilled and endorsed the prevailing Cause Victorious mythology. Hence, as historians sought, rather self-consciously, to contribute to a national unity, they saw little of those convolutions that did not conform to that end. With characteristic clarity of vision, W. E. B. Du Bois recognized this process with a bitter commentary: "War and especially civil strife leave terrible wounds. It is the duty of humanity to heal them. It was therefore soon conceived as neither wise nor patriotic to speak of all the causes of strife and the terrible results to which sectional differences in the United States had led. And so, first of all, we minimized the slavery controversy which convulsed the nation from the Missouri Compromise down to the Civil War. On top of that, we passed by Reconstruction with a phrase of regret or disgust."[49]

Certainly, there was much that was genuine about the reunion efforts occurring on a variety of fronts, especially among economic and political concerns. But these efforts have been made to answer for the entire spectrum of American expression throughout this tortured period. And the documentation of the era has been skewed largely to give pride of place to that effort that in hindsight seems the proper course for history to have taken. Such a bias improves the narrative, but it does an injustice to all those who mourned and would not be reconciled in their grief.

In short, there were many cracks in the plaster of national unification. While many sought to avoid actions sure to arouse indignant response, others were not so inclined. In 1888, a small syndicate of Chicago businessmen purchased the Libby Prison in Richmond, Virginia. That massive building stood second in infamy only to Andersonville as a source of antagonism between former Confederate and Union soldiers. Between 1861 and 1865, approximately forty thousand Union soldiers and officers were incarcerated within its masonry walls. One of its many notorious traditions concerned its heavily barred windows. On the order of the prison commandant, Major Thomas P. Turner, anyone approaching those windows was shot by snipers arrayed across from the building. In the heavy, close summers of Richmond, without other relief from the oppressive heat, many prisoners risked the dangers for a breath of fresh air, and many died for their violation of orders.[50]

Having purchased the former prison, the syndicate ordered the building dismantled, loaded into 132 twenty-ton railroad cars, shipped to Chicago, and there painstakingly rebuilt and stocked with a miscellany of Civil War–related artifacts, photographs, and exhibits. Any large building would have sufficed to contain the museum artifacts; the transplantation of Libby Prison to Chicago made the edifice itself an exhibit, one that was prominent at the 1892 World's Fair. The purpose was to instruct visitors in a painful lesson of war. However, in a guidebook printed to advertise the war museum, the anonymous author defended the enterprise as the act of "illustrating American heroism": "It is quite the fashion now to decry all just sentiment regarding the late war. There is raised the objection of fostering sectional feeling if honor is paid to the deeds of our country's saviors. This is a mistaken idea. The country is a whole." More important, the author continued, "The questions settled and the questions raised by that great struggle are not trivial. Any honorable means of keeping these questions in mind is permissible. If the United States took an ignoble stand in that memorable strife, or if the strife itself were wrong, then banished be every remembrance of it. But if the purpose was right and its accomplishment needful, then lapse of time should not dim the brightness of its lessons."[51]

The assertion that the nation was "whole" and therefore that nothing in the war museum project should be construed as harping on a long-dead sectionalism amounts to a late-season and formulaic assertion of the Cause Victorious. Moreover, the declaration that the justice of the cause makes permissible the renewal of questions raised by the war in public discourse is, of course, an inversion of a long-held Confederate position. By this point in time, Southerners argued passionately that, despite the outcome of the military decision, the righteousness of the Confederate cause remained undimmed and would be redeemed by history. This extension of the early proposition that the South had not lost the war but been overwhelmed by an enemy possessing greater resources held that the correctness of the Confederacy had not been invalidated by military defeat. The Libby Prison exhibit provides a Northern twist on that theme, stating that, since the Union armies' efforts had secured the nation, their enterprise could not have been an ignoble one. Therefore, all Americans, including Southerners, should agree in the appropriateness of honoring the Union war effort, even in ways in which the Confederate war effort would never be celebrated. The unidirectional flow of this argument becomes apparent if we speculate about the possible reaction had a stockade from the Union prison at Point Lookout, Maryland, or Elmira, New York, been removed to Atlanta and reopened as a Southern museum and commentary on the war.

In addition, the pattern of unapologetic candor in Memorial Day observances and other orations persisted in spite of, or perhaps because of, the resurgence in Confederate militancy. In August 1888, the chief justice of Tennessee's Supreme Court, Peter Turney, addressed the Tennessee Association of Confederate Veterans. He concluded his remarks by affirming, "A new government had been built upon the downfall of the old ones. We have promised our allegiance to it. . . . The element of evil and discord has been removed. Old things have passed away, and there will be, we venture to hope, no other cause for sectional jealousy." But his talk had been a thorough defense of secession, proving it to have been a constitutional act, and thereby removing the opprobrium of rebellion from the Confederate cause. Turney had opened his comments by stating, "We retract nothing, and believe the cause in which our comrades fell was just; that they and we were not traitors or rebels against the authorized action of that government from which we seceded; otherwise it would be *unlawful and immoral* to attempt to keep alive and perpetuate the memories of those who fell, or to preserve for history the records of their deeds of heroism. Nothing unpatriotic, immoral, unlawful or treasonable should be the basis of any association." It is not recorded what inspired Turney's address, but he did note that "we cannot and must not in anywise in the least sympathize with that spirit of seeming apology we sometimes meet."[52]

Still, the dead were the measure of the living, and reshaping their memory to a focus on the virtues of duty, dedication, and sacrifice served this end well. In 1893, at the Memorial Day exercise at Charleston, South Carolina, John Kershaw reminded the several thousand in attendance, "For vain will be our memorial days, vain these oblations of nature's revived life, vain all this pomp and circumstance, unless we are found translating the virtues of our dead into action and consecrating ourselves to the perpetuation and emulation of the sincerity, courage, self-sacrifice and devotion to duty which our soldier dead so grandly illustrated in their life and by their death." In a manner well suited to the most puritan of jeremiads, Kershaw pointed to corrupting influences that lured white Southerners from the true path. "There are many," he said, "who for lust of office sacrifice honor and violate conscience to feel for a passing moment the fickle breath of popular applause; there are many more who are selling their souls for greed of gold." In Charleston's Memorial Day service of 1915, the Reverend P. L. Duffy directed his audience's thoughts "to the dead, in our solemn declaration over their garlanded graves that their death was righteous, that their Cause was righteous, [and] that their immolation was a consecration of the Southland."[53]

Such repudiation of treason and the rehabilitation of Confederate soldiers drew comment from Union orators at Northern Memorial Day observances. African American veterans were particularly sensitive to any attempt to cloud the relevant issues of the day. In 1871, the Reverend Dr. Rankin, speaking at the Congregational Church in Washington, D.C., noted that "it is asked" why adverse feelings should persist in the commemoration of the dead: "Why should not memorial flowers be put indiscriminately upon the graves of the loyal and the disloyal? Why carry hostility beyond the portals of the dead?" "It is," he said, "a specious inquiry, destined to be put year by year; and we ought to know how to answer it. And in general it may be said that such a failure to discriminate between right and wrong, such an obliteration of the past, such a compounding of the principles involved in our recent struggle, defeats the end of history." This was far more, for Rankin, than a politically or sectionally inspired choice of action—it had a more fundamental significance. The outcome of the war "was not a sham result": "It was a contest in which He set His seal to a cause. We cannot honor their dead, we cannot honor their cause, without being untrue to that history which for four years God was writing for us."[54]

During the services of 30 May 1879, William H. Lambert stood among the Union dead in Monument Cemetery of Philadelphia. Lambert noted that in the fourteen years since the war many things had worked to efface the war from the landscape and from the halls of politics. He pointed out that no Southerner languished in prison as a result of the war. The national capital had no monument celebrating victory but Memorial Day, set aside to remember the dead, not the defeated. Lambert's passionate rebuttal to recent Southern celebrations, indeed, to the entire process of nationalist negotiation, bears quoting at length:

> We respect the sincerity of our late enemies, and we admire the bravery with which, in the face of great discouragements, they so long upheld their cause; but we cannot allow our belief in their honesty

and our admiration for their valor to beguile us into forgetfulness of the fact that they were utterly in the wrong.

Cherishing such faith, justice to ourselves and to the memory of these dead demands that we protest against the sentimentality which seeks to promote harmony by belittling the cause for which we fought and these died.

We cannot admit that "the sword has been sheathed between the North and the South; the banners of the Blue and Gray have been furled"—and we deprecate pictorial representations of our flag and that of the rebellion gracefully draped in trophy, as though flags of co-ordinate powers once warring, now at peace.

True, geographical lines divided loyal from the disloyal States; but the war was not a struggle between rival sections for supremacy, but between the Government and citizens in rebellion, for the life of the Nation.

The war ended, not by reason of mutual exhaustion, not by compromise and treaty, but because of the absolute victory of the Government, and the utter defeat of the insurgent.

No flag was furled, for ours still floats in triumph, whilst the flag of treason was annihilated.[55]

Note that Lambert expressly confronts and disdains the trend toward "forgetfulness." In the face of such emotionally powerful language, it is tempting to dismiss Lambert as a disgruntled Union veteran and any equally impassioned Southern rhetoric as the words of the "unreconstructed." But Lambert's comments recall that the shifting of a social interpretation in public memory can clash with personal memory, often painfully. The tides of intellectual change accompanying a negotiation of memory and interpretation were never impersonal. There is no possible means of quantifying a response, but the alterations were no doubt resisted by as many as those who willingly fell into the newer orbits of social interaction.

Lambert's speech should serve as a caution to those who would attribute the negotiation of memory to motives that can all too easily be interpreted as cynical and superficial, motives like political power or economic investment alone. Instead, genuine sentiments that incorporated each individual's sense of identity, nationalism, patriotism, and the war continued to struggle with personal and public memory for years to come. In 1905, Senator Joseph B. Foraker of Ohio, who had gained a reputation for conciliating Southern veterans, stood among the Union dead on Memorial Day at Arlington and echoed Lambert's concerns almost exactly: "In the first place, it was made plain that there was a right and a wrong side to the great controversy that had been so long in progress, and that the right side had triumphed and been vindicated. And that is as true to-day, and will be forever, as it was then. The fact that those who fought against the Government fought bravely and gallantly, and believed they were right, does not change the facts that they were nevertheless in the wrong, and that their defeat was a blessing for them as well as for us and all concerned."[56] Such sentiments tended not to fade, but to exist—at times uneasily, as Lambert shows—alongside the larger flow of public interpretation and memory.

But, as was always the case, the rhetoric of the resurgent South was in the main careful to avoid invoking such commentary as Lambert's and was never intended to renew the rift of sectional controversy. In a highly partisan defense of the South and its place in American history, South Carolina Chief Justice Eugene B. Gary cautioned: "We disclaim any intention to criticise the North, or to arouse sectional feeling. We are now a united people; and God grant that we may so remain until time shall be no more." Although the remainder of the text recounted the noble Americans that had been sons of the South and reasserted the long-formalized arguments that secession had been constitutionally sound, Gary opened his comments with a wish that the nation would follow the sentiments of Scripture: "May the North and the South ever utter, the one to the other the words of the Jewish daughter . . . 'Entreat me not to leave thee, or to return from following after thee; for whither thou goest, I will go; and where thou lodgest, I will lodge; thy people shall be my people, and thy God, my God. Where thou diest, will I die, and there will I be buried.'"[57] Of course, the vow of companionship even unto burial held particular poignancy in the light of the persistent separation of the Union and Confederate dead.

The central problem in the reunification of the American nation lies in the fact that, at its core, the process was predicated on a willingness and an ability selectively to remember the war and its human consequences. Anything that provoked memory was therefore antithetical to any attempt toward reunion based on forgetting the injuries of the past. Death, the greatest of all injuries, remained the one aspect of the war that could not be turned to the purpose of reunion. The commemoration of Civil War death, from monuments to Memorial Day, served to belie the rhetoric of reconciliation. The problems of monuments and the dead were the exact source of sectional tensions at Gettysburg. Gettysburg could never be embraced fully by Southerners, for too many of its memories were tragic. As one Virginian wrote in 1887: "Gettysburg is too sad a field to attract many Southerners."[58] Moreover, there never had been much reason for Southerners to travel to Gettysburg, or any of the national cemeteries, since there were no lost Confederates interred there in honored graves. As the battlefield became a tourist attraction in the late nineteenth century, the lessons that the undulating grounds taught were essentially the lessons of Northern national supremacy. Moreover, it cannot be overstated how influential the existence of the national cemeteries was on the desire to preserve and set aside the grounds of the battlefields that lay nearby. Throughout the late-nineteenth-century heyday of park and battlefield preservation, the various government agents, surveyors, veterans, historians, and entrepreneurs who were chiefly responsible for the establishment of the battlefield parks laid out their plans and walked off the battle lines in the shadow of the soldier dead.

At Gettysburg, the notion of preserving the landscape for its historical significance emerged nearly simultaneously with the drive to create the national cemetery. David McConaughy speculated with his own funds to buy up some of the more prominent features of the battlefield. He and other town leaders formed the Gettysburg Battlefield Memorial Association (GBMA). With sentiments that no doubt ranged from the noble wish to preserve lands sanctified by combat and death to the crass desire to attract tourist dollars, the GBMA set about removing important sections of the local landscape from the flow of time in order that future generations would have a chance to see the battlefield and to profit from the experience.[59]

Part of the process of preservation necessarily included the shaping of the lessons that future visitors would take away from the park; hence the GBMA's first thoughts were toward commemoration and monumentalization. The first monument to the military units that had fought there was placed in 1867, within the confines of the Soldier's National Cemetery. The process of placing monuments, and, hence, an interpretation of the war, on the land was costly, and the commemorative activities of the GBMA languished. Not until 1878 was a monument placed on the battlefield itself, a tablet to General John F. Reynolds erected by survivors of his corps. About this time, the Pennsylvania Post of the GAR held its annual meeting at Gettysburg and began to see the possibilities of a more fully developed commemorative effort. Members of the GAR—not just from Pennsylvania, but from across the country—purchased GBMA stock, more than doubling the association's assets and membership. And, in the elections of 1880, the GAR members had sufficient strength to elect their own to the steering committee, largely displacing the local civilian leadership that had guided the GBMA since the war. The GAR thereby assured that a particular pattern of commemoration and interpretation would prevail at the most notable battlefield in the nation.[60]

Naturally enough, following its beliefs about what was right and just, the GBMA ensured that, in its design, interpretation, and monumentation, the Gettysburg park reflected a particularly Northern perspective of the three days' events in 1863. Under GAR guidance, the GBMA had adopted a rule preventing Pickett's veterans from placing a monument at the point of farthest advance, close to the heart of the Union battle lines. After federal control of the park was established in 1895, the three-member commission appointed by the War Department to oversee the park's commemorative activities affirmed that rule. The commission also stipulated that all new monuments be placed only on the "lines of battle." This meant that any markers or monuments that Southern veterans wished to erect could be placed only in what they considered rearline areas, places that the Confederate troops had used for encampment and the mustering of forces. Thus Southern commemoration was excluded from the grounds of actual combat, the points of furthest advance into enemy territory, many of which had been marked for the Union forces already. The "line-of-battle" rule effectively checked any inclination that Southern veterans might have had to participate in the commemoration of the battle. Even former Confederate Major William M. Robbins of Alabama, who sat on the commission, could not win his fellow Southerners over to marking only the lines that were permitted them, the lines of least presence on the battlefield. During Robbins's tenure on the commission, which lasted from its establishment until his death in 1905, only one Confederate marker was placed on the field, commemorating the Fourth Alabama Infantry—Robbins's own unit—erected in 1886 and paid for by Robbins himself.[61]

Thus, at Gettysburg, and certainly at other battlefields as well, Northern gestures toward Confederates must always be viewed critically. The generosity of the efforts must be viewed in the light of the frustration of Union veterans and other visitors who, while standing on Little Round Top or at the Highwater Mark, looked westward and found no trace of an enemy. In a very real sense, the opening of the park to markings of the enemy's battle lines was prompted by the need to demonstrate the purpose of the defensive line, to identify the enemy that was repulsed.

When Confederate monuments and positions were traced on the landscape, it was done in a selective manner. Roads were constructed along the lines of both the Union and the Confederate positions, permitting visitors to travel either the "fishhook" of the Federal lines from Cemetery Ridge to Little Round Top or the long road shadowing the line of deployment of Southern troops. But, whereas the roads on the Union side came to bear the names of Union officers—Meade, Reynolds, Hancock, and so on—that marking the Southern line was not named after Lee, or Longstreet, or Pickett. It was named, and remains, simply Confederate Avenue.

Even for Southern battlefields the differing rates of memorialization continued. The battlefield of Shiloh, Tennessee, had been a reburial center for Union soldiers in the years following the war, producing Shiloh National Cemetery. Confederate soldiers buried on the field remained in their mass graves, and no efforts were ever made to disinter them or individualize their graves. In 1894, Congress established the site as a military park, one that encompassed most of the battlefield and the cemetery. Commissions from various states gathered to erect monuments to the valor of their native sons who had fought there. Roads, monuments, and black metal markers detailing the course of battle were all in place for the dedication services held on 6 and 7 April 1903. Indiana's state commission, reporting the results of its efforts to the state legislature, observed that "of the Southern States [whose soldiers fought at Shiloh], Tennessee had the greatest number of troops in the battle, and as Shiloh National Park is located in that State, *it will no doubt be the first* of the Southern States to join this National memorial."[62]

Nearly nine years after the park was established by Congress, not a single Southern state had erected a monument or had otherwise participated in the construction of the park. By 1911, only 3 Confederate monuments had been installed, at a cost of $14,000. By comparison, the Union states had by then erected 114 monuments and markers, spending $238,000 (over and above the nearly $1 million that the government had spent in constructing the park itself).[63] In both the creation of cemeteries to honor the dead and the preservation and memorialization of the battlefield on which they died, the overriding principle was the commemoration of a particularly Northern perception of the war.

After Memorial Day and national military parks, the aspect of late-nineteenth-century commemorative activity most celebrated by historians as evidence of the fading acrimony between sections was the reunion movement. However, the reunions were less than they have been made out to be. Although the reunion of living veterans lies largely outside the parameters of this work, the significance that it holds in the current scholarship requires some comment. While the manufactured tradition of reunion is important, focusing on it has prevented historians from assessing what has been obscured by it—the fact that only a minority of veterans participated in it. Reunion, and its attendant rituals, were widespread, but still only a facade. Also, reunion was possible only for the living; the dead remained permanently unreconciled, and any serious attempt to remember and commemorate them inevitably involved a confrontation with the tenets of the Cause Victorious.

By stressing reunion and the ease with which we assume it took place, we miss the persistence of antagonism, of bitterness, of animosity. We wrench out of its proper context the deep division that remained for many years after the war ended. And we misinterpret the sharp retreat from Reconstruction, assuming that Northerners tired of championing black rights in the face of Southern resistance when, in truth, they had no very advanced position from which to retreat. Similarly, we underestimate the power of a reconciliationist position as a manipulative tool in the hands of Southerners who had no reunion sentiment. The Northern nationalist myth provided emotional and political leverage to Southerners, who used that pry bar to open up intellectual and social spaces (not to mention political opportunities) in which to reassert a Confederate nationalism in ways that otherwise would have been impossible.

With the exception of a handful of national examples, most reunions across the color line of Blue and Gray were local and regional. Richmond held both the Robert E. Lee Camp, No. 1, of the United Confederate Veterans (UCV) and the Phil Kearny Post, No. 10, of the GAR. Cheek by jowl, the two fraternal groups shared meeting space, which a visiting GAR member described as "oddly decorated, [with] Confederate and Union flags and trophies being mingled impartially together."[64] In 1883, during the Confederate memorial exercises at Hollywood Cemetery, Union veterans of the Kearny Post joined in the ceremonies, standing in a show of respect for the Confederate dead. The Richmond *Daily Dispatch* reported that the GAR men marked General George E. Pickett's grave with a "floral monument" and presented to the cemetery "a broken column, mounted upon an appropriate pedestal, the whole wreathed and garlanded with evergreens and fresh flowers" and inscribed with "a tender testimonial of the feeling that these veterans held in a matter of so much sentimental moment." The actions of the Union veterans "warmed the blood of kindliness in every southern breast and reflected vast credit upon the gentlemen who so generously conceived and so pleasantly executed their fraternal purpose." A week later, on 30 May, the former Confederates joined the GAR post and "tenderly assisted" in its memorial ceremonies at the national cemetery.[65]

Later that same year, the members of New Jersey's GAR, Lincoln Post, No. 10, proposed to extend the hand of fraternity to their former foes in Richmond. The group's historian, C. H. Benson, attested to the shared sentiment that "each deserved from the other the respect which is always due to valor." "Add to this," he continued, "the fact that all are citizens of one common country, that all are Americans, the conclusion is unavoidable, that each must rejoice in the glory of the other." So great was Benson's desire to act decently and without the possibility of misinterpretation that he even acknowledged concerns expressed in certain quarters that the title given to his account of the reunion, *"Yank" and "Reb,"* might insult the feelings of "our ex-Confederate friends": "Some timid ones feared that those feelings would be injured by this title, but the writer is fully persuaded, that men who fought as they fought, on a cracker with a little grease, as their per diem rations are not so easily hurt. The writer has therefore no apology to offer, convinced that none is needed."[66]

Of the 198 members in good standing of the Lincoln Post, No. 10, only 91 made the trip to Richmond. Counting civilian guests, a band, and GAR members from other posts, however, the party totaled 188 men and 1 woman. For four days in October 1883, this group was toasted, feted, and carried about Richmond to see the sights, which included Libby Prison, Hollywood Cemetery, and at least two of the seven national cemeteries in and around Richmond. In all, the trip went smoothly, a paragon of genuine reconciliation among veterans. There were only minor slips: for example, a visitor was given a black and tan dog, which he accepted and then—"incontinently," according to Benson—named "Jeff." There were also other reminders of past disparities. During a trip to the battlefields of the Seven Pines, Benson found occasion to remark on the separate burials of the soldier dead that remained even after twenty years had passed: "The United States Government, by dint of paying $3.50 for every body of a Union soldier found, has gathered most of its fallen heroes into a National Cemetery near by. The Confederate dead, as brave as their more fortunate foes, lie where they fell, with only the night winds to sing their requiem, and without even the slight honor of sepulture." When the battlefield guide mentioned that he still occasionally found a soldier's body, he was asked by one of the party, "Why do not the Confederates bury their dead?" Why, in other words, was there not an extensive plan of reinterment like the one the federal government had instituted two decades earlier? The reply was simple: "'We are too poor.'—It told the whole sad story." Unstated in the account was the intolerable symbolism that would have been associated with such a large-scale effort. Benson concluded his thoughts by stating, "The Government refuses to recognize the Confederate dead in any manner whatever. It is a sad illustration of the remorselessness of war to see those white bones mutely appealing for the poor honor of a grave."[67]

Such small Blue-Gray reunions were fairly common, particularly among groups that shared a particular bond. In 1905, at the urging of the Ninth Regiment Veteran Volunteer Association, the state of New Jersey funded and placed a monument to that state's soldier dead in the national cemetery at New Berne, North Carolina. While there, the New Jersey contingent was warmly hosted by New Berne's Camp No. 1162 of the UCV. On the night of their arrival, 17 May, the members of the Ninth emphasized the bond between themselves and their hosts. During the war, in the Battle of New Berne, they and the rest of the regiment had been instrumental in overcoming the defenses of the town, defeating in the process the Beaufort County Plowboys, whose battle flag they had captured. Now, some forty years later, they returned that battle flag to New Berne. At the reception in the Confederate Veterans meeting hall later that same evening, they also presented their hosts with a silk national flag. The presentation of those two banners made the evening a particularly symbolic one, and the next night, when the battle flag was placed back into the hands of the woman who had created it, the connection between the two flags was noted. Speaking on behalf of the flag's creator, Mrs. E. N. Joyner pointed out that there was "no dishonor" in having lost the flag in the war, for it was carried "until the hand that held it had yielded to a soldier's death." Moreover, "none but Americans could have fought so fiercely for it, none but Americans could have wrested it from Americans."[68] Few sentiments express how thoroughly the Northern mythology of national unity and federal supremacy had penetrated the inheritors of the postwar South.

True and genuine sentiments of reunion and reconciliation often held sway at such gatherings. But the more celebrated national reunions, normally touted as the exemplars of reconciliation, usually fell short when it came to displaying a similar level of enthusiasm. The focal point for many national reunions was Gettysburg, and the 1887 reunion there marks the first attempt to court the participation of Confederate veterans at an ostensibly national reunion. In 1886, veterans of Brigadier General Alexander S. Webb's Pennsylvania troops—having formed themselves into the Philadelphia Brigade Association—began to consider setting monuments to their Sixty-ninth and Seventy-first Regiments at the high-water mark on the Gettysburg battlefield. As they finalized their plans, they learned that representatives of Pickett's Virginians were researching the possibility of placing a monument in the same general area—to mark the extent of the famous charge into destruction—and, therefore, extended an invitation to Pickett's men to meet again on the battlefield, but this time under the GAR rubric of values encapsulated into their motto: Fraternity, Charity, and Loyalty.[69]

The Southern veterans' reaction was not entirely positive. For one thing, the GBMA denied the Virginians permission to place their monument at the point of their farthest advance into Union-held territory, instructing them instead that all monuments must be placed at the original point of organization for battle—which in this case amounted to a distance of nearly a mile and a half from the point where Webb's and Pickett's men had clashed. For another, despite having faced Webb's men across the stone wall at the climax of Pickett's Charge, the Southern veterans likely found the issues raised by the proposed reunion as daunting as they had found the Union infantry. Certainly many questioned the propriety of the reunion, as did some Union veterans, ultimately deciding that returning to Gettysburg under such circumstances would be too painful. In the end, perhaps only two hundred Confederate veterans attended.[70]

While the reunion was accounted a success by all in attendance, Northern soldiers, editors, and politicians loudly disparaged the sentiments of reconciliation that the reunion had depicted. The following year, the Virginians invited the Philadelphians to Richmond for the unveiling of a monument to George Pickett. The same sorts of irritations and accusations surrounded those ceremonies. At one point, the Philadelphians refused abruptly to march in the parade to the cemetery. They explained that the ornamental national flag that they carried had been loaned to them under the condition that it not be paraded with any Confederate flag. The mayor of Richmond negotiated a quick compromise: Webb's veterans repacked their banner, the

Confederate flag was similarly furled, and the two groups marched together under a national flag owned by the Richmond camp of Southern veterans.[71]

During the highly anticipated twenty-fifth anniversary of the Battle of Gettysburg in 1888, about three hundred Southern veterans attended, but none as part of an official delegation from a Confederate veterans' group. Although Southern veteran attendance was up from the year before, the celebration was essentially a reunion of the Army of the Potomac. Local papers termed the reunion a "failure," particularly because most of the Southern representatives refused to participate in some of the planned festivities, including the parade in review. In the words of the park historian Kathleen Georg: "There was not much peace and unity pronounced at this anniversary where Union veterans still remembered that secession was treason and that the battlefield was a shrine to the Union victory."[72] The high point in attendance at a national reunion was the Gettysburg fiftieth anniversary in 1913. Estimates vary, but perhaps fifty thousand veterans attended the three-day festival of national patriotism, although only approximately eight thousand (or about 16 percent) were from the South. In fact, in covering the event, the *Confederate Veteran* refused to call it a reunion and labeled it instead "the Gettysburg gathering."[73] Significantly, in the same year, at a GAR encampment in Chattanooga, the Union veterans refused the participation of the Nathan Bedford Forrest Camp of the UCV. "The invitation it seems," the *Veteran* reported, was unauthorized, coming from "some impulsive Ohio veterans." The *Veteran* admitted that, in rejecting the Confederate camp, the GAR commander "simply conformed to the rule established some years ago, when the G.A.R. rarely did anything that was commendable." The *Veteran* article concluded by quoting the opinion of Washington Gardner, once Michigan's secretary of state, voiced several years earlier: "I wonder if the time will not come when somewhere on the borderland we may have a joint reunion of the survivors of the two great armies which would result in pleasure and profit to all concerned."[74] Clearly, to the editor of the *Veteran*, that time had not arrived even fifty years after Gettysburg.

Four years later, in the midst of world war, many thought that Vicksburg might be the place for such a reunion. Sponsored and organized by the national government, the National Memorial Celebration and Peace Jubilee was held from 16 to 19 October 1917 "in commemoration of a half century of peace and good fellowship which happily exists throughout the Republic." Many features of the Celebration, or National Memorial Reunion, as it was also called, displayed a strong sense of reunion. According to Willard D. Newbill, who organized the event on behalf of the Quartermaster Department, film and still photographers worked the crowds, with "the favorite poses being Blue and Gray veterans arm-in-arm or with a young soldier in khaki between them." On the night of the seventeenth, Union veterans formed in a body and marched to the Confederate portion of the camp for a "love feast," including the passage of joint resolutions supporting Woodrow Wilson in his war policies. In response to the critics who decried the expense and celebration in time of war, Newbill asserted that "no one can deny that it increased the patriotic spirit, now particularly needed and more precious than money, and that it contributed materially toward cementing widely separated sections of our country in a common cause." A display of portraits, with images of Lincoln, Grant, Davis, and Lee side by side, "was particularly commented upon by the veterans from the North and South as a significant feature of the reunion."[75]

However, all this effort was not rewarded with fulfilled expectations. From early attendance estimates that ranged from an upper limit of eighteen to twenty thousand down to twelve to fifteen thousand, it is clear that no more than seventy-five hundred attended on any one day. The government reports do not indicate how many of that number were Southern and how many Northern. Alone among the states of the former Confederacy, only Arkansas made an appropriation, of $5,000, to the general Celebration fund. Mississippi authorized Warren County and the city of Vicksburg to contribute $2,500 each, but, according to Newbill, "these sums particularly applied to decorations and city entertainment." Northern states, meanwhile, appropriated more than $159,750 in all. The reunion's program of events also ended up reflecting a particularly Northern bias. Two of the dignitaries representing Mississippi, Governor Theodore Bilbo and Congressman Byron P. Harrison, did not attend even though scheduled to speak. Former Mississippi Governor J. K. Vardaman did attend, but did not give his scheduled address. Even the commander in chief of the UCV failed to attend, his absence effectively permitting Northern orators to dominate the speaker's podium. Significantly, and perhaps as an intentional concession to Southern veterans, the program does not indicate that any events were scheduled to be held at the national cemetery, six miles distant, which of course contained only Union dead. Still, it appears that the National Memorial Reunion was embraced less than enthusiastically by most Southerners.[76]

Honoring the Civil War Dead

To be sure, many who attended these and other reunions felt as passionately about reconciliation as did those who did not attend, but the latter always constituted the larger number. Unfortunately, there is no way to know the reasons behind nonattendance. What is clear from the numbers alone is that the majority of reunions took place among veterans of the same uniform. Yearly meetings, reunions, and encampments within the GAR, the UCV, and numerous smaller organizations commanded far greater attendance than did the Blue-Gray efforts that attracted the national press. In 1897, the UCV numbered nine hundred active camps, and its annual reunion held that year at Nashville was attended by thousands. Precise attendance figures do not survive, but the Confederate Hotel served 36,800 meals a day, and this was only one of several places serving the veterans and their guests. In the same year as the Gettysburg fiftieth anniversary, the UCV held its reunion in Chattanooga, Tennessee, and the review of veterans mustered nearly a thousand gray-headed soldiers on horseback, in addition to those who walked and rode in automobiles along the parade route. Clearly, for most veterans of both sides, efforts were spent on reuniting with comrades first and former enemies second.[77]

Certainly, there had been genuine attempts at reconciliation, and not every oration that contained the mythic rhetoric of either the Cause Victorious or the Lost Cause was without sincere reconciliatory emotion. But the gestures toward a genuine reunification were largely predicated on the attempt to forget the underlying political and social tensions that had led to war. But memory was not so easily displaced when entering a cemetery to commemorate the dead or placing monuments on the proliferating battlefield parks. A. S. Billingsley of the U.S. Christian Commission recognized that the war could be forgotten, but for the presence of poignant spurs to memory: "But thanks be to a kind Providence, our God-protected republic, then unconscious of her strength, withstood the severe storm, and came out of the awful conflict with her columns of constitutional liberty stronger than ever. And so great has been our progress since, that, were it not for the old battle-fields, the maimed soldiers, their graves, and the mourning widows and orphans, you would scarce know that there had been any war."[78] Billingsley was exactly correct. So, while the maimed veterans, and even their widows and children, would eventually pass beyond human experience, the results of three decades of commemoration remained. In addition, the dead abided, resisted political and intellectual fashion, and stubbornly refused to be forgotten.

Given this perspective, it is important to note that one of the great gestures upon which national reunification was established has so far received less attention than it deserves. Many scholars have pointed to the Spanish-American War as the keystone in the arch that was the reunited country. As the sons of Union and Confederate veterans marched side by side in the same blue uniforms, the national division surely seemed resolved. In a rich moment of irony, Southern soldiers were suspect until they took up arms for the protection of American interests, just as, in every war this nation has ever fought, its black soldiers were held in suspicion and contempt until proving themselves on the battlefield. But overlooked in the military experience of the Spanish-American War was that, in addition to fighting together, Northern and Southern sons died together and were then buried together. The staunch separation of Union and Confederate soldiers had no counterpart in the interment of fatalities from the Cuban campaigns.

6

The Congregation of the Dead

The man that wandereth out of the way of understanding shall
remain in the congregation of the dead.
—*Proverbs 21:16*

A T THE ATLANTA PEACE JUBILEE IN 1898, President William McKinley
made the most tangible gesture on the part of the federal government
toward the South and the Southern dead when he proposed that the marking and care of Confederate graves, as with Union cemeteries, should become
the responsibility of the national government. In an address before Georgia's
state legislature, McKinley asserted that "sectional lines no longer mar the
map of the United States. Sectional feeling no longer holds back the love we
bear each other." Emphasizing the concerns of the Cause Victorious, he pronounced "The Union is once more the common altar of our love and loyalty, our devotion and sacrifice." Most important, the eminence of the nation
was reflected in the soldiers who had sacrificed all on its behalf: "What an
army of silent sentinels we have, and with what loving care their graves are
kept! Every soldier's grave made during our unfortunate Civil War is a tribute to American valor. And while, when those graves were made, we differed
widely about the future of this Government, those differences were long ago
settled by the arbitrament of arms; and the time has now come, in the evolution of sentiment and feeling under the providence of God, when in the spirit
of fraternity we should share with you in the care of the graves of the Confederate soldiers."[1]

But McKinley seems to have erred in expressing this most conciliatory
of sentiments, at least in the eyes of Southerners. He had framed his offer
within the language of the Cause Victorious, including an assertion that
American nationality had been settled by the arbitrament of arms. While most
in the audience might have acknowledged that the war's end had been ac-

complished through those means, they might not have so readily embraced the nationality he confidently projected. Nor did he resist the possessive language that had been the hallmark of Northern political rhetoric, stating that *we* should join *you* in caring for *your* graves even as he suggested that *we* are all Americans. For these reasons, McKinley's gesture was not without its detractors among the very people he had hoped to appease. For example, R. T. Owen, a Southern veteran, wrote the *Confederate Veteran:* "I wish you would file away in your papers that I don't think a Yankee tombstone would fit my grave."[2]

McKinley's oration falls at a particularly significant confluence of social and cultural trends in America. Northerners had by this point become convinced of Southern acquiescence in the Northern nationalist mythology. For thirty years, there had not been a credible whisper advocating the sundering of the nation into sectional fragments, the longest such period in U.S. history. Union, the first and always the most important of Northern war goals, was secure. This confident assurance that the Cause Victorious had been the correct interpretation of the war's significance made it all the easier to define the second war goal—the abolition of slavery—all the more narrowly. Although Southerners had imposed a number of social and economic restrictions on African Americans throughout the South, many Northerners comforted themselves that the original ideal of the war had been to destroy an immoral institution, not to bring social and political equality to black Americans. Satisfied with the state of affairs, and reassured by Booker T. Washington that Southern blacks were also satisfied with the nation that the war had produced, Northern whites eagerly embraced any opportunity to express their magnanimity to Southern veterans and their relations. The opportunity afforded by the Spanish-American War to display national union and international prowess easily lent itself to such interpretations. When contrasted against the memories of Civil War veterans, the imperialist lark against Spain, to that time the briefest, least costly war in American history, gave ample evidence that only other Americans could have forced a contest so fierce as to last four years and consume the lives of 620,000 men. Having praised their soldiers in guarded terms for so long, Southerners entered a vigorous new phase in the commemoration of the Confederate dead at the very moment when, seeking to shore up his political fortunes in the South, McKinley offered to extend federal government protection to include those who had most wanted to escape its influence when living.

Honoring the Civil War Dead

The first major change in national cemetery interment policy took place in June 1900, when Congress authorized a separate section for the burial of Confederate soldier dead in Arlington National Cemetery. With the resurgence of Southern political power over the previous decade, Washington had become host to a number of former Confederates, enough to sponsor two separate United Confederate Veterans (UCV) camps, not to mention five chapters of the United Daughters of the Confederacy (UDC), one camp of the recently founded Sons of Confederate Veterans, and the Southern Relief Society, dedicated to assisting indigent Confederate veterans. The second of the two UCV camps, No. 1191, named for Charles Broadway Rouss, was something of a splinter movement. In the 1890s, a small group of Southern veterans in Washington felt that there was more to be accomplished than dinners and other social functions. Among them, Samuel E. Lewis worked to focus the new camp's agenda on the problems faced in the District of Columbia by living veterans. This focus inevitably led him to consider the burial needs of dying veterans and—within a relatively short time—the burial of Confederate soldiers lost a generation before.[3]

Lewis's research formed the basis of, first, a series of inquiries to the War Department and the Quartermaster Department and finally a petition to President McKinley. During the war, more than 500 Confederate soldiers had been buried in the cemeteries of Washington. During the modest relocation efforts of the early 1870s, organized largely by state Ladies' Memorial Associations, 241 of the dead were removed and relocated to Virginia and the Carolinas for reburial in their native lands. But the remaining soldiers were, in Lewis's estimation, neglected and unrecognized. The burials were divided between the Soldiers' Home Cemetery, northeast of Washington proper, and Arlington, where they were scattered in three separate sections. Seeking a solution, Lewis urged the military, the Congress, and the president to set aside a number of acres within the Arlington property for the honored burial of Confederate soldiers and to see that the Confederate soldiers from both cemeteries were disinterred, recoffined, and reburied in this new cemetery section. Following McKinley's lead two years before, Congress appropriated $2,500 for the purposes of removing, transporting, and reburying Southern soldiers into a circular plot situated at that time about as far from the main gates as it was possible to be.[4]

Lewis's reasoning for the relocation and reburial efforts was complex and, ultimately, reflected a new direction in Lost Cause argumentation. In the first place, not only would such actions satisfy Southerners, but they would also, as Lewis noted in the petition to McKinley, please "many good people in the North, who no longer cherishing animosity, would be gratified at the removal of Confederate Dead from the midst of the Federal Graves." More specifically, Lewis and a committee of like-minded veterans were concerned about the proximity in Arlington of Confederate soldiers and black civilians. Although those soldiers had been decently buried, Lewis complained about the way their graves were marked. "They have thin marble head-stones," he wrote, "which bear no mark whatever to distinguish them from the Contrabands and Refugees, whose graves are marked by exactly the same description of stones." At the Soldiers' Home Cemetery the contrast seemed even more stark, since Confederate prisoners had been buried near solders, not civilians, yet the Southern graves "have head-stones exactly like those of the Confederate Dead, the Contrabands and Refugees at Arlington." Clearly, Lewis and other members of his UCV camp feared that Southern graves could not be recognized among those of the hundreds of black citizens buried in the northern sections of Arlington. In the petition to McKinley, Lewis argued that Southern graves should be marked by distinctive headstones, but, even if this easier step were taken, removal remained an imperative since "many of them [the headstones] are in exposed places, near low fences, and are liable to be stolen or mutilated by evil minded persons."[5]

Lewis also introduced into the debate the concept of an obligation on the part of the federal government to the soldiers who had died opposing it. Acknowledging the government's claim that Confederate prisoners in Washington had been decently buried, Lewis wrote Julian Moore, "We are willing to concede so much in the sense that they were given *individual* graves, and marking, and record, at a time when there was great rush to and fro, with much to do, and little time to do anything in order." But it was now time, he felt, for Southerners to do far more than ensure that they were simply decently buried. He invoked Southerners' "sacred duty, too long deferred," to see that the Confederate dead "shall have that honorable and loving care by us, and respect of the Government, to which they are entitled, which will save, not only our children, but those of our one-time foes, from the blush of shame in generations to come."[6] Thus, for Lewis, these Confederate soldiers deserved honorable interment in Arlington by virtue of their being American citizens; the cause for which they had died had been so far subsumed in the process of commemoration that the nation they had sought to defeat in war should now embrace them as fellow citizens in the most sacred of national burial sites.

Although Congress followed McKinley's stated sentiments in their endorsement of Lewis's plan and had appropriated the necessary funds, some questioned the plan's propriety, even some Southerners. For example, when news of the congressional appropriation circulated, the Southern Memorial Association, a multistate organization that had largely become the inheritor of the Ladies' Memorial Associations, expressed its alarm that Southern soldiers would remain in the custody of the federal government and continue to lie in Northern soil. Writing on behalf of the association, Janet H. W. Randolph of Richmond urged that, once the bodies were disinterred, the remains be restored to Southern cemeteries. "They must . . . exhume these bodies, and place them in boxes of some kind. Why could we not then ask that they be turned over to us, it would cost them that much less than [re]burying and placing headstones." Randolph's plan was to have the bodies then transported to Hollywood Cemetery in Richmond, to lie near the Confederate dead of Gettysburg, which had been moved there nearly thirty years earlier. The following week, Randolph again contacted the veterans' leadership, specifically criticizing Lewis and his intentions to mark the Arlington burial site with a large, ornamental urn: "We want our dead and notwithstanding the extreme generosity of the government in allowing Dr. Lewis out of *Our Taxes* the magnificent sum of $2500.00, we are going to have our dead. [A]nd we are not going to place *Grand Urns* over them, but a monument to tell how & where & for what they died."[7] No testimony more eloquently demonstrates that the didactic nature of commemoration was evident to all.

Lewis, for his part, was less than sanguine about the efforts of Southern women to reclaim their dead. In a lengthy letter to Julian G. Moore, Lewis bemoaned the activities of the Southern Memorial Association, "the patriotic women . . . with their well-meant but ill-advised and ill-timed interference; going so far as to bring to their aid the influence of their local members of Congress and other influential persons to have our local work set at naught, and their disturbing, impractical schemes laid before the government and brought to the attention of the county and made much of in the public press."[8] At this point, it is clearly Lewis who is out of step, or at least proceeding in a new direction. The concerns of the Southern Memorial Association represent continuity with earlier practices in commemoration; it is Lewis who is advocating the novel idea that Northerners should care for Southern bodies. Janet Randolph so obviously seeks the traditional, hence separate, course of

Southern memorialization; it is Lewis who is ironically employing the language of the Cause Victorious.

Despite the "interference" and the misunderstandings, Lewis and the Charles Broadway Rouss Camp succeeded in carrying out the relocation and reburial of Confederate soldiers in Arlington. Section 16, Confederate Circle, would eventually contain 482 officers and soldiers, wives and civilians, 12 of them unknown. The graves were marked with substantial marble headstones, similar in size and overall shape to the thousands of Union headstones scattered across the grounds, but with a distinct point at the top. Legend holds that this design was adopted specifically to keep Yankees from sitting on them.[9] In addition to the distinctive headstone design, however, the physical arrangement and placement of Section 16 are also significant. Confederate Circle lies at the westernmost edge of the cemetery grounds, high on the hillside above the other graves, farthest from the main gates on the eastern side bordered by the Potomac and isolated by a circular drive. The graves are arranged in concentric circles, with the gravestones all facing inward. One observer commented that, from the center of the plot, with a good spyglass, every inscription could be easily read.[10] Across the road on three sides, north, west, and south, only landscaped lawns surround the graves. Across the road to the east, running tangentially in north-south lines, the graves of Union soldiers, mostly black servicemen of the U.S. Colored Troops, fall away in serried ranks down the hill toward the river. Their gravestones face east, downhill, toward the national capital and away from Confederate Circle.

Eventually, perhaps in response to Janet Randolph's protests against symbolically neutral "*Grand Urns*," the plot was ornamented with a heroic statuary monument in 1914. The immense construction was designed and executed by Moses Ezekiel, who now also rests in the cemetery section. At the top, an idealized South stands with her head bowed but her right hand extending a laurel wreath of victory south toward Richmond. Inscribed on the plinth is the phrase VICTRIX CAUSA DIIS PLACUIT SED VICTA CATONI [The victorious cause was pleasing to the gods, but the lost cause to Cato]. This extraordinary monument, within the sacrosanct grounds of Arlington, serves, not only as a commemoration of the Southern soldier dead, but also as a monument to their survivors, the veterans and women who championed the resurgent Lost Cause. In addition to scenes of soldiers leaving family and sweethearts to go to war, bas-relief sculptures also depict a faithful mammy lifting an infant to kiss her departing father, her voluminous skirts sheltering

Honoring the Civil War Dead

The Confederate Monument, executed by Moses Ezekiel, erected in Arlington
National Cemetery 4 June 1914—the 106th anniversary of Jefferson Davis's birth.
Theodor Horydczak Collection, Library of Congress

Confederate veterans leaving Confederate Circle, Section 16 of Arlington National Cemetery, 1914. Note the distinctively "pointed" Confederate headstone in the foreground.
Library of Congress

an older, grieving child. Despite years of insisting that all soldiers of the war be remembered for their mutually respectable qualities, instead of invoking the valor, bravery, and dedication common to all American soldiers, Southerners continued to preserve the sentiments of sectionalism in the commemoration of the Confederate reburials at Arlington. In the conflict between reconciliation and memory, in the presence of the dead, memory reigned supreme.

Initially, the interment of Confederate soldiers at Arlington seemed to hold out the promise of an ever-increasing reconciliation between North and South, at least in the crucial arena of care for the dead. Although the first response had been mixed, most Southerners embraced the gesture eventually. Spurred by this success, former Confederate General Stephen D. Lee resurrected McKinley's Atlanta Peace Jubilee gesture by advancing the following resolution at the May 1901 UCV reunion in Memphis, Tennessee: "*Resolved,* That we respectfully request that Congress take appropriate action

looking toward the care and preservation of the graves of the Confederate dead
now in the various cemeteries of the Northern states." The veterans adopted
the resolution unanimously even though—as Samuel Lewis noted—"there
were active workers against it." Lewis supposed the opposition stemmed from
misunderstanding: "Some of our friends in the South, unaware of the facts,
supposed that Congress had made appropriations for the removal of Confederate dead from battle fields in Maryland, Pennsylvania, and elsewhere into
National Cemeteries. *Very naturally and properly* they objected to such pro-
cedures, and requested that the remains be sent to Southern Cemeteries."[11]

However, there seems to have been no thought given to extending federal care to Confederate graves in Southern states. Just as Northern anxiety
had—immediately following the war—focused on Union graves in the South,
nearly forty years later Southerners were every bit as anxious for their own
dead buried in Northern soil. Presumably, federal care for Confederate graves
in the South was unnecessary since they were already well tended. At least an
article in the *Confederate Veteran* confidently asserted: "So far as has been
ascertained, the graves of our Confederate dead within the boundaries of the
Southern states have been cared for chiefly by the ministrations of our Southern women, who have also from time to time made appeals in behalf of those
graves situated outside the Southern states, which their faithful services thus
far have been unable to reach."[12]

UCV Camp 1191, which had been instrumental in the creation of the
Confederate section of Arlington, forwarded its resolution, additional testi-
monials, and its own independent research into the potential logistics of the
proposed task to Senator Joseph B. Foraker. The senator had earned a reputation as a "broad-minded and liberal man" for his actions while governor of
Ohio promoting the preservation and care of two Confederate prisoner cemeteries, Camp Chase, near Columbus, and Johnson's Island, near Sandusky.[13]
Although Foraker introduced to Congress a statute based on the UCV resolution in early 1904, political wrangling and delays, failures to get reports out
of committee on time, and a certain reluctance on the part of some all con-
spired to postpone congressional action. The proposed statute even competed
with two other, nearly identical bills, each of which had to be investigated,
sent to committee, and reported on. Finally, Congress passed the Foraker Bill
in 1906, creating a temporary commission within the War Department, the
Commission for Marking Graves of Confederate Dead.[14]

Over the course of its existence, the commission was chaired by former Confederate officers. There was no stipulation in the law for this, only that "some competent person" be named for the job. However, some congressmen must have suspected that former Confederates would be appointed to the position. Although there is no overt indication in the tenor of the debate that any legislators feared setting up a permanent sinecure for former Confederates, an early amendment to the bill spelled out that the work of the commission, and hence the position of commissioner, was only temporary.[15] These successive commissioners—William Elliott, William C. Oates, James H. Berry, and later Samuel E. Lewis—in turn undertook the laborious process of implementing the designs of Congress, which authorized the commission to mark only the graves of Confederates who had died in Union custody, either while prisoners of war or in Union hospitals, and only those graves located in Northern states. The graves of soldiers who had died in combat, while under arms opposing Federal authority, were not eligible, nor were the graves of those who had died in Union field hospitals or encampments and been buried in Southern states. Such restrictions had always prevailed in the national cemeteries. Even the Confederates just reinterred in Arlington had all died while in Union custody or after the war's conclusion.[16]

These restrictions were simultaneously both lesser and greater than they first appear. In the first place, there were very few Confederate soldiers who had died in combat still remaining on Northern battlefields. The efforts of the Ladies' Memorial Associations had removed all that could be found from Gettysburg, the most notable of Northern battles. But the restrictions were still keenly felt, for the gesture of marking Confederate graves was a consciously selective one. Although federal government efforts on behalf of the Union dead encompassed the entire country, these late efforts on behalf of the Southern dead ignored the states of the former Confederacy. Also, in spite of the fact that eligibility requirements for burial in national cemeteries had been regularly relaxed, eventually including Union veterans and even army nurses who had died after the war, they were never broadened far enough to include Confederate veterans.

In the process of lobbying for the passage of the Foraker Bill, Samuel Lewis and others again resorted to the new, more assertive formulation about federal obligations to the dead first expressed during the Arlington reinterments. In a letter to a Kentucky veterans' group, Lewis outlined his favorite arguments for convincing reluctant congressmen. In addition to underscoring the "reason-ableness" of the appropriation amount and the possibility that, without fed-eral protection many Confederate graves might become obscured and lost, Lewis again suggested an obligation due the Southern dead. He recommended the argument that Southern taxes had funded the national cemeteries as well as Northern pensions, both of which were unavailable to Southern veterans. Furthermore, he urged his correspondent, "Emphasize the fact that it is the duty of the Southern people and especially of their public representatives to demand as a *right* but not as charity or favor in any sense, that the U. S. Gov-ernment give all proper and honorable care to the graves of the Confederate dead in the North."[17] Forty years after Appomattox, Lewis argued that South-ern soldiers dying in opposition to the Federal Union had a right to expect that same government to honor and protect their graves. Lewis went so far as to inform William Loeb, secretary to President Theodore Roosevelt, that "it is a lasting disgrace to our county that those American soldiers of the South, animated as they were . . . by the most exalted ideas of patriotism, should have been permitted to lie in unhonored graves for forty years."[18]

By 1900, the National Cemetery System had grown far beyond its origi-nally intended purpose, blossoming to eighty-three cemeteries. Twenty-three of those already had either small Confederate sections or, more often, a col-lection of Southern soldiers buried indiscriminately among civilian admin-istrators, employees, the relations of military personnel, and in some cases, African American "contrabands." Other than those Confederate burial sites already on national cemetery property, the Commission for Marking Graves of Confederate Dead located at least sixty additional sites that had never been incorporated into any form of federal custody. The commission also over-saw the cataloging and marking of the graves of Southerners who had died in prisoner-of-war camps such as Rock Island, Illinois, Point Lookout, Mary-land, and Elmira, New York. However, the enabling legislation did not per-mit, nor was funding available for, the collection of remains into centralized locations, as had been done on behalf of Union soldiers after the war. Hence, small cemetery grounds, such as those at Lafayette, Indiana, with twenty-eight burials, Gallipolis, Ohio, with four graves, and Covington, Kentucky, with ten interments in three locations, all remained in their original disposition. When, during the congressional investigation of the Foraker Bill, it was sug-gested that the commission's charter be expanded, one member of the Mili-tary Affairs Committee bluntly stated, "We made ample appropriation for marking the graves of deceased Confederate soldiers buried in the North; and that I think is as far as we ought to go."[19]

The restrictions, although they chafed, were upheld faithfully by the commissioners. Occasionally in their correspondence a somewhat defensive tone appears to be fending off criticism from fellow Southerners. Commissioner James H. Berry, replied to an inquiry from Elizabeth Thompson Sells, president of her UDC chapter. "I wish to assure you," Berry wrote, "that my whole heart is in this work, and having lost a limb in the Confederacy, shall do everything in my power to beautify the last resting place of my Comrades who died in these prisons in the North." Berry had been required to explain that, while the commission could mark the graves of the Confederate dead, it could not purchase outright the property in which they were buried, much to Elizabeth Sell's disappointment. Such problems and nuances were plentiful in the commission's work. In one case, a vault containing the remains of nine Confederate soldiers, placed by the local UCV chapter, was marked by the commission with a bronze tablet listing only six of the names. When asked why this was so, Commissioner Berry replied, "The reason for limiting the number of names to be placed on the tablet to six, is due to the fact that under the law providing for this marking only those names of Confederate soldiers who died as prisoners of war can be included in the list to appear on the tablet, the other three whose remains also repose in this vault not having died as prisoners of war."[20] In many such situations, the limitations of federal efforts were clear.

Overall, Southerners seemed pleased with the commission's efforts. "The Confederate soldiers everywhere regard it as a most generous act on the part of the United States," Berry wrote to a UDC chapter in Philadelphia. But there still existed suspicion of the government's efforts. In Lexington, Kentucky, James Nicoll, the superintendent of the local cemetery, complained to the commission that he had hoped that all his Confederate graves would be marked. But L. Frank Nye, a clerk for the commission, had been informed on a recent visit to the site that the local UCV camp opposed the work, having previously erected a large monument in the cemetery in honor of the Confederate dead, and, therefore, resenting the intrusion. Commissioner Berry informed Nicoll that the local veterans "were not so enthusiastic for markers, feeling that the graves were sufficiently marked by the monument and the terra cotta numbers at the graves." If Nicoll could obtain permission, Berry would authorize headstones for all of the dead that "can be determined as having died in federal prisons or military hospitals." Perhaps hoping to mollify Nicoll or entice the veterans, Berry added, "This number has not yet been determined, but I will say that in case of a doubt I shall be inclined to give you the benefit of the doubt and order headstones for the doubtful ones."[21]

By and large, the efforts of the commission were well rewarded, nearly thirty thousand Confederate soldier graves having been identified and marked (see appendix B). It seemed to be a successful and significant gesture. The graves of Southern soldiers buried in the North were brought into uniformity with the honored dead of the Union army, although marked with that distinctively pointed headstone. The efforts of the commission seemed to fulfill the hopes of McKinley, and they did so fully within the parameters of the Cause Victorious, more than a generation after war's end.

But too much should not be read into a Northern gesture at so late a date. By the 1920s, sentiments that the graves of Confederates should be honored began to wear thin. In the course of his research, Commissioner William Elliott had identified Camp Morton, just outside Indianapolis, as the repository of more than sixteen hundred Confederate prisoner dead. Following the war, the prison graveyard was abandoned and became overgrown, the headboards decayed and lost. In the 1870s, the officers of the Vandalia Railroad requested the use of the north end of the prison grounds to construct an engine house and sidings. In exchange, they gave up a small landholding on the west side of the cemetery. Two rows of the Confederate dead buried in the camp cemetery were disinterred and moved to the new grounds, but without any attempt to preserve the grave order or the individual identities of the dead. However, the remaining rows of undisturbed graves apparently had retained their identities, although probably only through record books rather than grave markers.[22]

In subsequent years, Camp Morton proved to be emblematic of Southern concerns about neglected burial grounds. The land that had become the cemetery had before the war been the city's fairgrounds, and after the war Indianapolis approved an expenditure of $3,000 to rehabilitate it to once again serve that purpose. Until the 1890s, the camp cemetery grounds were the scene of country fairs and picnics. As the town expanded, the nearby drainage ditch that had served the prison was torn up and replaced with a branch of the city sewer system, an excavation that very likely resulted in the removal of still more graves. The area was finally redeveloped as a residential district at the turn of the century. In the course of its work, the commission was able to preserve the names of the dead but unable to identify any individual graves. In 1912, since specific headstones could not be placed, the cemetery was marked with a large memorial listing the deceased, and the commission declared its work to be completed.[23]

However, the expansion of Indianapolis continued to disturb the dead of Camp Morton. In 1928, local residents petitioned Congress for permission to remove the memorial that the commission had placed over the dead to a park in town, "where it can be readily seen and receive proper care." With the consent of Congress the monument was relocated separating once again the graves from any record of their identity. In 1931, all 1,639 graves, apparently from both lots, were removed to nearby Crown Hill Cemetery. At some point, an unknown clerk in the War Department retrieved the records that William Elliott and the commission had prepared in 1912 and drew a heavy pencil line through all the names listed in the Camp Morton graves register. At the end of that section was penciled the explanation: "Remains of above removed to lot 285, Sec 32, Crown Hill Cemetery, Indianapolis, Ind and reinterred as Unknowns on Oct. 27, 1931."[24] While loss of identity was all too common during the war itself, two generations after the war's end Civil War graves remained vulnerable.

In the 1930s, the numbers of Civil War veterans, North and South, dwindled as they joined their lost comrades of decades before. Of course, as they died, Union veterans continued to find interment in national cemeteries but Confederate veterans did not. National cemetery regulations printed in 1911, while the Commission for Marking of Confederate Graves still operated, did not allow for their general interment.[25] Not until 1931 do the regulations even mention the word *Confederate*—and even then only to permit their burial in Section 16 of Arlington National Cemetery, under special circumstances.[26] Except for a few exceptions, national cemeteries remain to this day what they were originally designed to be—the honored ground of national, and, hence, Union, burials alone.

Occasionally, acting as potent spurs to memory, the scattered Civil War dead continued to turn up on the battlefields now preserved as parklands. As throughout the late nineteenth century, the response of the living to the dead tells much about their relationship to the war and to the American nation. On 16 August 1933, a *Philadelphia Ledger* article reported the discovery of the skeletal remains of two soldiers on the battlefield at Gettysburg. From the location and the type of ammunition found on the bodies, the dead were thought to have been Confederates, possibly from Alabama. The article mentioned that the park custodians would try to contact a chapter of the UDC for final disposition of the remains. Mrs. Arthur E. Shaw, president of the Philadelphia chapter, contacted the park to ascertain which UDC branch was taking the matter in hand. At the request of the park superintendent, she supplied the address of an Alabama UDC chapter.[27] James R. McConaghie, the park's superintendent, wrote the Alabama organization: "In many similar cases the remains were reburied deeply in the spot where discovered. The thought being that since definite information was lacking to identify the most honorable action would be to permit the remains to lie where they had honorably died. Should such be your desire, in view of the possible doubt as to identification, we will so act." The grounds upon which McConaghie based his proposal are unclear. There is no record at Gettysburg of any bodies being reburied where they lay after the establishment of the national cemetery and the removal of the Confederate dead in the 1870s. In three earlier but similar accounts, two in 1890 and one in 1899, all the remains were relocated. At any rate, perhaps because McConaghie now seemed tentative about the identity of the bodies or because he implied an honored battlefield burial, the Alabama UDC granted permission for McConaghie to bury the remains on the battlefield.[28]

However, McConaghie must eventually have realized that what he had proposed was not possible, for the remains were not reburied on the field. In a rather distressed letter, Mrs. Gustave Mertins, president of the Alabama women's chapter, wrote McConaghie six months after their first correspondence: "On Sept. 20th I replied to your letter, stating that action taken by the Board was that we would agree to your plan for the Government to bury them there again in Gettysburg on Nov. 12th[.] I talked with you personally in the Gettysburg Hotel, ratifying the former statements. Today, Mar 13th 1934, the Director of the Archives and History of the State of Ala[bama] phoned me saying that her nephew in Washington wrote her that 'these two bodies were lying in a paste board box [on?] the shelf,' at Gettysburg—and that the authorities there wished to know what disposition to make of them." Understandably concerned, Mrs. Mertins had also contacted Alabama Senator Hugo L. Black, who then contacted the park to inquire about the lack of attention in the matter of the reburial.[29] Unable either to reinter the remains on the field or to move them into the national cemetery, McConaghie had, simply and literally, shelved the problem. He finally solved the problem by arranging to have the bodies carried across the state border into Maryland and there interred in the Confederate Cemetery at Hagerstown, where the Southern dead of Antietam had ultimately been buried. He happily reported to Senator Black that the burial would be accomplished with military honors and assured him of his "deep regret" and that "there will be no further cause for criticism" since "every effort will be exercised by this office to properly expedite the final disposition."[30]

Five years later, as workmen were trenching for drainage pipes, another body was discovered. The grave was researched, the bones collected and boxed, and they too eventually wound up in the Park's library. In the trench the park representatives had found two blouse buttons: the first a Confederate button, near the skull, and the second a Union button, about four yards away. The body was also uncovered near a spot where, after the battle, Southern soldiers were thought to have been buried in a mass grave. Proximity, therefore, encouraged McConaghie and the park historian, Frank Tilberg, to rule that it was that of a Confederate soldier, but even McConaghie had to admit that the identification was uncertain: "While we cannot positively so identify [the remains] as such we do have enough evidence to warrant the belief."[31] Like the remains found in 1933, this body too was carried across the border into Maryland and interred at Hagerstown.

These examples make park policy clear: unless it could be proven that the dead were Union soldiers and therefore entitled to burial in the national cemetery, they were assumed to be Confederate and removed to Hagerstown. Throughout the history of Gettysburg National Military Park, every effort has been made to ensure that no Confederate soldier is buried in the national cemetery. How many Union soldiers might have been transported to the Hagerstown Confederate cemetery is unknowable. The preservation of the burial grounds as a Union cemetery remained the dominant concern.

These circumstances were apparently an uncomfortable subject at times for park personnel. Superintendent E. E. Davis employed some convoluted reasoning in answering a letter inquiring about Southern burials in the Cemetery at Gettysburg. "There are none," he admitted. Nor were there "memorials to Confederate dead in the Cemetery." But Davis also pointed out that "all laws regulating the Cemetery and all appropriations for its maintenance are made by Congress in which the South is proportionately represented." Perhaps hoping to demonstrate the absence of any continuing legacy of sectionalism, Davis continued: "This [national cemetery] (and other National Cemeteries) is under the immediate jurisdiction of the Quartermaster General of the Army who is a native of Tennessee. The officer under him directly in charge of National Cemeteries was born in West Virginia. The officer in the office of the Secretary of War most concerned with National Cemetery matters was born in Virginia."[32] Whatever ameliorating influences such native-born Southerners might have had, the policies of the park's administration with respect to the national cemetery indicate that it was permissible to err and bury a Union soldier in Southern soil but that it was not possible to err and bury a Confederate in a national cemetery.

However, recent events perhaps indicate that the sharp distinctions that had continually marked the commemoration of the Civil War soldier dead may be easing, more than a century after the war. In 1996, skeletal remains were again discovered at Gettysburg, this time eroding out of an embankment. After so much time had passed, little could be ascertained with any certainty. Forensic examination conducted at the Smithsonian Institution confirmed that the remains were male, had almost certainly died of a gunshot wound to the head, and dated to the period of the Civil War. Yet no evidence was discovered that might indicate for which side he had died. Although the situation with which park personnel were presented seems to mirror almost exactly those discussed earlier, the results in the 1990s were very different from those in the 1930s. Since it was conjectured from the location of the body that this soldier had been killed on the first day of the battle, the body was buried, with military honors, as unknown remains in Gettysburg National Cemetery on the presumed anniversary of his death, 1 July 1997. Noted Civil War historian James McPherson gave the eulogistic address to crowds that were actually quite small for so notable an event. National news coverage almost completely ignored the burial itself, focusing instead on the symbolic meeting of the oldest living Confederate and Union widows, both of whom placed flowers on the coffin before it was lowered into nationally sanctified ground.[33] Thus it is possible that, for the first time, a Confederate soldier who died while under arms opposing Union forces was interred with honors in a national cemetery, but the primary media coverage emphasized, as it had in the past, the moment when North and South—this time in the form of widows, not veterans—clasped hands across the stone wall near the Bloody Angle.

Following the centennial anniversary of the war, the Civil War historian Bruce Catton wrote: "The memory of our Civil War has not been a divisive force in this country. On the contrary, it has been a source of unity —something that ties us together and gives us a new depth of mutual understanding. Incredibly, the greatest and most terrible war we have ever fought—the one we fought with each other—has given us greater strength and a more enduring unity. It has given us a common tradition, shared memories that go to the very roots of our existence as a people."[34] While it is true that we all have shared memories of the war, we do not all share the same memories. Our perceptions of the past remain divisive and distinct. And, while it cannot be said that memory was ever so potent as to prevent reunification, it was only through an abridgment of memory that unity was successfully achieved. But the dead denied any such abridgment and continue to influence the ways in which we understand our past.

Of course, Americans have never hesitated to reinvent their past when memories prove to be uncomfortable. In 2002, as a result of legal challenges to administrative policy, the Veterans Administration (VA) essentially crafted a new interpretation of the origins and intent of the national cemeteries. A member of the Sons of Confederate Veterans filed suit to protest current restrictions on the display of Confederate flags in the cemeteries. The burial ground in question was Point Lookout Confederate Cemetery, created originally to receive those who died while prisoners of war. Maintained throughout the nineteenth century by the state of Maryland, the cemetery was turned over to the federal government in 1910, perhaps in response to the activities of the Confederate graves commission that had surveyed and marked the cemetery's approximately thirty-four hundred burials. Contrary to VA regulations, a Confederate flag had from 1994 to 1998 flown daily in the cemetery in addition to the U.S. flag mandated by law. The VA was unaware of the unauthorized display until an individual (unconnected with the subsequent legal proceedings) complained that the Confederate flag should be the only flag flown at Point Lookout and that the U.S. flag should be removed. Somewhat at a loss to explain how the Confederate flag came to be flying daily, the VA had it removed, prompting the local Sons of Confederate Veterans camp to petition for its daily display. The VA refused, pointing out that current regulations permitted the Southern flag to fly only two days a year, on Memorial Day and, in certain states, on Confederate Memorial Day. At that point, a former commander in chief of the Sons of Confederate Veterans filed suit, claiming an infringement of the First Amendment protection of free speech. The District Court of Maryland agreed and compelled the VA to restore the Confederate flag.[35]

On appeal, in two concurrent decisions in the Federal Circuit Court of Appeals and the Fourth Circuit Court of Appeals, the VA's arguments prevailed, and the lower court decision was overturned. Ultimately, the VA based its appeal on a fairly obscure portion of the *United States Code,* a statute detailing veterans' benefits, specifically a paragraph that permits national cemeteries to establish memorial areas honoring soldiers not physically interred. According to the statute: "All national and other veterans' cemeteries under the control of the National Cemetery Administration shall be considered national shrines as a tribute to our gallant dead and, notwithstanding the provisions of any other law, the Secretary is hereby authorized to permit appropriate officials to fly the flag of the United States of America at such cemeteries twenty-four hours each day."[36] The VA argued that, under this definition, its mission was to ensure the honored memorialization of *all* soldiers buried in the national cemeteries, even Confederate soldiers. Although the purpose of the statute has nothing to do with the historical creation of the cemeteries, the VA argued—and the appeals court agreed—that flying a Confederate flag in this small cemetery containing only Confederate soldiers was inimical to its larger mission of honoring those same soldiers as *Americans.*[37] The VA's successful appeal marks the latest triumph of the Cause Victorious; union has been accomplished through the subjugation of Confederate soldiers to the national purpose, creating a situation in which an agency of the national government utilized the bodies of the Southern dead to counter an effort to memorialize them as Southerners. That all those soldiers died while imprisoned for committing the crime of rebellion against that same government seems to have been lost in the shuffle.

Although once crucial to the negotiations between North and South, the process of forgetting may no longer serve us well in our interpretations of the war and its presence in our lives. Historian Allan Nevins once sagely advised:

> We should probe more deeply into [the Civil War's] roots, a process that will expose some of the weaknesses of our social fabric and governmental system. We should pay fuller attention to its darker aspects, and examine more honestly such misrepresentations as the statement it was distinguished by its generosity of spirit, the magna-

nimity with which the combatants treated each other; a statement absurd on its face, for no war which lasts four years and costs 600,000 lives leaves much magnanimity in its later phases. We should above all examine more closely the effects of the great and terrible war not on the nation's politics—we know that; not on its economy—we also know that; but on its character, the vital element of national life.[38]

The struggle to establish an inclusive, nonsectional nationalism following the most horrendous civil war of the nineteenth century should be acknowledged as one of the noblest ideals that this nation has ever embraced. It was accomplished unevenly, imperfectly, because it clashed with public and private memories of war and of death. It was also hindered by the reluctance on the part of both North and South to extend that assertion of nationalism to all, especially African Americans. Even after 140 years, the promise of that nationalist myth—a promise valorized by the death of Lincoln and more than half a million Americans—requires, not that we forget the war, but instead that we understand more clearly how the pain that it inflicted shaped the memory and meaning of it. Until the issues that ignited such passions become culturally irrelevant, we will continue to be tested by that legacy that requires that we both honor and remember the Civil War and its costs. Until we have reached an understanding of that war's place within our national identity, we, like Americans a century ago, will remain hopelessly, willingly, and reverently among the congregation of the dead.

Appendix A
National Cemeteries Created for the
Civil War Soldier Dead, 1861–1875

THE FOLLOWING TABLE LISTS THE NATIONAL CEMETERIES incorporated under the provisions of Congress by the year 1875. The interments are broken down into known and unknown burials among three categories: white Union soldiers; black Union soldiers; and Confederate soldiers. These are the distinctions that appear to have been most important to those compiling the records at the time. One other distinction, that between officers and soldiers, has not been repeated: the numbers listed here include all military ranks. Another category that sometimes appears in the cemetery records is civilians. These individuals range from the families of officers stationed at army posts, to employees, servants, "contraband" fugitive slaves, and prisoners. Where possible, they have not been represented in these lists so as to give a clearer picture of military deaths and burials.

The division of Union states, border states, and Confederate states demonstrates the centers of military struggle and the overriding concern for the protection of the Union soldier dead. By 1875, national cemeteries in Southern states greatly outnumbered those in the other two categories combined. Note also that identity becomes generally more vulnerable the further South a soldier is buried. Much of this is due to the delay in the creation of the Southern national cemeteries, which was postponed until after the war. But the percentage of unknown black soldiers to known black soldiers rises even more dramatically, from only 11.3 percent in Union states, to 55.7 percent in border states, to a staggering 63.5 percent in Southern states. Such a sharp and secular trend invites speculation, but little can now be known for certain.

This is not a complete picture of Union burials, for it lists only those interred in national cemeteries. Untold thousands were also buried in city and town cemeteries, churchyard burial grounds, and even private cemeteries. In 1872, Quartermaster General Montgomery C. Meigs reported to Congress that Union soldiers were buried in 285 cemeteries other than the national cemeteries. Some national cemeteries, like those at Fort McPherson, Nebraska, and Fort Gibson, Indian Territory (Oklahoma), are not included since, although they contain military deaths, they were not established to contain the Civil War soldier dead.

Name and Location	White Union, Known	White Union, Unknown	Black Union, Known	Black Union, Unknown	Confederate, Known	Confederate, Unknown	Total
Cemeteries in Union States (14)							
Battleground, D.C.	40						40
Soldiers' Home, D.C.	5,092	278			125		5,495
Keokuk, Iowa	600	27					627
Camp Butler, Ill.	549	165			454[a]	189	1,357
Mound City, Ill.	2,060	2,460	307		41		4,868
Rock Island, Ill.	226	9	54		1,913	15	2,217
New Albany, Ind.	1,341	490	757	208			2,796
Fort Leavenworth, Kans.	354	731					1,085
Fort Scott, Kans.	306	101			14		421
Beverly, N.J.	137	10					147
Cypress Hills, N.Y.	2,890	69	199	3	461		3,622
Gettysburg, Pa.	1,931	1,633					3,564
Philadelphia, Pa.[b]	1,516	55	340[c]		29		1,940
Grafton, W.V.	639	613					1,252
Cemeteries in Border States (12)							
Camp Nelson, Ky.	1,494	1,184	867	5			3,550
Cave Hill, Ky.	3,317	405		157			3,879
Danville, Ky.	346	8					354
Lebanon, Ky.	582	281					863
Lexington, Ky.	762	101	53	4			920
Mill Springs, Ky.	319	356	20	11			706
Annapolis, Md.	2,343	129	14	5			2,491
Antietam, Md.[d]	2,894	1,793					4,687
Loudon Park, Md.	1,480	166			139		1,785
Jefferson Barracks, Mo.	6,693	843	23	1,044	1,010		9,613
Jefferson City, Mo.	331	313			3		647
Springfield, Mo.	832	689					1,521

Cemeteries in Confederate States (46)

Mobile, Ala.	613	33	165	91			902
Fayetteville, Ark.	456	754					1,210
Fort Smith, Ark.	497	936	68	3	17	108	1,629
Little Rock, Ark.	2,724	1,953	438	324			5,439
Barrancas, Fla.	491[e]	496	154	98	60	12	1,311
Andersonville, Ga.	12,762	839	16	95	118		13,830
Marietta, Ga.	6,857	2,966	158	67			10,048
Alexandria, La.	445	622	62	141			1,366[f]
Baton Rouge, La.	2,258	489	173	3			2,923
Chalmette, La.	5,156	5,307	1,622	177			12,262
Port Hudson, La.	281	3,262[g]	256				3,799
Corinth, Miss.	1,905	3,474		288			5,667
Natchez, Miss.	203	399	50	2,434			3,086
Vicksburg, Miss.	3,482	6,953	147	6,004			16,856
New Bern, N.C.	1,878	856	209	195			3,138
Raleigh, N.C.	600	533	20	6			1,159
Salisbury, N.C.	85	12,027[h]					12,112
Wilmington, N.C.	643	839	55	502			2,039
Beaufort, S.C.	3,796	3,462	795	950			9,003
Florence, S.C.	30	2,773					2,803
Chattanooga, Tenn.	7,810	4,169	861	20			12,860
Fort Donaldson, Tenn.	153	503	4	8			668
Knoxville, Tenn.	1,990	1,007	73	68			3,138
Memphis, Tenn.	4,852	4,852	250	3,959			13,913

Name and Location	White Union, Known	White Union, Unknown	Black Union, Known	Black Union, Unknown	Confederate, Known	Confederate, Unknown	Total
Nashville, Tenn.	10,338	3,509	1,447	463			15,757
Shiloh, Tenn.	1,227	2,358		1			3,586
Stone River, Tenn.	3,750	2,202	85	102			6,139
Brownsville, Tex	540	245	973	950			2,708
San Antonio, Tex.	171	81	7	4			263
Alexandria, Va.	3,277[i]		243	6	33		3658
Arlington, Va.	7,024	3,848	175	229	347		11,623
Ball's Bluff, Va.	1	53					54
City Point, Va.	2,937	850	782	587	151		5,307
Cold Harbor, Va.	676	1,275					1,951
Culpeper, Va.	448	901					1,349
Danville, Va.	1,125	131	37	12			1,305
Fort Harrison, Va.	239	575					814
Fredericksburg, Va.	2,395	12,842	2	2			15,241
Glendale, Va.	230	949	6	4			1,189
Hampton, Va.	3,610	408	985	57			5,060
Poplar Grove, Va.	1,969	3,888	60	226	15	23	6,181
Richmond, Va.	805	5,665					6,470
Seven Pines, Va.	141	1,209		7			1,357
Staunton, Va.	231	518					749
Winchester, Va.	2,083	2,332	3	6			4,424
Yorktown, Va.	731	1,424	6	5			2,166
Recapitulation							
Union States Total	17,681	6,641	1,657	211	3,037	204	29,431
Border States Totals	21,393	6268	977	1226	1,152		31,016
Confederate States Totals	103,915	104,863	10,387	18,094	737	143	238,139
Combined Totals	142,989	117,772	13,021	91,531	4,926	347	298,586

Sources: U.S. Congress, Senate, "Letter of the Secretary of War Communicating . . . the Report of the Inspector of the National Cemeteries of the United States for 1869," 41st Cong, 2d sess., 1870, S.Ex.Doc. 62, serial 1406; U.S. Congress, Senate, "Letter of the Secretary of War Communicating . . . the Report of the Inspector of the National Cemeteries of the United States for 1870 and 1871," 42d Cong., 2d sess., 1872, S.Ex. Doc. 79, serial 1479; U.S. Congress, House, *Annual Report of the Secretary of War*, 42d Cong., 3d sess., 1872, H.Ex.Doc. 1, pt. 2, serial 1558; U.S. Congress, Senate, "Letter of the Secretary of War Communicating . . . the Report of the Inspector of the National Cemeteries of the United States for 1874," 43d Cong, 2d sess., 1875, S.Ex. Doc. 28, serial 1629.

ªThese numbers were derived from the inspection report of 1869 and confirmed by the inspection report of 1874. The report for 1871 does not distinguish between the known and the unknown "rebel" dead.

ᵇThe Philadelphia National Cemetery was actually seven individual cemeteries that had received the dead of area hospitals throughout the war. Afterward, they were united administratively and designated a national cemetery.

ᶜExcept for one, all the black Union soldiers in Philadelphia are segregated into Lebanon Cemetery, described in the inspection report as "a small cemetery, used by colored people." The remaining black soldier is buried in the Odd Fellow's Cemetery.

ᵈAntietam and Loudon Park, Maryland, had not yet become national cemeteries, at least officially. They are included in this list because their inclusion was nearly contemporaneous with the inspection report to Congress in 1875.

ᵉIn this cemetery, the counts for both white known and white unknown contain a number of pre–Civil War burials of naval personnel.

ᶠThis number includes ninety-six interments listed in the inspection reports as Union soldiers but "unknown and unclassified," implying that no racial determination was possible. That a separate category was created speaks to the importance of such classifications.

ᵍAll 3,262 burials are listed as "unclassified."

ʰThis is an estimation, predicted to be under the actual count. No death records of this prison survived the war, and the unidentified dead were buried in eighteen trench graves. Administrators arrived at this number by counting the dead in a sample excavation and extrapolating on the basis of the surface area of the trenches.

ⁱThe inspection reports for 1869 and 1874 both distinguish between known and unknown soldiers, but the report for 1871 does not. The numbers listed for black soldier burials do not change over that period, so the figures taken from the 1869 and 1874 reports are listed here. There is significant change in the reported numbers of white burials, so no determination is possible for 1871.

Appendix B
Numerical Abstract of the Commission for Marking Graves of Confederate Dead, 1906–1912

T HE FOLLOWING TABLE REPRESENTS A NUMERICAL ABSTRACT COMPUTED from the 1917 commission report. Although the 665-page report listed every individual's name, rank, organization, and burial location, it did not offer any numerical accounting of its work. The table lists the number of eligible Confederate dead alphabetically by state. The difference between "Total Marked" (total graves listed in cemetery records and marked by the commission) and the bracketed number listed under "Total on Record" (total graves recorded by the commission) represents burials for which the commission found records but could not find graves, because of either actual loss or removal of the body by relatives or friends at some point between burial and the activities of the commission. Bracketed numbers, therefore, represent the upper limit of the commission's planned activities. These numbers by no means account for all the Confederate dead buried in the North, only those determined to be eligible for grave markings under the terms set down by Congress. The relatively low incidence of unknown soldier burials is due to the nature of prisoner-of-war incarceration. Prison deaths were far more likely to retain identity on burial, although instances like Camp Morton, Indiana, indicate that, even though once known, the identity of prisoners was vulnerable over time.

Cemetery	Known	Unknown	Lost or Removed by Family	Total on Record	Total Marked
District of Columbia					
Congressional Cemetery	30		1	[31]	30
Mount Olivet	1			1	1
Rock Creek Cemetery	1			1	1
Totals	32		1	[33]	32
Illinois					
Confederate Cemetery, Alton	1,386			1,386	1,386
Smallpox Island, Alton	146			146	146
Unlocated [presumed Smallpox Island], Alton			95	[95]	0
Removed			12	[12]	0
Alton Cemetery	1			1	1
Catholic Burying Ground, Alton	1			1	1
Confederate Section, Camp Butler, Springfield	866			866	866
Camp Douglas, Chicago(Oakwoods Cemetery)	4,276	32	148	[4,456]	4,308
Mound City National Cemetery	36		9	[45]	36
Rock Island Confederate Cemetery	1,951	10		[1,961]	1,951
Totals	8,863	42	264	[8,969]	8,695
Indiana					
Camp Morton, Indianapolis		1,639		[1639]	0
Oak Hill Cemetery, Evansville	24			24	24
Greenbush Cemetery, Lafayette	28			28	28
Fairview Cemetery, New Albany	1	3		[4]	1
Woodlawn Cemetery, Terre Haute	13			13	13
Thornton Cemetery, Thornton	1			1	1
Totals	67	1,642		[1,709]	67

Iowa					
Keokuk National Cemetery	8			8	8
Totals	8			8	8
Kansas					
Fort Leavenworth National Cemetery	7			7	7
Fort Scott National Cemetery, Confederate Section	14			14	14
Totals	21			21	21
Kentucky					
Fairview Cemetery, Bowling Green			4	[4]	0
Nicholasville Cemetery, Camp Nelson	30		6	[36]	30
Cave Hill National Cemetery, Louisville	43			43	43
Cave Hill National Cemetery, Confederate Section	225	3	12	[240]	228
Linden Grove Cemetery, Covington	8			8	8
Camp Nelson National Cemetery, Covington	2			2	2
Spring Hill Cemetery, Harrodsburg	4			4	4
Spring Hill Cemetery, Confederate Lot	15		78	[93]	15
Spring Hill Cemetery, Masonic Lot	3			3	3
Spring Hill Cemetery, Mrs. Thompson's Lot	2			2	2
Lexington Cemetery, Confederate Lot	97		5	[102]	97
Williams Farm Perryville	1			1	1
Goodknight Farm, Perryville	1			1	1
Perryville Cemetery	1		2	[3]	1
Totals	432	3	107	[542]	435
Massachusetts					
Fort Warren (Deer Island), Boston	1		12	[13]	1
Totals	1		12	[13]	1

Cemetary	Known	Unknown	Lost or Removed by Family	Total on Record	Total Marked
Maryland					
Maryland National Cemetery, Annapolis	10		1	[11]	10
Loudon Park Cemetery, Confederate Lot	198	5	30	[233]	203
Loudon Park National Cemetery, Baltimore	3			3	3
Loudon Park National Cemetery, Fort McHenry Section	33			33	33
Rose Hill Cemetery, Confederate Lot, Cumberland	6			6	6
Mt. Olivet Cemetery, Confederate Lot, Frederick	277	29	5	[311]	306
Point Lookout Confederate Cemetery	3,429			3,429	3,429
Totals	3,956	34	36	[4,026]	3,990
Missouri					
Jefferson Barracks National Cemetery, St. Louis	1,090	15	154	[1,259]	1,105
Penitentiary Cemetery, St. Louis	1			1	1
Union Cemetery, Kansas City	15			15	15
Totals	1,106	15	154	[1,275]	1,121
New Jersey					
Finn's Point National Cemetery	2,475			2,475	2,475
Totals	2,475			2,475	2,475
New Mexico					
Santa Fe National Cemetery	5			5	5
Totals	5			5	5
New York					
Congregational Cemetery, Barryville	2			2	2
Cypress Hills National Cemetery, Brooklyn	479	5	31	[515]	484
Woodlawn Cemetery, Elmira	3,013	7	2	[3,022]	3,020
Totals	3,494	12	33	[3,539]	3,506

Ohio

Cemetery					
Confederate Cemetery, Camp Chase	2,182		34	[2,216]	2,182
Pine Street Cemetery, Confederate Section, Gallipolis		4		4	4
Confederate Cemetery, Johnson's Island, Sandusky	172	52	22	[246]	224
Totals	2,354	56	56	[2,466]	2,410

Pennsylvania

Cemetery					
Chambersburg			1	[1]	0
City Cemetery, Soldiers' Lot, Harrisburg	13			13	13
Philadelphia National Cemetery, Confederate Section	183	4	14	[201]	187
Philadelphia Odd Fellow's Section	8			8	8
Glenwood Cemetery	1			1	1
Mt. Moriah Cemetery	2			2	2
Allegheny Cemetery, Pittsburgh	8		7	[15]	8
Totals	215	4	22	[241]	219

West Virginia

Cemetery					
Clarksburg			1	[1]	0
New Creek (Keyser)			4	[4]	0
Harper's Ferry, WV			2	[2]	0
Green Hill Cemetery, Martinsburg	1			1	1
Wheeling			3	[3]	0
Totals	1		10	[11]	1

Wisconsin

Cemetery					
Forest Hill Cemetery, Confederate Lot, Camp Randall	140			140	140
Totals	140			140	140
Cumulative Totals				[25,473]	23,126

Source: United States, War Department, Office of the Commission for Marking the Graves of Confederate Dead, *Register of Confederate Soldiers, Sailors, and Citizens Who Died in Federal Prisons and Military Hospitals in the North, 1861–1865*, National Archives Microfilm Publications M918 (Washington, D.C.: National Archives and Records Administration, General Services Administration, 1972).

Notes

Abbreviations

    FSSP   Freedmen and Southern Society Project, University of Maryland,
            College Park
    FSNM   Fort Sumter National Monument, Fort Sumter Island, S.C.
GNMP Library Gettysburg National Military Park Library, Gettysburg, Pa.
    NARA   National Archives and Records Administration, Washington, D.C.
Official Records U.S. War Department, *The War of the Rebellion: A Compilation of the
            Official Records of the Union and Confederate Armies*

Introduction

1. Meigs to Secretary of War [William W. Belknap], 5 August 1871, in Record Book, Letters Sent 1871–1889, vol. 1, 204–5, RG 92, Textual Records of the Office of the Quartermaster General—Cemeterial, 1828–1929, Central Records, and Correspondence and Issuances, 1864–1923, E 567, National Archives and Records Administration (hereafter NARA).

2. John Cox Underwood, *Report of the Proceedings Incidental to the Erection and Dedication of the Confederate Monument* (Chicago: Wm. Johnston Printing Co., 1896), 2–9, 20–31; George Levy, *To Die in Chicago: Confederate Prisoners at Camp Douglas, 1862–1865* (Evanston, Ill.: Evanston, 1994). Permission was required since the federal government had purchased the plot from the Oakwoods Association in 1867. The exact number of deaths at Camp Douglas is difficult to ascertain since a fire in 1871 consumed at least some of the prison records. In 1896, Underwood submitted a report to the United Confederate Veterans indicating his belief that the number approached 6,300 (*Report of the Proceedings*, 11–13). After the turn of the century, a government commission reported 4,456 burials in Oakwoods Cemetery, including 148 removals (U.S. War Department, Office of the Commission for Marking the Graves of Confederate Dead, *Register of Confederate Soldiers, Sailors, and Citizens Who Died in Federal Prisons and Military Hospitals in the North, 1861–1865,* National Archives Microfilm Publications, M918 [Washington, D.C.: National Archives and Records Administration, General Services Administration, 1972 (originally 1912)], 145–252; Underwood, *Report of the Proceedings,* 6, 14–15).

3. See Paul Fussell, *The Great War and Modern Memory* (New York: Oxford University Press, 1975); J. M. Winter, *Sites of Memory, Sites of Mourning: The Great War in European Cultural History* (New York: Cambridge University Press, 1995); Thomas

Laqueur, "Memory and Naming in the Great War," in *Commemorations: The Politics of National Identity,* ed. John R. Gillis (Princeton, N.J.: Princeton University Press, 1994), 150–67; and Alex King, *Memorials of the Great War in Britain* (Oxford: Berg, 1998).

4. Paul Buck pioneered the study of reunion in his *The Road to Reunion* (Boston: Little, Brown, 1937). More recent works include Nina Silber, *Romance of Reunion: Northerners and the South, 1865–1900* (Chapel Hill: University of North Carolina Press, 1993); and Carol Reardon, *Pickett's Charge in History and Memory* (Chapel Hill: University of North Carolina Press, 1997). David W. Blight's *Race and Reunion: The Civil War in American Memory* (Cambridge, Mass.: Harvard University Press, 2001) particularly charts the abandonment of what Blight calls *the emancipationist vision* in favor of reconciliation.

5. Drew Gilpin Faust, "The Civil War Soldier and the Art of Dying," *Journal of Southern History* 67, no. 1 (February 2001): 3–38, 36; Blight, *Race and Reunion,* 23, 84–97, and passim; Buck, *Road to Reunion,* 121 (see 116–21 generally).

6. Blight, *Race and Reunion,* 50–51, 95–96, 149, 316–17, 389.

7. The leading scholarship exploring the Lost Cause is Rollin G. Osterweis, *The Myth of the Lost Cause, 1865–1900* (Hamden, Conn.: Archon, 1973); Charles Reagan Wilson, *Baptized in Blood: The Religion of the Lost Cause, 1865–1920* (Athens: University of Georgia Press, 1980); Gaines M. Foster, *Ghosts of the Confederacy: Defeat, the Lost Cause, and the Emergence of the New South, 1865 to 1913* (New York: Oxford University Press, 1987); and Alan T. Nolan, "The Anatomy of the Myth," in *The Myth of the Lost Cause and Civil War History,* ed. Gary W. Gallagher and Alan T. Nolan, 11–34 (Bloomington: Indiana University Press, 2000).

8. This view conflicts with the interpretation of William C. Davis, who argues that "losers" invariably create more myths than "winners" ("Myths and Realities of the Confederacy," in *The Cause Lost: Myths and Realities of the Confederacy* [Lawrence: University Press of Kansas, 1996], 175).

9. "The Tone and Temper of the North and South," *New York Herald,* 2 April 1865.

10. See Joseph Campbell, *The Hero with a Thousand Faces,* Bollingen Series 17, 2d ed. (Princeton, N.J.: Princeton University Press, 1968), 256–60, and "Mythological Themes in Creative Literature and Art," in *The Mythic Dimension: Selected Essays, 1959–1987,* ed. Antony Van Couvering (New York: HarperCollins, 1997), 180–82.

11. Walt Whitman, "The Death of Abraham Lincoln," in *Walt Whitman: Complete Poetry and Prose,* ed. Justin Kaplan (New York: Literary Classics of the United States, 1982), 1036–47, 1046.

12. See, for example, Maurice Halbwachs, *The Collective Memory,* trans. F. J. Ditter and V. Y. Ditter (New York: Harper & Row, 1980), and *On Collective Memory,* ed. and trans. Lewis A. Coser (Chicago: University of Chicago Press, 1992); Paul Connerton, *How Societies Remember* (Cambridge: Cambridge University Press, 1989); and James Fentress and Chris Wickham, *Social Memory* (Oxford: Blackwell, 1992). The work of Pierre Nora has been particularly helpful in my understanding of the cultural value of commemora-

tions. See his "Between History and Memory: *Les Lieux de mémoire*," *Representations* 26 (Spring 1989): 7–25. See also the discussions of memory and its relation to national identity in Gillis, ed., *Commemorations*.

13. Abraham Lincoln, *The Collected Works of Abraham Lincoln*, ed. Roy P. Basler, 9 vols. (New Brunswick, N.J.: Rutgers University Press, 1953), 4: 261–62, 271 (emphasis added).

Chapter 1

1. Bvt. Major Haskins to Col. Lorenzo Thomas, 13 February 1857, photocopy, and Daniel Hough, Enlistment Papers, 1849, 1854, and 1859, photocopies, Daniel Hough Papers, Fort Sumter National Monument, Fort Sumter Island, S.C. (hereafter FSNM).

2. Report of P. G. T. Beauregard, in U.S. War Department, *The War of the Rebellion: A Compilation of the Official Records of the Union and Confederate Armies* (hereafter *Official Records*), ed. Robert N. Scott et al., 70 vols. in 128 pts. (Washington, D.C.: U.S. Government Printing Office, 1880–1901), ser. 1, 1: 32.

3. Abner Doubleday later reported that the cartridges were stacked under at least one gun, apparently Hough's (*Reminiscences of Forts Sumter and Moultrie in 1860–'61* [New York: Harper & Bros., 1876], 171). See also *Official Records,* ser. 1, 1: 13, 14–15; and Samuel Wylie Crawford, *The Genesis of the Civil War: The Story of Sumter, 1860–1861* (New York: Charles L. Webster & Co., 1887), 435, 437, 442–43, 446.

4. *New York Herald,* 19 April 1861, 2. See also E. Milbury Burton, *The Siege of Charleston, 1861–1865* (Columbia: University of South Carolina Press, 1970), 56–57; and W. A. Swanberg, *First Blood: The Story of Fort Sumter* (New York: Charles Scribner's Sons, 1957), 327–28.

5. Crawford, *Genesis,* 446, 470; Doubleday, *Reminiscences,* 171; Swanberg, *First Blood,* 328. The exact cause of the accident is still a disputed point. A common explanation for the premature discharge is that Hough had not sponged out the cannon tube thoroughly and a spark or smoldering powder residue from the previous discharge remained (Burton, *Siege of Charleston,* 56–57). However, Abner Doubleday later wrote that, when the salute was begun, the air was still filled with ashes and debris from the fire that had destroyed the wooden buildings of the fort. Thus, the salute, Doubleday wrote, "was a dangerous thing to attempt" (*Reminiscences,* 171). "It happened," Doubleday explained in a different account, "that some flakes of fire had entered the muzzle of one of the guns [Hough's] after it was sponged" ("From Moultrie to Sumter," in *Battles and Leaders of the Civil War,* 4 vols. [1887–1888; reprint, Secaucus, N.J.: Castle, 1991], 1: 48). Historian William Marvel conjectures that it was more likely that the crewman at the rear of Hough's gun did not block the vent hole with his thumbstall, allowing air to rush through the tube as Hough was ramming the charge home and, thus, flare the powder residue, causing the explosion ("The First to Fall: The Brief and Bitter Life of Daniel Hough" [unpublished typescript], 9, Daniel Hough Papers, FSNM).

6. *The Battle of Fort Sumter and First Victory of the Southern Troops* (Charleston, S.C.: Evans & Cogswell, 1861), 24; Diary of W. B. Yates, photocopied excerpts, Daniel Hough Papers, FSNM.

7. Walker quoted in William C. Davis, *"A Government of Our Own": The Making of the Confederacy* (New York: Free Press, 1994), 198. Chestnut quoted in James M. McPherson, *Battle Cry of Freedom: The Civil War Era* (New York: Oxford University Press, 1988), 238.

8. Maris Vinovskis, "Have Social Historians Lost the Civil War? Some Preliminary Demographic Speculations," *Journal of American History* 76, no. 1 (June 1989): 34–58.

9. Note the distinction between *casualties* and *fatalities*. The term *casualties* as defined by military historians indicates a loss of soldiers from active duty because of death, wounds, illness, accident, capture, desertion, or any other means. See, for example, John Whiteclay Chambers II et al., eds., *The Oxford Companion to Military History* (New York: Oxford University Press, 1999), 106–8 (s.v. "casualties"), where the term is defined as "soldiers killed or rendered unable to fight by enemy weapons, disease, or accident," thus "reduc[ing] combat strength and sap[ping] the morale." This commonplace usage reflects the priority of the military and its historians to quantify fighting strength by subtracting anyone unable to participate in combat, whatever the reason.

10. McPherson, *Battle Cry of Freedom*, 735; Herman Hattaway and Archer Jones, *How the North Won: A Military History of the Civil War* (Urbana: University of Illinois Press, 1991), 577–80; Allan Nevins, *The Organized War to Victory, 1864–1865*, vol. 4 of *The War for the Union* (New York: Charles Scribner's Sons, 1971), 39–43.

11. Eric T. Dean Jr. has also pointed to the appropriateness of a Civil War–Vietnam comparison (see *Shook over Hell: Post-Traumatic Stress, Vietnam, and the Civil War* [Cambridge, Mass.: Harvard University Press, 1997]).

12. Frank W. Z. Barrett, *Mourning for Lincoln* (Philadelphia: John C. Winston Co., 1909), 52–53. While making no attempt to dispute Barrett's assessment, such averaging can mask the sometimes disproportionate impact of Civil War death, for recruitment and volunteering were never uniform across states and regions.

13. The study of death culture fairly begins with the work of Philippe Ariès, who delineated the contours of the changing social and intellectual responses to death in Europe (see *Western Attitudes toward Death: From the Middle Ages to the Present*, trans. Patricia M. Ranum [Baltimore: Johns Hopkins University Press, 1974], and *The Hour of Our Death*, trans. Helen Weaver [New York: Knopf, 1981]). For studies of death culture in America, see David E. Stannard, ed., *Death in America* (Philadelphia: University of Pennsylvania Press, 1975); David E. Stannard, *The Puritan Way of Death: A Study of Religion, Culture, and Social Change* (New York: Oxford University Press, 1977); James J. Farrell, *Inventing the American Way of Death, 1830–1920* (Philadelphia: Temple University Press, 1980); and Lewis O. Saum, *The Popular Mood of Pre–Civil War America* (Westport, Conn.: Greenwood, 1980), chap. 4. The pioneering work in the history of the American funeral industry is Robert W. Habenstein and William M. Lamers, *The History of American Funeral Directing* (Milwaukee: Bulfin, 1955). Recently, Faust and

Laderman have argued, as does the present work, that the Civil War did have a significant effect on American death culture. See Gary Laderman, *The Sacred Remains: American Attitudes toward Death, 1799–1883* (New Haven, Conn.: Yale University Press, 1996); and Drew Gilpin Faust, *"A Riddle of Death": Mortality and Meaning in the American Civil War* (Gettysburg, Pa.: Gettysburg College, 1995), and "Civil War Soldier."

14. Phillip S. Paludan, *"A People's Contest": The Union and Civil War, 1861–1865* (New York: Harper & Row, 1988), 439 n. 50; David Charles Sloane, *The Last Great Necessity: Cemeteries in American History* (Baltimore: Johns Hopkins University Press, 1991), 113. In part, Sloane's assessment is shaped by the connections that he draws between cemetery development and the growth of urban culture. In this light, since "the Civil War brought a dramatic halt to reformers' attempt to create a better society, but proved only a small halt in the urbanization of society" (ibid., 112), it would logically also have only a small influence on cemetery development within that urban context. The development and importance of cemeteries is also discussed in Blanche Linden-Ward, *Silent City on a Hill: Landscape of Memory and Boston's Mount Auburn Cemetery* (Columbus: Ohio State University Press, 1989). For the national cemeteries, see Edward Steere, *Shrines of the Honored Dead: A Study of the National Cemetery System* (Washington, D.C.: U.S. Army, Office of the Quartermaster General, [1954?]); Munro MacCloskey, *Hallowed Ground: Our National Cemeteries* (New York: Richard Rosen, 1968); and Dean W. Holt, *American Military Cemeteries* (Jefferson, N.C.: McFarland, 1992).

15. Computed from U.S. Army, Quartermaster Department, *Outline Description of Military Posts and Reservations in the U.S. and Alaska, and of the National Cemeteries* (Washington, D.C.: U.S. Government Printing Office, 1904), 571–623. The first battlefield parks, Chattanooga and Antietam, were both established by the government in 1890. The figures presented in the text do not include the national cemeteries, like Custer Battlefield, Mont., or Fort Gibson, Okla., which were not created specifically for the dead of the Civil War.

16. Although professional mortuary services were practically nonexistent, throughout this period "there was an evolving profession" of funeral care givers, largely women, who offered body preparation and other mortuary services to an ever-increasing circle of neighbors and clients (Habenstein and Lamers, *American Funeral Directing,* 235–38, 245). With increasing industrialization, workers were increasingly exposed to life-threatening situations. The innovations that such deaths made in epitaphs are recounted in Thomas C. Mann and Janet Greene, *Sudden and Awful: American Epitaphs and the Finger of God* (Brattleboro, Vt.: Stephen Greene, 1967). The cultural response to railroad accidents is discussed in Katie L. Lyle, *Scalded to Death by the Steam* (Chapel Hill, N.C.: Algonquin, 1983).

17. The best exploration of the cultural standards associated with Civil War death is Faust, "Civil War Soldier," esp. 6–8. See also Saum, *Popular Mood of Pre–Civil War America,* 96; Paludan, *"A People's Contest,"* 365; Reid Mitchell, *The Vacant Chair: The Northern Soldier Leaves Home* (New York: Oxford University Press, 1993), 142–43; and Laderman, *Sacred Remains,* 27–38.

18. Lewis O. Saum, "Death in the Popular Mind of Pre–Civil War America," in Stannard, ed., *Death in America,* 30–48, quote from 41; Faust, "Civil War Soldier," 12–13.

19. Earl J. Hess, *The Union Soldier in Battle: Enduring the Ordeal of Combat* (Lawrence: University Press of Kansas, 1997), 38; Faust, "Civil War Soldier," 12; Laderman, *Sacred Remains,* 109.

20. A notable exception to this time-honored practice is Hess, *Union Soldier in Battle,* 37–44. The accounting of the dead and wounded can be found in, for example, William F. Fox, *Regimental Losses in the American Civil War, 1861–1865* (1898; reprint, n.p.: Press of Morningside Bookshop, 1974); and Thomas L. Livermore, *Numbers and Losses in the Civil War in America, 1861–65,* 2d ed. (Boston: Houghton Mifflin, 1901). A few monographs address the dead of a particular battle directly. For Gettysburg, see Gregory A. Coco, *Wasted Valor: The Confederate Dead at Gettysburg* (Gettysburg, Pa.: Thomas, 1990), and *A Strange and Blighted Land: Gettysburg, the Aftermath of Battle* (Gettysburg, Pa.: Thomas, 1995). For Antietam, see Steven R. Stotelmyer, *The Bivouacs of the Dead: The Story of Those Who Died at Antietam and South Mountain* (Baltimore: Toomey, 1992).

21. *Official Records,* ser. 1, 39, pt. 1: 767. For other "Cemetery Hills," see ibid., ser. 1, 5: 202–3 (at Mechanicsburg), ser. 1, 21: 589, 599 (at Fredericksburg), ser. 1, 25, pt. 1: 610 (at Chancellorsville), ser. 1, 29, pt. 1: 433 (at Bristoe, Va.), ser. 1, 31, pt. 1: 19 (at Barton's Station, Ala.), ser. 1, 40, pt. 1: 170 (at Petersburg), and ser. 1, 42, pt. 2: 795 (at Richmond [near the Crater]). For similar renamings, see ibid., ser. 1, 16, pt. 1: 951, and 39, pt. 1: 767.

22. Soldier quoted in Wiley Sword, *Shiloh: Bloody April* (New York: Morrow, 1974), 429; Ulysses S. Grant, *Ulysses S. Grant: Memoirs and Selected Letters* (New York: Library of America, 1990), 238–39; Alpheus Williams quoted in Gerald F. Linderman, *Embattled Courage: The Experience of Combat in the American Civil War* (New York: Free Press, 1987), 125; on Fredericksburg, see James Longstreet, "The Battle of Fredericksburg," in *Battles and Leaders,* 3: 80–81; Daniel McCook quoted in Hess, *Union Soldier in Battle,* 8.

23. Col. Henry Morrow, *Official Records,* ser. 1, 27, pt. 1: 269; *History of the Antietam National Cemetery, Including a Descriptive List of All the Loyal Soldiers Buried Therein* (Baltimore: John W. Woods, Steam Printer, 1869), 201.

24. Brig. Gen. John E. Smith, *Official Records,* ser. 1, 31, pt. 2: 644. See also Mitchell, *Vacant Chair,* 143; and Linderman, *Embattled Courage,* 124–28, 248–49.

25. Ledger, 331, 335–58, and passim, Cain and Cornelius Papers, Special Collections, Perkins Library, Duke University, Durham, N.C. Prior to and during the war, Cain and Cornelius provided coffins and burial cases, as well as hearse services, mourning goods, and even crepe decorations. This firm seems to be typical of the intermediate development between a firm providing strictly carpentry services and one providing undertaking as a specialization, an evolution discussed in Habenstein and Lamers, *American Funeral Directing,* 227–35.

26. *Official Records,* ser. 1, 30, pt. 1: 1057. It was also often noted that soldiers were buried with the meager "honors of war" (see, for example, ibid., ser. 1, 24, pt. 2: 630).

27. Frederick Phisterer, *Statistical Record of the Armies of the United States* (New York: Charles Scribner's Sons, 1883), 77. See also General Order No. 75, *Official Records,* ser. 3, 1: 498.

28. MacCloskey, *Hallowed Ground*, 17–18.

29. Lorenzo Thomas, Adjutant General's Office, General Order No. 33, *Official Records*, ser. 3, 2: 2–3.

30. Joshua Lawrence Chamberlain, ibid., ser. 1, 27, pt. 1: 626. Occasionally, the burial of the dead revealed surprises. For example, in a burial report of the enemy dead, under "Remarks," one Union officer reported: "One female in rebel uniform (private)" (William Hays, Commanding Corps, 17 July 1863, copy, Vertical Files, file 7–17 "Confederate Reinterments," Gettysburg National Military Park Library [hereafter, GNMP Library]).

31. Leman W. Bradley, *Official Records*, ser. 1, 27, pt. 1: 406.

32. Ibid., ser. 1, 42, pt. 1: 732. Drew Gilpin Faust suggests that the drive for religious services fostered a remarkable ecumenism across Protestant, Catholic, and Jewish denominational lines: "Civil War death thus proved a great equalizer in its effect of minimalizing—or perhaps more accurately, marginalizing—theological and denominational differences" ("Civil War Soldier," 9–10).

33. Quartermaster General Montgomery C. Meigs, *Official Records*, ser. 3, 4: 434–35.

34. Chaplain James Peet, Fiftieth U.S. Colored Infantry, to Adj. Gen. L[orenzo] Thomas, 1 August 1864, P-945 (1864), Ser. 12, Letters Received, 1805–1889, RG 94: Records of the Adjutant General's Office, 1780s–1917, NARA [FSSP K-549] (emphasis in original). The brackets at the end of this and similar notes indicate that this document was made available through the kindness of the Freedmen and Southern Society Project, University of Maryland, College Park, and indicates their catalog number.

35. J. E. B. Stuart, *Official Records*, ser. 1, 27, pt. 2: 684. See also ibid., ser. 1, 22, pt. 1: 727–28, and 31, pt. 3: 253; and Laderman, *Sacred Remains*, 98.

36. Harry W. Pfanz, *Gettysburg: The Second Day* (Chapel Hill: University of North Carolina Press, 1987), 433.

37. Darius N. Couch, "Sumner's 'Right Grand Division,'" in *Battles and Leaders*, 3: 116. See also Hess, *Union Soldier in Battle*, 38–39.

38. Lorenzo Thomas to Edwin Stanton, *Official Records*, ser. 3, 2: 2.

39. Couch, "Sumner's 'Right Grand Division,'" 118. See also John R. Brooke, *Official Records*, ser. 1, 21: 261–62.

40. S. H. Lockett, "The Defense of Vicksburg," in *Battles and Leaders*, 3: 489. See also Col. Thomas Rose, *Official Records*, ser. 1, 38, pt. 1: 288; Maj. Gen. Earl Van Dorn, ibid., ser. 1, 8: 193–94; and Laderman, *Sacred Remains*, 105.

41. Wade Hampton, *Official Records*, ser. 1, 42, pt. 2: 1231. See also David M. Gregg, ibid., ser. 1, 42, pt. 2: 550–51.

42. G. B. Cuthbert, ibid., ser. 1, 1: 56; untitled newspaper excerpt, Daniel Hough Papers, FSNM. The report as printed indicated that the burial took place before the "departure of the Palmetto Guard *for* Fort Sumter" (emphasis added). This must be a confusion on the part of either the report's author or the printers. The Palmetto Guard was the first to occupy the fort after its surrender and was on hand immediately after Hough's death. As written, the report would seem to imply that Hough had been transported to shore immediately upon his death and buried before the Palmetto Guard left to garrison, briefly, the fort. This contradicts too many other accounts of witnesses reporting

Hough's burial at the fort. There is also a curiosity attached to the religious ceremonies provided for Hough. While stationed at Fort Moultrie on the Charleston Harbor before the war, Hough had served as a witness to the christening of a comrade's daughter, as listed in the parish record. It is tempting to presume that he was Catholic, like the majority of Irish in the regiment. However, a priest was not summoned from the parish to administer extreme unction, and Hough died apparently unshriven. If Hough was Catholic, this ignorance of his religion by those who tended him in death reflects another disadvantage of being buried by the enemy. Copy of the parish record, Daniel Hough Papers, FSNM.

43. Robert D. Hoffsommer, "The Aftermath of Gettysburg," *Civil War Times Illustrated* 2, no. 4 (July 1963): 50.

44. Henry W. Slocum, *Official Records,* ser. 1, 27, pt. 1: 761. See also Charles Candy, ibid., ser. 1, 27, pt. 1: 837.

45. J. B. Robertson, ibid., ser. 1, 27, pt. 2: 406; John Lane, ibid., ser. 1, 27, pt. 2: 641 (emphasis added).

46. J. B. Gordon, ibid., ser. 1, 27, pt. 2: 493. This is almost certainly not the only instance of Union burials on the part of Southern troops, but it may be the only recorded instance.

47. Charles Candy, ibid., ser. 1, 27, pt. 1: 837. The paucity of digging implements slowed the work except where pioneer corps constituted a portion of a unit's organization. These troops, primarily road and bridge builders carrying shovels and picks, facilitated the work considerably (Rufas Ingalls, ibid., ser. 1, 33: 596).

48. W. Roy Mason, "Notes of a Confederate Staff-Officer," in *Battles and Leaders,* 3: 101.

49. Benjamin Harrison, *Official Records,* ser. 1, 38, pt. 2: 347; correspondence between Lee and Grant, ibid., ser. 1, vol. 36, pt. 3: 638–40, 666–67; Grant, *Memoirs and Selected Letters,* 587.

50. Stotelmyer, *Bivouacs of the Dead,* Samuel Compton quoted on 5.

51. Mason, "Notes of a Confederate Staff-Officer," 101.

52. Stotelmyer, *Bivouacs of the Dead,* 5.

53. Laderman, *Sacred Remains,* chap. 11 passim, esp. 137, 138, 142–43 (emphasis added).

54. On the ubiquity of fatalism, see James M. McPherson, *For Cause and Comrades: Why Men Fought in the Civil War* (New York: Oxford University Press, 1997), 62–67.

55. Soldier quoted in Coco, *Wasted Valor,* 21.

56. Michael Deady quoted in Stotelmyer, *Bivouacs of the Dead,* 4.

57. John T. Young, *Official Records,* ser. 1, 32, pt. 1: 595; Charles W. Anderson, ibid., ser. 1, 32, pt. 1: 597.

58. The damage was regretted by their commanding officer, who ordered workmen to obtain materials to repair the despoiled graves (Samuel Breck, ibid., ser. 1, 12, pt. 1: 53). Earl Hess quotes a Union soldier on burial duty describing the burial of both Union and Confederate troops in mass graves, but interring one's own comrades in such a fashion was almost certainly reserved for the unidentifiable dead. Hess does assert that burial parties were scrupulous in separating Union and Confederate burials (*Union Soldier in*

Battle, 41). At times, the opportunity to inter the dead properly was denied by the press of war. Guerrilla troops in Missouri had little time for such niceties when being closely pursued. Union Lieutenant Colonel T. T. Crittenden reported: "I was informed by several ladies of his own stripe that ['guerrilla chief' Thomas R.] Livingston buried 12 of his men in one grave—[the ladies were] present at the burial" (*Official Records,* ser. 1, 22, pt. 1: 329).

59. Paludan, *"A People's Contest,"* 365.

60. *The Times* quoted in Alan Trachtenburg, *Reading American Photographs: Images as History, Mathew Brady to Walker Evans* (New York: Hill & Wang, 1989), 73 (see also chap. 2 passim, esp. 72–74, 83). See also William A. Frassanito, *Antietam: The Photographic Legacy of America's Bloodiest Day* (New York: Charles Scribner's Sons, 1978), 21–26, and *Early Photography at Gettysburg* (Gettysburg, Pa.: Thomas, 1995).

61. "Brady's Photographs: Pictures of the Dead at Antietam," *New York Times,* 20 October 1862, 5.

62. Leonard Gardner quoted in Robert L. Bloom, "We Never Expected a Battle," *Pennsylvania History* 55 (1988): 182; Albertus McCreary, "Gettysburg: A Boy's Experience of the Battle," *McClure's Magazine,* July 1909, 251; Mrs. S. M. Stewart, "Hospital Reminiscences—Gettysburg's Presbyterian Church," "Miscellaneous Civilian Accounts," Vertical Files, file 8–3, GNMP Library.

63. John C. Wills, "Reminiscences of the Three Days Battle of Gettysburg at the 'Globe Hotel,'" 31, "Charles Wills Account (Globe Inn)," Vertical Files, file 8–17, GNMP Library.

64. Sarah Broadhead, "Diary of a Lady of Gettysburg, Pennsylvania," 23, "Sarah Broadhead Account, Chambersburg Street." Vertical Files, file 8–6, GNMP Library.

65. McCreary, "Boy's Experience of Battle," 253.

66. See W. Willard Smith to M[ontgomery] C. Meigs, 9 July, 23 July, 29 July 1863, copies, "US Army Quartermaster Reports after the Battle of Gettysburg (Clean-Up)," "US Army Quartermaster Reports after the Battle of Gettysburg (Clean-Up)." Vertical Files, file 7–18, GNMP Library.

67. Mark Hunt quoted in Gregory A. Coco, *Killed in Action* (Gettysburg, Pa.: Thomas, 1992), 40.

68. "Brady's Photographs," 5.

69. Asst. Adj. Gen Seth Williams, *Official Records,* ser. 1, 36, pt. 3: 28; communications between P. G. T. Beauregard and Grant, ibid., ser. 1, 10, pt. 1: 111.

70. Ernest B. Furgurson, *Ashes of Glory: Richmond at War* (New York: Knopf, 1996), 154–55.

71. Both women quoted in A. S. Billingsley, *From the Flag to the Cross; or, Scenes and Incidents of Christianity in the War* (Philadelphia: New-World Publishing Co., 1872), 111, 113.

72. Martha Wells to [T. W.?] Taggard, 24 December 1866, W-209 (1866), Ser. 366, Letters Received Relating to Recruiting, 1863–1868, Colored Troops Division, 1863–1889, RG 94: Records of the Adjutant General's Office, 1780s–1917, NARA [FSSP B-391]. The cemeterial record for Augustus Wells can be found in U.S. War Department, Quarter-

master General's Office, *Roll of Honor: Names of Soldiers Who Have Died in Defence of the American Union Interred in the National Cemeteries,* 27 vols. (Washington, D.C.: U.S. Government Printing Office, 1865–1871), 6: 20.

73. Habenstein and Lamers, *American Funeral Directing,* 267, 321, 331.

74. Ibid. Holmes dates his account 1862, but, as Grant did not take command in the East until 1864, this date—or the story—must be erroneous.

75. Advertisement quoted in ibid., 334. See also McCreary, "Boy's Experience of Battle," 252.

76. Advertisement quoted in Hoffsommer, "Aftermath of Gettysburg," 51 (*casket* was a recently developed synonym for *coffin* and drew on its earlier definition of a chest or container for something precious); Harry P. Farrow quoted in Guy R. Everson and Edward H. Simpson Jr., eds., *Far, Far from Home: The Wartime Letters of Dick and Tally Simpson, 3rd South Carolina Volunteers* (New York: Oxford University Press, 1994), 287 (emphasis in original).

77. On state agents, see *Report of the Select Committee Relative to the Soldiers' National Cemetery . . . as Reported to the House of Representatives of the Commonwealth of Pennsylvania, March 31, 1864* (Harrisburg, Pa.: Singerly & Myers, 1864), 65. For the citizen's recollection, see Wills, "Reminiscences," 31. Cornelius quoted in Christine Quigly, *The Corpse: A History* (Jefferson, N.C.: McFarland, 1996), 55.

78. Frey to Ryder quoted in Coco, *Killed in Action,* 95.

79. On the object of the Third Army Corps Union, see Robert B. Beath, *History of the Grand Army of the Republic* (New York: Bryan, Taylor & Co., 1889), 11. On Baker's orders re Wilson, see H. Hannahs, Acting Asst. Adj. Gen, St. Louis, *Official Records,* ser. 1, 41, pt. 4: 251. Hancock, Second Corps, ibid., ser. 1, 42, pt. 1: 243. On Chambliss's remains, see also ibid., ser. 1, 42, pt. 2: 253–54. The preferential treatment given officers extends far beyond American military experience. Michel Ragon writes that, before the nineteenth century, in French practice "soldiers, stripped of their uniforms, were buried on the spot in common graves, and the officers were buried in the nearest church" (*The Space of Death: A Study of Funerary Architecture, Decoration, and Urbanism,* trans. Alan Sheridan [Charlottesville: University Press of Virginia, 1983], 110–11).

80. Billingsley, *From the Flag to the Cross,* 110 (emphasis in original).

81. Parvin quoted in Coco, *Killed in Action,* 47. For other, similar accounts, see Laderman, *Sacred Remains,* 111–12.

82. Thomas De Witt Talmadge, "Oration," *Washington Daily Morning Chronicle,* 31 May 1873, 4. Gerald Linderman also emphasizes the service of women but suggests that, unable to do more, nurses "encourage[d] the soldiers to live—and especially to die—in harmony with soldierly values, to accept pain and death within the framework of those values" (*Embattled Courage,* 29 [see also 27–31]). As we have seen, the values associated with a good death transcended the ethical world of soldiers; hence, women acting as surrogates had larger motivations than those limited to the battlefield.

83. "The Battle Field at Gettysburg: Scenes after the Battle," *Berks and Schuylkill Journal* (Reading, Pa.), 18 July 1863, 1.

84. Nellie Aughinbaugh quoted in Bloom, "We Never Expected a Battle," 187. A

temperate soldier at Shiloh recorded his belief that "the rebels were all drunk for their dead has turned black and ours did not" (quoted in Sword, *Shiloh,* 429; see also Linderman, *Embattled Courage,* 126). One undertaker in Washington, D.C., responded to public concerns by asserting in his advertisements: "Bodies Embalmed by Us NEVER TURN BLACK" (quoted in Habenstein and Lamers, *American Funeral Directing,* 330 (emphasis in original).

85. Crotty quoted in Linderman, *Embattled Courage,* 127; Michigan soldier quoted in Faust, "Civil War Soldier," 23.

86. "Hollinger Family Account," Vertical Files, file 8–10, GNMP Library.

87. "Account of Margaret Bissell," 13, Vertical Files, file 8–9b, GNMP Library.

88. U.S. Congress, *Congressional Globe,* 37th Cong., 2d sess., 1862, 32, pt. 2: 1465 (Sumner's proposal); U.S. Congress, Senate, Joint Committee on the Conduct of the War, *Barbarities of the Rebels,* 37th Cong., 2d sess., 1862, S. Rept. 41, serial 1125, 1–40 (testimony before the committee). For an example of press coverage, see "The Conduct of the War: Ghoulism of the Rebels," *Chicago Tribune,* 5 May 1862, 2. For an account of the Committee on the Conduct of the War and its work (albeit one that gives scant attention to the atrocities report), see Bruce Tap, *Over Lincoln's Shoulder: The Committee on the Conduct of the War* (Lawrence: University Press of Kansas, 1998).

89. Ricketts testimony, U.S. Congress, Senate, Joint Committee on the Conduct of the War, *Barbarities of the Rebels,* 17–18; Homiston testimony, ibid., 28.

90. Northern minister quoted in Billingsley, *From the Flag to the Cross,* 301; committee report quoted in "The Conduct of the War," 2.

91. Franklin Aretas Haskell, *Haskell of Gettysburg: His Life and Civil War Papers,* ed. Frank L. Byrne and Andrew T. Weaver (Madison: State Historical Society of Wisconsin, 1970), 196.

92. J. T. Trowbridge, "The Field of Gettysburg," *Atlantic Monthly* 16 (November 1865): 618.

93. W. W. Lyle, *Lights and Shadows of Army Life* (Cincinnati: R. W. Carroll & Co., 1865), 373, 374.

94. See *Official Records,* ser. 1, 33: 175–80, 216–24, and ser. 4, 3: 326. Kilpatrick strenuously and repeatedly denied the authenticity of the documents, while Dahlgren's father asserted that the writing and signature were not in his son's hand. Indeed, the admiral later pointed out that the signature accompanying the documents had been misspelled (see [John A.] Dahlgren, *Memoir of Ulric Dahlgren* [Philadelphia: J. B. Lippincott & Co., 1872], 233). However, the commander of the Army of the Potomac, Gen. George G. Meade, expressed private reservations in a letter to his wife: "I regret to say Kilpatrick's reputation, and collateral evidence in my possession, rather go against this theory [that the orders were forged]" (George Meade, *Life and Letters of George Gordon Meade* [New York: Charles Scribner's Sons, 1913], 191).

95. The best account of Dahlgren's postmortem misadventures is Meriwether Stuart, "Colonel Ulrich Dahlgren and Richmond's Union Underground," *Virginia Magazine of History and Biography* 72 (April 1964): 152–204. See also Dahlgren, *Memoir of Ulric Dahlgren,* 225–26; and Furgurson, *Ashes of Glory,* 256–58.

96. *Richmond Whig* and *Examiner* quoted in Stuart, "Colonel Ulric Dahlgren," 154–55. See also John W. Atkinson, "Col. Ulric Dahlgren, the Defeated Raider," *Southern Historical Society Papers* 37 (1909): 351–53; and Dahlgren, *Memoir of Ulric Dahlgren,* 227. The *Examiner* exaggerated—the body was encoffined—but the purpose of such remarks was to insult, not report. Kilpatrick at one point argued that, rather than the reverse, the documents published as Dahlgren's orders were fabricated "only as an excuse for the barbarous treatment of the remains of a brave soldier" (see George E. Pond, "Kilpatrick's and Dahlgren's Raid to Richmond," in *Battles and Leaders,* 4: 95–96).

97. Benjamin Butler, *Official Records,* ser. 2, 6: 1034–35.

98. Atkinson, "Col. Ulric Dahlgren," 352–53.

99. Stuart, "Colonel Ulrich Dahlgren," 159–75; *Official Records,* ser. 1, 46, pt. 3: 712; Dahlgren, *Memoir of Ulrich Dahlgren,* 275.

100. Luis F. Emilio, *History of the Fifty-fourth Regiment of Massachusetts Volunteer Infantry, 1863–1865* (1894; reprint, New York: Johnson Reprint, 1968), 73–85; *Official Records,* ser. 1, 28, pt. 1: 362–63; Quincy A. Gillmore, "The Army before Charleston in 1863," in *Battles and Leaders,* 4: 56–60.

101. Emilio, *History of the Fifty-fourth Regiment,* 101; Joseph T. Glatthaar, *Forged in Battle: The Civil War Alliance of Black Soldiers and White Officers* (New York: Free Press, 1990), 140.

102. James Henry Gooding, *On the Altar of Freedom: A Black Soldier's Civil War Letters from the Front,* ed. Virginia M. Adams (Amherst: University of Massachusetts Press, 1991), 41, 42.

103. Francis G. Shaw quoted in Emilio, *History of the Fifty-fourth Regiment,* 103. The postwar visit of one Union veteran raises doubts about the thoroughness applied to the removal of remains from Morris Island, the site of Battery Wagner, to the national cemetery. In 1869, Russell Conwell recorded: "Human skeletons from which the sea had washed the sand lay grinning upon the shore and filled us with sad sensations" (Russell H. Conwell, *Magnolia Journey: A Union Veteran Revisits the Former Confederate States,* ed. Joseph C. Carter [University: University of Alabama Press, 1974], 76–77).

104. *Record of the Service of the Fifty-fifth Regiment of Massachusetts Volunteer Infantry* (1868; reprint, Freeport, N.Y.: Books for Libraries, 1971), 67.

105. Saum, "Death in the Popular Mind," 34. See also Laderman, *Sacred Remains,* 113–16.

106. Rebecca Harding Davis quoted in Paludan, *"A People's Contest,"* 366.

Chapter 2

1. *The Independent,* 20 April 1865, 1; *Official Records,* ser. 1, 47, pt. 3: 34, and ser. 1, 49, pt. 2: 343–44; E[dward] D[avis] Townsend, *Anecdotes of the Civil War in the United States* (New York: Appleton & Co., 1884), 210–18, 220; Swanberg, *First Blood,* 339. Daniel Hough, the first death of the war, had been buried originally on the parade ground of Fort Sumter, his grave marked as Daniel Howe. No more is known of his grave after the fort passed into Southern possession. The Union soldiers buried throughout South Carolina and

eastern Georgia were removed after the war to Beaufort National Cemetery. Beaufort contains no record of Daniel Hough, or Howe, being interred there. In all likelihood then, Daniel Hough lies either in a lost grave at Fort Sumter or among the more than 500 unknown Union dead collected from Morris Island, Charleston, and surrounding areas that were reinterred at Beaufort. Correspondence, Walter A. Gray Jr., Director, Beaufort National Cemetery, to author, 1 August 1997 and 25 August 1997. Beaufort does contain the remains of Private Daniel Howe of Company E, 21 United States Colored Troops, who died serving the Union occupation on 15 August 1865. Beecher's address can be found in *The Independent,* 27 April 1865, 2.

2. Wilbur F. Paddock, *A Great Man Fallen! A Discourse on the Death of Abraham Lincoln* (Philadelphia: Sherman & Co., 1865), 4. There may be good reason for the folk myth about the moon. Fred Espenak of NASA's Goddard Space Flight Center, Planetary Systems Branch, has calculated that, on 10 April 1865, the full moon was partially eclipsed. Revelers throughout the United States that night would have seen the moon in the half-light cast by the earth's shadow, with nearly 20 percent of the moon thoroughly darkened in the umbra. Even penumbral lunar eclipses often exhibit a reddish color, tinged by the light from the sun traveling through the earth's atmosphere. Afterward, the assassination and eclipse may have been conflated in memory. If so, this provides more evidence for the deep sense of foreboding that Lincoln's death produced. Two Bible verses, Joel 2: 31 and Rev. 6: 12, mention the discoloring of the moon, both times to the color of blood, and both times as a sign of coming judgment. As the war was interpreted as divine retribution for the sin of slavery, this sign of judgment and the chastisement through Lincoln's removal would have been potent symbols. It should be noted that weather may have obscured the eclipse for some: a Pennsylvania newspaper reported rain in Washington, D.C., and Pittsburgh that night, although the rain in Washington ended at 11:00, so clearing may have occurred in time to see some of the eclipse (*Pennsylvania Daily Telegraph* [Harrisburg], 11 April 1865, 1).

3. Joyce Appleby, *Capitalism and a New Social Order: The Republican Vision of the 1790s* (New York: New York University Press, 1984), 5.

4. John Lattimer, *Kennedy and Lincoln: Medical and Ballistic Comparisons of Their Assassinations* (New York: Harcourt Brace Jovanovich, 1980), 34–38; Charles A. Leale, *Lincoln's Last Hours,* in *Address Delivered before the Commandery of the State of New York Military Order of the Loyal Legion of the United States* ([New York?]: n.p., 1909, 5–8). Victor Searcher (*The Farewell to Lincoln* [New York: Abingdon, 1965], 31–32) quotes another attending physician, Charles S. Taft, as describing Lincoln's condition in the theater as "almost moribund" and credits Leale's quick actions with preventing the president's immediate death. Leale's account of the resuscitation suggests that Lincoln had died and was revived.

5. Charles E. Brigham, "The National Bereavement: A Discourse Delivered at the First Congregational Church, Taunton, Mass., on Sunday Morning, April 16, 1865," in *Lincolniana* (Boston: William V. Spencer, 1865), 10. See also Searcher, *Farewell to Lincoln,* 29–30; Thomas Reed Turner, *Beware the People Weeping: Public Opinion and the Assassination of Abraham Lincoln* (Baton Rouge: Louisiana State University Press, 1982),

26; and William Hanchett, *The Lincoln Murder Conspiracies* (Urbana: University of Illinois Press, 1986), 53–54, 56–58.

6. Whitman quoted in William E. Barton, *Abraham Lincoln and Walt Whitman* (Indianapolis: Bobbs-Merrill, 1928), 175.

7. Gideon Welles, *Diary of Gideon Welles, Secretary of the Navy under Lincoln and Johnson* (Boston: Houghton Mifflin, 1911), 2: 288; Matthew Simpson, *Funeral Address Delivered at the Burial of President Lincoln, at Springfield, Illinois, May 4, 1865* (New York: Carlton & Porter, 1865), 8.

8. Leale, *Lincoln's Last Hours,* 11; David Herbert Donald, *Lincoln* (New York: Simon & Schuster, 1995), 598.

9. Jean H. Baker, *Mary Todd Lincoln: A Biography* (New York: Norton, 1987), 244–45. Conversely, Lincoln scholars Benjamin P. Thomas and Harold Hyman assert that, "though Stanton disliked Mrs. Lincoln, he . . . treated her tenderly" during the vigil (*Stanton: The Life and Times of Lincoln's Secretary of War* [New York: Knopf, 1962], 397).

10. Baker, *Mary Todd Lincoln,* xiv, 245–46.

11. Leale, "Lincoln's Last Hours," 12.

12. *Chicago Tribune,* 17 April 1865, 1; *Cincinnati Daily Enquirer,* 17 April 1865, 2; Henry J. Raymond, *The Life and Public Services of Abraham Lincoln, Sixteenth President of the United States* (New York: Derby & Miller, 1865), 699.

13. The best account of the deathbed prints is Harold Holzer and Frank J. Williams, *Lincoln's Deathbed in Art and Memory: The "Rubber Room" Phenomenon* (Gettysburg, Pa.: Thomas, 1998). For discussions of Gardner and Littlefield in particular, see ibid., 24, 26. See also Harold Holzer, Gabor S. Boritt, and Mark E. Neely Jr., *The Lincoln Image: Abraham Lincoln and the Popular Print* (New York: Charles Scribner's Sons, 1984), 149–202; and Dorothy Meserve Kunhardt and Philip B. Kunhardt, *Twenty Days* (New York: Castle, 1965), 78–79.

14. Thomas and Hyman, *Stanton,* 404; Charles Hamilton and Lloyd Ostendorf, *Lincoln in Photographs: An Album of Every Known Pose* (Norman: University of Oklahoma Press, 1963), 392; Kunhardt and Kunhardt, *Twenty Days,* 164–65.

15. Searcher, *Farewell to Lincoln,* 53; Kunhardt and Kunhardt, *Twenty Days,* 93, 95; Lattimer, *Kennedy and Lincoln,* 34–38.

16. Reporter quoted in Searcher, *Farewell to Lincoln,* 63 (see generally 72–86); Clement M. Butler, *Funeral Address on the Death of Abraham Lincoln, Delivered in the Church of the Covenant, April 19, 1865* (Philadelphia: Henry B. Ashmead, 1865), 6 (emphasis in original).

17. Searcher, *Farewell to Lincoln,* 79–80; Raymond, *Life and Public Services of Abraham Lincoln,* 705.

18. *Chicago Tribune,* 20 April 1865, 1, and Searcher, *Farewell to Lincoln,* 80–81.

19. *Pennsylvania Daily Telegram* (Harrisburg), 15 April 1865, 2; *Cincinnati Daily Enquirer,* 17 April 1865, 2; Leonard Swain, *A Nation's Sorrow* (Providence, [N.H.?]: n.p., [1865]), 6; Baker, *Mary Todd Lincoln,* 252; Searcher, *Farewell to Lincoln,* 55–58.

20. *Pennsylvania Daily Telegram* (Harrisburg), 24 April 1865, 1; *Cincinnati Daily Enquirer,* 29 April 1865, 3.

21. *Pennsylvania Daily Telegram* (Harrisburg), 24 April 1865, 1.

22. Charles A. Page, *Letters of a War Correspondent* (Boston: L. C. Page & Co., 1899), 359; H. Frank Eshleman, "Lincoln's Visit to Lancaster in 1861; and the Passing of His Corpse, 1865," *Papers Read before the Lancaster County Historical Society* 13, no. 3 (5 March 1909), 78–79; *Cincinnati Daily Enquirer*, 1 May 1865, 2; Edward G. Longacre, ed., "With Lincoln on His Last Journey," *Lincoln Herald* 84, no. 4 (Winter 1982): 241.

23. Lloyd Lewis, *Myths after Lincoln* (1929; reprint, New York: Readers Club, 1941), 124–25.

24. *Pennsylvania Daily Telegraph* (Harrisburg), 4 May 1865, 2. See also Searcher, *Farewell to Lincoln*, 100, 118, 223. For examples of other mourning prints, see Harold Holzer, "Lincoln Heaven-Bound, on Washington's Shoulders," *Lincoln Herald* 80, no. 2 (Summer 1978): 102–3; Holzer, Boritt, and Neely, *The Lincoln Image*, 192–203; Henry S. Wilson to Bluford Wilson, 21 April 1865, quoted in *Concerning Mr. Lincoln: In Which Abraham Lincoln Is Pictured as He Appeared to Letter Writers of His Time*, comp. Harry E. Pratt (Springfield, Ill.: Abraham Lincoln Association, 1944), 125; and Champ Clark, *The Assassination: Death of the President* (Alexandria, Va.: Time-Life Books, 1987), 127, 131.

25. James T. Hickey, *Springfield, May, 1865* (Springfield, Ill.: [James T. Hickey?], 1968), 9–10.

26. Something of the Lincoln funereal expression was echoed in the responses to the funeral train that returned Franklin Roosevelt to Washington, D.C., following his death and the assassination and funeral of John F. Kennedy. Of course, radio and television made these two funerals—especially Kennedy's—accessible to the nation in a way impossible in the 1860s. A. C. Nielsen estimated that, over the course of the period 22–25 November 1963, as many as 166 million Americans in 51 million homes tuned in to coverage of the assassination and funeral, and during the highest viewing period 93 percent of all televisions were tuned to Kennedy's televised burial in Arlington National Cemetery on the twenty-fifth (Wilbur Schramm, "Introduction: Communication in Crisis," in *The Kennedy Assassination and the American Public: Social Communication in Crisis*, ed. Bradley S. Greenberg and Edwin B. Parker [Stanford, Calif.: Stanford University Press, 1965], 14; Mary Ann Watson, *The Expanding Vista: American Television in the Kennedy Years* [New York: Oxford University Press, 1990], 223).

27. Such observations were made by, for example, Marvin Richardson Vincent, *A Sermon on the Assassination of President Lincoln, Delivered in the First Presbyterian Church, Troy, on Sunday Morning April 23, 1865* (Troy, N.Y.: A. W. Scribner, 1865), 10–11. The thesis of a Confederate conspiracy has recently gained new currency (see William A. Tidwell, with James O. Hall and David Winfred Gaddy, *Come Retribution: The Confederate Secret Service and the Assassination of Lincoln* [Jackson: University Press of Mississippi, 1988]; and William Tidwell, *April '65: Confederate Covert Action in the American Civil War* [Kent, Ohio: Kent State University Press, 1995]).

28. Minister quoted in Billingsley, *From the Flag to the Cross*, 295; Paddock, *A Great Man Fallen!* 5. See also A. S. Twombly, *The Assassination of Abraham Lincoln; a Discourse Delivered in the State St. Pres. Church . . . 16 April 1865* (Albany, N.Y.: J. Munsell, 1865), 7–8.

29. Lloyd Lewis, "Memorial Day Is Born," *Liberty*, 2 June 1928, 33.

30. Morris C. Sutphen, *Discourse on the Occasion of the Death of Abraham Lincoln* (Philadelphia: Jas. B. Rogers, 1865), 6.

31. Raymond, *Life and Public Services of Abraham Lincoln*, 702.

32. Abraham Lincoln, Second Inaugural Address, in Basler, ed., *Collected Works of Lincoln*, 8: 333.

33. Phillips Brooks, *The Life and Death of Abraham Lincoln: A Sermon Preached at the Church of the Holy Trinity, Philadelphia, Sunday Morning, April 23, 1865* (Philadelphia: Henry B. Ashmead, 1865), 4. See also Turner, *Beware the People Weeping*, 51. Only a handful of scholars have treated the Lincoln funeral sermons in any detail. The first to do so was Charles Joseph Stewart, whose pathbreaking "A Rhetorical Study of the Reaction of the Protestant Pulpit in the North to Lincoln's Assassination" (Ph.D. diss., University of Illinois, 1963) deserves a larger audience. See also Turner, *Beware the People Weeping*, 77–89; and David B. Chesebrough, *No Sorrow Like Our Sorrow: Northern Protestant Ministers and the Assassination of Lincoln* (Kent, Ohio: Kent State University Press, 1994). Some funeral sermons are discussed in Chester Forrester Dunham, *The Attitude of the Northern Clergy toward the South, 1860–1865* (Philadelphia: Porcupine, 1974), but they are not treated as a separate category of inquiry.

34. Andrew Jackson was, in 1835, the first victim of attempted assassination, but his assailant's pistols misfired. The caning of Charles Sumner on the Senate floor in 1856 was the most notorious instance of political violence prior to Lincoln's death. The first senator killed was David C. Broderick of California, shot in a duel in 1859. Lincoln's murder was the nation's introduction to political assassination, and it was quickly followed by other such incidents of crime, as if the violence of the war sought other channels in peace. In 1867, state legislators became the object of political murder for the first time when three were killed in the Reconstruction South. Two judges were killed in each of the years 1867, 1868, and 1870. The year 1868 saw the first assassinations of a lieutenant governor and of a congressman, former Representative James Hines of Arkansas. The next year two more state legislators were murdered, and in 1873 former Senator Clark Pomeroy of Kansas became the second member of the Senate to die by violence. The year 1873 also marks the first assault on the life of a state governor; the second occurred in 1877. In 1881, James Garfield became the second president to be assassinated. The year 1893 saw the first city mayor killed, 1900 the first successful assassination of a state governor, and 1901 the third presidential assassination, that of William McKinley. See James F. Kirkham, Sheldon Levy, and William J. Crotty, *Assassination and Political Violence: A Report to the National Commission on the Causes and Prevention of Violence* (Washington, D.C.: U.S. Government Printing Office, 1969), 21–40.

35. Parke Godwin, in *Commemorative Proceedings of the Atheneum Club, on the Death of Abraham Lincoln, President of the United States, April, 1865* (New York: C. S. Westcott & Co., 1865), 15. See also Chesebrough, *No Sorrow Like Our Sorrow*, 106.

36. George W. Briggs, *Eulogy on Abraham Lincoln, by George W. Briggs, D.D., June 1, 1865, with the Proceedings of the City Council on the Death of the President* (Salem, Mass.: George W. Pease, 1865), 10; Alexander H. Bullock, *Abraham Lincoln: The Just Magistrate,*

the Representative Statesman, the Practical Philanthropist (Worcester, [Mass.?]: Charles Hamilton, 1865), 4; Richard S. Storrs, *An Oration Commemorative of President Abraham Lincoln: Delivered at Brooklyn, N.Y., June 1, 1865* (Brooklyn, N.Y.: War Fund Committee, 1865), 6.

37. Baltimore City Council, *Proceedings of the City Council of Baltimore, in Relation to the Death of Abraham Lincoln, Late President of the United States* (Baltimore: n.p., 1865), 7. See also Stewart, "Rhetorical Study of the Reaction," 9.

38. Order of United American Mechanics, State Council of Pennsylvania, *In Memoriam: Abraham Lincoln, President of the United States* (Philadelphia: Geo. Hawkes Jr., 1865), 34.

39. "Three Weeks at Gettysburg," in *The Civil War in Song and Story, 1860–1865*, ed. Frank Moore (New York: P. F. Collier, 1889), 493; Albert Barnes, *The State of the Country: A Discourse Delivered* . . . (Philadelphia: Henry B. Ashmead, 1865).

40. David Belden, *Obsequies of President Lincoln: An Oration Delivered in Nevada City in 1865* (Marysville, Calif.: Marysville Herald Press, [1865?]), 4. See also Adoniram J. Patterson, *Eulogy on Abraham Lincoln, Delivered in Portsmouth, N.H., April 19, 1865* (Portsmouth, N.H.: C. W. Brewster & Son, 1865), 17; and William Binney, in Providence City Council, *Proceedings of the City Council of Providence on the Death of Abraham Lincoln: With the Oration Delivered before the Municipal Authorities and Citizens, June 1, 1865, by William Binney, Esq.* (Providence, R.I.: Knowles, Anthony & Co., 1865), 53.

41. John McClintock, *Discourse Delivered on the Day of the Funeral of President Lincoln,* reported by J. T. Butts (New York: J. M. Bradstreet & Son, 1865), 22; Treadwell Walden, *The National Sacrifice* (Philadelphia: Sherman & Co., 1865), 25; Bullock, *Abraham Lincoln,* 45; John Chadwick, "Abraham Lincoln: A Sermon Preached to His Society in Brooklyn, N.Y.," in *Lincolniana,* 36–51, 50–51. See also Brigham, "The National Bereavement," 18. Some of the Christine mythological analogies from Lincoln's life have been summed up in Lloyd Ostendorf, "Lincoln and Christ Parallels," *Lincoln Herald* 86, no. 3 (Fall 1984): 177–78. Ostendorf and a colleague, David S. Keiser, compiled the Lincoln-Kennedy parallels, which have gained some renown (see, for example, "Lives of Kennedy, Lincoln Paralleled," *Dayton Daily News,* 25 November 1963, 29).

42. Henry Deming, *Eulogy of Abraham Lincoln* . . . (Hartford, Conn.: A. N. Clark & Co., 1865), 55–56.

43. Lewis, *Myths after Lincoln,* 86.

44. O. H. Dutton, "Sermon: Preached in the Second Congregational Church, Holyoke, Ma., Wednesday, 19th," in *Lincolniana,* 76–88, 84; Gordon Hall, *President Lincoln's Death: Its Voice to the People* (Northampton, Mass.: Trumbal & Gere, Printers, 1865), 10 (emphasis in original); J. T. Tucker, *A Discourse in Memory of Our Late President* (Holliston, Mass.: Plimpton & Clark, 1865), 4; Charles S. Robinson, *The Martyred President: A Sermon Preached in the First Presbyterian Church, Brooklyn, N.Y.* (New York: John F. Trow, 1865), 14. See also Sutphen, *Discourse,* 16.

45. Hiram P. Crozier, *The Nation's Loss: A Discourse upon the Life, Services, and Death of Abraham Lincoln, Late President of the United States* (New York: John A. Gray & Green, 1866), 29; Daniel Rice, *The President's Death—Its Import: A Sermon, Preached in the Sec-*

ond Presbyterian Church, Lafayette, Indiana, April 19, 1865 ([Lafayette, Ind.?]: n.p., [1865]),
3; McClintock, *Discourse*, 22; Andrew L. Stone, *A Discourse Occasioned by the Death of
Abraham Lincoln* (Boston: J. K. Wiggin, 1865), 15 (on Lincoln as too magnanimous); E. T.
Corwin, "Death of President Lincoln: A Discourse Delivered at Millstone, N.J., on Sun-
day Morning, April 16, 1865," in *Lincolniana*, 58 (on Lincoln as too gentle hearted); Francis
E. Abbot, "The Martyr of Liberty: A Sermon Preached in the Unitarian Church, Dover,
N.H., on Sunday, April 16, 1865," in ibid., 1–7, 5 (on Lincoln as "not stern enough"); Cephas
B. Crane, *Sermon on the Occasion of the Death of Abraham Lincoln* (Hartford, Conn.: Press
of Case, Lockwood, & Co., 1865), 28–29; Isaac Smith, "In Memory of President Lincoln
(1865)," in *Two Memorial Addresses Delivered on Foxboro Common* (Foxboro, Mass.: The
Print Shop Inc., 1923), 19.

46. Johnson quoted in W. E. B. DuBois, *Black Reconstruction in America, 1860–1880*
(1935; reprint, New York: Atheneum, 1992), 245. See also Turner, *Beware the People Weeping*, 45–46.

47. Brigham, "The National Bereavement," 10. It should be remembered that, while
speaking to a black audience in 1864, Johnson had presented himself in a more elevated
role than that of a Joshua: "I will indeed be your Moses and lead you through the Red
Sea of war and bondage to a fairer future of liberty and peace" (quoted in Eric Foner,
Reconstruction: America's Unfinished Revolution [New York: Harper & Row, 1988], 44;
see also Chesebrough, *No Sorrow Like Our Sorrow*, 71–72).

48. P. B. Day, *A Memorial Discourse on the Character of Abraham Lincoln* (Concord,
[Mass.?]: McFarland & Jenks, 1865), 17–18; Sutphen, *Discourse*, 17; Richard B. Duane, *A
Sermon Preached in Saint John's Church, Providence, on Wednesday, April 19, 1865* (Provi-
dence, [N.H.?]: H. H. Thomas & Co., 1865), 11.

49. George P. Putnam, in *Commemorative Proceedings of the Atheneum Club*, 23;
Samuel L. Crocker, *Eulogy upon the Character and Services of Abraham Lincoln, Late President of the United States* (Boston: John Wilson & Son, 1865), 27.

50. Samuel T. Spear, *The Punishment of Treason: A Discourse Preached April 23d, 1865,
in the South Presbyterian Church, of Brooklyn* (Brooklyn, N.Y.: "The Union" Steam Presses,
1865); L. Clark Seelye, in *The Nation Weeping for Its Dead: Observances at Springfield,
Massachusetts, on President Lincoln's Funeral Day, Wednesday, April 19, 1865, Including Dr.
Holland's Eulogy* (Springfield, Mass.: Samuel Bowers & Co., 1865), 31.

51. Robinson, *The Martyred President*, 18. See also Swain, *A Nation's Sorrow*, 5; Dutton,
"Sermon," 85–86; Samuel Cherney Damon, *Damon's Lincoln Sermon: A Sermon Preached
in Honolulu, Hawaii, 14 May 1865* (New York: William M. Clemens, 1917), 12.

52. Job E. Stevenson quoted in William T. Coggeshall, *Lincoln Memorial: The Journeys of Abraham Lincoln; from Springfield to Washington, 1861, as President Elect; and from
Washington to Springfield, 1865, as President Martyred . . .* (Columbus: Ohio State Journal, 1865), 245; Henry Badger, *The Humble Conqueror: A Discourse Commemorative to the
Life and Services of Abraham Lincoln* (Boston: n.p., 1865), 15.

53. Francis Abbot, "The Martyr of Liberty," 6–7; Swain, *A Nation's Sorrow*, 7; San
Francisco resolution quoted in Searcher, *Farewell to Lincoln*, 40.

54. Turner, *Beware the People Weeping*, 21.

55. Billingsley, *From the Flag to the Cross,* 296–97. For similar thoughts, see Rice, *The President's Death,* 4. On the Miller and Matthew's widows, see David T. Valentine, *Obsequies of Abraham Lincoln, in the City of New York, under the Auspices of the Common Council* (New York: Edmund Jones & Co., 1866), 61–62.

56. George Bancroft, in New York Citizens' Committee, *Obsequies of Abraham Lincoln in Union Square, New York, 25 April 1865* (New York: Van Nostrand, 1865), 20; Henry A. Nelson, *The Divinely Prepared Ruler, and The Fit End of Treason: Two Discourses Delivered at the First Presbyterian Church, Springfield, Illinois, by Invitation of the Session . . .* (Springfield, Ill.: Baker & Phillips, 1865), 27. See also William Ladd Chaffin, *The President's Death and Its Lessons: A Discourse on Sunday Morning, April 23d, 1865, before the Second Unitarian Society of Philadelphia* (Philadelphia: King & Baird, Printers, 1865), 14.

57. Stewart, "Rhetorical Study of the Reaction," 10.

58. N. L. Brakeman, *A Great Man Fallen: A Sermon Preached in the Methodist Church, Baton Rouge, Louisiana, April 23, 1865 . . .* (Baton Rouge: New Orleans Times, Book and Job Office, 1865), 23 (emphasis added).

59. Badger, *The Humble Conqueror,* 5; Swain, *A Nation's Sorrow,* 4. Some orators did include the South in their calculations: "The assassin struck at constitutional liberty, and thirty millions of people are to-day reeling and staggering under the severity of the blow" (George A. Jeremiah, in Valentine, *Obsequies of Abraham Lincoln,* 31).

60. Baltimore City Council, *Proceedings,* 11, 13; Charles G. Loring, in Boston City Council, *A Memorial of Abraham Lincoln, Late President of the United States* (Boston: City Council, 1865), 42; Duane, *Sermon Preached in Saint John's Church,* 12.

61. *Houston Tri-Weekly Telegraph,* 26 April 1865; *Galveston Daily News,* 27 April 1865; *Dallas Herald,* 4 May 1865. Note that, because of the war's disruption of its communications with the rest of the Confederacy, Texas did not learn of Lincoln's death until 26 April. For an account of the situation in Texas, see John M. Barr, "The Tyrannicide's Reception: Responses in Texas to Lincoln's Assassination," *Lincoln Herald* 91, no. 2 (Summer 1989): 58–64; and Ralph W. Steen, "Texas Newspapers and Lincoln," *Southwestern Historical Quarterly* 51 (January 1948): 199–212.

62. Kate Stone, *Brokenburn: The Journal of Kate Stone, 1861–1868,* ed. John Q. Anderson (Baton Rouge: Louisiana State University Press, 1955), 341; newspapers quoted in Barr, "The Tyrannicide's Reception," 60, 61. The parallels to Caesar and Marat were refuted in Abott A. Abott, *The Assassination and Death of Abraham Lincoln, President of the United States, at Washington, on the 14th of April, 1865* (New York: American News Co., 1865), 11.

63. See Wilson, *Baptized in Blood.*

64. Alfred S. Patton, quoted in Chesebrough, *No Sorrow Like Our Sorrow,* 42; Jos. B. Stratton, "President Lincoln's Death: A Sermon Delivered in the First Presbyterian Church, Natchez, Miss., Sunday April 23, 1865," in *Lincolniana,* 186–203 (Stratton's sermon was originally published in the Natchez *Courier,* 6 May 1865). Patton refers to Brooks's May 1856 attack on Charles Sumner on the Senate floor.

65. John L. Burrows, *Palliative and Prejudiced Judgements Condemned: A Discourse Delivered in the First Christian Church, Richmond, Va., June 1, 1865 . . . Together with an Extract from a Sermon, Preached on Sunday, April 23, 1865* (Richmond: n.p., 1865), 3.

66. Ibid.

67. Ibid., 9, 10 (emphasis added, except for "as in this case").

68. Ibid., 8.

69. *Washington National Intelligencer* quoted in Searcher, *Farewell to Lincoln,* 35 (emphasis in original); Hiram Sears, *The People's Keepsake: or, Funeral Address on the Death of Abraham Lincoln* (Cincinnati: Poe & Hitchcock, 1865), 11; George P. Putnam, in *Commemorative Proceedings of the Atheneum Club,* 24; Robinson, *The Martyred President,* 17; Peter Russell, *Our Great National Reproach, and The Counsel of Ahitophel Turned into Foolishness: Two Sermons Preached in St. James Church, Eckley, Penna., by Rev. Peter Russell, Rector . . .* (Philadelphia: King & Baird, Printers, 1865), 8. Sears is quoting David's lamentation over the death of Saul (2 Sam 1: 20). The "sick man" to whom Robinson refers is William H. Seward, then Lincoln's secretary of state, who was attacked by one of the conspirators while bedridden by injuries sustained in a carriage accident.

70. William T. Wilson, *The Death of President Lincoln: A Sermon Preached in St. Peter's Church, Albany, N.Y., on Wednesday, April 19, 1865* (Albany, N.Y.: Weed, Parsons, & Co., 1865), 23; Crozier, *The Nation's Loss,* 32; Crane, *Death of Abraham Lincoln,* 16.

71. Boardman quoted in Chesebrough, *No Sorrow Like Our Sorrow,* 76–77.

72. Bancroft, in New York Citizens' Committee, *Obsequies of Abraham Lincoln,* 20.

73. Arthur G. Thomas, *Our National Unity Perfected in the Martyrdom of the President: A Discourse Delivered in the Chapel of the Filbert Street U.S. General Hospital, on the Day of the Obsequies at Washington . . .* (Philadelphia: Smith, English & Co., 1865), 14. The troops under General Joseph Johnston did not surrender to General William Sherman until 26 April 1865. General Richard Taylor surrendered the remaining Confederate forces east of the Mississippi River to General Edward R. S. Canby on 4 May, and General E. Kirby Smith relinquished his command of the forces west of the Mississippi, also to Canby, a month after Johnston's surrender, on 26 May 1865.

74. Brooks, *The Life and Death of Abraham Lincoln,* 24.

Chapter 3

1. "American and Foreign Art," *Evening Post,* 23 November 1865; [Russell Sturgis,] "The Sixth Annual Exhibition of the Artist's Fund Society of New York," *Nation* 1, no. 21 (23 November 1865): 663. X-ray analysis reveals the alterations made in the painting (Marc Simpson, ed., *Winslow Homer: Paintings of the Civil War* [San Francisco: Fine Arts Museums of San Francisco/Bedford Arts, 1988], 220).

2. Many critics see *Veteran in a New Field* as a symbol of postwar prosperity and optimism. Marc Simpson asserts: "It is an image of productivity rather than destruction, a harmonious and natural reaping of the earth's bounty rather than the bringing of death to another man" (Simpson, ed., *Winslow Homer,* 219). For interpretations emphasizing the death metaphor, see Christopher Kent Wilson, "Winslow Homer's *The Veteran in a New Field:* A Study of the Harvest Metaphor and Popular Culture," *American Art Journal* 17, no. 4 (autumn 1985): 2–27; Robert Hughes, *American Visions: The Epic History of*

Art in America (New York: Alfred A. Knopf, 1997), 305–6; and Nicolai Cikovsky Jr., "A Harvest of Death: The Veteran in a New Field," in Simpson, ed., *Winslow Homer*, 83–101. None of these critics, however, make the connection that the grain, once too high, was meant to echo the height of men in the war.

3. Charles Cruft, in *The Army Reunion: With Reports of the Meetings of the Societies of the Army of the Cumberland; the Army of the Tennessee; the Army of the Ohio; and the Army of Georgia. December 15 and 16, 1868* (Chicago: S. C. Griggs & Co., 1869), 59, 61.

4. Richard Franklin Bensel, *Yankee Leviathan: The Origins of Central State Authority in America, 1859–1877* (Cambridge: Cambridge University Press, 1990); Roger L. Ransom, *Conflict and Compromise: The Political Economy of Slavery, Emancipation, and the American Civil War* (Cambridge: Cambridge University Press, 1989), chap. 8.

5. *An Act to Define the Pay and Emoluments of Certain Officers of the Army, and Other Purposes,* 12 *Statutes at Large* 596 (1863).

6. George H. Thomas, *Official Records,* ser. 1, 31, pt. 3: 487. E. B. Whitman ("Remarks on National Cemeteries—Original Military Division of the Tennessee," in *Army Reunion,* 227) reports that Thomas moved to create the Stone's River cemetery in the spring of 1864, more than a year after the battle there. However, this is contradicted by the report of Chaplain William Earnshaw, who stated that Thomas ordered him to take charge of disinterring Union soldiers and reinterring them in the Stone's River National Cemetery on 23 June 1865 (U.S. War Department, *Roll of Honor,* 11: 227). Unfortunately, no such order of that date seems to have survived to be included in the *Official Records.*

7. Elizabeth Thorn, "Elizabeth Thorn Account," 8, "Evergreen Cemetery Gate House." Vertical Files, file 8–15, GNMP Library.

8. Theodore Dimon, "From Auburn to Antietam: The Civil War Journal of a Battlefield Surgeon Who Served with the Army of the Potomac, 1861–1863," 141–42, "Establishment of the National Cemetery." Vertical Files, file 10–4, GNMP Library. See also *Report of the Select Committee Relative to the Soldiers' National Cemetery,* 62; and Harlan D. Unrau, *Administrative History: Gettysburg National Military Park and National Cemetery* (Washington, D.C.: U.S. Department of the Interior, National Park Service, 1991), 3–4. Kathleen Georg-Harrison, the research historian at Gettysburg National Military Park, champions Theodore Dimon as the originator of the idea for the soldiers' cemetery and David McConaughy as instrumental in the preservation and development of the battlefield park, in both cases at the expense of the traditional hero of Gettysburg's commemoration, David Wills (see Kathleen R. Georg, "Gettysburg—a Happy and Patriotic Conception," 2, GNMP Library, and "'This Grand National Enterprise': The Origins of Gettysburg's National Cemetery and Gettysburg Battlefield Memorial Association," 3–9, GNMP Library).

9. Georg, "'This Grand National Enterprise,'" 21–27; Unrau, *Administrative History,* 5–6.

10. Hoffsommer, "Aftermath of Gettysburg," 52; Unrau, *Administrative History,* 11. The burial contracts are reprinted in *Report of the Select Committee Relative to the Soldiers' National Cemetery,* 10–11.

11. *Report of the Select Committee Relative to the Soldiers' National Cemetery*, 10.

12. Garry Wills, *Lincoln at Gettysburg: The Words That Remade America* (New York: Simon & Schuster, 1992), 37; Gettysburg Address quoted in ibid., 263 (emphasis added).

13. "Report of Samuel Weaver," in *Report of the Select Committee Relative to the Soldiers' National Cemetery*, 39–41, 41.

14. Winthrop Jordan, *White over Black: American Attitudes toward the Negro, 1550–1812* (Chapel Hill: University of North Carolina Press/Institute of Early American History and Culture, 1968), see generally 44–98; *Gettysburg (Pa.) Star-Sentinel*, 2 February 1864, typescript copy, "Confederate Reinterments," Vertical Files, file 7–17, GNMP Library (emphasis added).

15. George Meade, in John Russell Bartlett, *The Soldiers' National Cemetery at Gettysburg* (Providence, R.I.: Providence Press Co., 1874), 86.

16. "The National Cemetery at Gettysburgh," *Hours at Home* 2 (December 1865): 183–84, quoted in Unrau, *Administrative History*, 21–22.

17. Kathleen Georg-Harrison, Research Notes from the Minutes of the Proceedings of the Evergreen Cemetery, "Evergreen (Citizen's) Cemetery," Vertical Files, file 9–G8, GNMP Library. In recent years, a few headstones recording the burial of Confederates have been erected on the slopes of Evergreen Cemetery, but the location of the graves remains conjectural.

18. Charles W. Snell and Sharon A. Brown, *Antietam National Battlefield and National Cemetery: An Administrative History* (Washington, D.C.: National Park Service, U.S. Department of the Interior, 1986), 2, 6.

19. Chapter 237, "An Act Entitled, an Act to Purchase and Enclose a Part of the Battle Field at Antietam for the Purposes of a State and National Cemetery," *Laws of Maryland* 1864, and chap. 203, "An Act to Repeal an Act Passed March the Tenth, [1864,] Entitled an Act to Purchase and Enclose a Part of the Battle Field at Antietam for the Purposes of a State and National Cemetery, Chapter [237], Acts of [1864], and to Incorporate the Antietam National Cemetery in Washington County," *Laws of Maryland* 1865, in Record Group 92, Records of the Office of the Quartermaster General, Records Relating to Functions: Cemeterial, 1828–1929, Entry 576, Box 5, NARA.

20. Snell and Brown, *Administrative History*, 5–7, 12.

21. "Antietam National Cemetery. Second Annual Report of the President, Sharpsburg, Maryland, June 5, 1867," broadsheet, Record Group 92, Records of the Office of the Quartermaster General, Records Relating to Functions: Cemeterial, 1828–1929, General Correspondence and Reports Relating to National and Post Cemeteries, 1865–1890, Annapolis to Antietam, Md. (1880–1909), Entry 576, Box 4, NARA; See also Snell and Brown, *Administrative History*, 12–14, 16.

22. *History of the Antietam National Cemetery*, 22.

23. Ibid., 30–47 (emphasis added).

24. Ibid., 5 (emphasis in original).

25. Matthew asserted that this purchase fulfilled the prophecies of Jeremiah and Zechariah. The former describes a land purchase and burial ground (Jer. 19: 11, 32: 6–9). The latter states: "So they weighed for my price thirty pieces of silver. And the Lord said

unto me, Cast it unto the potter" (Zech. 11: 12–13). Those particularly deft at Scripture perhaps made a further potent association by recalling that thirty pieces of silver was also the price of a slave (Exod. 21: 32).

26. *History of the Antietam National Cemetery,* 54.

27. "Annual Meeting of the Trustees of the Antietam National Cemetery, Sharpsburg, Maryland, June 5 1867," and Antietam National Cemetery, "Second Annual Report of the President," Sharpsburg, Maryland, June 5, 1867, Record Group 92, Records of the Office of the Quartermaster General, Records Relating to Functions: Cemeterial, 1828–1929, Entry 576, Box 5, NARA.

28. *Proceedings of the Trustees of the Antietam National Cemetery at Their Meeting Held in Washington City, December 5th, 1867* (Hagerstown, Md.: n.p., 1867), 4–7.

29. Ibid., 7.

30. Ibid., 8–10. Why, after funding the cemetery in part on behalf of its Confederate soldiers, West Virginia voted to table and then to oppose the resolution is unclear.

31. "The Antietam Cemetery," *Washington Chronicle,* 9 December 1867; "New Jersey," *Washington Chronicle,* 29 January 1868; *Washington Chronicle,* 15 December 1867; and *Hagerstown (Md.) State Guard,* n.d., (reprinted in *Washington Chronicle,* 14 June 1868), all in Record Group 92, Records of the Office of the Quartermaster General, Records Relating to Functions: Cemeterial, 1828–1929, Entry 576, Box 5, NARA.

32. *Proceedings of the Trustees of the Antietam National Cemetery at a Special Meeting Held in Washington City, May 6th, 1868* ([Hagerstown, Md.?]: n.p., n.d.), 4–5, 10–13.

33. U.S. Congress, House, Committee on Military Affairs, "J. P. L. Strong and Others," 40th Cong., 2d sess., 1868, H. Rept. 61, serial 1358. See also "Interment of Rebel Dead in the Antietam Cemetery," *Washington Chronicle,* 19 June 1868.

34. Commonwealth of Massachusetts Senate, "Proceedings of Meetings of the Board of Trustees of the Antietam National Cemetery," no. 11 ([Boston?]: n.p., 1869), 6–7, 8.

35. *Proceedings of a Meeting of the Board of Trustees of the Antietam National Cemetery, Held at Washington City, Dec. 9, 1869* (Hagerstown, Md.: A. G. Boyd, [1869?]), 4–5, 12–13.

36. *A Descriptive List of the Burial Places of the Remains of Confederate Soldiers, Who Fell in the Battles of Antietam, South Mountain, Monocacy, and Other Points in Washington and Frederick Counties, in the State of Maryland* (Hagerstown, Md.: "Free Press," n.d.), 10; "A Law to Establish a Confederate Cemetery Near Hagerstown, Maryland," Record Group 92, Records of the Office of the Quartermaster General, Records Relating to Functions: Cemeterial, 1828–1929, Entry 576, Box 5, NARA; U.S. Congress, Senate, "Letter of the Secretary of War Communicating . . . the Report of the Inspector of the National Cemeteries of the United States for 1874," 43d Cong., 2d sess., 1875, S. Ex. Doc. 28, serial 1629, 21. See also Stotelmyer, *Bivouacs of the Dead,* 33–45. Surprisingly, the *Administrative History* of Antietam Battlefield and Cemetery makes no mention of the difficulties stemming from Confederate interment; hence, the shortage of funds is not discussed, nor is the reduction in salaries explained (see Snell and Brown, *Administrative History,* 17 and passim).

37. Meigs's order as reported in Whitman, "Remarks on National Cemeteries," 227 (emphasis in original).

38. U.S. Congress, House, *Officers and Soldiers Buried Near Atlanta,* 39th Cong., 1st sess., 1866, H. Ex. Doc. 92, serial 1263, 2–3.

39. Whitman, "Remarks on National Cemeteries," 228.

40. Ibid., 229.

41. Jason M. Moore in U.S. War Department, Quartermaster General's Office, *Names of Officers and Soldiers Found on the Battle-Fields of the Wilderness and of Spotsylvania Court House, Va.* (Washington, D.C.: U.S. Government Printing Office, 1865), v.

42. Jennie Friend quoted in National Park Service, "Poplar Grove National Cemetery" (9 September 2002), http://www.aqd.nps.gov/synthesis/views/Sites/PETE/History/7_PoplarGrove/PG_History.htm (accessed 18 December 2002). See also Whitman, "Remarks on National Cemeteries," 228; U.S. Department of the Interior, National Park Service, Interagency Resources Division, Lawrence E. Aten et al., *Study of Civil War Sites in the Shenandoah Valley of Virginia, Pursuant to Public Law 101-628* (Washington, D.C.: U.S. Government Printing Office, [1992?]), 9.

43. Mason, "Notes of a Confederate Staff-Officer," 101.

44. U.S. War Department, Quartermaster General's Office, *Statement of the Disposition of Some of the Bodies of Deceased Union Soldiers and Prisoners of War, Whose Remains Have Been Removed to National Cemeteries in the Southern and Western States,* 4 vols. (Washington, D.C.: U.S. Government Printing Office, 1868); Whitman, "Remarks on National Cemeteries," 236.

45. Report, E. B. Whitman to Bvt. Maj. Gen. J. L. Donaldson, Chief Quartermaster, Military Division of the Tennessee, 30 April 1866, 3–4, U.S. Army, Quartermaster's Department, Papers 1865–1868, (emphasis in original), Folder 2, Department of the Savannah, Manuscript Collection, Library of Congress (hereafter LOC). See also U.S. War Department, *Roll of Honor,* 20: 1–117.

46. U.S. Congress, House, Committee on Military Affairs, *National Cemeteries in Tennessee,* (emphasis in original), 39th Cong., 1st sess., 1866, H. Misc. Doc. 127, serial 1271, 21, 14–15.

47. Report, E. B. Whitman to Bvt. Maj. Gen. J. L. Donaldson, Chief Quartermaster, Military Division of the Tennessee, April 1866, 4, U.S. Army, Quartermaster's Department, Papers 1865–1868, Folder 2, Department of the Savannah, Manuscript Collection, LOC; U.S. Congress, Senate, "Letter of the Secretary of War Communicating . . . the Report of the Inspector of the National Cemeteries of the United States for 1869," 41st Cong., 2d sess., 1870, S. Ex. Doc. 62, serial 1406, 95, and "Letter of the Secretary of War Communicating . . . the Report of the Inspector of the National Cemeteries of the United States for 1870 and 1871," 95, 42d Cong., 2d sess., 1872, S. Ex. Doc. 79, serial 1479, 95.

48. Report, E. B. Whitman to Bvt. Maj. Gen. J. L. Donaldson, Chief Quartermaster, Military Division of the Tennessee, 24 May 1866, 3–5, U.S. Army, Quartermaster's Department, Papers 1865–1868, Folder 2, Department of the Savannah, Manuscript Collection, LOC.

49. Whitman, "Remarks on National Cemeteries," 230.

50. U.S. War Department, Quartermaster General's Office, *Compilation of Laws, Orders, Opinions, Instructions, etc., in Regard to National Military Cemeteries* (Washing-

ton, D.C.: U.S. Government Printing Office, 1878), 5; *An Act to Establish and Protect National Cemeteries,* 14 *Statutes at Large* 399–401 (1867).

51. U.S. Congress, *Congressional Globe,* "National Cemeteries," 39th Cong., 2d sess., 18 January 1867, 37, pt. 1: 539.

52. *An Act to Establish and Protect National Cemeteries,* 399–401.

53. Billingsley, *From the Flag to the Cross,* 325.

54. Hans L. Trefousse, *Thaddeus Stevens: Nineteenth Century Egalitarian* (Chapel Hill: University of North Carolina Press, 1997), xi.

55. U.S. Congress, Senate, "Report of the Inspector . . . for 1869," 20–21, 31–32, passim, and "Report of the Inspector . . . for 1870 and 1871," 29, 35–36, passim. Not all the cemeteries that appear in the inspection reports became part of the National Cemetery System.

56. John W. Busey, *Last Full Measure: Burials in the Soldier's National Cemetery at Gettysburg* (Hightstown, N.J.: Longstreet, 1988), 149.

57. Statistics reported in *New National Era* (Washington, D.C.), 2 March 1871, 1; Whitman, "Remarks on National Cemeteries," 225 (emphasis in original).

58. Beath, *History of the Grand Army of the Republic,* 11.

59. Wallace Evan Davies, *Patriotism on Parade: The Story of Veterans' and Hereditary Organizations in America, 1783–1900* (Cambridge, Mass.: Harvard University Press, 1955); Stuart McConnell, *Glorious Contentment: The Grand Army of the Republic, 1865–1900* (Chapel Hill: University of North Carolina Press, 1992); Mary Dearing, *Veterans in Politics: The Story of the G.A.R.* (Baton Rouge: Louisiana State University Press, 1952); Jennings Hood and Charles J. Young, *American Orders and Societies and Their Decorations* (Philadelphia: Bailey, Banks & Biddle, 1917). Burial assistance programs continued to be important to veterans' groups (McConnell, *Glorious Contentment,* 131–33).

60. Quoted in Beath, *History of the Grand Army of the Republic,* 82.

61. For example, *Veterans in Politics,* Mary Dearing's seminal work on the GAR, makes no mention of concern for the decent interment of the war dead or veterans.

62. Quoted in Beath, *History of the Grand Army of the Republic,* 82.

63. McConnell, *Glorious Contentment,* 136–37.

64. U.S. War Department, *Compilation of Laws,* 33.

65. Beath, *History of the Grand Army of the Republic,* 91.

66. Quoted in ibid., 90–91 (emphasis added). See also McConnell, *Glorious Contentment,* 183–93, although I disagree with McConnell's position that Memorial Day was considered a time to commune with the fallen more than a time to proclaim the lessons of the war. The oratory that pertained at virtually every Memorial Day ceremony, both North and South, expressly interpreted the meaning of the dead and their sacrifices for the living.

67. Frank Moore, ed., *Memorial Ceremonies at the Graves of Our Soldiers, Saturday, May 30, 1868* (Washington, D.C.: Wm. T. Collins, 1869), 67–70, 101, and passim.

68. Blight, *Race and Reunion,* 65–71.

69. Charles Cowley, "Our National Cemeteries," *Bay State Monthly* 2, no. 1 (October 1884): 58; Moore, ed., *Memorial Ceremonies,* 31, 33–34.

70. *The People's Advocate* (Washington, D.C.), 1 July 1876, 2; Moses, "Another Day with Prejudice," *The People's Advocate,* 10 June 1876, 2.

71. Beath, *History of the Grand Army of the Republic,* 110, 113.

72. Although the federal government at times *acted* as if Memorial Day had become a legislatively mandated national holiday—for example, by granting government workers the day off in 1887 and by directing that the holiday be held the following Monday should 30 May fall on a Sunday—it was not until the 1971 Monday Holiday Law, changing the date of the observance from 30 May to the last Monday of the month, that Memorial Day was stipulated by Congress as a national holiday.

73. Ibid., 112–13.

74. Ibid., 120, 128, 141, 236 (emphasis added).

75. Circular, Quartermaster General R. N. Batchelder, Quartermaster General Orders and Circulars and Blank Forms Relating to National Cemeteries, 1874–1905, RG 92, Records of the Office of the Quartermaster General, E 590, NARA.

76. Whitman, "Remarks on National Cemeteries," 225, 226 (emphasis in original).

Chapter 4

1. Billingsley, *From the Flag to the Cross,* 114–15 (emphasis in original).

2. Gaines Foster prefers *tradition* to *myth* when describing the Lost Cause (*Ghosts of the Confederacy,* 7–8). I believe that *myth* more precisely defines the irrational and emotive content of postwar Southern reactions to defeat and that, while traditional elements are clearly present, at root the crafting of this set of ideas and values was far too spontaneous and reactionary to fall within the definition of *tradition,* at least as defined by Eric Hobsbawm and Terence Ranger, eds., *The Invention of Tradition* (Cambridge: Cambridge University Press, 1983).

3. In addition to the works cited in n. 7 of the introduction, my reading and understanding of the Lost Cause and its interpretation owe much to Gaines M. Foster, "The Lost Cause Found: Reflections on a Burgeoning Historical Literature" (paper presented at the Graduate Student Conference on Southern History, University of Mississippi, 2000).

4. Foner, *Reconstruction,* 176–97.

5. Ibid., 164–68, 198–204, 425–44.

6. U.S. Congress, House, *Congressional Globe,* 39th Cong., 1st sess., 4 June 1866, 36, pt. 4: 2945. Williams had first offered his resolution a week earlier, but, because it forced an executive response, by the rules it was laid over (ibid., 28 March 1866, 36, pt. 3: 2857). The report was returned with all department heads denying any knowledge of government involvement (U.S. Congress, House, *Honors to Rebels,* 39th Cong., 1st sess., 1866, H. Ex. Doc. 141, serial 1267).

7. "The First Memorial Service," in Mildred Lewis Rutherford, *Historical Records of the United Daughters of the Confederacy, Volume 41—Origin of Ladies' Memorial Association* (unpaginated), Mildred Lewis Rutherford Volumes, Eleanor S. Brockenbrough Library, Museum of the Confederacy, Richmond, Va.

8. Clement Evans, in *Ceremonies in Augusta, Georgia, Laying the Corner Stone of the Confederate Monument; with Oration by Gen. Clement A. Evans, April 26, 1875, and the Unveiling and Dedication of the Monument, with Oration by Col. Charles C. Jones, Jr., October 31, 1878* (Augusta, Ga.: Chronicle and Constitutionalist Job Printing Est., 1878), 9.

9. Drew Gilpin Faust, *Mothers of Invention: Women of the Slaveholding South in the American Civil War* (Chapel Hill: University of North Carolina Press, 1996); George C. Rable, *Civil Wars: Women and the Crisis of Southern Nationalism* (Urbana: University of Illinois Press, 1989).

10. R. E. Colston, "Address of R. E. Colston," *Southern Historical Society Papers* 21 (1893): 38–49, 41 (originally delivered at Wilmington, N.C., 10 May 1870). Similarly: "Now, after the smoke of battle has cleared away, where do we find these devoted women? Where were Mary Magdalene and the other Mary after the crucifixion? At the sepulcher with sweet spices. So these women of the South came, and they continue to come, to the soldiers' graves with choice plants and bright flowers" (newspaper clipping from Cheraw, S.C., in Rutherford, *Origin of Ladies' Memorial Association*).

11. "Caring for Our Dead: The Work of C. Irvine Walker Chapter, U.D.C., Summerville, S.C.," *Confederate Veteran* 7, no. 2 (February 1899): 84.

12. *A History of the Origin of Memorial Day as Adopted by the Ladies' Memorial Association of Columbus, Georgia* (Columbus, Ga.: Thos. Gilbert, 1898), 6, 18. The novel that inspired Rutherford was *Initials,* by Baroness Tautphoeus: "Hamilton was occupied with the tombstones and crosses, which were variously and tastefully decorated with wreaths, festoons, bouquets of flowers, and colored lamps. Even the graves of the poorest were strewn with charcoal, and ornamented with red berries and moss, while tearful groups surrounding those newly made, gave an additional shade of solemnity to a religious rite" (Baroness [Jemima Montgomery, Freifrau von] Tautphoeus, *The Initials: A Story of Modern Life,* 2 vols. [1850; reprint, New York: G. P. Putnam's Sons, 1892], 2: 6).

13. *History of the Origin of Memorial Day,* 7.

14. Williams quoted in ibid., 24–25. In a significant and meaningful gesture, the graves of both Rutherford and Williams—both of whom are interred in the same cemetery as the soldiers whose graves they tended—were in 1892 marked by headstones similar to those marking the soldiers' graves (ibid., 24).

Perhaps inevitably, controversy later emerged over whether Rutherford or Williams was the true originator of the idea of setting aside a day for commemoration. Years later, Williams's sister wrote, "Lizzie Rutherford . . . lived in Columbus too, and not a suggestion that she was the originator of Memorial Day ever was heard until years after both these most loyal and useful women were dead[.] For a long time every Memorial day a military salute was fired over sister Mary Anne [Williams]'s grave. *Why* a contradictory claim should ever have arisen has always been a puzzle and wonder to me" (Mrs. C. E. Howard to Mildred Lewis Rutherford, 11 May 1916 [emphasis in original], in Rutherford, *Origin of Ladies' Memorial Association*).

15. Mrs. Garland Jones, "History of the Ladies' Memorial Association, and Confederate Cemetery," in *History of the Wake County Ladies Memorial Association,* by [Charlotte B. G. Williams] (Raleigh, N.C.: n.p., 1938), 7–8.

16. *Official Records*, ser. 1, 11, pt. 1: 1037, 1042, 1043; W. T. Robins, "Stuart's Ride around McClellan," in *Battles and Leaders*, 2: 272; William W. Averell, "With the Cavalry on the Peninsula," in ibid., 2: 430; Mark E. Neely Jr., Harold Holzer, and Gabor S. Boritt, *The Confederate Image: Prints of the Lost Cause* (Chapel Hill: University of North Carolina Press, 1987), ix–x.

17. John R. Thompson, "The Burial of Latane," in *Bugle-Echoes: A Collection of the Poetry of the Civil War*, [ed. Francis Fisher Browne] (New York: Frederick A. Stokes & Bro., 1890), 114–16. See also Neely, Holzer, and Boritt, *The Confederate Image*, x–xi.

18. Drew Gilpin Faust, "Race, Gender, and Confederate Nationalism: William D. Washington's *Burial of Latané*," in *Southern Stories: Slaveholders in Peace and War* (Columbia: University of Missouri Press, 1992), 148–59; Neely, Holzer, and Boritt, *The Confederate Image*, xi–xiv.

19. Ladies' Hollywood Memorial Association, *Our Confederate Dead* (Richmond, Va.: Whittet & Shepperson, 1896), 5.

20. *Memorial Day, May 10th, 1875: Address of Col. B. H. Rutledge* (Charleston, [S.C.]: A. J. Burke, 1875), 1; [Williams,] *History of the Wake County Ladies Memorial Association*, 12. See also the account of first Memorial Day observances throughout the South in Rutherford, *Origin of Ladies' Memorial Association*, [1–4].

21. *Confederate Veteran* 1, no. 3 (March 1893): 84; no. 5 (May 1893): 149; and no. 11 (November 1893): 326.

22. The 1989 history quoted in Nora Fontaine M. Davidson, comp., *Cullings from the Confederacy: A Collection of Southern Poems, Original and Others, Popular during the War between the States, and Incidents and Facts Worth Recalling. 1862–1866. Including the Doggerel of the Camp, as Well as Tender Tribute to the Dead* (Washington, D.C.: Rufus H. Darby Printing Co., 1903), 156, 159–60; Mary [Simmerson Cunningham] Logan, *Reminiscences of the Civil War and Reconstruction*, ed. George Washington Adams (Carbondale: Southern Illinois University Press, 1970), 170–74. See also *Confederate Veteran* 1, no. 1 (January 1893): 20–21.

23. Mrs. John T. Sifford, "History of Memorial Day" [1913], in Rutherford, *Origin of Ladies' Memorial Association*). In 1966, by congressional and presidential order, Waterloo, N.Y., was declared "the Birthplace of Memorial Day." Waterloo held its first "village-wide" observance on 5 May 1866 (Henning Cohen and Tristam Potter Coffin, eds., *Folklore of American Holidays* [Detroit, Mich.: Gale Research, 1987]), 188.

24. *Address at the Decoration of the Graves of the Confederate Dead, in the Cemetery, Near Lexington, Ky., on May 26, 1868* (Lexington, Ky.: Observer & Reporter Print, 1869), 4–5 (emphasis in original).

25. Ibid., 5 (emphasis added). See also U.S. War Department, *Register of Confederate Soldiers, Sailors, and Citizens*, 498–501; U.S. War Department, *Statement of the Disposition*, 3: 29; and *Confederate Veteran* 1, no. 7 (July 1893): 214.

26. The *Confederate Veteran*, the self-proclaimed organ of the Southern fraternal organizations, frequently ran articles featuring various Confederate cemeteries throughout the United States, reporting on their condition, and often providing lists of those

interred. See, for example, "Graves at Danville, Ky.," *Confederate Veteran* 5, no. 11 (November 1897): 558; "Confederate Cemetery, Covington, Ga.," ibid. 6, no. 1 (January 1898): 9; "Confederate Dead at Hopkinsville, Ky.," ibid. 7, no. 2 (February 1900): 106; and "Officer Prisoners on Johnson's Island [Ohio]," ibid. 8, no. 7 (July 1900): 305–7.

27. "Memorial Day at Winchester, Va.," 6 June 1877, unidentified newspaper clipping, 6 June 1877, Alexander R. Boteler Papers, Clippings, 1852–1933, Special Collections, Perkins Library, Duke University, Durham, N.C.

28. Edward G. J. Richter, "The Removal of the Confederate Dead from Gettysburg," *Gettysburg*, no. 2 (1 January 1990): 113–14; Frassanito, *Early Photography at Gettysburg*, 396–402.

29. Richter, "Removal." Years later, the Ladies Memorial Association of Raleigh recorded 103 bodies recovered from the "thirsty soil of Gettysburg" (Jones, "History of the Ladies' Memorial Association," 8–9), but Richter's evidence asserts 137 eventually interred in 121 graves.

30. S. A. Cunningham, "The Carnage at Franklin, Tennessee, Next to That of the Crater," *Southern Historical Society Papers* 24 (1896): 189–92. See also McPherson, *Battle Cry of Freedom*, 812–13.

31. U.S. Congress, House, Committee on Military Affairs, *National Cemeteries in Tennessee*, 19. See also McGavock Confederate Cemetery Record Book, 1864–1900, Special Collections, Perkins Library, Duke University, Durham, N.C.; "McGavock Confederate Cemetery," *Confederate Veteran* 7, no. 1 (January 1899): 26.

32. Thomas L. Connelly, *The Marble Man: Robert E. Lee and His Image in American Society* (Baton Rouge: Louisiana State University Press, 1977), 46. The last days of Lee are recounted in Douglas Southall Freeman, *R. E. Lee: A Biography*, 4 vols. (New York: C. Scribner's Sons, 1935–1936), 4: 482–505; and Connelly, *Marble Man*, 11–12. For Lee on Southern commemorative activity, see Freeman, *R. E. Lee*, 4: 436–37. Alan T. Nolan has argued that the conciliatory Lee of "tradition" is historically inaccurate, citing Lee's continuing praise for the Confederacy, his sustained rancor toward Radical Republican Southern policies, and his unabated racial animus (*Lee Considered: General Robert E. Lee and Civil War History* [Chapel Hill: University of North Carolina Press, 1991], x, 134–52). However, Lee's continued enthusiasm for the Southern cause and his intense desire that his war not be remembered as a rebellion or as treason do not axiomatically make him inconsistent when he urged submission to the national government. At any rate, whether historically accurate or not, the tradition with which Nolan finds such fault prevailed in the contemporary Northern and even Southern perception of Lee's retirement. Those perceptions of Lee shaped the national and sectional response to his death, irrespective of their factual foundation.

33. Connelly, *Marble Man*, 43 (quote), 42–61 (generally).

34. Address of John B. Gordon, in *The Army of Northern Virginia Memorial Volume*, ed. J. Wm. Jones (Richmond: J. W. Randolph & English, 1880), 26.

35. John W. Daniel in *Ceremonies Connected with the Inauguration of the Mausoleum and the Unveiling of the Recumbent Figure of General Robert Edward Lee, at Washington*

and Lee University, Lexington, Va., June 28, 1883 (Richmond, Va.: West, Johnson & Co., 1883), 73. It was argued at least once that Lee's conciliatory manner was manipulated by a duplicitous North to broaden the depredations of Reconstruction. Speaking at a meeting of veterans, former Colonel Charles Marshall charged: "The Government knew well that the handful of troops sent ostensibly to overawe the South could repose securely upon that honor which they insulted by their presence. . . . [T]he Federal Government knew that the Southern people looked for guidance to their leaders, and that foremost among those leaders they looked to General Lee. He had given the pledge of his honor, and his people regarded his honor as their own" (Jones, ed., *Army of Northern Virginia Memorial Volume,* 29).

36. Linderman, *Embattled Courage,* 66–71, 236–39.

37. The series was reprinted in 1887–1888 in the four-volume *Battles and Leaders of the Civil War.*

38. Reardon, *Pickett's Charge,* 91. For examples from the Confederate point of view, see *Confederate Veteran* 2, no. 6 (June 1893): 177; and 3, no. 5 (May 1895): 130–31. The best recent discussion of the development of a "reminiscence industry" is Blight, *Race and Reunion,* 171–254.

39. Frank Johnston, "An Address by Frank Johnston, Decoration Day, April 26th, 1913, Jackson, Mississippi," 3, Miscellaneous Papers, 1910–1924, Box 2, *Confederate Veteran* Papers, Special Collections, Perkins Library, Duke University, Durham, N.C.

40. *Burial Ceremonies of Confederate Dead. Oration: By A. Y. P. Garnett, M.D.; Ode: by Rt. Rev. Wm. Pinkney. December 11, 1874* (Washington: S. & R. O. Polkinhorn, 1875), 5, 6.

41. Ibid., 6–7.

42. Ibid., 9, 12–13.

43. [J. A. P. Campbell], "The Lost Cause: A Masterly Vindication of It by Judge J. A. P. Campbell," *Southern Historical Society Papers* 16 (1888): 232–45, 233, 245 (emphasis in original) (originally delivered at Canton, [Ga.?], on Memorial Day, 1 May 1874).

44. Alexander Boteler in "Memorial Day at Winchester, Va.," 6 June 1877, unidentified newspaper clipping, Alexander R. Boteler Papers, Special Collections, Perkins Library, Duke University, Durham, N.C. (emphasis added).

45. Charles C. Jones in *Ceremonies in Augusta, Georgia,* 21.

46. Hudson Strode, *Jefferson Davis: Tragic Hero* (New York: Harcourt, Brace & World, 1964); William C. Davis, *Jefferson Davis: The Man and His Hour* (New York: HarperCollins, 1991); William J. Cooper Jr., *Jefferson Davis, American* (New York: Knopf, 2000).

47. The *New Orleans Picayune* and the *Times-Democrat* quoted in J. Wm. Jones, *The Davis Memorial Volume: or, Our Dead President, Jefferson Davis, and the World's Tribute to His Memory* (Richmond, Va.: B. F. Johnson & Co., 1890), 472–73, 474; *Augusta (Ga.) Chronicle,* 6 December 1889; *Columbus (Ga.) Enquirer-Sun,* 7 December 1889. See also *Atlanta Constitution,* 8 December 1889; and *Florida Times-Union* (Jacksonville), 7 December 1889. Northern newspapers ran essentially the same stories, although the later ac-

count of Davis never having lost consciousness prior to death appears to have been more widely reprinted. See, for example, *Boston Evening Transcript,* 6 December 1889; and *New York Times,* 7 December 1889.

48. Jones, *Davis Memorial Volume,* 491; *Atlanta Constitution,* 8 December 1889.

49. The *New Orleans Picayune* is quoted in Jones, *Davis Memorial Volume,* 494, 501.

50. Telegrams of Condolence, Box 30, Jefferson Davis Collection, Eleanor S. Brockenbrough Library, Museum of the Confederacy; *Atlanta Constitution,* 8 December 1889.

51. Robert Lowry in Jones, *Davis Memorial Volume,* 481, 484, 491; Varina Howell Davis to J. Taylor Ellyson, 21 December 1889, in Scrapbook E-2, J. Taylor Ellyson, President of the Jefferson Davis Memorial Association, J. Taylor Ellyson Papers, Eleanor S. Brockenbrough Library, Museum of the Confederacy, Richmond, Virginia.

52. Ishbel Ross, *The First Lady of the South: The Life of Mrs. Jefferson Davis* (1958; reprint, Westport, Conn.: Greenwood, 1973), 378–84; Eron Rowland, *Varina Howell, Wife of Jefferson Davis,* 2 vols. (New York: Macmillan, 1931), 2: 529–31.

53. Procter's comments were reprinted in many newspapers. See, e.g., *Atlanta Constitution,* 8 December 1889; *Florida Times-Union* (Jacksonville), 7 December 1889; and *Mobile (Ala.) Daily Register,* 7 December 1889. They also appear in Jones, *Davis Memorial Volume,* 509; and Strode, *Jefferson Davis,* 525.

54. *Newport (R.I.) Mercury,* 14 December 1889.

55. Charles C. Jones Jr., *Funeral Oration Pronounced in the Opera House in Augusta, Georgia, December 11th 1889, upon the Occasion of the Memorial Services in Honor of President Jefferson Davis, by Col. Charles C. Jones, Jr.* (Augusta, Ga.: Chronicle Printing, 1889).

56. *Atlanta Constitution,* 8 December 1889; *Richmond (Va.) Dispatch,* 10 December 1889; and unidentified and undated newspaper clipping, in Scrapbook E-2, J. Taylor Ellyson, President of the Jefferson Davis Memorial Association, Eleanor S. Brockenbrough Library, Museum of the Confederacy, Richmond, Va.

57. Mary Poppenheim et al., *The History of the United Daughters of the Confederacy* (Richmond, Va.: Garret & Massie, [1938]), 49–92, 135–41.

58. Ross, *First Lady of the South,* 349, 351–53, 355–58; "United Daughters of the South: Daughters of the Confederacy Perfect a General Organization," *Confederate Veteran* 3, no. 12 (December 1895): 374–78.

59. Foster, *Ghosts of the Confederacy,* 104–14; Poppenheim et al., *History of the Daughters of the Confederacy,* 181–89.

60. Ross, *First Lady of the South,* 380.

61. Ibid., 381; *Confederate Veteran* 1, no. 6 (June 1893): 176–77.

62. [Williams,] *History of the Wake County Ladies Memorial Association,* 24.

63. There has not been much scholarly attention paid to the funeral train of Jefferson Davis. See Edison H. Thomas, "Story of the Jefferson Davis Funeral Train," pamphlet reprinted from the February 1955 issue of the *L. and N. Magazine;* Michael B. Ballard, "Jeff Davis' Last Ride," *Civil War Times Illustrated* 32, no. 1 (March/April 1993): 32–39, 63, 66. The best contemporary account is found in the *New York Times* from 28 to 31 May 1893.

Chapter 5

1. Samuel Denny Smith, *The Negro in Congress, 1870–1901* (Port Washington, N.Y.: Kennikat, 1940), 5–6; Foner, *Reconstruction*, 352, 591.

2. For fuller treatments of the statue, see F. Lauriston Bullard, *Lincoln in Marble and Bronze* (New Brunswick, N.J.: Rutgers University Press/Abraham Lincoln Association, 1952), 64–72; and Kirk Savage, *Standing Soldiers, Kneeling Slaves: Race, War, and Monument in Nineteenth-Century America* (Princeton, N.J.: Princeton University Press, 1997), 89–128.

3. [Frederick Douglass], *Oration by Frederick Douglass, Delivered on the Occasion of the Unveiling of the Freedmen's Monument in Memory of Abraham Lincoln* (Washington, D.C.: Gibson Bros., 1876), 3. For an account of Douglass's struggle against the process of reunion at the expense of black America, see David Blight, *Frederick Douglass' Civil War: Keeping Faith in Jubilee* (Baton Rouge: Louisiana State University Press, 1989), 219–39.

4. [Douglass], *Oration*, 3.

5. Ibid., 3–4, 1.

6. The concept of imagined communities is borrowed from Benedict Anderson's *Imagined Communities: Reflections on the Origin and Spread of Nationalism,* rev. ed. (London: Verso, 1991).

7. Robert Stewart Davis, "Three Months around Charleston Bar; or, The Great Siege as We Saw It," *United States Service Magazine* 1, no. 2 (February 1864): 169–79, 178, and no. 3 (March 1864): 273–83, 281.

8. "Negro Troops," *Harper's Weekly,* 20 June 1863, 386.

9. T[homas] W[entworth] Higginson, "Regular and Volunteer Officers," *Atlantic Monthly* 14 (September 1864): 348–57, 356.

10. Benjamin Apthorp Gould, comp., *Investigations in the Military and Anthropological Statistics of American Soldiers* (New York: U.S. Sanitary Commission/Hurd & Houghton, 1869), 602; *Chicago Tribune* article reprinted in "Mortality in Our Army," *United States Service Magazine* 5, no. 6 (June 1866): 568–72. The *Tribune* article expands on a report of the U.S. Adjutant General's Office (*Official Records,* ser. 3, 5: 664–72) stating, in part, that the difference in disease rates "is moral rather than physical; that the greater susceptibility of the colored man to disease arose from lack of heart, hope, and mental activity, and that a higher moral and intellectual culture would diminish the defect" (ibid., 669).

11. *Chicago Tribune* article in "Mortality in Our Army."

12. *Official Records,* ser. 1, 47, pt. 3: 621; McPherson, *Battle Cry of Freedom,* 486.

13. Surgeon M. W. Fisk to Surgeon Gen. R. Weeks, 5 November 1863, #12830 F.D. 279 (1863), Series 391: Letters Received, 16th Army Corps, Record Group 393, Records of the U.S. Army Continental Commands, pt. 2, NARA [FSSP C-4912]. Miasmatic diseases were thought to arise from wetlands and fetid areas and included a variety of fevers, most seriously malaria (literally, "bad air").

14. Dudley Taylor Cornish, *The Sable Arm: Negro Troops in the Union Army, 1861–1865* (1956; reprint, New York: Norton, 1966), 266; Ira Berlin, ed., *Freedom: A Documen-*

tary History of Emancipation, 1861–1867, ser. 2, *The Black Military Experience* (Cambridge: Cambridge University Press, 1982), 521.

15. Henry W. Halleck to Edwin Stanton and Halleck to Ulysses S. Grant, *Official Records,* ser. 1, 46, pt. 3: 990, 1005.

16. Philip Sheridan, ibid., ser. 1, 48, pt. 2: 647 (emphasis added). See also Glatthaar, *Forged in Battle,* 218.

17. Randal Ross, "Correspondence," *United States Service Magazine* 5, no. 2 (February 1866): 172–77, 174.

18. *Official Records,* ser. 1, 34, pt. 2: 231.

19. Glatthaar, *Forged in Battle,* 220–21. See also Edward A. Miller Jr., *The Black Civil War Soldiers of Illinois: The Story of the Twenty-ninth U.S. Colored Infantry* (Columbia: University of South Carolina Press, 1998), 157–59, 164; and S. Hemenway, "Observations on Scurvy, and Its Causes among U.S. Colored Troops of the 25th Army Corps, during Spring and Summer of 1865," *Chicago Medical Examiner* 7 (October 1866): 582–586.

20. B. R. Catlin, Chaplain, 115th U.S.C.T., to L[orenzo] Thomas, A.G., 30 June 1865 (C-1166), 31 July 1865 (C-1290), and 29 September 1865 (C-1506), in Ser. 12, Letters Received, 1805–89, RG 94, Records of the Adjutant General's Office, 1780s–1917, NARA [FSSP K-511].

21. Statistics compiled from U.S. War Department, *Roll of Honor,* 6: 6–35. Not included are the 232 men who died as prisoners of war at Camp Ford in Tyler, Tex.

22. U.S. War Department, *Roll of Honor,* 6: 6; Whitman, "Remarks on National Cemeteries," 236.

23. There were also thirty-two white soldiers buried in San Antonio who did not need to be relocated and one black soldier buried in an undetermined location (U.S. War Department, *Roll of Honor,* 6: 8–35).

24. Ibid., 75, 106–7.

25. There is a great deal of uncertainty about how Arlington came to be selected for cemeterial purposes and what Meigs's motivations might have been. Most accounts assert Meigs acted on a particular animus for Lee. See Russell F. Weigley, *Quartermaster General of the Union Army* (New York: Columbia University Press, 1959), 296; David W. Miller, *Second Only to Grant: Quartermaster General Montgomery C. Meigs* (Shippensburg, Pa.: White Mane, 2000), 258–59; and James Edward Peters, *Arlington National Cemetery: Shrine to America's Heroes* (Kensington, Md.: Woodbine, 1986), 22–25.

26. M. C. Meigs to Secretary of War, 5 August 1871, in Record Book, Letters Sent 1871–1889, vol. 1, p. 204, RG 92, Textual Records of the Office of the Quartermaster General Cemeterial, 1828–1929, Central Records, and Correspondence and Issuances, 1864–1923, E 567, NARA. See also Peters, *Arlington National Cemetery,* 25–27.

27. *Washington Daily Morning Chronicle,* 31 May 1871, 4.

28. *New Orleans Semi-Weekly Louisianian,* 15 June 1871, 2, and 22 June 1871, 2; *Shreveport South-Western* quoted in *New Orleans Semi-Weekly Louisianian,* 2 July 1871, 2.

29. *New Era* (Washington, D.C.), 23 June 1870, 2.

30. Ibid.

31. M. C. Meigs to Secretary of War, 5 August 1871, in Record Book, Letters Sent

1871–1889, vol. 1, 204–5, RG 92, Textual Records of the Office of the Quartermaster General Cemeterial, 1828–1929, Central Records, and Correspondence and Issuances, 1864–1923, E 567, NARA.

32. Ibid.

33. Ibid., 204–5.

34. M. C. Meigs to Secretary of War, 14 April 1873, ibid., 3: 176–77.

35. A. Gladwin, Supt. of Contrabands, to Brig. Gen. John P. Slough, Mil. Gov. of Alexandria, Va., 16 December 1864, 2053 Letters Received, Chronological, Box 1, RG 393, pt. 4, Military Gov. of Alexandria, 1862–1865, NARA [FSSP C-4707].

36. Ibid.

37. M. C. Meigs to Secretary of War, 14 April 1873, in Record Book, Letters Sent 1871–1889, vol. 3, 176–177, RG 92, Textual Records of the Office of the Quartermaster General Cemeterial, 1828–1929, Central Records, and Correspondence and Issuances, 1864–1923, E 567, NARA.

38. "Dedication of Monument in Chicago," *Confederate Veteran* 3, no. 5 (May 1895): 145 (emphasis added).

39. *Official Records*, ser. 1, 37, pt. 1: 88, 96–97.

40. Underwood, *Report of the Proceedings*, 3.

41. Ibid., 4.

42. David Hunter Strother, *A Virginia Yankee in the Civil War: The Diaries of David Hunter Strother*, ed. Cecil D. Eby Jr. (Chapel Hill: University of North Carolina Press, 1961), 254–57.

43. James McPherson, "When Memorial Day Was No Picnic," *New York Times*, 26 May 1996, E11. See also the balanced account of the tides pushing veterans together as well as pulling them apart in Davies, *Patriotism on Parade*, 250–74.

44. See, for example, Buck, *Road to Reunion*, 306–7; and Davies, *Patriotism on Parade*, 275.

45. "The Better Angels of Our Nature," episode 9 of *The Civil War*, produced by Ken Burns and Ric Burns (Florentine Films/WETA-TV, 1989). For a critical look at Burns's vision of reconciliation, see Eric Foner, "Ken Burns and the Romance of Reunion," in *Ken Burns's "The Civil War,"* ed. Robert Brent Toplin (New York: Oxford University Press, 1996), 103–18.

46. Buck, *Road to Reunion*, 298.

47. Peter Novick, *That Noble Dream: The "Objectivity Question" and the American Historical Profession* (Cambridge: Cambridge University Press, 1988), 72, 73 (see generally 72–80). Novick sees the *mésalliance* between Northern and Southern historians founded on unbridled racism (ibid., 73–77). The second generation of Columbia scholars is exemplified by Ulrich B. Phillips, who, under Burgess's guidance, was awarded his doctorate in 1902; Walter L. Fleming, born in Alabama and taking his Ph.D. in 1904; Mississippian James W. Garner, who received his doctorate in 1906; and J. G. de Roulhac Hamilton, of North Carolina, who after his 1906 degree from Columbia returned to his native state and the University of North Carolina, establishing the Southern Historical Collection there in 1930. Blight's *Race and Reunion* is the most notable of the exceptions.

48. John Higham, *History: Professional Scholarship in America,* updated paperback ed. (Baltimore: Johns Hopkins University Press, 1990), 151, 168.

49. Du Bois, *Black Reconstruction in America,* 13–14.

50. Lonnie R. Speer, *Portals to Hell: Military Prisons of the Civil War* (Mechanicsburg, Pa.: Stackpole, 1997), 89–92.

51. Libby Prison War Museum Association, *A Trip through the Libby Prison War Museum, Chicago* ([Chicago?]: n.p., 1893), 1. See also Libby Prison War Museum Association, *Libby Prison War Museum Catalogue and Program* (Chicago: Libby Prison War Museum Association, [1889]), 1.

52. Peter Turney, "They Wore the Gray—the Southern Cause Vindicated," *Southern Historical Society Papers* 16 (1888): 319–39, 319, 338 (emphasis added).

53. John Kershaw, "Address," in *Memorial Day, May 10th, 1893* ([Charleston, S.C.?]: n.p., n.d.), 3–8, 5–6, 6–7; P. L. Duffy, "Address," 1, Miscellaneous Papers, 1910–1924, Box 2, *Confederate Veteran* Papers, Special Collections, Perkins Library, Duke University, Durham, N.C.

54. Rankin's comments reported in the *New National Era* (Washington, D.C.), 8 June 1871, 3. For more focused studies of black memory, see Blight, *Frederick Douglass' Civil War,* chap. 10, and *Race and Reunion,* chap. 9; W. Fitzhugh Brundage, "Race, Memory, and Masculinity: Black Veterans Recall the Civil War," in *The War Was You and Me: Civilians in the American Civil War,* ed. Joan E. Cashin (Princeton, N.J.: Princeton University Press, 2002), 136–56; and Donald R. Shaffer, *After the Glory: The Struggles of Black Civil War Veterans* (Lawrence: University Press of Kansas, 2004).

55. William H. Lambert, *Address before Post No. 2, Dep't of Penn'a, Grand Army of the Republic* (Philadelphia: Culbertson & Bache, 1879), 9, 10.

56. Joseph B. Foraker, *Address of Senator Foraker at Arlington, Memorial Day, May 30, 1905* (n.p., [1905?]), 5.

57. Eugene B. Gary, "A Vindication of the South," 3, Miscellaneous Papers, 1910–1924, Box 2, *Confederate Veteran* Papers, Special Collections, Perkins Library, Duke University, Durham, N.C. Gary quotes Ruth 1: 16–17.

58. Quoted in Reardon, *Pickett's Charge,* 92.

59. Georg, "Gettysburg—a Happy and Patriotic Conception," 2–4, and "'This Grand National Enterprise,'" 36–39.

60. Georg, "Gettysburg—a Happy and Patriotic Conception," 4; Unrau, *Administrative History,* 46–48.

61. Georg, "Gettysburg—a Happy and Patriotic Conception," 8, 9–10. Numerous iron tablets marking the positions of Confederate troops were placed in the 1890s, but these were sponsored by the federal government after Southern states proved reluctant to adhere to the line-of-battle rule (David G. Rule, *Confederate Monuments at Gettysburg,* Gettysburg Battle Monuments, vol. 1 [Hightstown, N.J.: Longstreet, 1986], 8–9, 238–40).

62. Indiana Shiloh National Park Commission, *Indiana at Shiloh: Report of the Commission* (Indianapolis: Indiana Shiloh National Park Commission, 1904), 20 (emphasis added). This lack of participation is in spite of early Southern interest in purchasing the battlefield (see *Confederate Veteran* 2, no. 2 [February 1894]: 56).

63. U.S. Congress, House, Committee on Military Affairs, Subcommittee on Army Legislation, *A Hearing on H.R. 27293, a Bill to Extend the Limits of Shiloh National Military Park* (Washington, D.C.: U.S. Government Printing Office, 1911), 12 and passim.

64. C. H. Benson, *"Yank" and "Reb": A History of a Fraternal Visit Paid by Lincoln Post, No. 11, G.A.R., of Newark, N.J., to Robt. E. Lee Camp, No. 1, Confederate Veterans and Phil. Kearny Post, No. 10, G.A.R., of Richmond, Va.* (Newark, N.J.: M. H. Neuhut, Printer, 1884), 32.

65. *Richmond (Va.) Daily Dispatch* quoted in ibid., 35, 36, 36–37.

66. Ibid., 9, 10–11.

67. Ibid., 22–25, 28, 92, 96–97.

68. New Jersey State Commission, *Report of State Commission for Erection of Monument to Ninth New Jersey Volunteers at New Berne, North Carolina* ([Philadelphia]: State Commission [J. C. Winston Co.], 1905), 11, 35, 48–53, 54–56, 89–93.

69. Reardon, *Pickett's Charge*, 91–93.

70. Ibid., 93–97.

71. Ibid., 97–105.

72. Kathleen R. Georg, Research Notes, "50th Anniversary and Grand Reunion 1913," Vertical Files, file 11–61, GNMP Library, 109–112.

73. *Confederate Veteran* 21, no. 6 (June 1913): 280. Reardon gives the numbers attending the reunion as approximately 35,000 Union veterans and "only a few more than 7,000" Confederates (*Pickett's Charge*, 188). Unrau has higher numbers—44,713 and 8,694, respectively (*Administrative History*, 110). Both estimates yield a proportion of Confederate veterans in the range 16.2–16.6 percent.

74. "Refusal of Forrest Camp in G.A.R. Parade," *Confederate Veteran* 21, no. 10 (October 1913): 468.

75. Willard D. Newbill, *General Report of the National Memorial Celebration and Peace Jubilee (National Memorial Reunion)* (Washington, D.C.: U.S. Government Printing Office, 1917), 3, 20, 21, 23.

76. Ibid., 3, 4, 16, 29–30. Even though no events were scheduled at the national cemetery, Newbill does note an "extreme desire on the part of the veterans to visit all parts of the battle field and the National Cemetery" (12).

77. *Confederate Veteran* 5, no. 4 (April 1897): 180; "The Reunion," *Confederate Veteran* 5, no. 7 (July 1897): 338; *Confederate Veteran* 21, no. 7 (July 1913): 332–33.

78. Billingsley, *From the Flag to the Cross*, 419.

Chapter 6

1. McKinley quoted in Charles S. Olcott, *The Life of William McKinley*, 2 vols. (Boston: Houghton Mifflin, 1916), 1: 226. See also Margaret Leech, *In the Days of McKinley* (New York: Harper & Bros., 1959), 348–49.

2. *Confederate Veteran* 7, no. 2 (February 1899): 76. Another, more positive Southern reception is detailed in "National Dignity and Confederate Honor," *Confederate Veteran* 6, no. 12 (December 1898): 546.

3. Confederate Dead Arlington Monument, Correspondence, 1901–1905, Box 14, Samuel E. Lewis Papers, Virginia Historical Society, Richmond, Va. (hereafter Lewis Papers).

4. Charles Broadway Rouss Camp, No. 1191, U.C.V., document set, 9 April 1901, Box 10—Reburial at Arlington Cemetery, Lewis Papers.

5. Petition, Charles Broadway Rouss Camp, No. 1191, U.C.V., document set, 9 April 1901, to William McKinley; and Samuel E. Lewis to Marcus J. Wright, 24 March 1900, Box 10—Reburial at Arlington Cemetery, Lewis Papers.

6. [Samuel E. Lewis] to Julian G. Moore, 15 April 1901, Box 10—Reburial at Arlington Cemetery, Lewis Papers (emphasis in original).

7. Janet H. W. Randolph to [John B.?] Gordon, 15 September 1900, and Janet H. W. Randolph to [?], 27 September 1900, extract, Box 10—Reburial at Arlington Cemetery, Lewis Papers.

8. [Samuel E. Lewis] to Julian G. Moore, 15 April 1901, Box 10—Reburial at Arlington Cemetery, Lewis Papers.

9. Peters, *Arlington National Cemetery*, 250–53.

10. *Report of the Re-Burial of the Confederate Dead in Arlington Cemetery* (Washington, D.C.: Judd & Detweiler, 1901), 20; see generally 36–41, 44.

11. Lee's resolution quoted in Samuel E. Lewis, "The Locations and Condition of the Graves of the Confederate Soldiers Who Died in Federal Prisons and Military Hospitals and Were Buried Near Their Places of Confinement," in U.S. Congress, Senate, *Marking the Graves of the Soldiers of the Confederate Army and Navy*, 57th Cong., 2d sess., 1903, S. Rept. 2589, serial 4411, 11; [Samuel E. Lewis?] to Stephen D. Lee, April 14, 1902, Box 10—Reburial at Arlington Cemetery, Lewis Papers (emphasis added). The concern for the graves of Confederates had been raised before at UCV conventions (see, for example, *Confederate Veteran* 5, no. 2 [February 1897]: 71).

12. "Graves of Confederates North," *Confederate Veteran* 6, no. 4 (April 1898): 147.

13. The description of Foraker is Marcus J. Wright's, quoted in U.S. Congress, Senate, *Marking the Graves*, 5–6.

14. U.S. Congress, *Congressional Record*, 58th Cong., 2d sess., 25 January 1906, 38, pt. 2: 1109–10.

15. U.S. Congress, *Congressional Record*, 59th Cong., 1st sess., 10 January 1906, 40, pt. 1: 900.

16. Both William Elliot and William Oates died while holding the office of commissioner. Despite his best efforts, Samuel E. Lewis failed to be named to the post during the commission's original term, which expired under James H. Berry, the commission's work incomplete. Lewis achieved his goal only when, after a lapse of two years, the commission was reestablished (telegram [Samuel E. Lewis] to Mrs. W. J. Behan, 16 March 1906; W. A. Milton to [Samuel E. Lewis], 14 December 1907; and Joseph B. Foraker to [Samuel E. Lewis], 14 December 1907, all in Box 12, Lewis Papers; Robert H. Gruber, introduction to U.S. War Department, *Register of Confederate Soldiers, Sailors, and Citizens*, 2).

17. Samuel E. Lewis to W. A. Milton, 31 July 1905, draft, Box 12, Lewis Papers (emphasis in original).

18. Samuel E. Lewis to William Loeb, May 1904, Box 12, Lewis Papers.

19. Information gathered from U.S. War Department, *Register of Confederate Soldiers, Sailors, and Citizens,* passim; and J. A. T. Hull to Theodore Roosevelt, 6 May 1904, Box 12, Lewis Papers.

20. James H. Berry, Commissioner, to R. Lichenstein, 7 February 1912, Book 7, 404–405; see also [William Elliott,] Commissioner, to the Secretary of War, 4 November 1907, Book 2, 48; and James H. Berry, Commissioner, to H. P. Bottoms, 28 July 1911, Book 7, 23; all in Record Group 92, Records of the Quartermaster General, Records of the Cemeterial Commissions, 1893–1916, Office of the Commissioner for Marking Graves of Confederate Dead, Confederate Correspondence File, 1908–1916, Entry 693, NARA.

21. James Berry to Mrs. W. K. Beard, n.d., Book 7, 181–82, and James Berry to James Nicoll, 22 September 1911, Book 7, 141, Record Group 92, Records of the Quartermaster General, Records of the Cemeterial Commissions, 1893–1916, Office of the Commissioner for Marking Graves of Confederate Dead, Confederate Correspondence File, 1908–1916, Entry 693, NARA.

22. Hattie Lou Winslow and Joseph J. R. Moore, "Camp Morton, 1861–1865: Indianapolis Prison Camp," *Indiana Historical Society Publications* 13, no. 3 (1940): 374; *Confederate Veteran* 2, no. 1 (January 1894): 18.

23. Winslow and Moore, "Camp Morton," 376. There is some disagreement as to when the two rows of graves were removed and where they were relocated. A memorandum dictated by William Elliott states that it was not the Vandalia Railroad, but the Terre Haute & Indianapolis Railroad that exchanged not a nearby landholding, but plots in the town's Greenwood Cemetery. But Winslow and Moore state that Elliott himself identified the nearby plot of land "forty-five feet wide by two hundred feet long" as the site of the reinterments in 1870, even going so far as to have that ground "enclosed by an iron fence" and marked with a memorial in 1912. (See Memorandum, William Elliott, Commissioner, "Construction of the Act of March 9, 1906," Record Group 92, Records of the Office of the Quartermaster General, Correspondence relating to Cemeteries for Confederate Soldiers and Sailors who died as Prisoners of War in Northern Prisons, 1907–1912, Camp Douglas, Ill.—Johnson Island, Ohio, Box 1, NM-81, E.698, NARA; and Winslow and Moore, "Camp Morton," 374.) Later, Senator Simeon D. Fess reported that the removal took place during the excavation of the sewer and made no mention of the earlier expansion of the railroad facilities. (See U.S. Congress, Senate, "Removal of Confederate Monuments," 70th Cong., 1st sess., 1928, S. Rept. 907, serial 8831.)

24. U.S. War Department, *Register of Confederate Soldiers, Sailors, and Citizens,* 253–93.

25. U.S. War Department, Quartermaster's Department, *Regulations for the Government of National Cemeteries* (Washington, D.C.: U.S. Government Printing Office, 1911).

26. U.S. War Department, *National Cemetery Regulations* (Washington, D.C.: U.S. Government Printing Office, 1931), 5–6.

27. See Mrs. Arthur E. Shaw to Superintendent of Gettysburg Cemetery, 25 August 1933 James R. McConaghie to Shaw, 30 August 1933 and Shaw to McConaghie, 6 September 1933, all in "Battlefield Burial Sites," Vertical Files, file 7–15, GNMP Library.

28. James R. McConaghie to Mrs. A. M. Grimsley, 7 September 1933, and Mrs. Gustave Mertins to McConaghie, 20 September 1933, in "Battlefield Burial Sites," Vertical Files, file 7–15, GNMP Library. For other instances of found bodies, see *Gettysburg (Pa.) Star and Sentinel,* 27 May 1890 and 18 November 1890, clippings, and William Robbins to Col. Nicholson, 23 September 1899, all in "Soldier's Remains Found Long after the Battle and Reinterments," Vertical Files, file 7–25a, GNMP Library.

29. Mrs. Gustave Mertins to James R. McConaghie, 13 March 1934, and McConaghie to Senator Hugo L. Black, 16 March 1934, "Battlefield Burial Sites," Vertical Files, file 7–15, GNMP Library.

30. James R. McConaghie to Senator Hugo L. Black, 16 March 1934; McConaghie to John K. Beckenbaugh, 12 April 1934 and McConaghie to Director, National Park Service, Department of the Interior, 17 April 1934, in "Battlefield Burial Sites," Vertical Files, file 7–15, GNMP Library.

31. Frank Tilberg to Director, National Park Service, 18 June 1938 McConaghie to Beckenbaugh, 22 November 1938, and Memorandum, McConaghie to Director, National Park Service, 29 December 1938, all in "Battlefield Burial Sites," Vertical Files, file 7–15, GNMP Library.

32. E. E. Davis to Mrs. Will J. Fogarty, 7 October 1929, copy, "Battlefield Burial Sites," Vertical Files, file 7–15, GNMP Library.

33. *New York Times,* 2 July 1997, A10.

34. Bruce Catton, "The End of the Centennial," in *A Portion of That Field: The Centennial of the Burial of Lincoln* (Urbana: University of Illinois Press, 1967), 81–93, 84.

35. *Griffin v. Department of Veterans Affairs,* 129 F. Supp. 2d 832 (D. Md. 2001).

36. 38 U.S.C. sec. 2403©.

37. See *Griffin v. Department of Veterans Affairs,* 274 F.3d 818 (4th Cir. 2001), 5–6; and *Griffin v. Secretary of Veterans Affairs* 228 F.3d 1309 (Fed. Cir. 2002).

38. Allan Nevins, "The Glorious and the Terrible," in *Myth and the American Experience,* ed. Nicholas Cords and Patrick Gerster (New York: Glencoe, 1973), 2: 354–65, 365.

Bibliography

Sources of the Epigraphs

[Introduction]. Herman Melville. *Moby-Dick.* In Herman Melville, *Redburn, White-Jacket, Moby-Dick,* 832. New York: Library of America, Literary Classics of the United States, 1983.

[Chapter 1]. Herman Melville. "The Armies of the Wilderness." In Herman Melville, *Battle-Pieces and Aspects of the War: Civil War Poems,* 93–104, quotes from 101, 103. New Introduction by Lee Rust Brown. New York: DaCapo Press, 1995.

[Chapter 2]. Walt Whitman. "When Lilacs Last in the Dooryard Bloom'd." In Walt Whitman, *Complete Poetry and Collected Prose,* 460. New York: Library of America, Literary Classics of the United States, 1982.

[Chapter 3]. Theodore O'Hara. "The Bivouac of the Dead." In *The Blue and The Gray: The Best Poems of the Civil War,* 221–23. Edited by Claudius Meade Capps. 1943. Reprint, Freeport, N.Y.: Books for Libraries Press, 1969.

[Chapter 4]. Henry Timrod. "Ode." In *The Collected Poems of Henry Timrod,* 129–30. Edited by Edd Winfield Parks and Aileen Wells Parks. Athens: University of Georgia Press, 1965.

[Chapter 5]. Sarah Shuften, "Ethiopia's Dead." *The Colored American,* 30 December 1865, 4.

[Chapter 6]. Proverbs, 21: 16. King James Version of the Bible.

Archival Collections

"Battlefield Burial Sites." Vertical Files, file 7–15. Gettysburg National Military Park Library, Gettysburg, Pa.

Bissell, Margaret. "Account of Margaret Bissell." Vertical Files, file 8–9b. Gettysburg National Military Park Library, Gettysburg, Pa.

Boteler, Alexander R. Papers. Clippings, 1852–1933. Special Collections, Perkins Library, Duke University, Durham, N.C.

Broadhead, Sarah. "Diary of a Lady of Gettysburg, Pennsylvania." "Sarah Broadhead Account, Chambersburg Street." Vertical Files, file 8–6. Gettysburg National Military Park Library, Gettysburg, Pa.

Cain and Cornelius Papers. Special Collections, Perkins Library, Duke University, Durham, N.C.

"Confederate Reinterments." Vertical Files, file 7–17. Gettysburg National Military Park Library, Gettysburg, Pa.

Confederate Veteran Papers. Special Collections, Perkins Library, Duke University, Durham, N.C.

Bibliography

Davis, Jefferson. Jefferson Davis Collection, Eleanor S. Brockenbrough Library, Museum of the Confederacy, Richmond, Va.

Dimon, Theodore. "From Auburn to Antietam: The Civil War Journal of a Battlefield Surgeon Who Served with the Army of the Potomac, 1861–1863." "Establishment of the National Cemetery." Vertical Files, file 10–4. Gettysburg National Military Park Library, Gettysburg, Pa.

Ellyson, J. Taylor. Papers. Eleanor S. Brockenbrough Library, Museum of the Confederacy, Richmond, Va.

Georg, Kathleen R. "Gettysburg—a Happy and Patriotic Conception." Gettysburg National Military Park Library, Gettysburg, Pa.

———. Research Notes. "50th Anniversary and Grand Reunion 1913." Vertical Files, file 11–61. Gettysburg National Military Park Library, Gettysburg, Pa.

———. Research Notes from the Minutes of the Proceedings of the Evergreen Cemetery. "Evergreen (Citizen's) Cemetery." Vertical Files, file 9–G8, Gettysburg National Military Park Library, Gettysburg, Pa.

———. "'This Grand National Enterprise': The Origins of Gettysburg's National Cemetery and Gettysburg Battlefield Memorial Association." Gettysburg National Military Park Library, Gettysburg, Pa.

"Hollinger Family Account." Vertical Files, file 8–10. Gettysburg National Military Park Library, Gettysburg, Pa.

Hough, Daniel. Daniel Hough Papers. Fort Sumter National Monument, Fort Sumter Island, S.C.

Lewis, Samuel E. Papers. Virginia Historical Society, Richmond, Va.

McGavock Confederate Cemetery Record Book, 1864–1900. Special Collections, Perkins Library, Duke University, Durham, N.C.

"Miscellaneous Civilian Accounts." Vertical Files, file 8–3. Gettysburg National Military Park Library, Gettysburg, Pa.

Pamphlet Collection. Heritage Room, A. K. Smiley Library, Redlands, Calif.

Record Group 92. Records of the Office of the Quartermaster General. Correspondence Relating to Cemeteries for Confederate Soldiers and Sailors Who Died as Prisoners of War in Northern Prisons, 1907–1912. Camp Douglas, Ill.—Johnson Island, Ohio, NM-81. Entry 698. National Archives and Records Administration, Washington, D.C.

———. Quartermaster General Orders and Circulars and Blank Forms Relating to National Cemeteries, 1874–1905. Entry 590. National Archives and Records Adminstration, Washington, D.C.

———. Records of the Cemeterial Commissions, 1893–1916, Office of the Commissioner for Marking Graves of Confederate Dead. Confederate Correspondence File, 1908–1916. 8 vols. Entry 693. National Archives and Records Administration, Washington, D.C.

———. Records Relating to Functions: Cemeterial, 1828–1929. Entry 576. National Archives and Records Administration, Washington, D.C.

———. Textual Records of the Office of the Quartermaster General—Cemeterial, 1828–1929. Central Records, and Correspondence and Issuances, 1864–1923. Entry 567. National Archives and Records Administration, Washington, D.C.

Record Group 94. Records of the Adjutant General's Office, 1780s–1917. Ser. 12, Letters Received, 1805–1889. National Archives and Records Administration, Washington, D.C.

———. Ser. 366, Letters Received Relating to Recruiting, 1863–1868, Colored Troops Division, 1863–1889, National Archives and Records Administration, Washington, D.C.

Record Group 393. Records of U.S. Army Continental Commands. Pt. 2, 16th Army Corps. Letters Received, Ser. 391. National Archives and Records Administration, Washington, D.C.

———. Pt. 4, Military Governor of Alexandria[, Va.]. Letters Received, Ser. 391. National Archives and Records Administration, Washington, D.C.

Rutherford, Mildred Lewis. *Origin of Ladies' Memorial Association*. Vol. 41 of *Historical Records of the United Daughters of the Confederacy*. Mildred Lewis Rutherford Volumes. Eleanor S. Brockenbrough Library, Museum of the Confederacy, Richmond, Va. This work is unpaginated.

"Soldier's Remains Found Long after the Battle and Reinterments." Vertical Files, file 7–25a. Gettysburg National Military Park Library, Gettysburg, Pa.

Thorn, Elizabeth. "Elizabeth Thorn Account." "Evergreen Cemetery Gate House." Vertical Files, file 8–15. Gettysburg National Military Park Library, Gettysburg, Pa.

U.S. Army. Quartermaster's Department. Papers, 1865–1868. Folder 2, "Department of the Savannah." Manuscript Division, Library of Congress, Washington, D.C.

"US Army Quartermaster Reports after the Battle of Gettysburg (Clean-Up)." Vertical Files, file 7–18. Gettysburg National Military Park Library, Gettysburg, Pa.

Wills, John C. "Reminiscences of the Three Days Battle of Gettysburg at the 'Globe Hotel.'" "Charles Wills Account (Globe Inn)." Vertical Files, file 8–17. Gettysburg National Military Park Library, Gettysburg, Pa.

Published Primary Sources

Abott, Abott A. *The Assassination and Death of Abraham Lincoln, President of the United States, at Washington, on the 14th of April, 1865.* New York: American News Co., 1865.

Abbot, Francis E. "The Martyr of Liberty: A Sermon Preached in the Unitarian Church, Dover, N.H., on Sunday, April 16, 1865." In *Lincolniana 1865*, 1–7.

Address at the Decoration of the Graves of the Confederate Dead, in the Cemetery, Near Lexington, Ky., on May 26, 1868. Lexington, Ky.: Observer & Reporter Print, 1869.

The Army Reunion: With Reports of the Meetings of the Societies of the Army of the Cumberland; the Army of the Tennessee; the Army of the Ohio; and the Army of Georgia. December 15 and 16, 1868. Chicago: S. C. Griggs & Co., 1869.

Atkinson, John W. "Col. Ulric Dahlgren, the Defeated Raider." *Southern Historical Society Papers* 37 (1909): 351–53.

Averell, William W. "With the Cavalry on the Peninsula." In *Battles and Leaders 1887–1888/1991*, 2: 429–33.

Badger, Henry. *The Humble Conqueror: A Discourse Commemorative to the Life and Services of Abraham Lincoln.* Boston: n.p., 1865.

Bibliography

Baltimore City Council. *Proceedings of the City Council of Baltimore, in Relation to the Death of Abraham Lincoln, Late President of the United States.* Baltimore: n.p., 1865.

Barnes, Albert. *The State of the Country: A Discourse Delivered . . .* Philadelphia: Henry B. Ashmead, 1865.

Bartlett, John Russell. *The Soldiers' National Cemetery at Gettysburg.* Providence, R.I.: Providence Press Co., 1874.

The Battle of Fort Sumter and First Victory of the Southern Troops. Charleston, S.C.: Evans & Cogswell, 1861.

Battles and Leaders of the Civil War. 4 vols. 1887–1888. Reprint, Secaucus, N.J.: Castle, 1991.

Belden, David. *Obsequies of President Lincoln: An Oration Delivered in Nevada City in 1865.* Marysville, Calif.: Marysville Herald Press, [1865?].

Benson, C. H. *"Yank" and "Reb": A History of a Fraternal Visit Paid by Lincoln Post, No. 11, G.A.R., of Newark, N.J., to Robt. E. Lee Camp, No. 1, Confederate Veterans and Phil. Kearny Post, No. 10, G.A.R., of Richmond, Va.* Newark, N.J.: M. H. Neuhut, Printer, 1884.

Billingsley, A. S. *From the Flag to the Cross; or, Scenes and Incidents of Christianity in the War.* Philadelphia: New-World Publishing Co., 1872.

Boston City Council. *A Memorial of Abraham Lincoln, Late President of the United States.* Boston: City Council, 1865.

"Brady's Photographs: Pictures of the Dead at Antietam." *New York Times,* 20 October 1862, 5.

Brakeman, N. L. *A Great Man Fallen: A Sermon Preached in the Methodist Church, Baton Rouge, Louisiana, April 23, 1865 . . .* Baton Rouge: New Orleans Times, Book and Job Office, 1865.

Brigham, Charles E. "The National Bereavement: A Discourse Delivered at the First Congregational Church, Taunton, Mass., on Sunday Morning, April 16, 1865." In *Lincolniana 1865,* 8–20.

Briggs, George W. *Eulogy on Abraham Lincoln, by George W. Briggs, D.D., June 1, 1865, with the Proceedings of the City Council on the Death of the President.* Salem, Mass.: George W. Pease, 1865.

Brooks, Phillips. *The Life and Death of Abraham Lincoln: A Sermon Preached at the Church of the Holy Trinity, Philadelphia, Sunday Morning, April 23, 1865.* Philadelphia: Henry B. Ashmead, 1865.

Bullock, Alexander H. *Abraham Lincoln: The Just Magistrate, the Representative Statesman, the Practical Philanthropist.* Worcester, [Mass.?]: Charles Hamilton, 1865.

Burial Ceremonies of Confederate Dead. Oration: By A. Y. P. Garnett, M.D.; Ode: By Rt. Rev. Wm. Pinkney. December 11, 1874. Washington: S. & R. O. Polkinhorn, 1875.

Burrows, John L. *Palliative and Prejudiced Judgements Condemned: A Discourse Delivered in the First Christian Church, Richmond, Va., June 1, 1865 ... Together with an Extract from a Sermon, Preached on Sunday, April 23, 1865.* Richmond: n.p., 1865.

Butler, Clement M. *Funeral Address on the Death of Abraham Lincoln, Delivered in the Church of the Covenant, April 19, 1865.* Philadelphia: Henry B. Ashmead, 1865.

[Campbell, J. A. P.]. "The Lost Cause: A Masterly Vindication of It by Judge J. A. P. Campbell." *Southern Historical Society Papers* 16 (1888): 232–45. (Originally delivered at Canton, [Ga.?], on Memorial Day, 1 May 1874.)

Ceremonies Connected with the Inauguration of the Mausoleum and the Unveiling of the Recumbent Figure of General Robert Edward Lee, at Washington and Lee University, Lexington, Va., June 28, 1883. Richmond, Va.: West, Johnson & Co., 1883.

Ceremonies in Augusta, Georgia, Laying the Corner Stone of the Confederate Monument; with Oration by Gen. Clement A. Evans, April 26, 1875, and the Unveiling and Dedication of the Monument, with Oration by Col. Charles C. Jones, Jr., October 31, 1878. Augusta, Ga.: Chronicle and Constitutionalist Job Printing Est., 1878.

Chadwick, John. "Abraham Lincoln: A Sermon Preached to His Society in Brooklyn, N.Y." In *Lincolniana* 1865, 36–51.

Chaffin, William Ladd. *The President's Death and Its Lessons: A Discourse on Sunday Morning, April 23d, 1865, before the Second Unitarian Society of Philadelphia.* Philadelphia: King & Baird, Printers, 1865.

Coggeshall, William T. *Lincoln Memorial: The Journeys of Abraham Lincoln; from Springfield to Washington, 1861, as President Elect; and from Washington to Springfield, 1865, as President Martyred....* Columbus: Ohio State Journal, 1865.

Colston, R. E. "Address of R. E. Colston." *Southern Historical Society Papers* 21 (1893): 38–49. (Originally delivered at Wilmington, N.C., 10 May 1870.)

Commemorative Proceedings of the Atheneum Club, on the Death of Abraham Lincoln, President of the United States, April, 1865. New York: C. S. Westcott & Co., 1865.

Commonwealth of Massachusetts Senate. "Proceedings of Meetings of the Board of Trustees of the Antietam National Cemetery." No. 11. [Boston?]: n.p., 1869.

"The Conduct of the War: Ghoulism of the Rebels." *Chicago Tribune*, 5 May 1862, 2.

Conwell, Russell H. *Magnolia Journey: A Union Veteran Revisits the Former Confederate States.* Edited by Joseph C. Carter. University: University of Alabama Press, 1974.

Corwin, E. T. "Death of President Lincoln: A Discourse Delivered at Millstone, N.J., on Sunday Morning, April 16, 1865." In *Lincolniana* 1865, 52–62.

Couch, Darius N. "Sumner's 'Right Grand Division.'" In *Battles and Leaders* 1887–1888/1991, 3: 105–20.

Crane, Cephas B. *Sermon on the Occasion of the Death of Abraham Lincoln.* Hartford, Conn.: Press of Case, Lockwood, & Co., 1865.

Crawford, Samuel Wylie. *The Genesis of the Civil War: The Story of Sumter, 1860–1861.* New York: Charles L. Webster & Co., 1887.

Crocker, Samuel L. *Eulogy upon the Character and Services of Abraham Lincoln, Late President of the United States.* Boston: John Wilson & Son, 1865.

Crozier, Hiram P. *The Nation's Loss: A Discourse upon the Life, Services, and Death of Abraham Lincoln, Late President of the United States.* New York: John A. Gray & Green, 1866.

Cunningham, S. A. "The Carnage at Franklin, Tennessee, Next to That of the Crater." *Southern Historical Society Papers* 24 (1896): 189–92.

Dahlgren, [John A.]. *Memoir of Ulric Dahlgren.* Philadelphia: J. B. Lippincott & Co., 1872.

Bibliography

Damon, Samuel Cherney. *Damon's Lincoln Sermon: A Sermon Preached in Honolulu, Hawaii, 14 May 1865.* New York: William M. Clemens, 1917.

Davidson, Nora Fontaine M., comp. *Cullings from the Confederacy: A Collection of Southern Poems, Original and Others, Popular during the War between the States, and Incidents and Facts Worth Recalling. 1862–1866. Including the Doggerel of the Camp, as Well as Tender Tribute to the Dead.* Washington, D.C.: Rufus H. Darby Printing Co., 1903.

Davis, Robert Stewart. "Three Months around Charleston Bar; or, The Great Siege as We Saw It." *United States Service Magazine* 1, no. 2 (February 1864): 169–79; no. 3 (March 1864): 273–83.

Day, P. B. *A Memorial Discourse on the Character of Abraham Lincoln.* Concord, [Mass.?]: McFarland & Jenks, 1865.

Deming, Henry. *Eulogy of Abraham Lincoln. . . .* Hartford, Conn.: A. N. Clark & Co., 1865.

A Descriptive List of the Burial Places of the Remains of Confederate Soldiers, Who Fell in the Battles of Antietam, South Mountain, Monocacy, and Other Points in Washington and Frederick Counties, in the State of Maryland. Hagerstown, Md.: "Free Press," n.d.

Doubleday, Abner. *Reminiscences of Forts Sumter and Moultrie in 1860–'61.* N.Y.: Harper & Bros., 1876.

———. "From Moultrie to Sumter." In *Battles and Leaders* 1887–1888/1991, 1: 40–49.

[Douglass, Frederick.] *Oration by Frederick Douglass, Delivered on the Occasion of the Unveiling of the Freedmen's Monument in Memory of Abraham Lincoln.* Washington, D.C.: Gibson Bros., 1876.

Duane, Richard B. *A Sermon Preached in Saint John's Church, Providence, on Wednesday, April 19, 1865.* Providence, [N.H.?]: H. H. Thomas & Co., 1865.

Dutton, O. H. "Sermon: Preached in the Second Congregational Church, Holyoke, Ma., Wednesday, 19th." In *Lincolniana* 1865, 76–88.

Everson, Guy R., and Edward H. Simpson Jr., eds. *Far, Far from Home: The Wartime Letters of Dick and Tally Simpson, 3rd South Carolina Volunteers.* New York: Oxford University Press, 1994.

Foraker, Joseph B. *Address of Senator Foraker at Arlington, Memorial Day, May 30, 1905.* N.p., [1905?].

Gillmore, Quincy A. "The Army before Charleston in 1863." In *Battles and Leaders* 1887–1888/1991, 4: 56–60.

Gooding, James Henry. *On the Altar of Freedom: A Black Soldier's Civil War Letters from the Front.* Edited by Virginia M. Adams. Amherst: University of Massachusetts Press, 1991.

Gould, Benjamin Apthorp, comp. *Investigations in the Military and Anthropological Statistics of American Soldiers.* New York: U.S. Sanitary Commission/Hurd & Houghton, 1869.

Grant, Ulysses S. *Ulysses S. Grant: Memoirs and Selected Letters.* New York: Library of America, 1990.

Hall, Gordon. *President Lincoln's Death: Its Voice to the People.* Northampton, Mass.: Trumbal & Gere, Printers, 1865.

Haskell, Franklin Aretas. *Haskell of Gettysburg: His Life and Civil War Papers.* Edited by

Frank L. Byrne and Andrew T. Weaver. Madison: State Historical Society of Wisconsin, 1970.

Hemenway, S. "Observations on Scurvy, and Its Causes among U.S. Colored Troops of the 25th Army Corps, during Spring and Summer of 1865." *Chicago Medical Examiner* 7 (October 1866): 582–86.

Higginson, T[homas] W[entworth]. "Regular and Volunteer Officers." *Atlantic Monthly* 14 (September 1864): 348–57.

History of the Antietam National Cemetery, Including a Descriptive List of All the Loyal Soldiers Buried Therein. Baltimore: John W. Woods, Steam Printer, 1869.

A History of the Origin of Memorial Day as Adopted by the Ladies' Memorial Association of Columbus, Georgia. Columbus, Ga.: Thos. Gilbert, 1898.

Indiana Shiloh National Park Commission. *Indiana at Shiloh: Report of the Commission.* Indianapolis: Indiana Shiloh National Park Commission, 1904.

[Jones, Charles C., Jr.] *Funeral Oration Pronounced in the Opera House in Augusta, Georgia, December 11th, 1889, upon the Occasion of the Memorial Services in Honor of President Jefferson Davis, by Col. Charles C. Jones, Jr.* Augusta, Ga.: Chronicle Printing, 1889.

Jones, Mrs. Garland. "History of the Ladies' Memorial Association, and Confederate Cemetery" (1893). In *History of the Wake County Ladies Memorial Association,* by [Charlotte B. G. Williams]. Raleigh, N.C.: n.p., 1938.

Jones, J. Wm., ed. *The Army of Northern Virginia Memorial Volume.* Richmond, Va.: J. W. Randolph & English, 1880.

———. *The Davis Memorial Volume; or, Our Dead President, Jefferson Davis, and the World's Tribute to His Memory.* Richmond, Va.: B. F. Johnson & Co., 1890.

Kershaw, John. "Address." In *Memorial Day, May 10th, 1893.* [Charleston, S.C.?]: n.p., n.d.

Ladies' Hollywood Memorial Association. *Our Confederate Dead.* Richmond, Va.: Whittet & Shepperson, 1896.

Lambert, William H. *Address before Post No. 2, Dep't of Penn'a, Grand Army of the Republic.* Philadelphia: Culbertson & Bache, 1879.

Leale, Charles A. *Lincoln's Last Hours: Address Delivered before the Commandery of the State of New York Military Order of the Loyal Legion of the United States.* [New York?]: n.p., 1909.

Libby Prison War Museum Association. *Libby Prison War Museum Catalogue and Program.* Chicago: Libby Prison War Museum Association, [1889].

———. *A Trip through the Libby Prison War Museum, Chicago.* [Chicago?]: n.p., 1893.

Lincoln, Abraham. *The Collected Works of Abraham Lincoln.* Edited by Roy P. Basler. 9 vols. New Brunswick, N.J.: Rutgers University Press, 1953.

Lincolniana. Boston: William V. Spencer, 1865.

Lockett, S. H. "The Defense of Vicksburg." In *Battles and Leaders* 1887–1888/1991, 3: 482–92.

Logan, Mary [Simmerson Cunningham]. *Reminiscences of the Civil War and Reconstruction.* Edited by George Washington Adams. Carbondale: Southern Illinois University Press, 1970.

Bibliography

Longstreet, James. "The Battle of Fredericksburg." In *Battles and Leaders* 1887–1888/1991, 3: 70–85.

Lyle, W. W. *Lights and Shadows of Army Life*. Cincinnati: R. W. Carroll & Co., 1865.

Mason, W. Roy. "Notes of a Confederate Staff-Officer." In *Battles and Leaders* 1887–1888/1991, 3: 100–101.

McClintock, John. *Discourse Delivered on the Day of the Funeral of President Lincoln.* Reported by J. T. Butts. New York: J. M. Bradstreet & Son, 1865.

McCreary, Albertus. "Gettysburg: A Boy's Experience of the Battle." *McClure's Magazine*, July 1909, 243–53.

Meade, George. *Life and Letters of George Gordon Meade*. New York: Charles Scribner's Sons, 1913.

Memorial Day, May 10th, 1875: Address of Col. B. H. Rutledge. Charleston, [S.C.]: A. J. Burke, 1875.

Moore, Frank, ed. *Memorial Ceremonies at the Graves of Our Soldiers, Saturday, May 30, 1868*. Washington, D.C.: Wm. T. Collins, 1869.

———, ed. *The Civil War in Song and Story, 1860–1865*. New York: P. F. Collier, 1889.

"Mortality in Our Army." *United States Service Magazine* 5, no. 6 (June 1866): 568–72.

The Nation Weeping for Its Dead: Observances at Springfield, Massachusetts, on President Lincoln's Funeral Day, Wednesday, April 19, 1865, Including Dr. Holland's Eulogy. Springfield, Mass.: Samuel Bowers & Co., 1865.

Nelson, Henry A. *The Divinely Prepared Ruler, and The Fit End of Treason: Two Discourses Delivered at the First Presbyterian Church, Springfield, Illinois, by Invitation of the Session . . .* Springfield, Ill.: Baker & Phillips, 1865.

New Jersey State Commission. *Report of State Commission for Erection of Monument to Ninth New Jersey Volunteers at New Berne, North Carolina*. Philadelphia: New Jersey State Commission [J. C. Winston Co.], 1905.

New York Citizens' Committee. *Obsequies of Abraham Lincoln in Union Square, New York, 25 April 1865*. New York: Van Nostrand, 1865.

Newbill, Willard D. *General Report of the National Memorial Celebration and Peace Jubilee (National Memorial Reunion)*. Washington, D.C.: U.S. Government Printing Office, 1917.

Order of United American Mechanics. State Council of Pennsylvania. *In Memoriam: Abraham Lincoln, President of the United States*. Philadelphia: Geo. Hawkes Jr., 1865.

Paddock, Wilbur F. *A Great Man Fallen! A Discourse on the Death of Abraham Lincoln*. Philadelphia: Sherman & Co., 1865.

Page, Charles A. *Letters of a War Correspondent*. Boston: L. C. Page & Co., 1899.

Patterson, Adoniram J. *Eulogy on Abraham Lincoln, Delivered in Portsmouth, N.H., April 19, 1865*. Portsmouth, N.H.: C. W. Brewster & Son, 1865.

Pond, George E. "Kilpatrick's and Dahlgren's Raid to Richmond." In *Battles and Leaders* 1887–1888/1991, 4: 95–96.

Pratt, Harry E., comp. *Concerning Mr. Lincoln: In Which Abraham Lincoln Is Pictured as He Appeared to Letter Writers of His Time*. Springfield, Ill.: Abraham Lincoln Association, 1944.

Proceedings of a Meeting of the Board of Trustees of the Antietam National Cemetery, Held at Washington City, Dec. 9, 1869. Hagerstown, Md.: A. G. Boyd, [1869?].

Proceedings of the Trustees of the Antietam National Cemetery at a Special Meeting Held in Washington City, May 6th, 1868. [Hagerstown, Md.?]: n.p., [1868?].

Proceedings of the Trustees of the Antietam National Cemetery at Their Meeting Held in Washington City, December 5th, 1867. Hagerstown, Md.: n.p., 1867.

Providence City Council. *Proceedings of the City Council of Providence on the Death of Abraham Lincoln: With the Oration Delivered before the Municipal Authorities and Citizens, June 1, 1865, by William Binney, Esq.* Providence, R.I.: Knowles, Anthony & Co., 1865.

Record of the Service of the Fifty-fifth Regiment of Massachusetts Volunteer Infantry. 1868. Reprint, Freeport, N.Y.: Books for Libraries, 1971.

Report of the Commissioner of Patents for the Year . . . Washington, D.C.: various printers, various years. *Reports* for the years 1847–1870 have been consulted.

Report of the Re-Burial of the Confederate Dead in Arlington Cemetery. Washington, D.C.: Judd & Detweiler, 1901.

Report of the Select Committee Relative to the Soldiers' National Cemetery ... as Reported to the House of Representatives of the Commonwealth of Pennsylvania, March 31, 1864. Harrisburg, Pa.: Singerly & Myers, 1864.

Rice, Daniel. *The President's Death—Its Import: A Sermon, Preached in the Second Presbyterian Church, Lafayette, Indiana, April 19, 1865.* [Lafayette, Ind.?]: n.p., [1865].

Robins, W. T. "Stuart's Ride around McClellan." In *Battles and Leaders* 1887–1888/1991, 2: 271–75.

Robinson, Charles S. *The Martyred President: A Sermon Preached in the First Presbyterian Church, Brooklyn, N.Y.* New York: John F. Trow, 1865.

Ross, Randal. "Correspondence." *United States Service Magazine* 5, no. 2 (February 1866): 172–77.

Russell, Peter. *Our Great National Reproach, and the Counsel of Ahitophel Turned into Foolishness: Two Sermons Preached in St. James Church, Eckley, Penna., by Rev. Peter Russell, Rector . . .* Philadelphia: King & Baird, Printers, 1865.

Sears, Hiram. *The People's Keepsake; or, Funeral Address on the Death of Abraham Lincoln.* Cincinnati: Poe & Hitchcock, 1865.

Simpson, Matthew. *Funeral Address Delivered at the Burial of President Lincoln, at Springfield, Illinois, May 4, 1865.* New York: Carlton & Porter, 1865.

Smith, Isaac. "In Memory of President Lincoln (1865)." In *Two Memorial Addresses Delivered on Foxboro Common.* Foxboro, Mass.: The Print Shop Inc., 1923.

Spear, Samuel T. *The Punishment of Treason: A Discourse Preached April 23d, 1865, in the South Presbyterian Church, of Brooklyn.* Brooklyn, N.Y.: "The Union" Steam Presses, 1865.

The Statutes at Large, Treaties, and Proclamations of the United States of America, from December 5, 1859 to March 3, 1863. Edited by George P. Sanger. Vol. 12. Boston: Little, Brown, 1863.

The Statutes at Large, Treaties, and Proclamations of the United States of America, from

December 1865 to March 1867. Edited by George P. Sanger. Vol. 14. Boston: Little, Brown, 1868.

Stone, Andrew L. *A Discourse Occasioned by the Death of Abraham Lincoln.* Boston: J. K. Wiggin, 1865.

Storrs, Richard S. *An Oration Commemorative of President Abraham Lincoln: Delivered at Brooklyn, N.Y., June 1, 1865.* Brooklyn, N.Y.: War Fund Committee, 1865.

Stratton, Jos. B. "President Lincoln's Death: A Sermon Delivered in the First Presbyterian Church, Natchez, Miss., Sunday April 23, 1865." In *Lincolniana* 1865, 186–203.

Strother, David Hunter. *A Virginia Yankee in the Civil War: The Diaries of David Hunter Strother.* Edited by Cecil D. Eby Jr. Chapel Hill: University of North Carolina Press, 1961.

Sutphen, Morris C. *Discourse on the Occasion of the Death of Abraham Lincoln.* Philadelphia: Jas. B. Rogers, 1865.

Swain, Leonard Swain. *A Nation's Sorrow.* Providence, [N.H.?]: n.p., [1865].

Tautphoeus, Baroness [Jemima Montgomery, Freifrau von]. *The Initials: A Story of Modern Life.* 2 vols. 1850. Reprint, New York: G. P. Putnam's Sons, 1892.

Thomas, Arthur G. *Our National Unity Perfected in the Martyrdom of the President: A Discourse Delivered in the Chapel of the Filbert Street U.S. General Hospital, on the Day of the Obsequies at Washington . . .* Philadelphia: Smith, English & Co., 1865.

Thompson, John R. "The Burial of Latane." In *Bugle-Echoes: A Collection of the Poetry of the Civil War* [ed. Francis Fisher Browne], 114–16. New York: Frederick A. Stokes & Bro., 1890.

Townsend, E[dward] D[avis]. *Anecdotes of the Civil War in the United States.* New York: Appleton & Co., 1884.

Trowbridge, J. T. "The Field of Gettysburg." *Atlantic Monthly* 16 (November 1865): 616–24.

Tucker, J. T. *A Discourse in Memory of Our Late President.* Holliston, Mass.: Plimpton & Clark, 1865.

Turney, Peter. "They Wore the Gray—the Southern Cause Vindicated." *Southern Historical Society Papers* 16 (1888): 319–39.

Twombly, A. S. *The Assassination of Abraham Lincoln; a Discourse Delivered in the State St. Pres. Church . . . 16 April 1865.* Albany, N.Y.: J. Munsell, 1865.

Underwood, John Cox. *Report of the Proceedings Incidental to the Erection and Dedication of the Confederate Monument.* Chicago: Wm. Johnston Printing Co., 1896.

U.S. Army. Quartermaster Corps. *Outline Description of Military Posts and Reservations in the U.S. and Alaska, and of the National Cemeteries.* Washington, D.C.: U.S. Government Printing Office, 1904.

U.S. Congress. *Congressional Globe.* 46 vols. Washington, D.C., 1843–73.

———. *Congressional Record.* Washington, D.C., 1873–.

———. House. *Honors to Rebels.* 39th Cong., 1st sess., 1866. H. Ex. Doc. 141, serial 1267.

———. *Officers and Soldiers Buried Near Atlanta.* 39th Cong., 1st sess., 1866. H. Ex. Doc. 92, serial 1263.

———. Committee on Military Affairs. *National Cemeteries in Tennessee.* 39th Cong., 1st sess., 1866. H. Misc. Doc. 127, serial 1271.

———. "J. P. L. Strong and Others." 40th Cong., 2d sess., 1868. H. Rept. 61, serial 1358.

———. Subcommittee on Army Legislation. *A Hearing on H.R. 27293, a Bill to Extend the Limits of Shiloh National Military Park.* Washington, D.C.: U.S. Government Printing Office, 1911.

———. Senate. "Letter of the Secretary of War Communicating . . . the Report of the Inspector of the National Cemeteries of the United States for 1869." 41st Cong., 2d sess., 1870. S. Ex. Doc. 62, serial 1406.

———. "Letter of the Secretary of War Communicating ... the Report of the Inspector of the National Cemeteries of the United States for 1870 and 1871." 42d Cong., 2d sess., 1872. S. Ex. Doc. 79, serial 1479.

———. "Letter of the Secretary of War Communicating ... the Report of the Inspector of the National Cemeteries of the United States for 1874." 43d Cong., 2d sess., 1875. S. Ex. Doc. 28, serial 1629.

———. *Marking the Graves of the Soldiers of the Confederate Army and Navy.* 57th Cong., 2d sess., 1903. S. Rept. 2589, serial 4411.

———. "Removal of Confederate Monuments." 70th Cong., 1st sess., 1928. S. Rept. 907, serial 8831.

———. Joint Committee on the Conduct of the War. *Barbarities of the Rebels.* 37th Cong., 2d sess., 1862. S. Rept. 41, serial 1125.

U.S. Department of the Interior. National Park Service. "Poplar Grove National Cemetery." 9 September 2002. http://www.aqd.nps.gov/synthesis/views/Sites/PETE/History/7_PoplarGrove/PG_History.htm (accessed 18 December 2002).

———. Interagency Resources Division. Lawrence E. Aten et al. *Study of Civil War Sites in the Shenandoah Valley of Virginia, Pursuant to Public Law 101-628.* Washington, D.C.: U.S. Government Printing Office, [1992?].

U.S. War Department. *The War of the Rebellion: A Compilation of the Official Records of the Union and Confederate Armies.* Edited by Robert N. Scott et al. 70 vols. in 128 pts. Washington, D.C.: U.S. Government Printing Office, 1880–1901.

———. *Regulations for the Government of National Cemeteries.* Washington, D.C.: U.S. Government Printing Office, 1911.

———. Office of the Commission for Marking the Graves of Confederate Dead. *Register of Confederate Soldiers, Sailors, and Citizens Who Died in Federal Prisons and Military Hospitals in the North, 1861–1865.* National Archives Microfilm Publications, M918. Washington, D.C.: National Archives and Records Administration, General Services Administration, 1972 (originally 1912).

———. Quartermaster General's Office. *Names of Officers and Soldiers Found on the Battle-Fields of the Wilderness and of Spotsylvania Court House, Va.* Washington, D.C.: U.S. Government Printing Office, 1865.

———. *Statement of the Disposition of Some of the Bodies of Deceased Union Soldiers and Prisoners of War, Whose Remains Have Been Removed to National Cemeteries in the Southern and Western States.* 4 vols. Washington, D.C.: U.S. Government Printing Office, 1868.

———. *Compilation of Laws, Orders, Opinions, Instructions, etc., in Regard to National Military Cemeteries.* Washington, D.C.: U.S. Government Printing Office, 1878.

Bibliography

———. Quartermaster General's Office. *Roll of Honor: Names of Soldiers Who Have Died in Defense of the American Union Interred in the National Cemeteries.* 27 vols. Washington, D.C.: U.S. Government Printing Office, 1865–1871.

———. *National Cemetery Regulations.* Washington, D.C.: U.S. Government Printing Office, 1931.

Valentine, David T. *Obsequies of Abraham Lincoln, in the City of New York, under the Auspices of the Common Council.* New York: Edmund Jones & Co., 1866.

Vincent, Marvin Richardson. *A Sermon on the Assassination of President Lincoln, Delivered in the First Presbyterian Church, Troy, on Sunday Morning April 23, 1865.* Troy, N.Y.: A. W. Scribner, 1865.

Walden, Treadwell. *The National Sacrifice.* Philadelphia: Sherman & Co., 1865.

Welles, Gideon. *Diary of Gideon Welles, Secretary of the Navy under Lincoln and Johnson.* 3 vols. Boston: Houghton Mifflin, 1911.

Whitman, E. B. "Remarks on National Cemeteries—Original Military Division of the Tennessee." In *The Army Reunion: With Reports of the Meetings of the Societies of the Army of the Cumberland; the Army of the Tennessee; the Army of the Ohio; and the Army of Georgia. December 15 and 16, 1868.* Chicago: S. C. Griggs & Co., 1869.

Whitman, Walt. "The Death of Abraham Lincoln." In *Walt Whitman: Complete Poetry and Collected Prose,* ed. Justin Kaplan, 1036–47. New York: Literary Classics of the United States, 1982.

[Williams, Charlotte B. G.] *History of the Wake County Ladies Memorial Association.* Raleigh, N.C.: n.p., 1938.

Wilson, William T. *The Death of President Lincoln: A Sermon Preached in St. Peter's Church, Albany, N.Y., on Wednesday, April 19, 1865.* Albany, N.Y.: Weed, Parsons, & Co., 1865.

Secondary Sources

Anderson, Benedict. *Imagined Communities: Reflections on the Origin and Spread of Nationalism.* Rev. ed. London: Verso, 1991.

Appleby, Joyce. *Capitalism and a New Social Order: The Republican Vision of the 1790s.* New York: New York University Press, 1984.

Ariès, Phillipe. *Western Attitudes toward Death: From the Middle Ages to the Present.* Translated by Patricia M. Ranum. Baltimore: Johns Hopkins University Press, 1974.

———. *The Hour of Our Death.* Translated by Helen Weaver. New York: Knopf, 1981.

Baker, Jean H. *Mary Todd Lincoln: A Biography.* New York: Norton, 1987.

Ballard, Michael B. "Jeff Davis' Last Ride." *Civil War Times Illustrated* 32, no. 1 (March/April 1993): 32–39.

Barr, John M. "The Tyrannicide's Reception: Responses in Texas to Lincoln's Assassination." *Lincoln Herald* 91, no. 2 (Summer 1989): 58–64.

Barrett, Frank W. Z. *Mourning for Lincoln.* Philadelphia: John C. Winston Co., 1909.

Barton, William E. *Abraham Lincoln and Walt Whitman.* Indianapolis: Bobbs-Merrill, 1928.

Beath, Robert B. *History of the Grand Army of the Republic.* New York: Bryan, Taylor & Co., 1889.

Bensel, Richard Franklin. *Yankee Leviathan: The Origins of Central State Authority in America, 1859–1877.* Cambridge: Cambridge University Press, 1990.

Berlin, Ira, ed. *Freedom: A Documentary History of Emancipation, 1861–1867.* Ser. 2, *The Black Military Experience.* Cambridge: Cambridge University Press, 1982.

Blight, David. *Frederick Douglass' Civil War: Keeping Faith in Jubilee.* Baton Rouge: Louisiana State University Press, 1989.

———. *Race and Reunion: The Civil War in American Memory.* Cambridge, Mass.: Harvard University Press, 2001.

Bloom, Robert L. "We Never Expected a Battle." *Pennsylvania History* 55 (1988): 161–200.

Brundage, W. Fitzhugh. "Race, Memory, and Masculinity: Black Veterans Recall the Civil War." In *The War Was You and Me: Civilians in the American Civil War,* ed. Joan E. Cashin, 136–56. Princeton, N.J.: Princeton University Press, 2002.

Buck, Paul S. *The Road to Reunion.* Boston: Little, Brown, 1937.

Bullard, F. Lauriston. *Lincoln in Marble and Bronze.* New Brunswick, N.J.: Rutgers University Press/Abraham Lincoln Association, 1952.

Burns, Ken, and Ric Burns, producers. *The Civil War.* 9 episodes. Florentine Films/WETA-TV, 1989. Videotape.

Burton, E. Milbury. *The Siege of Charleston, 1861–1865.* Columbia: University of South Carolina Press, 1970.

Busey, John W. *Last Full Measure: Burials in the Soldier's National Cemetery at Gettysburg.* Hightstown, N.J.: Longstreet, 1988.

Campbell, Joseph. *The Hero with a Thousand Faces.* Bollingen Series 17. 2d ed. Princeton, N.J.: Princeton University Press, 1968.

———. "Mythological Themes in Creative Literature and Art." In *The Mythic Dimension: Selected Essays, 1959–1987,* ed. Antony Van Couvering, 180–203. New York: HarperCollins, 1997.

Catton, Bruce. "The End of the Centennial." In *A Portion of That Field: The Centennial of the Burial of Lincoln,* 81–93. Urbana: University of Illinois Press, 1967.

Chambers, John Whiteclay, II, et al., eds. *The Oxford Companion to Military History.* New York: Oxford University Press, 1999.

Chesebrough, David B. *No Sorrow Like Our Sorrow: Northern Protestant Ministers and the Assassination of Lincoln.* Kent, Ohio: Kent State University Press, 1994.

Cikovsky, Nicolai, Jr. "A Harvest of Death: The Veteran in a New Field." In *Winslow Homer: Paintings of the Civil War,* ed. Marc Simpson, 83–101. San Francisco: Fine Arts Museums of San Francisco/Bedford Arts, 1988.

Clark, Champ. *The Assassination: Death of the President.* Alexandria, Va.: Time-Life Books, 1987.

Coco, Gregory A. *Wasted Valor: The Confederate Dead at Gettysburg.* Gettysburg, Pa.: Thomas, 1990.

———. *Killed in Action.* Gettysburg, Pa.: Thomas, 1992.

———. *A Strange and Blighted Land: Gettysburg, the Aftermath of Battle.* Gettysburg, Pa.: Thomas, 1995.

Bibliography

Cohen, Henning, and Tristam Potter Coffin, eds. *Folklore of American Holidays.* Detroit, Mich.: Gale Research, 1987.

Connelly, Thomas L. *The Marble Man: Robert E. Lee and His Image in American Society.* Baton Rouge: Louisiana State University Press, 1977.

Connerton, Paul. *How Societies Remember.* Cambridge: Cambridge University Press, 1989.

Cooper, William J., Jr. *Jefferson Davis, American.* New York: Knopf, 2000.

Cornish, Dudley Taylor. *The Sable Arm: Negro Troops in the Union Army, 1861–1865.* 1956. Reprint, New York: Norton, 1966.

Cowley, Charles. "Our National Cemeteries." *Bay State Monthly* 2, no. 1 (October 1884): 58–60.

Davies, Wallace Evan. *Patriotism on Parade: The Story of Veterans' and Hereditary Organizations in America, 1783–1900.* Cambridge, Mass.: Harvard University Press, 1955.

Davis, William C. *Jefferson Davis: The Man and His Hour.* New York: HarperCollins, 1991.

———. *"A Government of Our Own": The Making of the Confederacy.* New York: Free Press, 1994.

———. "Myths and Realities of the Confederacy." In *The Cause Lost: Myths and Realities of the Confederacy,* 175–90. Lawrence: University Press of Kansas, 1996.

Dean, Eric T., Jr. *Shook over Hell: Post-Traumatic Stress, Vietnam, and the Civil War.* Cambridge, Mass.: Harvard University Press, 1997.

Dearing, Mary. *Veterans in Politics: The Story of the G.A.R.* Baton Rouge: Louisiana State University Press, 1952.

Donald, David Herbert. *Lincoln.* New York: Simon & Schuster, 1995.

DuBois, W. E. B. *Black Reconstruction in America, 1860–1880.* 1935. Reprint, New York: Atheneum, 1992.

Dunham, Chester Forrester. *The Attitude of the Northern Clergy toward the South, 1860–1865.* Philadelphia: Porcupine, 1974.

Emilio, Luis F. *History of the Fifty-fourth Regiment of Massachusetts Volunteer Infantry, 1863–1865.* 1894. Reprint, New York: Johnson Reprint, 1968.

Eshleman, H. Frank. "Lincoln's Visit to Lancaster in 1861; and the Passing of His Corpse, 1865." *Papers Read before the Lancaster County Historical Society* 13, no. 3 (5 March 1909).

Farrell, James J. *Inventing the American Way of Death, 1830–1920.* Philadelphia: Temple University Press, 1980.

Faust, Drew Gilpin. *Southern Stories: Slaveholders in Peace and War.* U.S. War Department, *The War of the Rebellion: A Compilation of the Official Records of the Union and Confederate Armies* Columbia: University of Missouri Press, 1992.

———. *"A Riddle of Death": Mortality and Meaning in the American Civil War.* Gettysburg, Pa.: Gettysburg College, 1995.

———. *Mothers of Invention: Women of the Slaveholding South in the American Civil War.* Chapel Hill: University of North Carolina Press, 1996.

———. "The Civil War Soldier and the Art of Dying." *Journal of Southern History* 67, no. 1 (February 2001): 3–38.

Fentress, James, and Chris Wickham. *Social Memory.* Oxford: Blackwell, 1992.

Foner, Eric. *Reconstruction: America's Unfinished Revolution.* New York: Harper & Row, 1988.

———. "Ken Burns and the Romance of Reunion." In *Ken Burns's "The Civil War,"* ed. Robert Brent Toplin, 103–18. New York: Oxford University Press, 1996.

Foster, Gaines M. *Ghosts of the Confederacy: Defeat, the Lost Cause, and the Emergence of the New South, 1865 to 1913.* New York: Oxford University Press, 1987.

———. "The Lost Cause Found: Reflections on a Burgeoning Historical Literature." Paper presented at the Graduate Student Conference on Southern History, University of Mississippi, 2000.

Fox, William F. *Regimental Losses in the American Civil War, 1861–1865.* 1898. Reprint, n.p.: Press of Morningside Bookshop, 1974.

Frassanito, William A. *Antietam: The Photographic Legacy of America's Bloodiest Day.* New York: Charles Scribner's Sons, 1978.

———. *Early Photography at Gettysburg.* Gettysburg, Pa.: Thomas, 1995.

Freeman, Douglas Southall. *R. E. Lee: A Biography.* 4 vols. New York: C. Scribner's Sons, 1935–1936.

Furgurson, Ernest B. *Ashes of Glory: Richmond at War.* New York: Knopf, 1996.

Fussell, Paul. *The Great War and Modern Memory.* New York: Oxford University Press, 1975.

Gallagher, Gary W., and Alan T. Nolan, eds. *The Myth of the Lost Cause and Civil War History.* Bloomington: Indiana University Press, 2000.

Gillis, John R., ed. *Commemorations: The Politics of National Identity.* Princeton, N.J.: Princeton University Press, 1994.

Glatthaar, Joseph T. *Forged in Battle: The Civil War Alliance of Black Soldiers and White Officers.* New York: Free Press, 1990.

Golden, Claudia. "War." In *Encyclopedia of American Economic History: Studies of the Principal Movements and Ideas,* ed. Glenn Porter, 3: 935–57. New York: Charles Scribner's Sons, 1980.

Habenstein, Robert W., and William M. Lamers. *The History of American Funeral Directing.* Milwaukee: Bulfin, 1955.

Halbwachs, Maurice. *The Collective Memory.* Translated by F. J. Ditter and V. Y. Ditter. New York: Harper & Row, 1980.

———. *On Collective Memory.* Edited and translated by Lewis A. Coser. Chicago: University of Chicago Press, 1992.

Hamilton, Charles, and Lloyd Ostendorf. *Lincoln in Photographs: An Album of Every Known Pose.* Norman: University of Oklahoma Press, 1963.

Hanchett, William. *The Lincoln Murder Conspiracies.* Urbana: University of Illinois Press, 1986.

Hattaway, Herman, and Archer Jones. *How the North Won: A Military History of the Civil War.* Urbana: University of Illinois Press, 1991.

Hess, Earl J. *The Union Soldier in Battle: Enduring the Ordeal of Combat.* Lawrence: University Press of Kansas, 1997.

Hickey, James T. *Springfield, May, 1865.* Springfield, Ill.: [James T. Hickey?], 1968.

Bibliography

Higham, John. *History: Professional Scholarship in America*. Updated paperback ed. Baltimore: Johns Hopkins University Press, 1990.

Hobsbawm, Eric, and Terence Ranger. *The Invention of Tradition*. Cambridge: Cambridge University Press, 1983.

Hoffsommer, Robert D. "The Aftermath of Gettysburg." *Civil War Times Illustrated* 2, no. 4 (July 1963): 49–52.

Holt, Dean W. *American Military Cemeteries*. Jefferson, N.C.: McFarland, 1992.

Holzer, Harold. "Lincoln Heaven-Bound, on Washington's Shoulders." *Lincoln Herald* 80, no. 2 (Summer 1978): 102–3.

Holzer, Harold, Gabor S. Boritt, and Mark E. Neely Jr. *The Lincoln Image: Abraham Lincoln and the Popular Print*. New York: Charles Scribner's Sons, 1984.

Holzer, Harold, and Frank J. Williams. *Lincoln's Deathbed in Art and Memory: The "Rubber Room" Phenomenon*. Gettysburg, Pa.: Thomas, 1998.

Hood, Jennings, and Charles J. Young. *American Orders and Societies and Their Decorations*. Philadelphia: Bailey, Banks & Biddle, 1917.

Hughes, Robert. *American Visions: The Epic History of Art in America*. New York: Knopf, 1997.

Jordan, Winthrop. *White over Black: American Attitudes toward the Negro, 1550–1812*. Chapel Hill: University of North Carolina Press/Institute for Early American History and Culture, 1968.

King, Alex. *Memorials of the Great War in Britain*. Oxford: Berg, 1998.

Kirkham, James F., Sheldon Levy, and William J. Crotty. *Assassination and Political Violence: A Report to the National Commission on the Causes and Prevention of Violence*. Washington, D.C.: U.S. Government Printing Office, 1969.

Kunhardt, Dorothy Meserve, and Philip B. Kunhardt. *Twenty Days*. New York: Castle, 1965.

Laderman, Gary. *The Sacred Remains: American Attitudes toward Death, 1799–1883*. New Haven, Conn.: Yale University Press, 1996.

Laqueur, Thomas. "Memory and Naming in the Great War." In *Commemorations: The Politics of National Identity*, ed. John R. Gillis, 150–67. Princeton, N.J.: Princeton University Press, 1994.

Lattimer, John. *Kennedy and Lincoln: Medical and Ballistic Comparisons of Their Assassinations*. New York: Harcourt Brace Jovanovich, 1980.

Leech, Margaret. *In the Days of McKinley*. New York: Harper & Bros., 1959.

Levy, George. *To Die in Chicago: Confederate Prisoners at Camp Douglas, 1862–1865*. Evanston, Ill.: Evanston, 1994.

Lewis, Lloyd. "Memorial Day Is Born." *Liberty*, 2 June 1928, 33.

———. *Myths after Lincoln*. 1929. Reprint, New York: Readers Club, 1941.

Linden-Ward, Blanche. *Silent City on a Hill: Landscape of Memory and Boston's Mount Auburn Cemetery*. Columbus: Ohio State University Press, 1989.

Linderman, Gerald F. *Embattled Courage: The Experience of Combat in the American Civil War*. New York: Free Press, 1987.

Livermore, Thomas L. *Numbers and Losses in the Civil War in America, 1861–65.* 2d ed. Boston: Houghton Mifflin, 1901.

Longacre, Edward G., ed. "With Lincoln on His Last Journey." *Lincoln Herald* 84, no. 4 (Winter 1982): 239–41.

Lyle, Katie L. *Scalded to Death by the Steam.* Chapel Hill, N.C.: Algonquin, 1983.

MacCloskey, Munro. *Hallowed Ground: Our National Cemeteries.* New York: Richard Rosen, 1968.

Mann, Thomas C., and Janet Greene. *Sudden and Awful: American Epitaphs and the Finger of God.* Brattleboro, Vt.: Stephen Greene, 1967.

Marvel, William. "The First to Fall: The Brief and Bitter Life of Daniel Hough." N.d. Unpublished typescript. Daniel Hough Papers, Fort Sumter National Monument, Fort Sumter Island, S.C.

McConnell, Stuart. *Glorious Contentment: The Grand Army of the Republic, 1865–1900.* Chapel Hill: University of North Carolina Press, 1992.

McPherson, James. *Battle Cry of Freedom: The Civil War Era.* New York: Oxford University Press, 1988.

———. "When Memorial Day Was No Picnic." *New York Times,* 26 May 1996, E11.

———. *For Cause and Comrades: Why Men Fought in the Civil War.* New York: Oxford University Press, 1997.

Miller, David W. *Second Only to Grant: Quartermaster General Montgomery C. Meigs.* Shippensburg, Pa.: White Mane, 2000.

Miller, Edward A., Jr. *The Black Civil War Soldiers of Illinois: The Story of the Twenty-ninth U.S. Colored Infantry.* Columbia: University of South Carolina Press, 1998.

Mitchell, Reid. *The Vacant Chair: The Northern Soldier Leaves Home.* New York: Oxford University Press, 1993.

Neely, Mark E., Harold Holzer, and Gabor S. Boritt. *The Confederate Image: Prints of the Lost Cause.* Chapel Hill: University of North Carolina Press, 1987.

Nevins, Allan. *The Organized War to Victory, 1864–1865.* Vol. 4 of *The War for the Union.* New York: Charles Scribner's Sons, 1971.

———. "The Glorious and the Terrible." In *Myth and the American Experience,* ed. Nicholas Cords and Patrick Gerster, 354–65. New York: Glencoe, 1973. Originally published in the *Saturday Review,* 2 September 1961.

Nolan, Alan T. *Lee Considered: General Robert E. Lee and Civil War History.* Chapel Hill: University of North Carolina Press, 1991.

———. "The Anatomy of the Myth." In *The Myth of the Lost Cause and Civil War History,* ed. Gary W. Gallagher and Alan T. Nolan, 11–34. Bloomington: Indiana University Press, 2000.

Nora, Pierre. "Between History and Memory: *Les Lieux de mémoire.*" *Representations* 26 (Spring 1989): 7–25.

Novick, Peter. *That Noble Dream: The "Objectivity Question" and the American Historical Profession.* Cambridge: Cambridge University Press, 1988.

Olcott, Charles S. *The Life of William McKinley.* 2 vols. Boston: Houghton Mifflin, 1916.

Bibliography

Ostendorf, Lloyd. "Lincoln and Christ Parallels." *Lincoln Herald* 86, no. 3 (Fall 1984): 177–78.

Osterweis, Rollin G. *The Myth of the Lost Cause, 1865–1900.* Hamden, Conn.: Archon, 1973.

Paludan, Phillip S. *"A People's Contest": The Union and Civil War, 1861–1865.* New York: Harper & Row, 1988.

Peters, James Edward. *Arlington National Cemetery: Shrine to America's Heroes.* Kensington, Md.: Woodbine, 1986.

Pfanz, Harry W. *Gettysburg: The Second Day.* Chapel Hill: University of North Carolina Press, 1987.

Phisterer, Frederick. *Statistical Record of the Armies of the United States.* New York: Charles Scribner's Sons, 1883.

Poppenheim, Mary, et al. *The History of the United Daughters of the Confederacy.* Richmond, Va.: Garret & Massie, [1938].

Quigly, Christine. *The Corpse: A History.* Jefferson, N.C.: McFarland, 1996.

Rable, George C. *Civil Wars: Women and the Crisis of Southern Nationalism.* Urbana: University of Illinois Press, 1989.

Ragon, Michel. *The Space of Death: A Study of Funerary Architecture, Decoration, and Urbanism.* Translated by Alan Sheridan. Charlottesville: University Press of Virginia, 1983.

Ransom, Roger L. *Conflict and Compromise: The Political Economy of Slavery, Emancipation, and the American Civil War.* New York: Cambridge University Press, 1989.

Raymond, Henry J. *The Life and Public Services of Abraham Lincoln, Sixteenth President of the United States.* New York: Derby & Miller, 1865.

Reardon, Carol. *Pickett's Charge in History and Memory.* Chapel Hill: University of North Carolina Press, 1997.

Record of the Service of the Fifty-Fifth Regiment of Massachusetts Volunteer Infantry. 1868. Reprint, Freeport, N.Y.: Books for Libraries, 1971.

Richter, Edward G. J. "The Removal of the Confederate Dead from Gettysburg." *Gettysburg*, no. 2 (1 January 1990): 113–22.

Ross, Ishbel. *The First Lady of the South: The Life of Mrs. Jefferson Davis.* 1958. Reprint, Westport, Conn.: Greenwood, 1973.

Rowland, Eron. *Varina Howell, Wife of Jefferson Davis.* 2 vols. New York: Macmillan, 1931.

Rule, David G. *Confederate Monuments at Gettysburg.* Gettysburg Battle Monuments, vol. 1. Hightstown, N.J.: Longstreet, 1986.

Saum, Lewis O. "Death in the Popular Mind of Pre–Civil War America." In *Death in America*, ed. David Stannard, 30–48. Philadelphia: University of Pennsylvania Press, 1975.

———. *The Popular Mood of Pre–Civil War America.* Westport, Conn.: Greenwood, 1980.

Savage, Kirk. *Standing Soldiers, Kneeling Slaves: Race, War, and Monument in Nineteenth-Century America.* Princeton, N.J.: Princeton University Press, 1997.

Schramm, Wilbur. "Introduction: Communication in Crisis." In *The Kennedy Assassination and the American Public: Social Communication in Crisis*, ed. Bradley S. Greenberg and Edwin B. Parker, 1–25. Stanford, Calif.: Stanford University Press, 1965.

Searcher, Victor. *The Farewell to Lincoln.* New York: Abingdon, 1965.

Shaffer, Donald R. *After the Glory: The Struggles of Black Civil War Veterans.* Lawrence: University Press of Kansas, 2004.

Silber, Nina. *The Romance of Reunion: Northerners and the South, 1865–1900.* Chapel Hill: University of North Carolina Press, 1993.

Simpson, Marc, ed. *Winslow Homer: Paintings of the Civil War.* San Francisco: Fine Arts Museums of San Francisco/Bedford Arts, 1988.

Sloane, David Charles. *The Last Great Necessity: Cemeteries in American History.* Baltimore: Johns Hopkins University Press, 1991.

Smith, Samuel Denny. *The Negro in Congress, 1870–1901.* Port Washington, N.Y.: Kennikat, 1940.

Snell, Charles A., and Sharon A. Brown. *Antietam National Battlefield and National Cemetery: An Administrative History.* Washington, D.C.: National Park Service, U.S. Department of the Interior, 1986.

Speer, Lonnie R. *Portals to Hell: Military Prisons of the Civil War.* Mechanicsburg, Pa.: Stackpole, 1997.

Stannard, David E., ed. *Death in America.* Philadelphia: University of Pennsylvania Press, 1975.

———. *The Puritan Way of Death: A Study of Religion, Culture, and Social Change.* New York: Oxford University Press, 1977.

Steen, Ralph W. "Texas Newspapers and Lincoln." *Southwestern Historical Quarterly* 51 (January 1948): 199–212.

Steere, Edward. *Shrines of the Honored Dead: A Study of the National Cemetery System.* Washington, D.C.: U.S. Army, Office of the Quartermaster General, [1954?].

Stewart, Charles Joseph. "A Rhetorical Study of the Reaction of the Protestant Pulpit in the North to Lincoln's Assassination." Ph.D. diss. University of Illinois, 1963.

Stotelmyer, Steven R. *The Bivouacs of the Dead: The Story of Those Who Died at Antietam and South Mountain.* Baltimore: Toomey, 1992.

Strode, Hudson. *Jefferson Davis, Tragic Hero: The Last Twenty-five Years, 1864–1889.* New York: Harcourt, Brace & World, 1964.

Stuart, Meriwether. "Colonel Ulrich Dahlgren and Richmond's Union Underground." *Virginia Magazine of History and Biography* 72 (April 1964): 152–204.

Swanberg, W. A. *First Blood: The Story of Fort Sumter.* New York: Charles Scribner's Sons, 1957.

Sword, Wiley. *Shiloh: Bloody April.* New York: Morrow, 1974.

Tap, Bruce. *Over Lincoln's Shoulder: The Committee on the Conduct of the War.* Lawrence: University Press of Kansas, 1998.

Thomas, Benjamin P., and Harold Hyman. *Stanton: The Life and Times of Lincoln's Secretary of War.* New York: Knopf, 1962.

Thomas, Edison H. "Story of the Jefferson Davis Funeral Train." Pamphlet reprinted from the February 1955 issue of the *L. and N. Magazine.*

Tidwell, William. *April '65: Confederate Covert Action in the American Civil War.* Kent, Ohio: Kent State University Press, 1995.

Bibliography

Tidwell, William A., with James O. Hall and David Winfred Gaddy. *Come Retribution: The Confederate Secret Service and the Assassination of Lincoln.* Jackson: University Press of Mississippi, 1988.

Trachtenburg, Alan. *Reading American Photographs: Images as History, Mathew Brady to Walker Evans.* New York: Hill & Wang, 1989.

Trefousse, Hans L. *Thaddeus Stevens: Nineteenth Century Egalitarian.* Chapel Hill: University of North Carolina Press, 1997.

Turner, Thomas Reed. *Beware the People Weeping: Public Opinion and the Assassination of Abraham Lincoln.* Baton Rouge: Louisiana State University Press, 1982.

Unrau, Harlan D. *Administrative History: Gettysburg National Military Park and National Cemetery.* Washington, D.C.: U.S. Department of the Interior, National Park Service, 1991.

Vinovskis, Maris. "Have Social Historians Lost the Civil War? Some Preliminary Demographic Speculations." *Journal of American History* 76, no. 1 (June 1989): 34–58.

Watson, Mary Ann. *The Expanding Vista: American Television in the Kennedy Years.* New York: Oxford University Press, 1990.

Weigley, Russell F. *Quartermaster General of the Union Army.* New York: Columbia University Press, 1959.

Wills, Garry. *Lincoln at Gettysburg: The Words That Remade America.* New York: Simon & Schuster, 1992.

Wilson, Charles Reagan. *Baptized in Blood: The Religion of the Lost Cause, 1865–1920.* Athens: University of Georgia Press, 1980.

Wilson, Christopher Kent. "Winslow Homer's *The Veteran in a New Field:* A Study of the Harvest Metaphor and Popular Culture." *American Art Journal* 17, no. 4 (autumn 1985): 2–27.

Winslow, Hattie Lou, and Joseph J. R. Moore. "Camp Morton, 1861–1865: Indianapolis Prison Camp." *Indiana Historical Society Publications* 13, no. 3 (1940): 227–383.

Winter, J. M. *Sites of Memory, Sites of Mourning: The Great War in European Cultural History.* New York: Cambridge University Press, 1995.

Periodicals

Atlanta Constitution, 8 December 1889.

Augusta (Ga.) Chronicle, 6 December 1889.

Berks and Schuylkill Journal (Reading, Pa.), 18 July 1863.

Boston Evening Transcript, 6 December 1889.

Chicago Tribune, 5 May 1862–20 April 1865.

Cincinnati Daily Enquirer, 17 April 1865–1 May 1865.

The Colored American (Augusta, Ga.), 30 December 1875.

Columbus (Ga.) Enquirer-Sun, 7 December 1889.

Confederate Veteran, 1893–1913.

Dallas Herald, 4 May 1865.

Dayton Daily News, 25 November 1963.

Evening Post, 23 November 1865.

Florida Times-Union (Jacksonville), 7 December 1889.

Galveston Daily News, 27 April 1865.

Harper's Weekly, 20 June 1863.

Houston Tri-Weekly Telegraph, 26 April 1865.

The Independent, April 1865.

Mobile (Ala.) Daily Register, 7 December 1889.

The Nation, 23 November 1865.

New Era (Washington, D.C.), 23 June 1870.

New National Era (Washington, D.C.), 2 March 1871–8 June 1871.

New Orleans Semi-Weekly Louisianian, 15 June 1871–2 July 1871.

New York Herald, 2–19 April 1861.

New York Times, 20 October 1862, 7 December 1889–31 May 1893, 2 July 1997.

Newport (R.I.) Mercury, 14 December 1889.

Pennsylvania Daily Telegraph (Harrisburg), 11 April 1865–4 May 1865.

The People's Advocate (Washington, D.C.), 10 June 1876–1 July 1876.

Richmond (Va.) Dispatch, 10 December 1889.

United States Service Magazine, 1862–1866.

Washington Chronicle, 5 June 1867–19 June 1868.

Washington Daily Morning Chronicle, 31 May 1871, 31 May 1873.

Index

Index

Index

Index